# PIMLICO

## 759

# CLEOPATRA

Lucy Hughes-Hallett is a cultural historian and critic. She is the author of *Heroes: Saviours, Traitors and Supermen*, and is currently at work on a book about Gabriele d'Annunzio and the origins of fascism. She reviews regularly for the *Sunday Times* Books Section.

D0898909

# CLEOPATRA

## Queen, Lover, Legend

---

# LUCY HUGHES-HALLETT

PIMLICO

*In Memory of*
*Philip Llòyd-Bostock 1946-86*

Published by Pimlico 2006

2 4 6 8 10 9 7 5 3 1

Copyright © Lucy Hughes-Hallett 1990
Afterword copyright © Lucy Hughes-Hallett 2006

Lucy Hughes-Hallett has asserted her right under the Copyright,
Designs and Patents Act 1988 to be identified as the author of this work

This book is sold subject to the condition that it shall not, by way of trade or
otherwise, be lent, resold, hired out, or otherwise circulated without the
publisher's prior consent in any form of binding or cover other than that
in which it is published and without a similar condition including
this condition being imposed on the subsequent purchaser

Grateful acknowledgement is made to Faber & Faber Ltd to reproduce two lines
from *The Waste Land* from *Collected Poems 1909–1962* by T. S. Eliot.

First published in Great Britain in 1990 by Bloomsbury Publishing, Ltd
Vintage edition 1990
First Pimlico edition 1997

Second Pimlico edition 2006

Pimlico
Random House, 20 Vauxhall Bridge Road,
London SW1V 2SA

Random House Australia (Pty) Limited
20 Alfred Street, Milsons Point, Sydney,
New South Wales 2061, Australia

Random House New Zealand Limited
18 Poland Road, Glenfield,
Auckland 10, New Zealand

Random House South Africa (Pty) Limited
Isle of Houghton, Corner of Boundary Road & Carse O'Gowrie,
Houghton 2198, South Africa

Random House UK Limited Reg. No. 954009

A CIP catalogue record for this book is available from the British Library

ISBN 9781844139378 (from Jan 2007)
ISBN 1844139379

Papers used by Random House UK Ltd are natural, recyclable products
made from wood grown in sustainable forests. The manufacturing processes
conform to the environmental regulations of the country of origin

Printed and bound in Great Britain by Bookmarque Ltd, Croydon, Surrey

# CONTENTS

# ACKNOWLEDGEMENTS

My first thanks are due to Nicholas Ward-Jackson, who suggested I should take Cleopatra as my subject. I also owe especial debts of gratitude to the following: to Timothy Binyon, Kate Figes and Charity Scott-Stokes, who translated texts from languages inaccessible to me; to Peter Washington and Gray Watson, each of whom read parts of the book in manuscript – I am grateful for their comments and suggestions; to Richard Simpson for his invaluable help in my quest for visual representations of Cleopatra. Among the numerous people who have drawn my attention to Cleopatras I might otherwise have missed I am particularly grateful to Professor Bram Dijkstra, Professor Inga-Stina Ewbank and Henry Ford. Liz Calder of Bloomsbury has been an exemplary publisher, encouraging, sympathetic and scrupulous. Finally I must thank my husband, Dan Franklin. This book could certainly have been written without him, but its author would not have been so happy.

# NOTE

I have referred throughout to my three principal characters by the simplest forms of their names: Cleopatra, Antony and Octavius.

Cleopatra's full title was Cleopatra VII Thea Philopator (Goddess and Lover of her Father/Fatherland). Her other titles included Philadelphus (Brother-loving), Thea Neotera (Younger Goddess) and Regina Regum Filiorum Regum (Queen of Kings and of her Sons who are Kings). Antony's full name was Marcus Antonius. He appears in later sources variously as Antony or Mark Antony. Octavius was born Caius Octavius. Subsequently he called himself Caius Julius Caesar Octavianus and took the title Filius Divi Julii (Son of Julius the God). After Cleopatra's death he dubbed himself Imperator and assumed the name by which history knows him best: Caesar Augustus.

For clarity's sake I have used the appellation 'Caesar' only of Julius Caesar, never (except in quotation) of Octavius. I have modernized all spellings and I have chosen the most familiar variant for each proper name.

# INTRODUCTION

SHE IS 'THE wickedest woman in history';[1] she is a pattern of female virtue. She is a sexual glutton; she is a true and tender lover who died for her man. She is a royal princess whose courage is proof of her nobility; she is an untrustworthy foreigner whose lasciviousness and cunning are typical of her race. She is a public benefactor, builder of aqueducts and lighthouses; she is a selfish tyrant who tortures slaves for her entertainment. She is as playful as a child; she is as old as sin. She is Cleopatra VII, the Queen of Egypt who died in 30 BC, an historical person about whom a limited number of facts can be ascertained; but she is also, as Théophile Gautier wrote in 1845, 'the most complete woman ever to have existed, the most womanly woman and the most queenly queen, a person to be wondered at, to whom the poets have been able to add nothing, and whom dreamers find always at the end of their dreams'.[2]

This book is about all of these dream-Cleopatras, and about the reasons why they took their particular and diverse forms. Cleopatra, the Hellenistic queen, makes many appearances in it, but it is not primarily her biography. It is a book about sex, monarchy, masochism, the ethics of suicide and the rhetoric of racism. Above all, it is about propaganda and the persuasive power of narrative.

Cleopatra's legend has undergone many metamorphoses in the two millennia since her death. Lurid anecdotes have been added to it, dull details have been pared away. Its focus has shifted frequently. For the Elizabethans it was a story about

11

passion and fidelity; for eighteenth-century interpreters it was a political parable; for nineteenth-century Romantics it was a tale of sexual violence. Even when the narrative outline of the story has remained more or less stable its meaning switches. To Boccaccio, writing in the 1350s, Cleopatra was 'known throughout the world for her greed, cruelty and lustfulness'.[3] To Chaucer, writing only thirty years later and probably using Boccaccio's account as a source, she was an exemplar of chastity and steadfastness, the first and best of the 'Good Women' who demonstrated their virtue by dying for love.

A story is a protean thing, changing its nature as well as its shape when viewed from different angles. A single set of facts, arranged and rearranged, can point to a variety of contradictory conclusions. The vicissitudes of Cleopatra's legend, to which so many different morals have been attached, may act as a reminder that even the simplest piece of information can be made to serve a polemical purpose. Every story-teller, whether journalist, historian, poet or entertainer, is also – willy-nilly – something of a propagandist.

I myself am no exception to that rule. Although I have striven to achieve objectivity, this book cannot escape being yet another of the distorting mirrors in which Cleopatra's reflection appears tinted and reshaped by the glass which holds it. Its form has been determined, much though I might wish to pretend to originality, by intellectual fashion: the deconstruction of ancient narratives is a late twentieth century practice. Its content has been conditioned, not only by my own private inclinations, but also by the tastes and politics of my time. I acknowledge myself bound – however reluctantly – as all other interpreters of Cleopatra's story have been, by the rule that, in Oscar Wilde's words, 'Every portrait that is painted with feeling is a portrait of the artist, not of the sitter.'[4]

My intention in this analysis of the many portraits of Cleopatra – literary, visual and cinematic – is similar to that of an archaeologist who drives a narrow but deep shaft through the layered remains of an often-rebuilt city. Each image of Cleopatra (like the archaeologist's shard of pottery) provides clues to the nature of the culture which produced it, in particular to its sexual politics, its racial prejudices, its neuroses and its fantasies. Smug critics used to laugh at Hollywood anachronisms – at Cecil B. De Mille's 1934 *Cleopatra* in which Claudette Colbert inhabits an art deco, Egypto-style palace not dissimilar from the Odeons in which the film was shown, and at the pale peach lipstick and petalled bathing cap which stamp Elizabeth Taylor's Cleopatra (in the film directed by Joseph L. Mankiewicz) as being so unmistakably a product of the early 1960s. But Cleopatras (like Satans, like Christs, like the images of any character who has been frequently represented over a long period of time) are always shaped by the individuals imagining them and the societies within which those people live.

Painters of the European Renaissance depicted Cleopatra as a plump blonde (for she was believed, incorrectly, to have been a great beauty, and only those whose fair skins proclaimed them members of a social and racial élite were then deemed beautiful). Those of the nineteenth century placed her, a Hellenistic queen, in one or other of two equally inappropriate settings – Pharaonic Egypt or a prettified medieval Orient, a land of Turkish delights. Even those modern interpreters who strove most consciously to achieve historical accuracy have failed to keep their images pure of contemporary influences. De Mille and Mankiewicz both spent vast sums on 'authentic' sets. Gabriel Pascal, director of the 1945 film in which Vivien Leigh played Cleopatra, even hired a consultant astronomer to ensure that the electric stars lighting up his blue tulle sky should be in precisely the positions in which they would have appeared to an observer by the Nile in 48 BC.[5] To no avail. All three films could be dated to within five years by anyone with even the most cursory knowledge of the history of twentieth-century design. A greater naïvety than that of the film director who allows Cleopatra to use colloquial American slang is that of the critic who supposes there could ever be a representation of her which was not conditioned by the fashions and preconceptions of its time.

13

As with appearances, so with meanings. The ceaseless shifts in the structure and significance of Cleopatra's story mirror shifts in the emotional and intellectual condition of those who interpreted it. It has been justly questioned whether art and literature can be considered trustworthy sources for the social historian. It was assumed by seventeenth-century European writers that because Cleopatra was a woman she must be weak, even though many seventeenth-century European women – merchants, scholars, missionaries, fighters – were clearly as tough as their male contemporaries. In the nineteenth century Cleopatra became the heroine of a multitude of masochistic fantasies – yet women of the period were seldom really violent, nor did many nineteenth-century men wish, in actuality, to be killed by their mistresses. More recently Cleopatra, as embodied by Elizabeth Taylor, became fascinating for her reckless bad behaviour, even while such behaviour continued to be rigorously condemned outside the unreal sphere of film-fan gossip. But although fiction can provide only suspect evidence of actual social conditions, it must, of its very nature, make manifest the fantasies of the culture which spawns it. Images of Cleopatra may not tell us how their progenitors actually lived, but they do reveal much about those progenitors' prejudices, their systems of value and morality, and their desires.

In searching for these revelations I have been guided by the assumption that story-telling is never an innocent occupation. It may be that many of the anecdotes that make up the Cleopatra legend are based on fact – some of them undoubtedly are – but to say that an event or sequence of events actually occurred is never a sufficient answer to the question 'Why is this story being told now, and in this manner?' Even the most scrupulous historian selects and edits. Propagandists, poets, painters and film makers go further, using history as a store of raw material from which new images of reality can be produced.

I have treated all of my sources with equal respect, or lack of it, as evidence in an investigation. I have not made any distinction between my approach to the works of great artists

14

like Virgil, Shakespeare, Michelangelo or Tiepolo and to those of deservedly forgotten seventeenth-century playwrights or the makers of cinematic schlock. I have devoted a chapter to Shakespeare's play not because I consider it a work of genius (although I do) but because it contains the most complete expression of one of the important themes of Cleopatra's story – the danger inherent in passion. I have written only cursorily about Mary Butts's novel *Scenes from the Life of Cleopatra*, even though it is very fine, and I have given a great deal of attention to the film starring Elizabeth Taylor, even though it is not. I am not suggesting that works of art and literature should only, or even preferably, be viewed as documentary evidence in the history of the imagination – only that they can be, and that what they reveal when so viewed is often unexpected and illuminating.

The great majority of the sources to which I have referred are of Western origin. To the tenth-century Arab historian Al-Masūdī Cleopatra was a sage, the last exponent of Greek wisdom. To the Egyptian dramatist Ahmad Shawqui, writing in the 1920s, she was a nationalist heroine defending Egypt against the aggression of an imperial European power. But on the whole her legend is a Western one. There were, after all, several great queens of Egypt. What distinguishes Cleopatra's story from that of Hatshepsut or Berenice I or Arsinoe II – what makes her a legendary heroine and a household name in our society as those other, equally energetic and powerful leaders are not – is the fact that, unlike them, she played a crucial role in the political affairs of the West.

Cleopatra was Rome's enemy, and we in the West are Rome's heirs. The notion of Cleopatra that we have inherited identifies her primarily as being the adversary, the Other. Her otherness is twofold. She is an Oriental, and she is a woman. Even in her lifetime her legend was already shaped by the two overlapping chauvinisms of race and sex, for in a man's world every woman is a foreigner. According to the legend, Cleopatra and the people of her court are dishonest, self-indulgent, sex-fixated and quintessentially feminine (as the Oriental peoples of the Western imagination still tend to

15

be). Her Roman adversaries embody the 'masculine' virtues of patriotism, discipline, sexual abstemiousness and readiness for war. From Rome we have inherited not only this language of racial and sexual stereotyping (which has remained extraordinarily constant for over two thousand years) but also the habits and mind which decree not only that the 'Roman' qualities are peculiarly masculine, but also that they are virtues.

Yet Cleopatra, even in the most negative representations, remains alluring. 'Before the thought of Cleopatra every man is an Anthony,' wrote the Decadent critic Arthur Symons, who thought her 'perhaps the most wonderful of women'.[6] We do not always desire what we esteem, nor do we esteem what we desire. In this study I have repeatedly come across an ambivalence at the heart of our culture, a great divide between the cluster of qualities that I have labelled 'goodness' – the Christian virtues of obedience, humility and care for others – and those which constitute 'greatness' – the ancient warrior virtues of pride, strength, aggressiveness and loyalty. When Cleopatra is good, as for instance in the seventeenth-century plays which depict her as a pathetic, wronged mistress dreaming in vain of a wedding ring, then she is not great. But in the far more numerous versions of her story in which she is bad, her badness has frequently a kind of grandeur to it. She is a temptress, a *femme fatale*, an alien. As such she is perceived as being infinitely more attractive, and sometimes also more admirable, than the good woman, or the girl next door.

Even when she is most wicked, most depraved and bloodthirsty, she always fascinates. The nineteenth-century French writer Théophile Gautier imagined her as a kind of cypher, a vague figure at the end of all dreams, a blank screen on to which any number of desires could be projected. The forms in which she has been represented provide clues as to the nature of those often complicated desires. Cleopatra has been described as a great beauty, the supreme sexual prize, an exotic mistress up to all the tricks of the oldest of professions. But she has also been presented as a castrator and a killer.

It is not enough to write off these negative images as manifestations of sexism. A feminist consciousness is a useful tool with which to chip away at the image of Cleopatra. Using it, one uncovers a great deal of misogyny. But fantasists, male and female, create fantasy-figures shaped by their own needs and yearnings. Cleopatra is only threatening because she is alluring, and she is alluring because over and over again writers, painters and film makers have used her to personify something they seek. That something has little or nothing to do with enlightened self-interest. The core of Cleopatra's story is a double suicide. An analysis of her legend must simultaneously be an analysis of the suppressed human craving for frenzy, for the stranger and for death.

In 1819 the poet John Keats met a pretty Anglo-Indian girl at a tea party in Hampstead. Describing her with some excitement in a letter to a friend he candidly let slip what generations of Westerners have wanted from the queen of Egypt. 'She is not a Cleopatra but she is at least a Charmian. She has a rich eastern look. . . . When she comes into a room she makes an impression the same as the Beauty of a Leopardess. . . . I should like her to ruin me.'[7]

# PART ONE

# I

## FANTASY AND FACT

THERE WAS ONCE an Egyptian queen called Cleopatra. She was rich, unscrupulous and fascinatingly beautiful.

While she was still a young girl she fought a civil war against her brother King Ptolemy, who was also her husband. (Like most Oriental potentates Cleopatra was as depraved as she was seductive: incest was the least of her offences against chastity.) The war was going badly for her party when the great Julius Caesar arrived in Alexandria and took up residence in the royal palace. The troops loyal to King Ptolemy guarded all the entrances but, undeterred, Cleopatra resolved to win him to her cause. Being both audacious and cunning, she persuaded a merchant, Apollodorus, to smuggle her into the palace rolled up in a carpet. The bundle was carried safely into Caesar's apartment, and unrolled at his feet. Cleopatra sprang out, a vision as gorgeous as it was startling. Caesar was dazzled and Cleopatra, who had already seduced Cnaius Pompey, son of Pompey the Great, lost no time in making another conquest. Enchanted by her charms and her prodigious sexual talents Caesar lingered in Alexandria far longer than was politic, and intervened in the civil war on her behalf. Thus one of the world's wisest and most careful men was turned aside from duty and good sense by a scheming girl.

The war was decided by a battle in the harbour and, peace once restored, Caesar and Cleopatra addressed themselves to pleasure. They took an extended cruise up the Nile, travelling in the magnificent barge of the Pharaohs which was decorated with all the precious woods of the Orient and studded with jewels. By day Cleopatra showed Caesar the treasures of her ancient land. By night they dallied under the vast and luminous stars of Africa while sinuous, dark-skinned slaves served them with exotic delicacies.

The idyll ended. Urgent matters of state demanded Caesar's presence in Rome. Reluctantly he tore himself away from his bewitching mistress.

During the next six years Cleopatra did nothing of any interest.

In the meanwhile the world changed. Caesar was murdered. His assassins were defeated, and three men appointed themselves joint rulers of the Roman Empire. Lepidus was a foolish nonentity. Octavius, Julius Caesar's adopted son, was a cool and wily politician, ruthlessly ambitious and devoid of attractive human weaknesses. Antony, the third, who ruled the Eastern part of the empire, was charming but flawed. He was easily taken in and led astray by unscrupulous people, he had some very disreputable friends – actresses and the like – and he had a weakness for wine. These, though, are the failings of imprudence rather than of vice, and he was easily forgiven for them because he was a military commander of genius. He was generous, impetuous and brave. His soldiers loved him. He was, besides, very attractive to women.

One of his first actions on taking over the empire of the East was to summon Cleopatra to meet him on the River Cydnus near Tarsus in what is now southern Turkey. As soon as his messenger, Dellius, set eyes on Cleopatra he knew that Antony would fall in love with her. She was now a mature woman. To the beauty which had captivated Caesar was added the spicy allure that comes with experience and the exotic glamour of an Oriental queen. She hesitated, unsure whether Antony's intentions might not be hostile, but Dellius hinted to her that she would have no trouble subjugating her new overlord, as she had subjugated so many other men. Encouraged, she set sail for the Cydnus, and she travelled in style.

The barge in which she arrived for this first meeting with Antony was even more gorgeous than the one in which she had entertained Caesar. Its fittings were of gold and of silver. Its sails were of purple silk. From its decks rich perfumes and the sound of music spread across the waters. It was crewed by lovely boys and maidens, all half-naked and bedizened with jewels. But none of them could rival for beauty their mistress, Cleopatra. The entire population of Tarsus left the city and flocked to the riverbank to see her, leaving Antony, who was awaiting her in the marketplace, foolish and alone.

That night she invited him to a banquet the likes of which he had never seen before. The dinner was served on dishes of solid gold, the pavilion was carpeted with rose petals and a myriad lights made the night brilliant. But even in this setting Cleopatra's ripe, sensuous beauty outshone its surroundings. Antony fell madly in love, just as the cunning queen had intended that he should.

He was a married man, and he had public duties besides, but in his passion for Cleopatra he forgot all earlier ties and responsibilities. He allowed her to lure him back to Alexandria. There she tempted him to join her in a life of fabulous extravagance and fecklessness.

Life at Cleopatra's court was a ceaseless round of *louche* pleasure. Not only were the Egyptian royal family given to incest, their court was peopled with eunuchs and sexual deviants. No moral code restrained the debauches of the Alexandrians. Their religion was primitive: they worshipped brutish gods with cruel rites. They drank to excess. They feasted all night long. They wasted their wealth in a succession of immoral extravagances. Cultured they may have been, being proficient in effete decorative arts and clever enough to know how to deceive, but they never gave a thought to the serious, sober business of government or of family duty.

Cleopatra was a fitting mistress for this dissolute court. She was vain: she bathed in asses' milk while her people went hungry. She was sadistic: slaves and prisoners were tortured for her amusement. She was frivolous: she spent her days in silly pranks and fishing expeditions. She was rich beyond measure, but she squandered her wealth with reckless abandon. A cold-hearted voluptuary, she never loved Antony, but made use of him to further her ambitions and to satisfy her lust.

Antony, befuddled by ceaseless drunken debauchery and by the even more intoxicating pleasures of Cleopatra's bed, was dead to the world. The Queen's lasciviousness was matched by her sexual ingenuity. She was able to afford Antony pleasures that pious Roman matrons would never have dreamed of. Drugged by these baleful raptures, he cared nothing that in succumbing to her blandishments he stood to lose his share of the Empire.

Abruptly the spell was broken. Antony's wife Fulvia, distraught with jealousy, declared war on Octavius, calculating that this news would bring her husband hurrying home. She was right. Antony returned to Italy – but too late for Fulvia, who died shortly afterwards of a broken heart. Meanwhile Cleopatra, a spoilt princess whose unstable character was ill fitted to weather such a reverse, was left to vent her peevishness on her effeminate courtiers and to hatch vindictive plots against Rome. To relieve her boredom she took one lover after another, but none touched her heart. Each was allowed one night in which to enjoy the ecstasy of sexual intercourse with her; in the morning she would have him put to death.

Antony, away from Cleopatra's court, became once more clear-headed: the great commander and man of action revived. He made his peace with Octavius and married his new ally's sister, Octavia. In this he was magnificently rewarded for having returned to the path of virtue. Octavia was a paragon of a wife, a woman entirely without faults. She was unselfish, loyal, patient, brave, modest and affectionate. She was younger than Cleopatra. Her manner was demure and dignified, not overtly alluring, but although she did not have the Egyptian Queen's flashy glamour, anyone whose taste had not been corrupted could see that she was the more beautiful of the two.

Only a brief time elapsed before Antony, who had never

been able to forget Cleopatra, lost control of himself. Deserting his perfect wife, resigning the glory of ruling a third of the world, he returned to Alexandria. His passion had proved stronger than any motive of duty or proper, manly ambition. He should have been fighting Rome's enemies; instead he was revelling with a motley crowd of dissolute foreigners.

Octavius, in order to avenge the insult to his sister and for other, more complicated and prosaic reasons which have no place in this story, decided to go to war against Antony and Cleopatra. Their forces met at Actium, in the Peloponnese.

Octavius's victory was fore-ordained. He was better manned and better equipped than his opponents. Most importantly, his army and navy were composed of Romans – resolute, obedient, disciplined to almost machine-like efficiency, the greatest fighting men in the world. Antony, by contrast, though he had once been a military genius, was now sadly enfeebled by licentiousness and obliged to depend on untrustworthy foreign troops.

Worse still, Cleopatra, who had no sense of feminine decorum, insisted on joining him on the field of battle. Wilful and frivolous as ever, she counselled that they should not fight on land, where Antony had the clear advantage, but by sea, so that she could show off the mettle of her Egyptian fleet. The love-sick Antony allowed himself to be persuaded. The decision was disastrous. Antony and Cleopatra each took sails on board their ships. Sea battles of this period were normally fought by ships powered only by oarsmen, so this was a sure sign that they were ready to take the cowardly course and flee if they were defeated. Cleopatra, whose avarice was notorious (she even looted ancient temples in her greed for gold), took all her treasure on board as well.

For a while the battle was indecisive. Antony was holding his own when all of a sudden Cleopatra's flagship, its purple sails spread, burst through the battle lines. For all her meddling, the woman lacked the manly courage necessary to stand firm in battle. Cynically abandoning her men, her ships and the lover who had given up so much for her sake, she made all speed for Alexandria, whence, she calculated, she would be able to use the bargaining power her treasure afforded her to arrive at an understanding with Octavius.

Antony saw her go and, besotted as he was, he could not help but follow after. Thus he revealed to what vileness his association with her had degraded him. The erstwhile great commander was guilty of the most craven of all treacheries. He deserted his troops in the middle of a battle, fleeing like a woman while his men fought bravely on his behalf. His army, bewildered by this unprecedented action, refused to believe that their hero had so failed them and held out for another week. Antony's dishonour was total, and the shame he felt was savage.

The ill-starred pair arrived safely back at Alexandria and attempted to rally their forces, but they were now accursed and shunned by gods and men. Their former allies deserted them. A series of ill omens presaged their end. Reckless to the last, Cleopatra coaxed Antony to lay aside his moroseness and join her in a new drinking club, 'The Order of the Inseparable in Death'. Their orgies became more frenzied, their luxuries more excessive. Meanwhile Cleopatra prepared for the worst by testing a variety of poisons on prisoners; many of them died in agony while she watched unmoved. At the same time she ordered the building of a monument and had all her treasure carried into it.

Octavius invaded Egypt and camped outside Alexandria. Cleopatra secretly offered to hand Antony over to him in exchange for her own safety. Her lover caught her out in this treachery, but even then she was able to wheedle her way back into his good graces, for her skill in deception was prodigious.

Antony roused himself to a last effort. He led an attack on Octavius's troops and scored a brilliant success. He returned exultant, but both he and Cleopatra knew the respite was only temporary. That night he feasted his captains with especial splendour, and they all wept for love of him, and for the pity of his impending fate. Around midnight the guards at the city gates heard strange music, and knew that the gods were deserting them.

The next morning the Egyptian ships sailed out of harbour, supposedly to attack the Roman fleet. But, perfidious as their Queen, every single one of them surrendered. Seeing this, Antony's army lost heart and was put to fight. Cleopatra locked herself in her monument with her two attendants, Iras and Charmian, and sent a false message to tell Antony that she had killed herself. Persuaded by this lie that he had misjudged her, and ashamed to be so bested in heroism, Antony stabbed himself, but did not die immediately. Another messenger arrived to tell him that the Queen was in fact still alive. He asked to be carried to her monument. Cleopatra, selfish as ever, would not open the door even for him, but she and her maids let down ropes and hoisted him up to a high window. Once inside, he died in her arms.

Octavius sent more messengers, and finally came himself to negotiate with Cleopatra, keeping his eyes fixed on the floor as he spoke to her so as not to be tempted by her dangerous beauty. He had resolved to take her back to Rome and parade her, chained, through the streets in celebration of his Triumph. He was anxious, therefore, that she should not kill herself in earnest.

Whatever her vices, Cleopatra had her pride. She had contrived to make one of Octavius's commanders, Dolabella, fall in love with her. (Even in this crisis, her flair for seduction did not desert her.) He had warned her of Caesar's intentions. She could not tolerate the prospect of such a humiliation. She arranged for an old countryman to bring figs to her in the monument. The unsuspecting guards let him pass, but in his basket was concealed an asp, a snake whose venomous bite, as Cleopatra knew from her callous researches, caused a quick and painless death.

Nothing in her life became her like the leaving of it. She wrote a note to Octavius asking that she should be buried beside Antony. Then she ordered Iras and Charmian to dress her in her most magnificent robes and jewels, and to place her crown on her head. Seated on a golden throne, she calmly applied the asp to her breast. Iras and Charmian, loyal unto death, did likewise. As soon as Octavius received the note he hurried to the monument. Too late. The Queen was dead, Iras was dying and Charmian had only just enough life left in her to answer Octavius's stern question, 'Is this well done?'

'It is well done,' she said, 'and fitting for a princess descended of so many royal kings.'[1]

Such is the legendary story of Cleopatra. It is shot through with falsehood from beginning (Cleopatra was not Egyptian, she was Greek) to end (suspicious circumstances surrounding her suicide suggest that Octavius actually acquiesced in it, relieved to get such an inconveniently charismatic enemy off his hands).[2]

The story has been told and retold for over two thousand years, but in Cleopatra's case the gap between attested fact and legend is only partially the result of time's gradual blurring. Even in her lifetime she was already, several times over, an invention. Her own propaganda and that of her enemies depicted her in contrasting and equally fictive ways. In the imagination of the Romans she was a barbaric debauchee and a *femme fatale* who lured their generals off the path of duty. To her own Egyptian subjects she was a goddess and a universal mother. To the Hellenistic peoples of the eastern Mediterranean she was a Messiah and a liberator, come to free them from political oppression and to usher in a Golden Age. Each of these images was cleverly fostered. Octavius and his allies were astute manipulators of public opinion, and Cleopatra herself was a skilled self-publicist who stage-managed the crucial events of her own career with a consummate sense of the persuasive power of spectacle and symbolic action. Even her death was a show.

In the succeeding centuries her legend has undergone numerous variations, but before examining the construction of these many imaginary Cleopatras, ancient and modern, it would be as well to look first at the known facts about the historical person on whom they are all based. In the following account I have drawn on the works of Michael Grant, J. M. Carter, Jack Lindsay, M. Rostovtzeff, Ronald Syme, W. W.

Tarn and Hans Volkmann. They, in their turn, drew on the ancient poets and historians whose versions of the Cleopatra story I shall examine in more detail elsewhere in this book, as well as on inscriptions, papyri, coins and other archaeological evidence. Using these not always reliable witnesses and fragmentary material clues, they have pieced together a picture of Cleopatra and her career which is, within its limits, trustworthy; but in doing so they have had to grapple with a formidable epistemological problem: their prime authorities are writers whose testimony they themselves have proved to be frequently misleading. The conundrum is insoluble. When dealing with such distant times historians have to leave absolutes like truth and untruth alone and content themselves with sorting the probable from the unlikely. Such limitations accepted, here – as near as modern scholarship can establish them – are the plain facts about Cleopatra.


Cleopatra VII was born in 69 BC, the third child of Ptolemy XII, King of Egypt, nicknamed Auletes (the flute player). She was thus a descendant of the first Ptolemy, a Macedonian general who became ruler of Egypt after the death of Alexander the Great in 323 BC. It is not known for certain who her mother was, but as the Ptolemaic rulers had adopted the Pharaonic practice of incestuous brother–sister marriage she must have been of largely Greek descent.

Egypt, at the time of her birth, was a rich but politically unstable state. The Ptolemaic empire, which had once extended far into Asia Minor in the north and Syria in the east, had dwindled to the confines of Egypt itself. The increasing power of Rome had already engulfed many of the Ptolemies' former territories, and it was claimed on the Capitol that an earlier King Ptolemy, beholden to Rome for military and financial aid, had bequeathed his entire empire to the republic in his will. The threat of annexation was therefore everpresent, and Egypt, restive under an unpopular foreign dynasty, was increasingly unfit to defend itself.

Rather than challenge the bellicose Romans, Ptolemy Aule-

29

tes offered them his support. His strategy was motivated by his perception that Egypt no longer had the resources to function as a great and independent nation. Like many rulers of second-rank states throughout history, he sought the protection of a superpower. This willing acceptance of a dependent role earned him a reputation for weakness, but Cleopatra, for one, understood that his judgement was shrewd. She, too, was to base her foreign policy on Roman alliances.

In 59 BC, feeling insecure on a throne threatened both by internal unrest and by Rome's empire-building, Ptolemy Auletes implored Julius Caesar and Pompey (now ruling Rome, with Crassus, as the First Triumvirate) to declare publicly that they recognized his right to his own throne. This they did, proclaiming him a 'Friend and Ally of the Roman People', but they made him pay dearly for the favour. The price of this title was 6,000 talents, roughly the equivalent of Egypt's entire annual revenue. Knowing that raising such a sum from his already recalcitrant subjects would be impossible, Ptolemy Auletes borrowed it all from Gaius Rabirius Posthumus, a Roman money-lender. It was to prove a bad bargain for the King and his people. Unimpressed by his new titles, Ptolemy Auletes's subjects continued to conspire against him. Two years later, unable to impose his authority, he fled to Rome again – in search, this time, of military aid. It is possible that he took the twelve-year-old Cleopatra with him. In his absence his eldest daughter, Cleopatra VI Tryphaena, usurped his throne. In Rome he persuaded Gabinius, a supporter of Pompey's, to undertake his restoration, for which service Auletes promised to pay a further 10,000 talents.

Cleopatra VI Tryphaena's reign was short. By the time Gabinius reached Egypt she was dead, presumably assassinated by her father's supporters, and Auletes's second daughter, Berenice, had seized power in her turn. Gabinius, with the help of a young cavalry officer, Mark Antony, restored Ptolemy Auletes to power, whereupon the King promptly had Berenice executed. In 51 BC he died. His will named

Cleopatra and her brother Ptolemy XIII his joint heirs. The new Queen was eighteen years old; the King was ten.

No contemporary description of Cleopatra has survived. The Greek biographer Plutarch, who was writing nearly two hundred years after her death but had read the memoirs and histories (since lost) of several people who had actually seen her, asserts that she was not particularly good-looking, but that her voice was musical and her charm and 'force of character' such as to render her company delightful.[3] Her coins (minted on her orders and therefore more likely to flatter than otherwise) show a strong, bony face with a hooked nose and a jutting chin, pretty neither by the standards of Cleopatra's own day nor by those of ours. Her appearance thus seems to have been very far from that of the fabled seductress of legend. Her character can best be deduced from the way she conducted her career.

The first two years of her reign were troubled. The Nile failed to rise to the height necessary to flood the banks and ensure an adequate harvest. There were food shortages in the cities, and in the countryside labourers went into hiding to avoid paying taxes, leaving whole villages abandoned. International affairs posed further problems. Cleopatra agreed to send troops to help the Roman governor of Syria against the Parthians. The soldiers mutinied, refusing to go, but Cleopatra was from then on perceived as being an ally of the Romans, something which did not endear her to her nationalistically minded subjects. It must also have aroused the hostility of Pothinus, a eunuch who had achieved a position of considerable influence at court and who was now acting as the boy-king's regent. He was to prove inveterately hostile to all things Roman. By September of 49 BC Cleopatra had left Alexandria and Pothinus had begun to issue edicts in Ptolemy's name alone, as though she had been deposed.

Meanwhile, in Rome, Pompey and Julius Caesar had quarrelled. Civil war broke out. Cnaius Pompey, the son of Pompey the Great, came to Alexandria on behalf of his father asking for aid. The Egyptian government (now led by Pothinus) promised him ships, men and grain, but it seems unlikely

31

that the exiled Cleopatra ever met him, let alone made him her lover, as Plutarch and many later writers believed her to have done. A year later Caesar defeated Pompey at Pharsalus in central Greece. Pompey fled to Egypt, thinking he would find a friendly welcome there, but Pothinus had no wish to be identified with the losing side. When Pompey arrived off the Egyptian coast with his wife, Cornelia, he was surprised to see no fittingly pompous party waiting to greet him. Instead a small boat pulled out to his flagship. There were three men on board, one of whom was the Egyptian commander, Achillas. They offered to row Pompey through the shallows to the shore where, they said, he would be given an appropriate welcome. He consented, though with some misgivings. Silently, his escorts took up their oars. In the boat, as Cornelia watched from the deck of his ship, Pompey was overpowered and his head hacked off.

Four days later Julius Caesar reached Egypt. He was shown Pompey's severed head, but instead of thanking the Egyptians for ridding him of his enemy and leaving, as they had trusted he would, he expressed himself outraged by this treacherous murder of a great Roman and he showed no eagerness to depart. He needed money: the civil wars had been expensive. Now he claimed that he was empowered to collect the 6,000 talents (plus punitive interest) still owed by Ptolemy Auletes's heirs to the money-lender Rabirius. It was not the love of a sweet princess which induced him to stay in Alexandria, but his need for cash.

He landed in the insignia of a Roman consul. Thinking he had come to assert the power of Rome, the Alexandrians rioted. The situation was dangerous, but even had Caesar been willing to leave Egypt without his money he could not have done so, for the prevailing winds penned his ships in the harbour. He took up quarters in the royal palace and prepared to defend himself.

He was joined there by the boy-king Ptolemy XIII and Pothinus. A little later Cleopatra also arrived, making her way into the city and the palace past Pothinus's guards, to the latter's great displeasure. She and Caesar became lovers.

Perhaps influenced by this sexual bond, perhaps left no alternative by Pothinus's hostility, Caesar took her part in the power struggle between them. He decreed that brother and sister should reign jointly, and arranged that they should be formally married in accordance with the terms of their father's will. Ptolemy and Pothinus apparently acquiesced in this, but at the end of 48 BC Achillas (presumably acting on Pothinus's orders) marched on Alexandria with the Egyptian army and besieged the palace. Over the next two months a series of skirmishes in the city and the harbour all proved inconclusive. Meanwhile Caesar, Pothinus, Cleopatra, Ptolemy XIII and the rest of the royal family coexisted inside the palace in a situation which amounted to mutual house arrest.

The deadlock was broken when Cleopatra's younger sister, Arsinoe, left the palace to join Achillas's army and proclaim herself Queen. Caesar's barber meanwhile gave information that Pothinus was in league with her. Caesar, glad to have such a pretext, had the eunuch executed, and a little later he allowed the young King Ptolemy to leave the palace, perhaps in the hope of dividing the army's loyalties. Eventually reinforcements arrived for Caesar, and he defeated the Egyptian army at a battle near Lake Mareotis. Afterwards Ptolemy XIII was found drowned in the Nile, dragged down by the weight of his golden armour.

The way was now clear for a settlement. Caesar resisted the temptation to annex Egypt, perhaps on the grounds given by the historian Suetonius, that any Roman governor of Egypt would be so rich and powerful as to pose a serious threat to the central government in Rome,[4] perhaps (but less probably) because of his personal loyalty to Cleopatra. Instead he married his royal mistress to her youngest brother, Ptolemy XIV, who was by then about twelve years old, and proclaimed them joint rulers. This young Ptolemy had no powerful guardian like Pothinus to protect his interests, and from this time onward Cleopatra reigned effectively alone. To assist her, or perhaps to remind her that she held her throne on sufferance, Caesar left three legions behind in Alexandria.

Cleopatra and Caesar probably did travel up the Nile together, but the length of this journey is disputed. Some historians believe that he must have left Egypt for good within a fortnight of the Battle of Lake Mareotis,[5] in which case the celebrated cruise could have been scarcely more than a day trip. By the time he left, Cleopatra was pregnant.

For the next year Caesar was occupied with foreign campaigns. When he returned to Rome in the autumn of 46 BC he celebrated four Triumphs, the most splendid of which commemorated the Alexandrian War. The centrepiece of this show was the Princess Arsinoe, Cleopatra's sister, who was led, loaded with chains, at the head of a parade of prisoners. Her appearance was not a popular success: the people of Rome were shocked to see a young girl, and a princess to boot, so cruelly treated. It may have been as a result of their protests that Arsinoe was not executed after the Triumph, as the other prisoners were, but was allowed to seek asylum in the temple of Artemis at Ephesus.

Cleopatra may have witnessed this spectacle. She was certainly in Rome shortly afterwards, with her brother/husband and her baby, whom she had named Ptolemy Caesar (nicknamed Caesarion) so that his glorious parentage should be unmistakable. The name, though, proved insufficient to convince. Caesar never publicly acknowledged the child and it remains unproven to this day whether he really was the father. What is known is that Cleopatra stayed in Rome as Caesar's guest for well over a year, until the time of his assassination on the Ides of March, 44 BC.

Immediately after Caesar was killed she left Rome. By July she was back in Alexandria. By September Ptolemy XIV was dead. There is no hard evidence that Cleopatra had him murdered, but she cannot be cleared of the suspicion. Certainly she made political capital out of her renewed widowhood. She elevated her infant son Caesarion to share her throne as Ptolemy XV Caesar, thus assuring her position as sole ruler. It would be a long time before the child was likely to demand real power, as Ptolemy XIV might soon have done. Besides, Caesarion, who could be considered Julius Caesar's heir, made an illustrious partner for her: between them mother and son could lay claim to an hereditary right to rule the entire Mediterranean world.

During the next three years Cleopatra, now in her mid-twenties, devoted herself to the government of her country. This was no easy task. Again the Nile twice failed to rise sufficiently to irrigate the land. None the less Cleopatra contrived to keep the peace both in the countryside and in Alexandria.

Foreign affairs presented even greater dangers. In Rome Julius Caesar's assassination was followed by a period of confusion during which allegiances repeatedly shifted. Caesar's assassins, Brutus and Cassius, realizing that the people of Rome were not going to rise on their behalf, left Italy shortly after the Ides of March to seek funds and support in the eastern provinces of the empire. In Rome supreme power was disputed by Octavius, Caesar's nineteen-year-old great-nephew and adopted son, and Antony who, as consul at the time of Caesar's death, was by constitutional right the highest authority in Rome. The contest between these two formidable rivals led to the brink of civil war, but after the inconclusive battle of Mutina they agreed to join forces and govern with Lepidus (who held the important post of Master of Horse) as a Triumvirate, a dictatorship in three persons. Thus the friends of Julius Caesar were able to present a united front against his murderers.

Cleopatra, as ruler of the richest state in the eastern Mediterranean, received appeals for help from both parties. Once again Egypt's future security depended on picking the winning side in an internal Roman power struggle. Over the next year she played a dangerous but canny game of procrastination and prevarication. She told Cassius that famine and pestilence had depleted Egypt's resources to such an extent that she could send him neither ships nor men. Giving herself the lie, she then equipped a fleet and set out as though to join Antony and Octavius. A storm blew up. The Queen fell ill. The fleet turned back for Alexandria. Perhaps Cleopatra had never intended that it should reach its destination. In going to sea she had made a gesture of support for the Triumvirs, but it was safer to wait for the war's outcome before committing herself unequivocally to either side.

At the Battle of Philippi in 42 BC the Caesarian party was victorious. Brutus and Cassius both committed suicide, leaving the Triumvirs undisputed masters of all Rome's dominions except the small enclave controlled by Sextus Pompeius, another son of Pompey the Great, who had established control of Sicily. Octavius and Antony now split the Empire between them – because they suspected Lepidus of being in league with Sextus Pompeius they left him out of this division of the spoils. Octavius took western Europe; Antony took the east.

Antony was now about forty. He was married (for the third time) to Fulvia, an intelligent and ambitious woman. He was known primarily for his skill as a military commander, but in the months following Julius Caesar's death he had proved himself an adroit and charismatic politician, capable of containing a volatile situation and with a flair for imposing his will on his constituency without appearing to dictate. Now he resolved to launch an attack on the Parthian empire (roughly the geographical equivalent of modern Iran and Iraq). Julius Caesar had been about to lead just such an expedition when he was assassinated. In reviving the project Antony was taking on the role of champion of all the Romans, and was besides assuming Caesar's heritage.

Military expeditions require lavish funding. Antony, like Pompey, Caesar and Cassius before him (to name only the most recent), resolved to draw on the wealth of Egypt.

Cleopatra and Antony probably met for the first time when he came to Egypt with Gabinius, when she was in her early teens. During her long sojourn in Rome as Julius Caesar's guest she would certainly have encountered this friend and close associate of Caesar's. All the same, when he summoned her to meet him at Tarsus she would have had cause for misgiving. The invitation was not an entirely friendly one:

Antony was demanding that she answer charges of secretly assisting Cassius. Even if she could secure Antony's friendship, she knew that she would have to buy it. He needed money for his troops, and in all the east only Egypt had enough to supply him.

At Tarsus the two became lovers. They also did some hard bargaining. Cleopatra agreed to underwrite Antony's Parthian expedition in exchange for his support against her enemies. She demanded that various of her rivals should be killed, including her sister Arsinoe who, still in asylum in Ephesus, had defiantly had herself proclaimed Queen of Egypt. Thus the most substantial love token demanded and given at this supposedly so romantic meeting was the murder of Cleopatra's last surviving sibling.

No campaign could be launched until spring came; Antony went with Cleopatra to spend the winter in Alexandria. No doubt she did her utmost to impress him with the splendour of her court, and no doubt Antony, who had a reputation for sexual promiscuity and who was more at ease in the Hellenic world than most Romans, enjoyed himself with his new mistress-*cum*-ally. But after a few months he was gone. His wife Fulvia and his brother Lucius had raised a rebellion in Italy against Octavius; they had been defeated, and Fulvia had fled to Greece. As soon as he heard the news Antony left Alexandria. He and Cleopatra were not to see each other again for three and a half years.

Fulvia met Antony in Athens. She was ill already; shortly after their probably unhappy reunion she died. Antony's relations with Octavius were now seriously strained, but in October of 40 BC they patched up their differences and reconfirmed their division of the Empire at the Treaty of Brundisium. To seal the agreement Antony married Octavius's sister Octavia, who had conveniently just become a widow. The wedding took place within weeks of Cleopatra's giving birth to her twin children by Antony, later to be named Alexander Helios and Cleopatra Selene.

Three years followed during which Cleopatra lived in Egypt, busy with the government of her kingdom and the restoration of its economy. She is remembered as a voluptuary and as the heroine of a love story, but in fact by the time she died she had been celibate for more than half her adult life. She wintered with Julius Caesar in Alexandria in 47 BC. Over the next three years she was probably in Rome at the same time as him for a further eight months, but there is no evidence that their sexual relationship continued during that period (nor even any gossip to suggest it). She was with Antony for a little over six years (during much of which time he was absent on campaigns). It is most unlikely that either of her marriages, to younger brothers aged respectively fourteen and sixteen when they died (the first as her enemy in the civil war, the second allegedly murdered at her instigation), was consummated. The Augustan poets accused her of unbridled lust, and later authors avidly took up the theme, but as far as can be ascertained she had only two sexual partners, both of whom were chosen with a shrewd eye to the political advantages they could offer her. Cleopatra, who was to be made the heroine of many hundreds of fevered fantasies, seems to have been, by the standards of her age, a markedly abstemious lover.

Her energies were fully employed elsewhere. She appears to have been a tactful and efficient ruler, a tough negotiator and a thrifty manager. The Greek Ptolemies were not always popular with their Egyptian subjects. Nationalist uprisings were endemic throughout most of their three-hundred-year rule. Besides, Cleopatra came to the throne in the wake of a bitter civil war. Yet all the records agree that during her reign the country was internally at peace. She was, according to Plutarch,[6] the first ruler of her dynasty to have learnt to speak demotic Egyptian (Greek was the language of the court), and she observed the rites of the ancient Egyptian religion. Her subjects seem to have repaid her care with loyalty. It is also clear that under her management the economy was strong, despite the massive debts incurred by her father, and despite Julius Caesar's having so ruthlessly milked the country to pay for his own civil wars. By the end of her reign Egypt was once again rich enough for Cleopatra to be able to pay and provision Antony's army and to build a fleet to rival Rome's, and this vast expenditure on warfare seems scarcely to have dented her country's wealth. When, after her death, Octavius returned to Rome with her captured treasure, prices throughout the city soared and the interest rate fell from 12 per cent to 4 per cent.[7]

How this prosperity was achieved is not known in detail; ancient historians were not much interested in the nitty-gritty processes of government. It is known that Cleopatra came to an extremely profitable arrangement with the Nabataean Arabs over the oil rights in some territory at the southern end of the Dead Sea and that, having persuaded Antony to grant her some land around Jericho that was valuable for its dates and balsam, she subsequently leased it back to King Herod of Judaea, a deal that brought Egypt substantial revenues without any outlay of money or manpower. These transactions are recorded by Josephus,[8] the first-century Jewish historian who was one of the few ancient writers to see Cleopatra from anything other than a Roman point of view. They provide a unique and fascinating glimpse of a working queen, one more interested in the extraction of bitumen and the market price of dates than in the pleasures of love.

Antony, meanwhile, apparently untroubled by any fatal passion for Cleopatra, lived with Octavia in Rome and Athens. His relationship with his newly acquired brother-in-law was far from harmonious but the two remained nominally allied, partly thanks to Octavia's meditations. The Parthian campaign was postponed but not forgotten. While Antony consolidated his position in the eastern provinces by a series of agreements with client monarchs, his commander Ventidius fought a successful preliminary campaign, driving the Parthians out of Syria and Asia Minor.

In the autumn of 37 BC Anthony and Octavia left Italy together. Octavia was pregnant again (she had already borne Antony a daughter), and when they reached Corfu she was unwell. Antony suggested that she should return to Rome. His purpose in coming east this time was to make final preparations for the invasion of Parthia, provisionally scheduled for the following spring. She would not, in any case, be able to accompany him in the campaign and she would be safer (and possibly more useful to him) if she returned to Rome at once. She obeyed. Antony went on to Antioch in Syria and sent messengers to Cleopatra, requiring her to join him there.

This was to be expected. Before embarking on such an ambitious war effort in Asia he needed to be sure he could count on Egypt's support. He also needed money again. Even had he been firmly committed to his marriage with Octavia and his alliance with her brother, he would probably have wished to see Cleopatra at this point. But he was not. Repeatedly Octavius had broken promises to him, and had made it irritatingly plain that he had little respect for Antony. If they were to continue to rule as partners Antony was likely to find himself consigned with increasing regularity to the role of second-in-command. When partnership with Octavius seemed advantageous to him, Antony had deserted the pregnant Cleopatra. When he calculated that that partnership was of no further use, he deserted the pregnant Octavia with equal abruptness. No doubt he was glad to see his former mistress again and to meet two of his children for the first time. But the traditional explanation of Antony's actions – that he was impelled by passion, pure and simple – seems far-fetched. A passion which could wait so long, and only asserted itself at such a politically opportune moment, was scarcely an irresistible or a disinterested one.

Nor was Cleopatra's behaviour on this occasion that of a woman rapturously reunited with the one she loved. She struck a hard bargain. She asked Antony to give her extensive territories in the area now covered by the Lebanon, Syria, Jordan and southern Turkey. According to the legend Antony acceded to these demands out of pure love, handing over vast realms to her in the madness of his passion. In fact such grants were consistent with his policy of governing Rome's eastern dominions through alliances with client monarchs. Just as he had installed his protégé, King Herod, on the

40

throne of Judaea, so he deemed it to be in his interests that other strategically important areas should be controlled by another monarch who had hitherto proved friendly, Cleopatra. Besides, these land grants were not free — in exchange, Cleopatra agreed to build a fleet to protect Antony's interests in the Mediterranean, and to help him provision his army.

Their sexual relationship was resumed as well as their political alliance. Once again they passed a winter together, this time in Antioch. Once again, when spring came, Antony turned his attention back to business, leaving a pregnant woman behind him. In May 36 BC he departed with his army for Parthia. This campaign, Antony's great endeavour, which was intended to confirm his title to be counted among the greatest of the Romans, was in the event a catastrophic failure. His siege equipment proved too unwieldy and had to be left behind. A supposed ally betrayed him. In a surprise attack Antony's legions were terribly depleted. He had to turn back, but the homeward journey, with winter coming on, cost even more lives than had been lost in battle. By the time he reached Syria again two-fifths of his soldiers were dead.

He sent at once for Cleopatra. She was slow in coming — perhaps because she had just had another baby, Ptolemy Philadelphus, perhaps because she needed time to raise the money required, perhaps because she hesitated before publicly allying herself with a man who had just failed so signally. But in January 35 BC she arrived, bringing pay and winter clothing for the troops. A couple of months later Antony heard that Octavia was also on her way, bringing supplies and reinforcements from Rome.

Antony might now have left Cleopatra, as he had left her once before when her political and economic usefulness to him was temporarily exhausted, and made his peace with Octavia and her brother. Instead he wrote to Octavia, instructing her to return to Rome. He had cast in his lot with the Queen of Egypt.

There is no reason to doubt that he loved Cleopatra. She was an able colleague and a cultured companion, and she possessed as well the glamour of ancient royalty and

41

enormous wealth. She had borne him three children, two of them sons, whereas Octavia had given him only two daughters – such considerations weighed heavily with a Roman. But in choosing her rather than Octavia he was not only making a choice between two women. He was changing the course of his career.

When he marched against the Parthians he, as commander of the Roman forces in the east, was leading a Roman army to conquer new territory for Rome, a republic of which he was still officially the servant. After he dismissed Octavia his position was more ambivalent. Over the next six years, until Antony and Cleopatra's death, Octavius did all he could to persuade the Roman people that Antony was now their enemy, or at best their enemy's helpless tool, that he intended to establish his capital in Alexandria and to make Rome a mere dependency of an Oriental empire ruled jointly by himself and Cleopatra. There is some evidence that Octavius was right.

In the spring of 35 BC Cleopatra and Antony returned to Alexandria together, not to give themselves up to lotus-eating, but once again to raise money for a military campaign. Antony was deterred from renewing his attack on Parthia that year, not by an addiction to the pleasures of Cleopatra's bed, but by the need to deal with Sextus Pompeius, the younger son of Pompey the Great, who had been using his Sicilian base to launch piratical attacks on passing ships. He had seized a town in Asia Minor and was said to be negotiating with the Parthians. But in spring of 34 BC Antony marched east again, subdued Armenia, and brought its king, Artavasdes, back prisoner to Egypt.

The captives, Artavasdes among them, were led in chains through the streets of Alexandria while Antony, dressed as Dionysus, the god who ruled the east, rode behind in a splendid chariot. Octavius described this parade as a Triumph, which could only properly be held in Rome, and used it as evidence that Antony was no longer a true Roman. A few days later Antony gave Rome good cause for alarm on the occasion known as the Donations of Alexandria.

In a ceremony of spectacular magnificence he declared Cleopatra 'Queen of Kings' and Caesarion, her official co-ruler, 'King of Kings'. His own children by her, the six-year-old twins and two-year-old Ptolemy Philadelphus, were proclaimed kings and queen. To each of these juvenile monarchs Antony granted vast realms. These grants of land were only notional: all of the territories in question already had incumbent rulers. Some of them, like Asia Minor, which was granted to little Ptolemy Philadelphus, were ruled by client kings who already acknowledged Antony's overlordship. Others, like Parthia, which was granted to Alexander Helios, had yet to be conquered. But these proclamations had, all the same, great significance. When the kings of Asia Minor acknowledged Antony's sovereignty they were submitting to him not as an individual warlord but as the representative of Rome. When he made Ptolemy Philadelphus their overlord it became clear that he was annexing their realms not to the Roman Empire, but to the Ptolemaic one of Egypt. And in proclaiming Alexander lord of Parthia he made it abundantly clear that the much-deferred conquest of that empire was no longer to be undertaken on Rome's behalf.

All of this could perhaps have been explained away, but at the same ceremony Antony made a declaration which was an overt challenge to Octavius. Not only did he dub Caesarion King of Kings. He also stated categorically that the boy, now aged thirteen, was Julius Caesar's legitimate son. This could not possibly be literally, legally true, as Antony was fully aware, since Caesar was married to Calpurnia from well before he first met Cleopatra until the time of his death, and neither Roman nor Ptolemaic law sanctioned bigamy. But such a matter-of-fact detail would not have bothered Antony, whose purpose was grand. He meant to claim Rome for Caesarion on the grounds that he, not Octavius, was Julius Caesar's rightful heir.

The Donations make plain the scope of Antony and Cleopatra's ambitions. Caesarion would be ruler of Rome and the west. Cleopatra, either directly or through her children, would govern an immensely enlarged version of the Ptolemaic empire in the east. And Antony, who had so graciously bestowed these realms on her and her family, would be overlord to them all. Shakespeare's Cleopatra, lamenting her dead lover, recalls his days of splendour:

> . . . in his livery
> Walked crowns and crownets: realms and islands were
> As plates dropp'd from his pocket.[9]

At the time of the Donations that fantasy looked very like reality. There was just one small snag: those 'realms and islands' were never really Antony's to give away.

From this time onward relations between Octavius and Antony steadily worsened. A year after the Donations, in the autumn of 33 BC, Antony and Cleopatra moved to Ephesus and began to assemble all their fleets and armies there. In the spring of 32 BC the consuls, Cnaeus Domitius Ahenobarbus and Gaius Sosius, and between two and three hundred senators left Rome to join Antony. Their loyalty suggests that he still had a sizeable and important following in Rome, but their leaving demonstrates that the city was increasingly hostile to him. That same spring he divorced Octavia.

There was friction in Ephesus. Ahenobarbus and other Romans objected to Cleopatra's presence. While they supported Antony in his rivalry with Octavius, they were not party to the ambitions implicit in the Donations. Cleopatra refused to be sent home, arguing that her fleet owed its loyalty to her, not to Antony. In April Antony and Cleopatra sailed first to the island of Samos, where they held a festival, and then to Athens. They were followed by their fleet and army. Octavius was meanwhile struggling to raise the money, and the troops, to meet the threat they posed. Had they invaded Italy that summer they could very possibly have defeated him, but they held back, and they had good reason. If Antony invaded Italy in partnership with Cleopatra, a foreign monarch, he was likely to lose all the Italian support he had, as rival factions closed ranks to repel the outsider. If he went without her he would not be able to count on the loyalty of her navy. So they preferred to wait in Greece, intending to defeat Octavius on neutral territory and travel peacefully on to Rome as victors. They had 500 warships, 75,000 legionaries, 25,000 light armed infantry and 12,000 cavalry. They had every reason to believe they they could afford to wait.

The dénouement was very slow in approaching. In the autumn Antony and Cleopatra moved to Patrae, west of Athens, distributing their fleet between half a dozen sites on the western seaboard of the Greek archipelago, from Corfu to Crete. That winter Octavius, his preparations nearing completion, finally declared war – not on Antony, but on Cleopatra. In March of 31 BC the first action took place. A large part of Octavius's fleet, under Agrippa – by all accounts an outstanding admiral – appeared at Methone, Cleopatra's naval post at the southernmost tip of the Peloponnese, and took it. This was a catastrophic blow. Using Methone as a base Agrippa was able to launch attacks on all of the other Egyptian naval stations. Even worse, he could intercept the supply ships from Alexandria. Meanwhile Octavius landed his army on the Greek mainland opposite Corfu and marched southwards as far as another of his opponents' bases, at Actium on the gulf of Ambracia, and established his camp nearby. A few days later Antony and Cleopatra arrived at Actium themselves and set up their camp across the gulf from Octavius's.

It was not long before they found themselves trapped there. Agrippa took all their other strongholds in rapid succession. Supplies could no longer reach them by sea; Agrippa's fleet blocked the exit from the gulf, and Octavius's army menaced them from the north. In waiting too long they had lost their advantage. Demoralized by food shortages and by the epidemics which plagued military camps in antiquity, their supporters began to desert. Ahenobarbus was among the defectors. He had himself rowed across to Octavius's headquarters. A few days later he died, probably of malaria or dysentery, both of which were rife in Antony's camp.

Time was now on Octavius's side. Antony and Cleopatra called a council of war. Canidius Crassus, Antony's military commander, was in favour of abandoning the fleet and marching northward to face Octavius's army in Macedonia. He had strong arguments, notably that while Agrippa was a gifted and experienced admiral, possibly unbeatable at sea, Antony was more than his match on land. Cleopatra was inevitably opposed to this plan. The fleet was hers; its cost had been enormous, and no doubt she was reluctant to abandon it. Besides, it was where her power lay. It was her contribution to the war effort, and her hold over Antony.

Antony took her part. The traditional tale tells us that he was blinded by love. Possibly his personal feelings for Cleopatra were a factor in his decision, but their relationship was by now far more complicated than that of private lovers. If he lost her he would not only lose a woman with whom he had been living for six years; he would also have to relinquish his dream of an empire of the east. All his diplomacy, all his campaigns of the previous decade would be rendered futile. They were now, irrevocably, partners. If the only way they could fight together was in a naval battle, then a naval battle it must be.

They planned not to fight to win, but simply to fight a way out of the trap they were in. Their highest priority was the protection of the treasure, which had been loaded on to Cleopatra's flagship. This would allow them to raise another fleet, if necessary, and fight again. Antony, accordingly, ordered that sails should be taken on board, an order which sparked off a rumour that he and Cleopatra were planning to flee from the battle. The rumour was correct, but its implications, that they were craven and treacherous, were not.

On 2 September 31 BC, the Battle of Actium was fought; Antony and Cleopatra got away with their treasure, leaving many of their ships to be captured by Octavius. So much is certain. Almost everything else about the battle is disputed. Most modern historians subscribe to one of two possible versions of the day's events. W. W. Tarn believed that Antony was fighting resolutely on the north wing of the fleet, but that he was let down by the ships in the centre and on his left wing, who all either surrendered or refused to leave the harbour. Cleopatra, seeing that all was lost, sailed off with her squadron of sixty ships and Antony followed after. J. M. Carter, R. Syme and Michael Grant are unconvinced by this theory, believing that the whole fleet fought loyally, though unsuccessfully. They believe that Agrippa and Octavius lured Antony to bring his fleet much further out to sea than he had intended, so that his lines were weakened. Cleopatra and her squadron were able to make their getaway, protected by the rest of the fleet, and Antony was able to follow, but the remaining ships, although under orders to withdraw after Antony and Cleopatra, who had no intention of abandoning them, were blocked by their opponents. Thirty or forty of them were sunk before the remainder retreated into the gulf. There they were trapped, and the following day they all surrendered.

All was not yet lost. The Egyptian treasure was sufficient to pay for another fleet as splendid as the one Cleopatra had just lost and, as far as she and Antony knew, their all-important land forces were still intact. But much worse was to follow. Canidius Crassus led Antony's army northwards, only to be quickly overtaken by a column of Octavius's troops. Tempted by offers of money and land, the soldiers surrendered. Canidius and other generals escaped by night and made their way to Antony to give him the news. This bathetic defeat, with not a blow struck, not an heroic gestured sketched, was a far more serious blow to Antony and Cleopatra than the loss of their ships at Actium.

As they sailed south they heard of more defections. Asia Minor was now solid for Octavius. Fearing pursuit Antony stopped on the borders of Egypt, ready to waylay any sea attack on Alexandria, while Cleopatra went ahead, anxious to reach the capital before news of the battle's outcome reached her enemies there.

A curious lull followed. Octavius, in Greece, received news of unrest in Italy. Paradoxically his very successes threatened to undo him. His soldiers, and those of his defeated enemies, had heard news of his victory and were demanding their pay and their promised land grants, and threatening to rebel if not satisfied. First Agrippa and then Octavius himself were obliged to return to Rome to deal with the crisis. His homecoming was far from being the celebration he might have wished. At Brundisium he was met by the veterans' angry demonstrations.

This distraction gave Antony and Cleopatra a few months' grace, but Antony seems to have been too dejected to make use of the interlude. Perhaps his depression was compounded by Cleopatra's very different behaviour. She raised all the money she could. She sent Caesarion away with his tutor, intending that he should travel up the Nile, cross the desert to a port on the Red Sea and then sail to India. She planned to follow him there, and to that end she had ships dragged overland from the Nile to the Red Sea. This astonishing labour provided futile: no sooner were the ships afloat again than the Nabataean Arabs burnt them.

Her plan of escape foiled, Cleopatra resigned herself to wait. She still had money, and as long as she could protect it she had power: Octavius's only hope of paying his troops depended on his getting possession of her treasure. She might still be able to dictate terms. In the spring of 30 BC Octavius returned to the east. One after another Antony and Cleopatra's former allies went over to him. By the summer he was closing in on Egypt. Cleopatra sent a messenger offering to abdicate if he would allow her children to rule in her stead. Antony sent his son Antyllus to deliver a large bribe to Octavius and convey his father's offer to retire from public life. Cleopatra sent again, once more asking that her children might succeed her. All of these approaches Octavius ignored. Cleopatra had all her wealth carried into the mausoleum she had had built for herself, and made preparations for setting it on fire. Now it was Octavius's turn to send messages, anxiously trying to reassure the Queen that there was no need for such a desperate measure as the incineration of the wealth of the Ptolemies. Antony, in a final, despairing gesture, sent to tell Octavius that he was prepared to kill himself if his doing so would save Cleopatra.

Octavius reached the suburbs of Alexandria. Antony attacked his advance guard and put it to flight, but his advantage did not outlast the night. The next day, 1 August 30 BC, the Egyptian fleet sailed out from Alexandria and promptly surrendered to Octavius. Antony's cavalry, hearing the news, surrendered as well. His infantry, disheartened and bewildered, fled back into the city, followed by Octavius's victorious army. Cleopatra shut herself up in her monument with three attendants. Antony, believing her to be dead, stabbed himself, but the wound was not immediately mortal. A messenger arrived from the Queen to tell him that she was still alive. He was carried to her monument and was hoisted into it to be with her as he died.

Octavius's representative soon arrived at the monument, and found a way in. Cleopatra attempted to stab herself with a dagger she had hidden in her clothes, but she was overpowered and taken prisoner. She was permitted to attend Antony's burial, but otherwise she was kept under close guard. Octavius allowed it to be believed that he was keeping her alive so that he could display her in his Triumph when he returned to Rome. Possibly the story was deliberately circulated in order to hasten her inevitable suicide: if so, the ruse was successful. She asked the man guarding her to take a letter to Octavius; he acceded to her request with suspicious ease and departed, leaving her conveniently unwatched. The letter contained a request that she might be buried next to Antony. Octavius sent men to find out what was happening (but perhaps he did not hurry to do so). By the time they arrived, the Queen was dead.

It is not certain how she killed herself. Plutarch had read the memoirs of her private physician, but even he was not sure. It seems likely to have been by the bite of a snake brought to her in a basket of figs, but it may be that she had some poison ready prepared and hidden in a hollow hair comb, or that she pricked herself with a poisoned hairpin. The only marks found on her body were two tiny scratches on her arm.

Octavius had Caesarion and Antyllus put to death. The

three children of Antony and Cleopatra's union were spared. The twins, Alexander and Cleopatra, were carried in Octavius's Triumph, but afterwards little Cleopatra was married to Prince Juba of Numidia and her two brothers were allowed to live with her at her husband's court. Mindful, no doubt, of their parents' and half-brothers' fate, they seem to have led quiet and unassuming lives. At all events, history forgot them. Octavius annexed Egypt on behalf of Rome. He was to count this one of the most glorious achievements of his long life. In 27 BC he took the name Augustus Caesar, and decreed that the sixth month of the Roman calendar should be named August, because it was then that he had vanquished the most formidable of all his enemies, Cleopatra.

'So obscure are the greatest events,' wrote the Roman historian Tacitus, 'as some take for granted any hearsay, whatever its source, others turn truth into falsehood, and both errors find encouragement with posterity.'[10] Such has certainly been Cleopatra's case. But the discrepancies between her story and the known facts of her life cannot be attributed simply to the truth's obscurity. Her legend did not just grow. It was fabricated rapidly, while the events on which it was based were still current, and it was constructed for a precise purpose – that of denigrating its heroine. Cleopatra's friends and allies have left few written records. The idea of her which passed into the *musée imaginaire* of Western culture is derived almost entirely from the propaganda of her enemies. That idea has been subjected to an infinite variety of adaptations, but in nearly all of them its outline remains discernible – the outline of the monstrous but enticing character which was invented for Cleopatra by her opponent, Octavius.

In the circumstances what surprises is not the hostility implicit in the resulting image of Cleopatra but that hostility's curious lapses. It is notable, for instance, that the legend makes little of Cleopatra's two incestuous marriages (conventional among Egyptian royalty but not among Romans). Her sister Arsinoe's death at her request is seldom mentioned, her brother Ptolemy XIV's probable murder never. These offences have not been stressed, because they were not directed against Romans. We have inherited a version of the Cleopatra story in which she is identified primarily as being Rome's enemy; what she did to her own people was not Rome's affair.

It is partly for this reason that her competent and successful government of Egypt forms no part of her legend, but there are other motives more complex than straightforward hostility for this omission. Certainly it was no part of Octavius's purpose to point out that his great adversary was an efficient ruler; but that aspect of her character seems to have been of equally little interest to those more kindly disposed towards her. Ancient historians and poets dealt in stories, and Cleopatra's story, like the majority of others before or since, was about sex and violence, love and war. Topics like taxation, harvests good or bad, the policing of Alexandria (a notoriously volatile, polyglot city) and the adminstration of justice do not feature in this story. In the years when she lived loverless in Egypt and devoted herself to the important but prosaic work of government, Cleopatra slips from sight. Just as a country will drop out of the news during periods of peace and prosperity, so Cleopatra, the able administrator with a scandal-free private life, was not good copy.

A story needs a beginning, a middle and an end. Cleopatra had two lovers, therefore her life contains two stories, each of which has been given a structure which contradicts the actual facts. The story of her relationship with Julius Caesar has frequently been related as though it ended when he sailed away from Egypt. Her subsequent visit to Rome spoils the neatness of that conclusion; therefore it is ignored. Similarly her affair with Antony is imagined as having begun with love-at-first-sight when she sailed up the Cydnus in her gilded barge. The fact that the pair must already have been old acquaintances reduces the impact of that dramatic opening. Again, aesthetics have demanded that the truth be suppressed.

Few of the artists and writers who have reimagined Cleopatra have had any scruples about such fact-fudging. The notion that an historian's duty is to relate the events of the past without altering anything is as old as Thucydides, but it is only in the last three centuries that it has been widely accepted, and already doubts are being cast on its feasibility. In our own time researchers in fields as various as physics and literary theory are coming to see the ideal of absolute objective truth as a chimera, insisting that a perception is always conditioned and distorted by the personality and ideology of the perceiver. Throughout most of the two millennia which separate us from Cleopatra the majority of historians have been brazen in their biases, unashamedly selecting and suppressing material for the greater glory of their masters, or of God, or for the better entertainment of their readers.

Appian, the second-century Alexandrian historian whose *Roman History* contains several references to Cleopatra, unabashedly declares the principles he used in choosing material from the mass available to him. He refers, he says, only to those incidents 'which are most calculated to astonish by their extraordinary nature or to confirm what has already been said'.[11] Not a practice which a modern historian would approve, but one which has held sway for centuries (and which, incidentally, is still followed by the popular press). Appian was unashamed because he saw his business not as truth-telling but as story-telling. In the Christian era authors have had even less respect for historical accuracy. In a world which was but a vale of tears and a pale shadow of the glorious Yonder, factual truth had frequently to be subordinated to spiritual truth (however that might be defined). Playwrights, poets, painters and so-called historians alike have treated historical data as raw material which could be guiltlessly adapted to serve the interpreter's purpose, to point a moral or adorn a tale. In the sixteenth century Montaigne expressed sentiments which Appian would have cheerfully endorsed, and which would have found enthusiastic support in all of the fifteen hundred years which separated them. 'Fabulous testimonies, provided they are possible, serve like true ones . . . and of the different readings the historians often given, I take for my use the one that is most rare and memorable.'[12]

Rare and memorable tales have thus attached themselves to the idea of Cleopatra, constituting a legend which is a patchy fabric of uncertain facts and certain lies. This book traces the process of their accumulation and, in so doing, attempts to bring to light the fears and desires which have created and kept alive Cleopatra the harlot queen, the serpent of the Nile, the dream-woman for whose sake the world was well lost.

# 2

# THE STORY ACCORDING TO OCTAVIUS

WHEN JULIUS CAESAR first met Cleopatra in Alexandria in 48 BC she was a woman without a story. Few people outside her own country had heard of her; her adult life was only just beginning; her character was unknown. When he came to write his own account of the time he spent in her country Caesar mentioned her only briefly and coldly. 'He decided', he wrote, referring to himself as always in the authoritative third person, 'that King Ptolemy and his sister Cleopatra should dismiss their armies' and agree to reign jointly.[1] So Cleopatra enters written history, unobtrusively, with no attendant ceremony, as somebody else's sister.

Caesar's sojourn in Alexandria was to become the stuff of many stories, romantic, picturesque and erotic. But in his own account there is no bewitching princess, no love interest at all, nor indeed any reference to the financial demands he made of the Egyptians. He admits that he took an interest in the dispute between the young Queen and King, but he suppresses any sexual or commercial motive for so doing, admitting only to having done his duty, 'thinking that the quarrels of the royal family concerned both the Roman people and himself as consul'.[2]

Caesar had good reasons for reticence on the subject of Cleopatra. He was writing for the edification of generations to come, not for the amusement of friends. He had the reputation of a lady-killer. Suetonius records that his soldiers, marching back into Rome after a successful campaign, used to sing:

> Home we bring our bald whoremonger;
> Romans lock your wives away!
> All the bags of gold you lent him
> Went his Gallic tarts to pay.[3]

But his amorous conquests were for idle moments. They formed no part, apparently, of his self-image. Certainly they were allowed no place in the account of himself and his exploits which he gave to posterity.

He would have had nothing to gain from advertising his affair. If it were to be said (as it later was) that he had lingered in Alexandria – thus endangering his own and his army's safety – for the sake of a pretty princess, the story would damage his reputation both as a wise commander and as a man of honour. Besides, Caesar was a married man. When he returned to Rome he returned to his wife, Calpurnia. When Cleopatra followed him there she lived in a palace south of the Tiber where she held court not as Caesar's consort, but as a visiting queen. She may have hoped that Caesar would set aside Calpurnia and marry her. She certainly must have wished that he would acknowledge Caesarion, and make the child his heir. But when Caesar died these hopes were still unrealized. He never publicly proclaimed their partnership in his lifetime; it is not surprising that he did not want a record of it to survive his death.

Finally and, for the purposes of this book, most significantly, he probably considered it a matter of little importance. Cleopatra was not his only mistress, nor even his only royal mistress (Suetonius asserts that he had affairs with 'several queens', and mentions especially Eunoë, wife of King Bogudes the Moor).[4] When he came to Egypt she was powerless and in exile. When he left she had regained her throne, but only because it had pleased Caesar that she should. However impressed he may have been by her personal attractions she was, for him, only a human being.

Had he lived another twenty years he would have found

that the person he remembered had acquired the reputation of a fabulous temptress. His intimacy with her would already be envied and deplored as a taste of erotic bliss, a reckless adventure, a fearful test. Such is the stuff of legend. However attractive Caesar found Cleopatra, however remarkable a girl he may have thought her, however pleasant their relationship may have been, he would surely have found that legend ludicrous. When he came to Alexandria he could have had no special expectations of their meeting. And even after he came to know her, even if he was in love with her for a time, the statesman in him would have perceived her still as one of the many client monarchs through whom he administered his conquests. She was the last representative of a tired and debt-ridden dynasty. Her father had bought the right to rule his own kingdom from Rome; she inherited it on Rome's sufferance. Only one circumstance marked her out in Caesar's lifetime as an important mover in the world's affairs (and it was a circumstance he chose to suppress): she, not Calpurnia, claimed to have given birth to his son.

What Caesar wrote of her reflects his assessment of her public standing (not his private feelings for her; those remain hidden). To him she appeared insignificant. In his book, therefore, she is a cypher, a blank, only a name.


By the time Cleopatra killed herself, eighteen years after her first encounter with Julius Caesar, she had become legendary. The young monarch whom Caesar felt obliged to introduce to his readers died famous throughout the Mediterranean world. People who had never laid eyes on her knew, or thought they knew, a great deal about her. They had an idea of her character and of her significance in the international affairs of the time. That idea was based, not on fact and experience, but on a cluster of prejudices and on a largely fictional narrative. Even before her life was over its events were being selected, falsified and otherwise tailored to fit the contours of a story – a story loosely based on actual events, but deliberately and drastically misrepresenting them.

That story was devised by Octavius, Cleopatra's enemy, as the main vehicle for his propaganda against her and Antony. It is a brilliant creation, one which owes its plausibility partly to its references to archetypes and preconceptions already ancient when Cleopatra was born, and partly to the perfection of its form. Even in the histories it has a discernible tragic structure. That structure has earned it a two-thousand-year life, but it was first developed for an immediate and cynical purpose. Like all tragic plots, this one is teleologically determined. It seems to lead inevitably to the conclusion which it was designed to hasten: Antony's downfall, Cleopatra's despair and Octavius's triumph.

It is the story of a great but flawed hero undone by his passion for a cunning queen. It tells how Antony, maddened by his intemperate love for the spellbinding Cleopatra, lost command of himself. It relates how Cleopatra used her sexual power to subordinate his will to hers, and how she so dazed and bewildered him with her deceitful tricks and her intoxicating charms that he surrendered his personal sovereignty and became her creature. It is in the context of this story that Cleopatra's character, as it passed into legend, assumed its shape. That character was formed to some extent by crude hostility – hence the representation of Cleopatra as a devious, barbaric libertine – but the Octavian propaganda project made use as well of subtler strategies than simple invective. Cleopatra owes it in part to her enemies that the image posterity received of her was so attractive and so strong. It was her opponent, Octavius, who, in his campaign to discredit and defeat her, ascribed to her the persona of a beautiful and ingenious temptress, one for whose love's sake a great man might be glad to abdicate his greatness.

This imaginary Cleopatra was designed to eclipse Antony, to subsume him and render him invisible. The contest between Octavius and Antony, the contest which was decided when Antony's army surrendered after Actium and which ended with Antony's death, was primarily a domestic struggle, a competition between two Romans for supreme power in Rome. Ideologically there was little to choose between the contestants. Their strategies and their rhetoric differed, but they were both would-be dictators happy to pay lip service to the proprieties of republicanism so long as doing so served their ends. The triumvirate in which they had ruled together was unconstitutional, only supposedly justified by a state of emergency. After they fell out there was no legal or moral reason why the people of Rome should rally behind either of them. Only because Octavius happened to be based in Italy did he appear to be the guardian of Rome against aggression from abroad.

It did not suit Octavius that these facts should be too generally understood. Few Romans, after two generations of civil war, were willing to fight yet again in order to aid one ambitious fellow-countryman against another. They were, however, ready to defend Rome in a patriotic war against a foreign enemy. And, fortunately for Octavius, when Antony allied himself with Cleopatra he provided one. It was against Cleopatra, the alien queen, that Octavius declared war, not against Antony the Roman. He proposed a scenario, which was widely accepted as being a simple description of current events, in which the meaning of those events was radically altered. In this scenario Antony's role was minimized. Far from being a dangerous and potent threat to Octavius's power he was represented as a man fatally debilitated by love, the infatuated tool of a woman. Cleopatra's influence was correspondingly inflated. She was not just Antony's ally and lover, a client monarch who derived her power from his; she was the woman who led him by the heartstrings, whose lightest caprice became his law. Thus the legend of Cleopatra the all-powerful temptress was first elaborated to mask another, truer, but uglier story. It served its immediate purpose. After Octavius's victory, records the second-century Greek historian Dio Cassius, 'the Romans forgot all their unpleasant experiences and viewed his triumph with pleasure, quite as if the vanquished had been all foreigners'.[5] And so dazzling, so beguiling was it, that it has continued to persuade. Historians may know better, but cinema and theatre audiences and the readers of popular novels are still pitying

58

and envying Antony, the man who threw a world away for Cleopatra's kisses.

In the context of this legend Octavius appears in a misleadingly flattering light. His opponent is foreign; he is Roman. His opponent is female; he is male. On both these counts, according to the racial and sexual prejudices prevalent in Rome in his time, he is both the more righteous and also the stronger. He deserves to triumph, and, what is more, he is bound to do so. In the story he fabricated he himself is cast as the hero, the man predestined to usher in the happy ending, for he is conducting a campaign whose dual purpose is so virtuous, so popular, that he must surely have right and all the gods on his side. On behalf of Rome, and of all men, he is fighting (as he proclaims in Dio Cassius's account) 'to conquer and rule over all mankind, and to allow no woman to make herself equal to a man'.[6]

His version of the story of Cleopatra was to become the dominant one. The tale was frequently told in the two centuries which followed the events on which it was based. By no means all the interpreters were Octavius's lackeys; nor indeed were they all Roman – though they did, to varying degrees, owe some allegiance to Rome. All of them, though, with the exception of the Jewish historian Josephus, wrote mainly from the Roman point of view. All of them are to be suspected of mingling invention with reportage: when Dio Cassius quotes long speeches verbatim he is clearly being truer to the spirit of the story, as he understood it, than he is to the letter of any actual words spoken. All of them brought to the story preoccupations of their own. But in these frequently untrustworthy histories and poems Octavius's story is repeated, with many variations but always retaining its tripartite moral: that Cleopatra was dangerous, Antony was unfit to rule, and Octavius, by contrast, was just, competent and fortunate – just the kind of man, in short, by whom Romans might wish to be governed.

In this story Cleopatra and Antony are both allotted characters so precisely tailor-made for their roles in its plot that it is impossible to separate them from it. Antony's personality is that of a man who is bound to fall in love with Cleopatra, and to be destroyed by that love. This personality is imaginary. The real Antony appears generally to have been motivated more by ambition than by sentiment. Accounts of the earlier part of his career, of the period before Octavius had cast him as the male lead in the Antony-and-Cleopatra story, reveal him to have been an energetic and canny politician (the astute, silver-tongued Mark Antony of Shakespeare's *Julius Caesar* is true to the spirit of the ancient sources). But within the context of the Cleopatra story he appears as a predestined victim. He is brave, generous and open-hearted. His faults are not incompatible with his status as a tragic hero, but they are precisely those which will allow Cleopatra to be his undoing. He is over-susceptible to women, he has a taste for things foreign, he is occasionally debauched and, most significant of all, he is easily led. Writing in the second century Plutarch, who gives the fullest of all ancient accounts of the Octavian story (although he juxtaposes it with elements drawn from a very different tradition), makes much of his dependency, first on male friends and subsequently on his wife Fulvia. 'In fact Cleopatra was indebted to Fulvia for teaching Antony to obey a wife's authority, for by the time he met her he had already been quite broken in and schooled to accept the way of women.'[7]

The Cleopatra of the story, by contrast, is cunning and manipulative. She knows a thousand kinds of flattery. She is a deceiver whose every apparent emotion is feigned for a purpose. Outstandingly beautiful, she has an irresistible power over men and she uses it always to her own advantage. Once enamoured of her, Antony is no longer his own master. As soon as they meet on the Cydnus he is lost. His love for her, wrote Plutarch, 'excited to the point of madness many passions which had hitherto lain concealed, or at least dormant, and it stifled or corrupted all those redeeming qualities in him'.[8] At once he loses all sense of responsibility. Cleopatra 'carries him off'[9] to Alexandria where she coaxes him to waste his time in pleasure. He is like a man drugged or bewitched. He 'became her captive',[10] wrote Appian. 'He obeyed her every wish,'[11] wrote Josephus. 'He gave not a thought to honour,' wrote Dio Cassius, 'but became the Egyptian woman's slave and devoted his time to his passion for her. This caused him to do many outrageous things.'[12] He loses his Roman identity and begins to dress and behave like an Oriental. He showers Cleopatra with presents, 'no mere trinkets'[13] but great dominions. His Parthian campaign is botched and over-hasty. His army is of tremendous size, 'And yet,' write Plutarch,

> We are told that this immense concentration of strength, which alarmed even the Indians beyond Bactria and made all Asia tremble, was rendered useless to Antony because of his attachment to Cleopatra. Such was his passion to spend the winter with her that he took the field too early. It was as if he were no longer the master of his own judgement, but rather under the influence of some drug or magic spell.[14]

When he regains the Levantine coast he is so absurdly eager to see her again that he cannot even sit through a meal without repeatedly leaping up to scan the horizon for her approaching sails.[15] He is a 'slave to passion and the witchery of Cleopatra'.[16] He is 'a mere tool in Cleopatra's hands'.[17] His passion for her robs him of will and of courage. At Actium he fights at sea merely to please her, and when she leaves the battle he demonstrates the extent to which he had lost his individuality.

> And it was now that Antony revealed to all the world that he was no longer guided by the motives of a commander, nor of a brave man, nor indeed by his own judgement at all. He allowed himself to be dragged along after the woman, as if he had become a part of her flesh and must go wherever she led him ... He hurried after the woman who already ruined him and would soon complete his destruction.[18]

Destroyed he is. Cleopatra, the siren who has brought him to this sorry pass, attempts after his death to seduce the victorious Octavius; but he, being without any of Antony's fatal weaknesses, is impervious to her wiles. With no future in a world dominated by such a firm Roman she concedes defeat and takes her own life.

Octavius did not propagate this version of the Cleopatra story single-handed, but he was energetic in its promotion. He appears to have been an adroit publicist. Dio Cassius relates that at his coming-of-age ceremony, when he was barely adolescent, his tunic was accidentally torn and fell around his ankles. This looked like a grim omen but, boy as he was, he was quick-witted enough to turn it to his advantage. 'It occurred, however, to Octavius to say "I shall have the whole senatorial dignity beneath my feet" . . . Caesar accordingly founded great hopes upon him.'[19] Anecdotes about the boyhood exploits of men who grow up to wield enormous power tend to be tinged with flattering hindsight, but it is tempting to believe this one. The child capable of turning a torn tunic into a good omen grew up to be a man adept at manipulating public opinion.

During the two years which preceded the Battle of Actium the propaganda war between the two parties was intense, and Octavius took it upon himself to do much of his own dirty work. 'By repeatedly denouncing Antony in public,' wrote Plutarch, 'he did his utmost to rouse the Roman people's anger against him.'[20] His friends and allies joined in the chorus. Then, as now, once a person had become identified with a particular pattern of behaviour, anecdotes illustrating that pattern accumulated around his or her name. For the public has always, as Appian so shrewdly remarked, preferred stories which 'confirm what has already been said'. One Calvisius, a friend of Octavius's, circulated a whole series of stories designed to illustrate Antony's subjection to Cleopatra. He had presented her with the famous library of Pergamum. He had anointed her feet at a banquet. He had allowed the Ephesians to salute her as a monarch,

and on many occasions, while he was seated on the tribunal administering justice to kings and tetrarchs, he would receive love-letters from her written on tablets of onyx or crystal and read them through in public; and on another occasion . . . Cleopatra happened to pass through the Forum, whereupon

Antony leaped to his feet from his tribunal, walked out of the trial, and accompanied Cleopatra on her way, hanging on to her litter.[21]

It was Octavius himself who described the Donations of Alexandria to the Senate. And it was he who made Antony's secret will public. According to Plutarch two unfaithful friends of Antony's informed Octavius that he had deposited a will in the safe-keeping of the Vestal Virgins. Octavius demanded to see it. The Chief Vestal refused. Octavius obtained it by force and 'read it through privately and marked the passages which would serve best to discredit Antony, and later he summoned a meeting of the Senate and read it aloud to them'.[22] He may have done more: it seems unlikely that Antony would really have left such a will in Rome.[23] But whether Octavius forged the document, tampered with it, or simply selected from it, he certainly made use of it to illustrate and support one of the recurrent themes of his propaganda. 'Octavius singled out for special emphasis the clause which dealt with Antony's burial, for he had left instructions that even if he were to die in Rome, his body should be carried in state through the Forum and then sent to Cleopatra in Egypt.'[24] In other words he was no longer a true patriot, but a debased being so subservient to a foreign woman that he would even choose to make his last resting place a country far from Rome.

Octavius's assiduity as a propagandist, and the power that his victory gave him to doctor the historical record (after Cleopatra's death he not only wrote and published his own autobiography, he 'edited' the Sibylline oracles and had over two thousand documents burnt),[25] ensured that his version of the Cleopatra story was given ample publicity. Once known, it was really believed, because it catered so precisely to its public's prejudices.

Four basic premises underlie the Cleopatra story, as told by Octavius: firstly, foreigners are inferior; secondly, women resemble foreigners in many respects, not least in their common inferiority to the Roman male; thirdly, a man who allows himself to be dominated by a woman is no longer a real man, and is most certainly not a real Roman; and fourthly, such a man cannot be considered accountable for his own actions – the guilt for his misdeeds is solely his female partner's. These premises gave shape to the Cleopatra story. And because that story seemed to affirm them, it gained credence: a story encapsulating what are believed to be universal truths will itself be easily taken for truth.

Octavius's Cleopatra story is a brazenly racist one. It is the story of European men and a woman from the southeast. Or, to translate that simple geographical statement into a language of racial stereotyping which has changed little in two thousand years, it is the story of brave, public-spirited, straight-dealing men (masculinity being a northern and Occidental attribute) and a craven, wily, self-indulgent female (in the terms of this language the Orient is always effeminate). Julius Caesar, Octavius's adoptive father, took his pleasure with Cleopatra (for a hero is permitted his reward, and that reward frequently takes the form of a 'native woman') and then, as befits a hero, went on his way. Antony stayed, succumbed (went native) and was ruined.

Octavius claimed to represent Rome in his struggle against Antony. He was to write that 'the whole of Italy voluntarily took an oath of allegiance to me and demanded me as its leader'.[26] Before setting sail at the beginning of the campaign which ended at Actium he summoned all the Roman knights and men of influence to see him off, an exercise designed, according to Dio Cassius, 'to show all the world' that he was acting as Rome's chosen representative,[27] the representative of the best people on earth. Ignoring the fact that Antony's legions constituted a large proportion of his opponents' manpower, he presented his bid for power as a patriotic war. And having once identified his enemy as a foreign one he was able to play on his public's racial prejudices to devastating effect.

In a speech assigned to him by Dio Cassius, Octavius defines what, in Roman eyes, was wrong with foreigners. First and foremost among their failings is, simply, their foreignness. Romans cannot 'meekly bear the insults of this throng, who, oh heavens! are Alexandrians and Egyptians (what worse or what truer name could one apply to them?)'.[28] To be anything other than Roman was to be vile. In the first century BC, as now, simple descriptions of nationality were used as insults. Virgil refers to Cleopatra as 'Egyptian', an imprecision which may look like innocent carelessness since, though Greek herself, she was after all Queen of Egypt, but one which had a vituperative purpose. As W. W. Tarn has pointed out, Virgil uses the term Egyptian 'as a term of abuse like "dago" '.[29]

In the *Aeneid*, the great epic which provided Octavius's Rome with its defining myth, Virgil describes the Battle of Actium as depicted on Aeneas's wonderful shield. On one side is 'Augustus Caesar leading Italians into battle, having with him the senate and populace, the little Gods of Home and the Great Gods of the race'. Opposing him is Antony supported by 'Egyptians and the whole strength of the East even to the most distant Bactria . . . the wealth of the Orient . . . the nations of the Dawn and Red Sea's shore, followed – the shame of it! by an Egyptian wife'.[30] Raymond Schwab, the French cultural historian, has suggested that this passage is the first ever articulation of a sense of the East as a place in which each part resembled all the others while being absolutely different from (and inferior to) the West. In his view it marks the inception of the Western discourse of Orientalism, of the body of fables, stock characters and images in which Westerners have given expression to their fantasies about the East.[31] True, it refers to hostilities and suspicions at least as old as Alexander's Persian wars, but Octavius, in his propaganda attack on Cleopatra, marshalled those ancient prejudices and gave them new vitality and a clear, pragmatic focus.

Besides the inferior status which their non-Romanness conferred on them the Egyptians had specific vices, ones they were supposed by Romans to share with Greeks and other Orientals. Foremost among these was duplicity. 'Caesar was well aware that this was a deceitful nation, always given to dissimulating their real intentions,'[32] wrote the anonymous author of *De Bello Alexandrino*, the chronicle of Julius Caesar's sojourn in Egypt. In the same work Cleopatra's brother, Ptolemy XIII, is described as shedding crocodile tears 'so as to live up to the character of his countrymen, for he was well-trained in wiles'.[33] The refrain is constant. 'If I had to defend the Alexandrians as being neither deceitful nor foolhardly I should merely be wasting a lot of words . . . No one can doubt that this breed is most apt to be treacherous.'[34] 'Egypt was a treacherous kingdom,' wrote the first-century Roman poet, Lucan, apropos of Cleopatra.[35] 'Seditions with them, are very numerous,' agreed Dio Cassius.[36] This was clearly a popular prejudice; Octavius was to put it to good use.

Cleopatra is imagined by all those writing within the Roman tradition to be incapable of genuine emotion. When she first met Julius Caesar she was an exile whose life was in danger, one who had good reason to be distraught. Yet in his poem *Pharsalia*, Lucan decribes her distress as a meretricious trick. 'Though she pretended to tear her hair in grief, it was not sufficiently disarranged to lose its attraction.'[37] Plutarch recounts how she feigned passion when she feared that Antony might leave her and return to Octavia.

> She adopted a rigorous diet, and succeeded in making her body waste away. Whenever Antony came near her she would fix her eyes on him with a look of rapture, and whenever he left she would appear to languish and be on the verge of collapse. She took great pains to arrange that he should often see her in tears, and then she would quickly wipe them away and try to hide them as if she did not wish him to notice.[38]

Dio Cassius gives a similarly cynical account of her behaviour after Antony's death, suggesting that her apparent grief is part of a calculated attempt to seduce Octavius: 'Her mourning garb wonderfully became her . . . she bewailed her fate in musical accents and melting tones.'[39] The cunning and insincerity that these authors, following Octavia's lead, ascribed to Cleopatra found ready credence, for was she not an Egyptian, a wily Oriental, an untrustworthy foreigner? 'Noxious Alexandria!' exclaimed the poet Propertius, echoing an Octavian theme in a contemporary poem on Cleopatra, 'Land most skilled in guile!'[40]

Land most unskilled, on the other hand, in the admirable, masculine, quintessentially Roman arts of war. Dio Cassius describes the Alexandrians as being blusterers 'ready to assume a bold front . . . but for war and its terrors they are utterly useless'.[41] This was a conventional opinion. Vitruvius, a protégé of Antony's wife Octavia, wrote that 'while the southern peoples are of acute intelligence and infinite resource in planning, they give way when courage is demanded, because their strength is drained away by the sun'.[42] The *canard* that Cleopatra fled from Actium because she was afraid, and that she subsequently betrayed Antony over and over again, secretly negotiating with Octavius and encouraging her fleet to surrender, fits neatly with this estimate of Egyptian cowardice. A craven and treacherous Cleopatra is precisely the character a normally racist Roman would expect.

So ignoble, so deficient in the prime manly virtues of frankness and courage, were the Egyptians perceived to be that in the context of Octavius's propaganda their very humanity begins to be called in doubt. They 'worship reptiles and beasts as gods,'[43] accuses Dio Cassius's Octavius. Both Propertius and Virgil, in their descriptions of the Battle of Actium, dwell on the zoomorphic Egyptian gods, Propertius opposing 'yapping Anubis', the jackal-headed guardian of the Egyptian underworld, with Jove, and Virgil surrounding Cleopatra with 'monster forms/of gods of every race, and the dog-god/Anubis barking'.[44] These animal deities were clearly part of the hostile contemporary image of the Egyptian Queen, one which Octavius seems to have prompted. When, after Cleopatra's death, it was suggested to him that he might wish to pay his respects to Apis, the bull-god, he retorted, 'I worship gods, not cattle.'[45]

The implication is that the Egyptians, whose gods are beasts, are themselves bestial. It is the common purpose of wartime propaganda to dehumanize the enemy. Opponents are described as brutes, monsters, fighting machines. Thus soldiers are presented with an imagined enemy whom they can kill without transgressing the normal inhibition against murder. Octavius's troops could be relied on to be more ruthless, more staunch, if they could be persuaded that the Egyptians (and by extension, Antony's Roman supporters fighting on the Egyptian side) were utterly unlike them, that they were aliens, barbarians, not fully civilized human beings in the way that the Romans were. In his Actium poem Propertius draws a series of comparisons between things Egyptian, which he perceives as being primitive, ugly and potentially contaminating, and their Roman counterparts, which are by contrast dignified, orderly and pure. Like Virgil he describes Cleopatra's fleet made noisy by the 'clattering rattle' or sistrum, and compares this cacophonous instrument with the grand Roman trumpet, the playing of which requires skill and discipline. He claims that 'punted barges' challenged the Roman ships, a fanciful image conflating the Nile, where the barge was indeed the normal form of transport, and Actium, where Cleopatra's fleet was made up of warships every bit as solid as, and somewhat heavier than, Octavius's.[46] These imaginary Egyptian barges are something like the savage canoes of a much later racist discourse. They are frightening but impotent, tokens of 'savagery' in both senses of the word. Those who punt or paddle them are wild and cruel, but they are not really threatening because, primitive and sub-human as they are, they cannot hope to match the power of European civilization.

Their gods are weird, their music bizarre, but what stamps the Egyptians most surely as a backward and degraded people is their monarchical constitution. Cleopatra, simply by being a queen, could be used to typify everything the Romans found most politically abhorrent. Octavius, who was, after her defeat, to dub himself Emperor Augustus and to subject Rome and its dominions to forty years of autocratic government, cynically made use of the rhetoric of the all but defunct tradition of Roman republicanism. The image of Cleopatra, seated on her golden throne on the occasion of the Donations of Alexandria, seemed to embody both the outmoded tyranny of a Tarquin and the frightening otherness of the Parthian monarchs, those long-standing rivals of Rome who had within living memory inflicted a traumatic defeat on Rome when Crassus and his legions were slaughtered by their armies. It is a tableau on which, as we have seen, Octavius dwelt in his propaganda, and it was preserved by the writers who followed his lead as a salient scene in Cleopatra's story (although one which, once its political function was past, dropped out of her legend). Plutarch and Dio Cassius both describe it.[47] Her monarchy, in Roman eyes, was Cleopatra's most subversive attribute. Lucius Florus, in a second-century epitome of Livy's lost account, asserts that under her influence Antony appeared in public with a golden sceptre, a scimitar and a purple robe studded with gems. 'A crown only was lacking to make him a king dallying with a queen.'[48]

Cleopatra, the politically decadent foreigner, and Antony, who had succumbed to her influence to such an extent that her faults were also his, were not fit to govern Rome, or anywhere else. Only Roman males, according to the solipsistic Roman myth, were born to rule. In a key passage in the *Aeneid*, Aeneas meets his father, Anchises, in the underworld. Anchises foretells the rule of Cleopatra's adversary, 'Caesar Augustus, son of the deified, who shall bring once again an Age of Gold', and goes on to describe the special calling of the Roman:

> Others will cast more tenderly in bronze . . .
> And bring more lifelike portraits out of marble;
> Argue more eloquently . . .
> And accurately foretell the rising stars.
> Roman, remember by your strength to rule
> Earth's peoples – for your arts are to be these:
> To pacify, to impose the rule of law,
> To spare the conquered, battle down the proud.[49]

Neither the artistry of the Greeks nor the scientific

achievements of the Egyptians could save them from subjection. With dignified reluctance, even grimacing slightly under the weight, the archetypal Roman shouldered the White Man's Burden, the arduous but fabulously profitable task of governing those whom, despite all evidence to the contrary, the Romans judged incapable of governing themselves.

Not only, therefore, was it a foregone conclusion that Octavius, self-appointed representative of Rome, should defeat Cleopatra and her rabble of treacherous, cowardly foreigners; it was right that he should do so. At Actium, wrote Velleius Paterculus in the first century AD, Octavius and Cleopatra were fighting, respectively, 'one to save, the other to ruin the world'.[50]

If Cleopatra's race made her unfit to rule, so, even more emphatically, did her sex. Dio Cassius's Octavius enumerates the despicable and repugnant characteristics of the Egyptians – their foreignness, their superstition, their effrontery in daring to oppose the Romans, their cowardice – and then ends on a crescendo: 'Worst of all, they are slaves to a woman and not to a man!'[51] Here, for by no means the last time in the iconology of Cleopatra, the two chauvinisms, of race and sex, elide and intertwine. Orientals, who are ruled by queens, are effeminate. To submit to them would be tantamount (oh, horror) to submitting to a woman. A Roman's determination to dominate other nations was intimately linked with his concern for his own virility, for it was part of the definition of manhood that a man must be master over women and over womanish aliens. Just as the character that Octavius imagined for Cleopatra is shaped and endorsed by racist expectations, so is it conditioned by sexual prejudice. Femaleness and foreignness overlap in bewildering ways, for women and foreigners are both inferior beings. All of the attributes inseparable from Cleopatra's foreign status – cowardice, duplicity, animality and administrative incompetence – belong also to her gender. When she flees at Actium she does so 'true to her nature as a woman and an Egyptian'.[52] The two natures are all but identical. Taken together, as they are in Cleopatra, they add up to a perfect image of otherness, of all the vices and weaknesses that a good Roman soldier-male must shun.

Cleopatra, according to the Octavian story, was an entirely frivolous person. Her only statesmanlike characteristic is a greed for territory, and though she repeatedly requires new dominions from Antony, she is interested in them not as useful additions to her empire but as proofs of his slavish love. When she carries him away to Alexandria it is to make him her companion in a round of feasts and follies. 'Straightaway Antony's former interest in public affairs began to dwindle,' declares Appian.[53] 'He was so under the sway of his passion and his drunkenness,' agrees Dio Cassius, 'that he gave not a thought either to his allies or to his enemies.'[54] Cleopatra's court is a land of Cockaigne peopled by cooks, soothsayers and hairdressers, where entertainment is the only business. There, as Plutarch recounts, she and her lovers play dice, dance, drink and hunt.[55] Their only politically significant actions are those of dressing up in gorgeous, absurdly pompous robes. Their only alliances take the form of drinking clubs. Even when the might of Rome is arming against her, Cleopatra, so the story runs, can think of nothing but parties. On the island of Samos, the year before Actium, she and Antony hold a festival of glittering extravagance. Kings vie with each other in the magnificence of their gifts 'and, while almost the whole world round about was filled with sighs and lamentations at the impending war, this single island echoed for many days with the music of strings and flutes'.[56] There is, as will be seen, another way of understanding the festivities on Samos, but according to the Octavian story they illustrate and confirm Cleopatra's feminine lack of seriousness. Even in defeat, according to the story, her taste for futile pleasure doesn't desert her. Back in Alexandria after the débâcle at Actium she and Antony plunge once again into a round of banquets and revels, resolving with their friends 'to charm away the days with a succession of exquisite supper parties'.[57]

This flibbertigibbet behaviour is only to be expected of a woman and, given that women are so shallow-minded and so silly, it is clearly a man's duty to guide, protect and govern them. A man who omits to do so, who allows a woman to rule him, as the Egyptians allow Cleopatra to do, incurs immediate disgrace and runs, besides, a terrible risk — that of forfeiting his manhood altogether.

Romans had some cause to mock Egyptians for their unmanly failure to keep women in subjection. Cleopatra married both her brothers in turn because dual rule was customary, not because her own claim to the throne depended on her being their wife. Nor were women of the Egyptian royal family alone in being entitled to inherit, own and dispose of power and property. Papyri show that during the Hellenistic period women in Egypt bought and sold houses, borowed and lent money, paid taxes, made legacies and submitted petitions to the government and police — all in their own names.[58] Roman women, by contrast, could conduct no legal or financial business on their own account. All their affairs were handled by a male guardian (usually a husband or father), and his signature was required to ratify any deal or agreement.[59] There is a nugget of historical truth in the Roman perception that Alexandria was a city of women, where conventional gender roles were under threat.

Cleopatra, queen and, effectively, sole ruler, personified that threat. The effect she was imagined to have had on her subjects was calculated to strike horror into the heart of every Roman male. In his ninth epode, written soon after the Battle of Actium, the poet Horace laments: 'Alas when Romans . . . bear stakes and weapons for a woman!' and goes on to refer with evident disgust to the 'withered eunuchs' under whom these renegades are imagined to have served.[60] The stress which the writers of the Roman tradition placed on the fact that some of the officials of the Egyptian court were castrated ex-slaves is not just a matter of factual accuracy. The juxtaposition of a dominant woman with emasculate men forms a powerfully disturbing image. The subliminal suggestion is that the 'withered eunuchs' have been reduced to this condition by the Queen's unwomanly self-assertiveness. In modern parlance, she is a ball-breaker, and what she

72

has done to her own courtiers she can also do to Romans. Propertius, in a poem celebrating her defeat, holds up the horrid prospect of centuries of virile achievements annulled by the shame of submitting to a female conqueror.

> What use now to have shattered Tarquin's axes? Whose proud
>   life brands him with that same name Proud
> If a woman must be endured?[61]

Castration was forbidden on Roman soil, although the Romans were quite capable of mistreating their slaves in other ways. Agricultural work on large estates was commonly performed by slaves working in chain-gangs, a fact which Virgil and Horace, in their idyllic descriptions of country life, omit to mention. Slaves worked the mercury mines in Asia Minor where, as Strabo noted, 'in addition to the harshness of the work, the air is deadly, so that workmen very soon die'.[62] Octavius himself was considered to be a lenient slave-master, even though he had some 'arrogant, greedy' attendants flung into the river with weights tied round their necks and was said to have punished a slave who ate a prize-fighting quail by having him nailed to a ship's mast.[63] Masters less 'lenient' were permitted to, and did, discipline and punish their slaves in ferocious ways. But they did not make eunuchs of them. Naturally they were reluctant to impair a slave's breeding capacity, but it appears that this prohibition had motives other than the purely commercial. To deprive a man of his freedom, his health, his limbs or his life might be permissible, but to deprive him of his manhood was anathema.

This is the transgression of which Cleopatra stands accused by Octavian propaganda. Attended by the wretched and repulsive victims of her improper dominance, she has trapped Antony, once a paragon of masculine, militaristic virtue, and – according to the story – she has feminized him. She plays the man, ruling alone and organizing her own sexual and political affairs without deferring to any male protector. And the mate of a man is a woman, a subordinate person of trivial

73

interests and weak will. This is the degrading role into which Antony is forced by Cleopatra's unladylike independence.

Cleopatra chose her own lovers. No father or brother gave her to her partners, as Octavius gave his sister to Antony. This sexual self-determination was enough to procure her the reputation of a nymphomaniac. For a woman who frankly proposed or consented to a sexual union (rather than submitting to one on the order of a male relation) was inevitably judged to be possessed of gross appetites and unseemly boldness. Cleopatra's actual political power is ignored in the story that Octavius elaborated. It is tacitly recognized that she is an adversary capable of mounting a serious challenge to Rome, but otherwise her potency is perceived as being entirely sexual. Into the descriptions of her supposed lechery are poured all the insecurity and anger that her real personal autonomy aroused.

One of the forms in which Egyptian animality manifests itself is that of sexual promiscuity. Lucan described Egypt as 'that abode of luxury'[64] and Cleopatra, Egypt's queen, is in this respect even more abandoned than her subjects. Josephus relates a story about Cleopatra attempting to seduce King Herod 'for she was by nature used to enjoying this kind of pleasure without disguise'.[65] Lucan imagines two Egyptian officials plotting while she feasts with Julius Caesar. Their lives are at stake, urges Pothinus the eunuch, for Cleopatra will always bear them a grudge for having omitted to gratify her lust. 'We are guilty in her eyes – like every other man who has not slept with her.'[66] The myth of her sexual voracity was already current in her lifetime. Propertius calls her 'lecherous Canopus's prostitute queen', describes her union with Antony as 'filthy' and alleges (outrageously, in view of the fact that Cleopatra came of a family so proud of their royalty and divinity that they habitually committed incest rather than mingle their blood with that of mere mortals) that she had been worn out by sexual intercourse with her household slaves.[67]

This allegation of sexual intemperance is an ancient and long-lived cliché of misogynist rhetoric. Similar accusations

74

have been made against powerful female rulers from Semiramis to Catherine the Great.[68] Romans gave it ready credence. When Propertius calls Cleopatra 'prostitute queen' he is not only referring to the widely held view that foreigners are morally lax, he is also leaping to the conclusion (to which most of his contemporaries would also have leapt) that a woman who took an active part in political life was probably promiscuous. Fulvia, Antony's wife, an energetic politician who made war on Octavius in her husband's absence and, according to the disapproving Velleius Paterculus, 'had nothing of the woman about her but her form',[69] was the subject of similar rumours. Cicero inveighed against her 'hot eyes and free way of talking'.[70] Octavius himself is credited with the composition of some verses suggesting that her rebellion is a kind of sexual challenge:

> Fuck or else fight! she cries. But still I've found
> Dearer than life my prick. Let trumpets sound.[71]

When she and her army were besieged, the enemy soldiers lobbed obscene messages over the walls ('Give it to Fulvia!'),[72] implying that her political and military endeavours were merely expressions of frustrated lust.

Sex gives a woman power over a man. It befuddles and infatuates him. Thus it scrambles gender. A sexually active woman becomes preternaturally virile (powerful, independent). A sexually active man is feminized (made weak). Propertius's poem about Cleopatra begins with a defiance of those who mock him for doting so abjectly on his lover, Cynthia. 'What wonder that a woman steers my life, and drags a man enslaved beneath her laws: Why trump up the nasty charge of cowardice because I can't smash my yoke and burst my chains? ... Learn now to be afraid by my example.' The poet goes on to compare his own humiliating servitude to that with which Cleopatra threatened Rome, and he compares Cleopatra with other dominant women, Medea, the Amazon queen Penthesilia, Semiramis and – most significantly – Omphale.[73]

The legend of Omphale and Hercules was a recurrent motif

of Octavius's propaganda against Cleopatra. The story goes that, after performing his twelve famous labours, Hercules agreed to be sold into slavery in expiation of the crimes of murdering a guest and descrating the oracle of Apollo at Delphi. He was bought by Omphale, Queen of Lydia, in whose service he performed many heroic exploits and whose lover he became.[74] The crucial part of the story is related by Ovid.[75] Omphale commanded her slave Hercules to lay aside his lion pelt and to dress in women's clothes and jewellery. So attired, he was set to spin along with the rest of the slave girls and, as he worked, the great hero and lion-slayer trembled lest his mistress should scold him. When he crushed the spindle with his big, clumsy fingers she would strike him with her golden slipper and, to emphasize the fact that she had stolen his manly power from him, she dressed herself in the lionskin, his trophy and distinctive badge.

This legend was frequently referred to in Greek and Roman literature as the prototype of a relationship within which a woman had subjugated a man. Roxanne was said to have played Omphale to the Hercules of Alexander the Great.[76] Pericles's mistress Aspasia was known as 'the new Omphale' because the Athenian ruler was so immoderately fond of her that, according to Plutarch, 'he would kiss her both when he left for the marketplace and when he returned home each day'.[77] The comparison was a commonplace of the Roman propaganda directed against Cleopatra. Plutarch refers to it as well as Propertius: 'Antony, like Heracles in paintings where Omphale is seen taking away his club and stripping off his lion-skin, was often disarmed by Cleopatra, subdued by her spells, and persuaded to drop from his hands great undertakings and necessary campaigns only to roam and play with her on the seashores by Canopus and Taphosiris.'[78] Reliefs on an earthenware drinking vessel found in Italy and produced at about the time of Actium show Omphale/Cleopatra carrying the hero's club and Hercules/Antony in women's dress, accompanied by maids carrying a parasol, a fan and a ball of wool.[79] This is the feminized Antony who, according to the Octavian story, was transformed by his

76

association with Cleopatra into a ludicrously feeble creature, negligible as an enemy, fit only, as Dio Cassius's Octavius has it, 'to execute a ridiculous dance or cut a lascivious fling'.[80]

Sexual love was the agency through which a woman could so turn the tables on a man, and it was primarily for this reason that Antony's love for Cleopatra was so deplored by Octavius and his allies. Suetonius quotes a letter which Antony must have written to Octavius during the height of their propaganda war. 'What's come over you?' asks Antony, referring to the allegations of depravity being levelled against him.

> Is it because I go to bed with the queen [Cleopatra]? ... And what about you, is Livia the only woman you go to bed with? I congratulate you, if at the time you read this letter you haven't also had Tertullia or Terentilla or Rufilla or Salvia Titisenia or the whole lot of them. Does it really matter where you get a stand – or who the woman is?[81]

No doubt the list of Octavius's mistresses was designed to embarrass him but, whatever his other motives for writing, Antony was asking a real and pertinent question. Certainly there was a discrepancy between the ideal of continence to which public figures were expected to conform and the far laxer sexual morality actually obtaining, and generally condoned, in Roman society. But more fundamentally, the link between sexual conduct and political competence is by no means a simple and obvious one. Antony might well ask what one had to do with the other.

To the Romans sexual morality was not a matter of badness and goodness, but of weakness and strength. The libertine was not sinful, but he was lacking in self-control. Promiscuity was indulged in a man. Julius Caesar's soldiers called him 'whoremonger' with affectionate pride. Plutarch writes of Antony that 'his weakness for the opposite sex showed an attractive side of his character, and even won him the sympathy of many people, for he often helped others in their love affairs and always accepted with good humour the jokes they made about his own'.[82] Promiscuity is associated with openheartedness in an apparently libertarian and tolerant judgement. But it is one thing for a man to enjoy women, to take them as he takes cities, and quite another for him to be ruled by his desire. Love is of man's life a thing apart; when, womanishly, he allows it to dictate his actions, he forfeits the respect of his fellow-men.

According to Octavius's story, Antony's love for Cleopatra reduced and degraded him. When he returns to Cleopatra, in Plutarch's account, he acts 'just like the rebellious and unmanageable horse which Plato describes when he compares the human soul to a chariot team. So Antony flung away all those nobler considerations of restraint which might have saved him.'[83] Plutarch is referring to the passage in Plato's *Phaedrus* in which Socrates describes the two horses pulling the chariot of the soul. One is disciplined and dependable: 'His thirst for honour is tempered by restraint and modesty'; the other is 'hairy-eared and deaf, hardly controllable even with whip and goad'. Their erotic behaviour is typical of each. When the loved one approaches,

> the obedient horse, constrained now as always by a sense of shame, holds himself back from springing on the beloved; but the other, utterly heedless of the driver's whip and goad, rushes forward prancing, and to the great discomfiture of his yoke-fellow and the charioteer, drives them to approach the lad and make mention of the sweetness of physical love.[84]

Antony, in his love for Cleopatra, behaves like this undisciplined horse, the epitome of uncivilized, brutish appetite. As such he is not a man to trust.

The government of the self and the government of the state are linked. A man who is incapable of the one is incapable of the other. Ancient philosophers from Plato to Marcus Aurelius concluded that the self-control of which sexual abstemiousness was a test was necessary to one who would be a good ruler, and that passionate love was a sign of unreliability.[85] This is the significance of the stories about Antony leaving the law courts to follow Cleopatra's litter,

78

about his jumping up from a meal to scan the horizon for her ships, about his deserting his fleet at Actium in order to follow her sails. These anecdotes illustrate the folly of passion, but more precisely, and more to Octavius's purpose, they illustrate the way that Cleopatra has stripped Antony of the virtues (rationality, self-command, coolness) necessary for the exercise of power. And so Cleopatra's influence over him, and his love for her, are deliberately exaggerated. If it were to be understood, for instance, that he had made her grants of territory as part of his consistent and generally efficient policy of ruling the Middle East through dependent local monarchs, then he would still be perceived as being a competent statesman. But if, as the Octavian story has it, he gave her those lands simply because he loved her, then he was clearly unfit to rule Rome.

Unfit because self-indulgent, light-minded, carnal – in short, feminine. Antony was not the only person to be subjected to virulent sexual slander in the first century BC; the histories of the period are foul with slung mud and raked muck. Julius Caesar, Cicero (whose *Philippics* did much to dirty Antony's name), Octavius himself – all were accused, at one time or another, of sexual depravity. And in these prurient accusations certain themes recur. Julius Caesar's enemies put it about that he used to have the hairy parts of his body depilated with tweezers, and that he had had sexual relations with King Nicomedes of Bithynia.[86] Antony's friend Calenus charged Cicero with effeminacy: 'Who does not scent your carefully combed grey locks?'[87] Antony accused Octavius of having submitted to 'unnatural relations' with Julius Caesar as the price of his adoption. Sextus Pompeius 'jeered at his [Octavius's] effeminacy'. Antony's brother alleged 'that after sacrificing his virtue to Caesar, Augustus [Octavius] sold his favours to Aulus Hirtius in Spain for 300 gold pieces and that he used to soften the hair on his legs by singeing them with red-hot walnut shells'.[88] These repetitive, formulaic accusations speak of more than simple sexual profligacy. A passive homosexual who has had his bodily hair removed is guilty of something far more subversive, more despicable, than promiscuity. Like Antony/Hercules at the court of Cleopatra/Omphale, he has allowed himself to become a woman.

The Cleopatra of the Octavian story unmanned Antony by a dual strategy. Not only did she refuse to play a properly feminine role, thereby denying him the right to act the man; she also seduced him, drawing him into a realm of sensual and sexual pleasure which was perceived as being essentially gynocratic. She didn't make him impotent – quite the contrary – but she compromised his masculinity and so destroyed him. The word 'virility' is now commonly understood to signify male sexual potency; 'manhood' is a euphemism for penis, and the stud is the manliest of men. But there is a much older tradition, one which is still to some extent current, which decrees that the proper business of a man is not sex but warfare, and that it is a short step from stud to gigolo, from conqueror of women to woman's toy. This is the tradition Octavius invoked when he claimed that Cleopatra made a woman, a nothing, of Antony. By every sexual act his perceived virility is reduced. 'Now that the occasion calls for arms and battle what is there about Antony that anybody should fear?' asked Octavius in Dio Cassius's account. 'He plays the woman and has worn himself out with lust.'[89]

Such a debased creature cannot be held accountable for his actions. Not only, according to the story, was Antony bewitched, intoxicated, drugged, seduced and enslaved by Cleopatra, he was also, to all political intents and purposes, annulled. Unmanned, he is unpersoned, for in Rome only a man had full civil rights and civic responsibilities (Cleopatra, by taking an active part in public affairs, proved herself monstrous). He cannot be judged or blamed for his craziness in allying himself with Cleopatra against Octavius, for he is no more responsible for his own actions than one of the Roman women who were barred from making any contract without the endorsement of a male guardian. So Octavius abolished his power and erased him from the scene, declaring, as Plutarch reports, 'that the Romans were fighting this war against Mardian the eunuch, Pothinus, Iras, who was Cleopatra's hairdresser, and Charmian, her waiting-woman, since it was they who were mainly responsible for the direction of affairs'.[90]

Antony vanishes: and the conjuring trick with which Octavius contrived to make him do so would not have been much questioned, for it was well known that a man in the clutches of a lovely woman was helpless. It is always the temptress, whether or not she has deliberately set out to seduce, who is to blame for his fall. Homer's Odysseus, explaining why he and his sailors lingered so long on Circe's island, succinctly pleads the case for male innocence. 'As we were men, we could not help consenting.'[91] Lucan, in *Pharsalia*, compares Cleopatra with Helen, whose 'dangerous beauty' led to the destruction of Troy and Mycenae. So Cleopatra 'fanned the frenzy of Italy'; her 'unchastity cost Rome dear'. She has joined Helen in the catalogue of scapegoat women whose beauty is so maddening that men cannot be held accountable for their actions while possessed by desire for them. 'Who can refuse pardon to the infatuation of Antony,' wrote Lucan, 'when even the stubborn heart of Caesar took fire?'[92]

At its ugliest this notion that men are powerless to control themselves when exposed to sexual temptation becomes a rapist's defence. A woman, simply by being female and attractive, is asking for it. A man possessed, as men are supposed to be possessed, by unmasterable sexual cravings, is not to be blamed if he grabs what she seems to offer. This pernicious fallacy underlies the Roman vision of Antony helpless in the toils of an enchantress; underlies it and seems to validate it. Why should Octavius's public question the story that Antony had lost his reason and his willpower, when it was well known that no man could be answerable for what he might do when under the spell of love?

So Cleopatra is credited with the ability to take Antony over and to make him one of her creatures. Under her influence he becomes as foreign as she is. Both Plutarch and Dio Cassius repeat the allegation that he left off his Roman clothes and 'dressed in a manner not in accordance with the customs of his native land'.[93] 'Henceforth,' proclaims Dio Cassius's Octavius, 'let nobody consider him to be a Roman citizen, but rather an Egyptian: let us not call him Antony, but rather Serapis. He has discarded all the august titles of his native land and become a cymbal player from Canopus.'[94] No longer a Roman, he is no longer brave or trustworthy. He flees from Actium, as cowardly and dishonest as all his new countrymen. No longer a stalwart Roman republican, 'he referred to his headquarters as "the palace", sometimes carried an Oriental dagger in his belt ... and appeared in public seated upon a gilded couch or chair'.[95] 'He aspired to sovereignty,' wrote Lucius Florus, 'forgetting his country, name, toga and fasces, and degenerating wholly, in thought, feeling, and dress, into a monster.'[96] Or rather, into an Egyptian. By brilliant sleight of hand Octavius had transformed his Roman rival into a foreign woman's plaything, and thence into a foreigner and a woman himself. For 'it is impossible for anyone who indulges in a life of royal luxury and coddles himself like a woman to have a manly thought or do a manly deed'.[97] Roman xenophobia and misogyny could thus be turned against an enemy who was both a Roman and a man. The sheer audacity of such a propaganda campaign compels, if not respect, at least some wonder.

Once Cleopatra and Antony had been defeated. Octavius began to look around for a poet who could celebrate his talents and achievements in appropriately grand style. The search should not have been hard, for one of his closest associates was Maecenas, history's most celebrated literary patron, but Maecenas's protégés were sophisticated poets with tastes and opinions of their own, not docile hacks. Horace had fought on the side of Julius Caesar's assassins at Philippi. He was ready and willing to celebrate the Battle of Actium with a couple of short lyrics. But his republicanism, his irony and his ambivalent relationship with the court combined to disqualify him from undertaking the task of writing the Augustan epic. Propertius was equally ill suited to it. If fate had granted him the talent 'to lead heroic squads to war', he assures Maecenas in verse, he would have used that talent to 'commemorate the wars and deeds of Caesar' and to sing 'of kings' necks collared with chains of gold and the beaks of Actium gliding along the Sacred Way', but every man must find the work to which his skill is adapted, and Propertius's is that of the erotic poet. 'The soldier enumerates wounds, the shepherd sheep, but I – writhing fights in a narrow bed.' He wrote two poems on the occasion of Cleopatra's defeat, but it was left to Virgil to do what Propertius would not: 'in epic verse to build the name of Caesar back to his Phrygian forebears',[98] back, that is, to the Trojan Anchises and the son that Venus bore him, Aeneas, the legendary founder of Rome.

Virgil began work on the *Aeneid* shortly after the death of Cleopatra. It was still unfinished when he died eleven years later. In the interim rumour and speculation about it grew. The subject matter was widely known: it was to be precisely the epic account of recent history that neither Horace nor Propertius had wished to write. Virgil himself announced it in his *Georgics*. He intended, he wrote, to depict 'the enormous stream of Nile a-surge with a naval battle'.[99] The first Latin epic was to have as its central subject the triumph of Octavius over Antony and Cleopatra at Actium. The author himself had said so, and he was believed. Propertius, generously giving his fellow-poet's work some excellent advance publicity, sketches a similar synopsis, 'Let Virgil tell of Actium's shore which Phoebus guards, and Caesar's sturdy vessels . . . Give place, you Roman authors, Greeks, give place! Now is born something greater than the *Iliad*.'[100]

Roman readers must have been surprised when, after Virgil's death in 19 BC, the complete but uncorrected draft of the *Aeneid* was made public. For the poem contains only a few brief (though certainly adulatory) references to Octavius, and the Battle of Actium is described only, as it were, in miniature, as one of the scenes depicted on Aeneas's shield. And yet in a sense Virgil did precisely what he set out to do. He provides the society of Augustan Rome with a myth which defines and sanctions it, while contrasting it with everything for which, in Roman eyes, Cleopatra stood. Duty to family and country, service, loyalty, obedience, self-denial – these are the ideals to which the *pius* Aeneas owes allegiance. His faithfulness to them makes him a worthy father of Rome. And they appear to most dramatic effect in the episode in which he rejects the temptation posed by the love of an African queen.

After the fall of Troy, so Virgil relates, Aeneas wanders for years over the sea with a little band of refugees. A storm drives him ashore on the African coast. There he and his men are made welcome by Dido, Queen of Carthage. Dido, a widow, is noble and gracious, but Aeneas's mother Venus is suspicious of her and, with the help of the boy-god Cupid, infects her with love for Aeneas.

It is clear from the outset that this love is a curse. Passion's victim, Dido roams through the city where, so recently, she dispensed order and oversaw construction, as witless and distracted as a wounded deer. As she is reduced and degraded, so is her state. Passionate love stifles creativity. Carthage, once thriving, atrophies. 'Projects were broken off, laid over, and the menacing huge walls with cranes unmoving stood against the sky.' Aeneas lingers. When a day's hunting is interrupted by a rainstorm, he and Dido take shelter in the same cave and there become lovers. 'That day was the first cause of death, and first of sorrow.' Rumour reports 'how they revelled all the winter long, unmindful of the realm, prisoners of lust'. The insidious evil generated by their love spreads, disturbing the equilibrium of the commonwealth and fostering discord: as the news of Dido's affair with the stranger prince travels through north Africa, neighbouring kings begin to think of war.

Jupiter is aghast to see how Aeneas is neglecting his destiny. He was not fated to be a lady's man but 'ruler of Italy, potential empire, armourer of war'. He was to father male children and to 'bring the whole world under law's dominion'. Jupiter sends Mercury to remonstrate with him. The divine messenger finds him ignobly employed, laying the foundations of Carthage like a 'tame husband', made shamefully subservient to an alien woman by the dangerous power of love. Mercury entreats him, if he cares no more for his own honour, to think of his son, whose great destiny he will throw away with his own. At once Aeneas is shaken awake. 'He now burned only to be gone.'

He orders his men to prepare for an instant departure. Dido upbraids him, she pleads, she reproaches him. His heart is moved, but his resolution is immovable. He answers her courteously but coolly: he is not her legitimate husband; his duty is not to her but to his father, his son and his god-given destiny to found Rome. 'There is my love; There is my country.' 'Duty-bound', he orders the launching of his ships. At dawn Dido sees them leaving. Beside herself, she calls down curses on Aeneas, and prays that there should be eternal enmity and ruinous war between the Carthaginians and his people. Then, with wildly beating heart, bloodshot eyes and quavering cheeks, she bursts out into the courtyard, climbs the pyre she has had built and there, on Aeneas's bed, she kills herself with Aeneas's sword.[101]

The *Aeneid* is not a *roman à clef*. But the story of Dido and Aeneas, the story of a Roman hero seduced by a north African queen who all but prevails upon him to forget his national identity and his proper work and to stay for ever with her, thus shaming himself and betraying Rome, is full of echoes. No Roman alive when the poem was written could have read it without thinking of Cleopatra, of Julius Caesar who, 'duty-bound' like Aeneas, returned from Africa to Rome, and of Antony who did not.

Dido is a lover, and her love is an affliction from which Aeneas himself is exempt. He is not impervious to feeling: Dido's reproaches cause him agony. Her pleas make his brave heart grieve, but he knows love to be no part of life's serious business. That business is not personal but civic. Aeneas owes his duty to his father and his son, for the heritage of property and reputation, passing through the male line, is the fibre of the state. If Dido had been his legal wife he would have owed duty to her as well, for it is part of a man's honourable work to protect the women of his household and to respect the mother of his sons. But extra-marital affairs are futile recreations. Private emotions, which lead individuals to hanker after something for themselves, something which is not necessarily of benefit to the larger social group, must be guarded against, repressed, harshly condemned.

This is the code against which Antony and Cleopatra are imagined to have transgressed. When Plutarch describes Antony, waiting for Cleopatra to join him on the Levantine coast after his retreat from Parthia, repeatedly jumping up from the table and running out to see if she has yet arrived, he describes behaviour which, to readers who had learnt to admire the firm Aeneas, must seem at best undignified, at worst depraved.

We can question the actual and emotional facts of that anecdote, as of so many of those which make up the Cleopatra story. Antony had brought a hungry and demoralized army to the coast. Cleopatra was bringing him supplies, ships and money to pay troops who, if left unpaid much longer, were likely to become mutinous. His impatience was probably not entirely that of a lover eager to be reunited with his mistress.

We can also question the assumptions which determine the story's meaning, the value system which found Antony wanting and Cleopatra wicked. Antony had been campaigning for eight months. He had seen thousands of his own soldiers die and had himself been frequently in danger. Say that, on returning to relative safety, he allowed his thoughts to turn to Cleopatra, his lover and friend, who had already borne him twins and who was pregnant again when he had parted from her so many months ago, who was cultured and clever, who was the only one of his associates who knew, as he did, what is was like to wield enormous power. Suppose that as he thought of her he began to long to be with her. Suppose that, as day by day her arrival was delayed, he became quite frantic with yearning, so that even in the middle of a meal he would get up from the table and search the horizon for her sails. Would that really be so ridiculous, so reprehensible? Must we accept that the destiny Jupiter designed for Aeneas, that of fighting, governing and fathering sons, spans the complete range of human possibility? Must private emotion always be subordinated to the stern demands of the patriarchal, nationalist state? Must sexuality serve only to spawn dynasties? Must Dido always be left to die?

Octavius thought so, or so the story runs. Dio Cassius relates how he visited Cleopatra after Antony's suicide. 'Sweet were the glances she cast at him and the words she murmured.' He was 'not insensible to the ardour of her speech and the appeal to his passions', but he was not to be swayed. Throughout their interview he kept his eyes fixed on the floor.[102] Thus (how like Aeneas, how unlike Antony!) he foiled the temptation which might have kept him from his duty and his reward, a life of ruling Rome. Like Dido, Cleopatra, in the Octavian version of her story, comes to stand for everything that a man who wishes to be truly great, truly manly, must reject.


Like any temptation worthy of the name, Cleopatra, she-who-must-be-renounced, is all but irresistible. She is femininity, exoticism, sex and self-indulgence. She is also luxury, pleasure and peerless beauty. She is Woman epitomized. 'On the one hand', wrote the psychoanalyst Jacques Lacan, 'woman becomes, or is produced, precisely as what man is not, that is sexual difference: on the other as what he has to renounce, that is *jouissance*.'[103] Octavius and his allies laboured the point of Cleopatra's difference – sexual, ethnic, cultural and moral – from the ideal Roman male. In doing so, willy-nilly, her enemies made of her not only the adversary, but also the longed-for other, the object of desire. In presenting her as a dangerous siren they glorified her attractions. In condemning her depravity, they inadvertently associated her with Lacan's *jouissance*, with ineffable pleasures, with superfluity and with bliss.

Octavius had created a character too alluring to be forgotten. The memory of his imagined Cleopatra – queen

87

of an exotic wonderland, seductress of unbridled appetite and blinding beauty – was in the centuries to come to shine brighter even than his own. He made his rejection of her and all she signified the touchstone of his own virtue, but few have wished to emulate him. As with so many fables of temptation it is not the abstemious nay-sayer who is of interest, but the delights on which he turns his back. In the late classical period and the early Middle Ages one particular tableau, a single frozen still from the varied narrative of Cleopatra's life, was preserved and elaborated. It is the image of her banquet, an image which epitomizes the forbidden luxury she had come to represent. It was first drawn in detail by Lucan, nearly a hundred years after her death. In his *Pharsalia* he describes a dinner Cleopatra gives for Julius Caesar in the palace at Alexandria. Later imaginary banquets are differently placed in Cleopatra's story. For Plutarch and Pliny, for the third-century historian Athenaeus and his source, Socrates of Rhodes, it is Antony who is the guest of honour at the fantastic feast.[104] But at whichever chronological point it is supposed to have occurred, the banquet's nature remains the same. It is a spectacle of sensuality and excess, and its purpose is seduction.

The banquet is an ancient metaphor for sexual temptation, one which has not yet lost is force. Courtship still conventionally begins with an invitation to dinner. Lovers eat together before they sleep together. The carnal satisfactions of eating and sex are, by long tradition, symbolically associated. Circe feasted Odysseus. Dido feasted Aeneas. Cleopatra feasts both Caesar and Antony, parading her wealth before them, offering them food and, by the same token, offering them herself. Odysseus and Aeneas both succeeded in escaping from the woman at whose tables they had eaten, but only with difficulty, and by dint of their heroic willpower. So did Julius Caesar, but not Antony. On the Cydnus, according to Plutarch, Cleopatra captivated Antony by inviting him to dinner and then, when he had taken the bait, bore him off to Alexandria where 'each day they gave banquets for one another of an almost incredible extravagance'.[105] So Antony's ruin is accomplished. Like Persephone, who ate a pomegranate seed and lost one half of each year's sunlight, like Adam who ate an apple and lost Paradise, he traded things immeasurably precious – his personal sovereignty and his great future – for the ephemeral pleasures of the flesh.

Cleopatra's banquet is more than a mere meal, it is a digest of all earthly delights. The classical writers who first described it and the medieval ones who elaborated on the theme place it in a splendid setting, cluttered with beautiful and costly things. Lucan describes the banqueting hall 'as large as a temple' and itemizes it fixtures and fittings. The ceilings are encrusted with jewels, the rafters gold-plated. All the building materials are expensive: agate, porphyry, onyx, ivory, jasper. Lucan, whom Robert Graves has described as 'the father of yellow journalism and of the costume film',[106] notes their precise use with an interior decorator's eye. 'The doors were inlaid with tinted tortoise-shell, the dark patches concealed by emeralds . . . The walls were marble, not merely marble-faced . . . similarly the great door-posts were solid ebony, not common timber with an ebony veneer.' This is the pornography of wealth. The poet proceeds to further transports over the gem-studded furniture, the coverlets of 'Tyrian purple repeatedly dyed and either embroidered in gold or shot with fiery thread of cochineal in Egyptian style', and the attendants. The latter are as numerous and obviously expensive as the soft furnishings, and, like them, come in attractively varied colours. 'Some had black Numidian hair, some hair so blond that Caesar swore he had never seen the like even in the Rhineland: others were negroes, notable for dusky skins, receding foreheads and kinky curls.'[107]

Other writers added to the details that Lucan provides. Plutarch repeats a story told him by his grandfather, who had a friend who had visited Cleopatra's kitchens.

After he had seen the enormous abundance of provisions and watched eight wild boars being roasted, he expressed his astonishment at the size of the company for which this vast hospitality was intended. The cook laughed aloud and explained that this was not a large party, only about a dozen people, but that everything must be cooked and served to perfection, and that the whole effect could be ruined by a moment's delay.

Thus a whole succession of meals are cooked, one after the other, throughout the evening, until Cleopatra and Antony finally decide that they are ready to eat.[108] This prodigal hospitality is indecorous, uneconomic, exhilarating. It owes its first notoriety to the allegations of frivolity and self-indulgence that Octavius levelled against Cleopatra. It grew and branched into ever more fantastic forms because Cleopatra's posterity was entranced by it. 'Nothing was enough for this extravagant woman,' wrote Josephus. 'She was enslaved by her appetite so that the whole world failed to satisfy the desires of her imagination.'[109] Such vast desires, however reprehensible, have a kind of magnificence. As the legend of Cleopatra grew, her limitless depravity was transmuted into a luxury equally without limit.

When she entertained Antony on the Cydnus, writes Plutarch, her temporary lodgings were made splendid by a myriad lights hanging from the ceiling 'in such ingenious patterns . . . some in squares and some in circles, that they created as brilliant a spectacle as can ever have been devised to delight the eye'.[110] According to Athenaeus, whose *Deipnosophistae* was written around the turn of the second century AD, the walls were hung with tapestries of purple and gold and the floor was strewn knee-deep with roses. The dinner service was 'of gold and jewelled vessels made with exquisite art' and – wonderful to relate – it is all to be given away.[111] At Cleopatra's legendary banquet there is no place for good housekeeping, no thought for the morrow. Plutarch tells of servants scandalized by old and exquisite gold cups being recklessly given to a guest.[112] In Athenaeus's account the feasting lasts for four days. On the first Antony declares himself overwhelmed by the richness of the display. Cleopatra 'quietly smiled and said that all these things were a gift for him'. The next day the vessels are so massive and so finely worked as to make those of the first day look paltry.

Again Cleopatra gives them all away. On the third day each of Antony's officers is presented at the end of the feast with the couch on which he has reclined, and Cleopatra sends them all home in splendour, providing Ethiopian torch-bearers, litters and bearers for those of highest rank and, for the rest, 'horses gaily caparisoned with silver-plated harness'.[113]

Octavius proved himself, wrote Suetonius, to be free of 'over-luxurious tastes by his conduct at the capture of Alexandria, where the only loot he took from the Palace of the Ptolemies was a single agate cup. He melted down all the golden dinner services.'[114] Those dinner services! Octavius could melt them down, thus signalling his disapproval (and, incidentally, converting them into negotiable currency), but he could not erase their memory. Zenobia, the third-century Queen of Palmyra, is said to have 'used vessels of gold and jewels that once belonged to Cleopatra',[115] thus annexing to herself some of the glamour of those fabulous cups and dishes. In Roman verses and Greek histories, in chronicles of the Middle Ages and paintings of the Renaissance, they surround Cleopatra, glittering props expressing plenitude, munificence and pleasure.

More even than for her golden tableware, Cleopatra is remembered for her pearls. To the Romans pearls were emblems of opulence. Julius Caesar collected them and loved to weigh them in his hand, a taste which was cited as evidence of his inordinate extravagance. It was even said that 'pearls were the lure that prompted his invasion of Britain'; they were prizes for which it was worth travelling to the ends of the earth.[116] 'The topmost rank among all things of price', wrote Pliny the Elder, 'is held by pearls.' Pompey the Great is said to have had his portrait rendered in pearls; the Emperor Caligula wore pearl-embroidered slippers; and Nero had sceptres, masks and travelling litters encrusted with pearls. But 'the two pearls, the largest of all time', wrote Pliny, 'both belonged to Cleopatra'.[117]

Lucan's Cleopatra is resplendent with Red Sea pearls, so many that she is weighed down by them. Thus adorned, she is the picture of female vanity and extravagance for, as Pliny says, pearls are 'wasteful things meant only for women'.[118] They were to become inextricably connected with Cleopatra's name. In the sixteenth century Rabelais imagined an afterlife for her as an onion-seller in Hell: a pun, for the word onion derives from the Latin *unio*, meaning an exceptionally large pearl.[119]

The story of Cleopatra and her pearls was first related towards the end of the first century AD by Pliny the Elder. Antony is daily gorging himself on sophisticated delicacies at Cleopatra's table. He is dazzled by such splendid fare, but the Queen tells him haughtily that what he has so far seen is as nothing. She knows how to spend ten million sesterces on one banquet. He does not believe her. They lay bets. The next day another marvellous feast is served, but it seems not so greatly different from those they eat every day. Antony scoffs at it. But then a cup of vinegar is placed before Cleopatra. She takes off her pearl ear-ring, tosses it in the cup, waits for it to dissolve and then, as Antony watches wonderstruck, she swallows it.[120]

This story is not only implausible (vinegar does not dissolve pearls, and an acid which did would wreak havoc on the stomach of anyone who drank it), it is also a stock anecdote, a parable of reckless extravagance. Suetonius tells it of Caligula.[121] Horace and the historian Valerius Maximus both tell it of one Aesopus's son.[122] But of the various people proposed as its protagonist Cleopatra is the one with whose name it has remained associated, perhaps because when juxtaposed with her legendary character the pearl's erotic significance can become part of the story, for pearls are frequently associated with female lubricity. The second-century Christian theologian Clement of Alexandria was to rail against women who wore them.[123] The great whore seen by St John the Divine in his vision is decked with pearls,[124] and Pelagia, the fifth-century saint who was the proudest prostitute in Antioch before her conversion, was also known as Margarita, the Pearl.[125]

'Oh God,' wrote Jean de Tuim, the thirteenth-century author of *Li Hystoire de Julius Cesar*, 'how happy would he be who could hold that lady naked and willing in his arms!"[126] As the historical Cleopatra, with her big nose and her (according to Plutarch) otherwise less-than-pretty face, receded into the past Octavius's depiction of her as a depraved lecher capable of infatuating a hero was transmuted into the image of a beauty yielding her lovers rapturous delights. Her fabled banquet is a metaphor for the glory of her person. According to the Octavian story, Cleopatra's attractions were of Medusa-like potency. Octavius could save himself from ruin only by refusing to look at her. Lucan asserts that Julius Caesar agreed to give her the crown of Egypt because 'her face supported her petition and her wicked beauty gained her suit'.[127] Dio Cassius imagines her setting out to seduce Caesar, 'being brilliant to look upon and to listen to, with the power to subjugate everyone, even a love-sated man already past his prime'.[128] As she was lovely, so was she disposed to love. Cleopatra's sexual avidity was a byword throughout the classical period. Fragments of a piece of Latin pornography, ascribed (for no good reason) to Petronius, have survived; entitled *Priapism: Or Queen Cleopatra's Disgraceful Lusts*, it asserts that 'in truth the ancient writers repeatedly speak of Cleopatra's insatiable libido'.[129]

This wanton Cleopatra, with her complement of beauty, inspires voluptuous longing. Gradually the terrifying character of sexual predator that Octavius had ascribed to her gave way to one more passive, that of an idealized object of erotic fantasy. Lucan describes her as 'grossly over made-up', with her white breasts revealed by diaphanous stuff. Later interpreters were to preserve the enticing image but to discard the disapproving tone. Two medieval translators of *Pharsalia* were both to dwell gloatingly on Cleopatra's clothes and physical charms. The anonymous Italian author of the thirteenth-century *I Fatti di Cesare* itemises her snakeskin belt, her silken shoes, her 'cape of curious white samite lined with ermine', her red lips, her jutting breasts and small white teeth.[130] The author of the thirteenth-century French version, *Li Fait des Romains*, evokes a similar picture. He imagines

Cleopatra unfastening her cloak to display her body, a body which he lingeringly describes: full hips, slim waist, neat little ears, firm little breasts, a fresh rose-red complexion and whiter-than-ivory teeth glistening between parted lips.[131] Happy indeed were he who enjoyed such a lady's charms!

Temptation resisted is also an opportunity missed, a fool's paradise lost before ever gained. Octavius made of Cleopatra the epitome of everything the Roman male resolved to forgo in the interests of good government (of self and others), of male supremacy and of military fitness. The sacrifice was a stern one, and so alongside a horror of Cleopatra's vices grew up a regret for her fabled but prohibited beauty and all it represented. Even Octavius, so the story runs, wept for Antony and mourned Cleopatra. The *Aeneid*, the poem whose hero denied Dido, Cleopatra's surrogate, is full of the pity of wasted life and stifled emotion: Virgil's attitude to his Aeneas and the queen he rejected is ambivalent. As Cleopatra receded from living memory, as new generations of writers took up her story, she acquired the melancholy glamour of something irrevocably lost. After the Battle of Actium, wrote Lucius Florus, 'the vast fleet, being shattered in the engagement, spread the spoils of the Arabians and the Sabaeans and a thousand other nations of Asia over the face of the deep. The waves, driven onward by the winds, were continually throwing up purple and gold on the shore.'[132] The legend of Cleopatra, like that gorgeous flotsam, continues to dazzle. The ambition that motivated its invention was ugly, and so were the misogyny and racism that shaped it. But from that murky inception a perennially alluring image grew. Like a fragment of wave-brought golden treasure it is the trace of something deemed outlandish and outcast, something deliberately submerged by Rome and Rome's inheritors, but still rich, still bright.

# 3

## CLEOPATRA'S VERSION

TO THE ROMANS and their successors Cleopatra was a callous if fascinating vamp, famous, as Boccaccio was to write in the fourteenth century, 'for nothing but her beauty',[1] but to the worshippers of a cult still flourishing three hundred years after her death she was a goddess.[2] To John of Nikiu, a seventh-century Coptic bishop from Upper Egypt, she was 'the most illustrious and wise among women ... great in herself and in her achievements in courage and strength'.[3] To Al-Masūdī, the tenth-century Arab historian, she was 'the last of the wise ones of Greece'.[4]

When Rome ruled the Mediterranean world Greeks, Levantines, Jews and north Africans (among them the non-Roman writers – Plutarch, Dio Cassius, Appian and Josephus – who perpetuated the Roman version of Cleopatra's story) all learned to identify themselves as Romans, accepting that to do so gave them superior status. They rejoiced in Rome's triumphs and revered her heroes, especially Octavius, who had lived to become Augustus Caesar, the founder and patron deity of the empire. 'A Roman thought hath struck him,'[5] says Shakespeare's Cleopatra of Antony when she feels he eludes her. During the period when Cleopatra's image was being shaped it was hard for anyone living in Rome's dominions to entertain a thought of any other kind. And yet, in fragmentary texts and later footnotes, in surprising anecdotes embedded in otherwise pro-Roman histories, enough hints and clues have survived to allow us to glimpse images of Cleopatra quite different from the one fostered by her Roman enemies. Besides the real-life ruler, the shrewd diplomat and hard-headed economist already referred to, there are two further ancient images of Cleopatra – the one that her subjects and their Hellenic and Arabic posterity admired, and the one that she herself invented. For Cleopatra, no less than Octavius, was a propagandist of genius.

When Octavius was marching on Egypt, according to an Alexandrian scholar of the second century, nationalist groups offered to rise on Cleopatra's behalf (she dissuaded them because she was still hoping to negotiate an agreement for the protection of her children).[6] After her death a loyal supporter ransomed her statues, offering Octavius a large sum if he would refrain from tearing them down, as he had torn down Antony's.[7] Josephus, in the first century AD, accused her of anti-Semitism in an attempt to counter the claims of an Alexandrian writer, Apion, in whose book (long-lost) she was highly praised.[8] Among Cleopatra's subjects there were clearly many who felt not only respect for her, but also affection. Their idea of the Queen is preserved in scraps and snippets in the work of later writers and, most vividly, in Plutarch's *Life of Mark Antony*, where it lies alongside the Roman version of her. If Cleopatra has become known for her changefulness it is largely because in Plutarch's account, on which the vast majority of post-Renaissance versions are based, two mutually contradictory images are juxtaposed. In his text they can still be seen lying separately side by side, like the pieces in a mosaic. In Shakespeare's play, and in the works of most interpreters who have followed him, they are synthesized, making Cleopatra's most consistent characteristic her inconsistency and winning her a reputation for capriciousness which seems to have been quite undeserved.

Octavius and his allies suggested that Cleopatra's court was a site of barbarism, where a depraved, subhuman race worshipped grotesque gods, but to the Alexandrian eye, whose vision was affected by a very different set of racist assumptions, it was the Romans who appeared uncivilized. When, in Plutarch's account, Cleopatra meets Antony on the Cydnus, she does not only outdo him in the 'splendour and elegance' of her hospitality; 'Cleopatra saw that Antony's humour was broad and gross and belonged to the soldier rather than the courtier, and she quickly adopted the same manner towards him and treated him without the least reserve.'⁹ In this version Antony and Cleopatra's relationship becomes that of a crude soldier, representative of a young, unpolished society, and a wise, cultured and aristocratic woman who indulges him and tries, with infinite tact, to educate him to her level.

Back in Alexandria Plutarch's Cleopatra entertains her guests. 'Whether Antony's mood was serious or gay, she could always invent some fresh device to delight or charm him.' Antony amuses himself by dressing up as a slave. 'He liked to wander about the city, stand by the door or windows of ordinary citizens' houses and make fun of the people inside.' He is indulged. 'The Alexandrians had a weakness for his buffoonery and enjoyed taking part in these amusements in their elegant and cultivated way.' Sometimes Cleopatra disguises herself as well and accompanies him on his nocturnal rambles through the city, but it appears that these childish pleasures pall quickly on her. Plutarch relates an anecdote about a fishing party during which she orders one of her servants to attach a salted fish to Antony's line. 'The whole company burst out laughing . . . and Cleopatra told him: "Emperor, you had better give up your rod. . . . Your sport is to hunt cities and kingdoms and continents." '¹⁰ Far from enticing him to waste time in self-indulgence this Cleopatra, impatient of play, is urging him on to great endeavours.

According to the Alexandrian tradition Cleopatra was notable, not for her sex life and her party-giving, but for her scholarship and her public benefactions. There is no reason to suppose that this idea of her is any more factually accurate than the Roman notion of the prostitute queen. Bishop John of Nikiu, who claimed that 'she executed many noble works and created many important institutions. . . . There was none of the kings that preceded her who wrought such achievements as she', believed her to have died 'in the fourteenth year of the reign of Caesar Augustus'.[11] Al-Masūdī, who praises her scientific knowledge, asserts, even more wildly, that the asp that killed her, a fabulous two-headed serpent capable of bounding several feet in the air, hid itself, after stinging her, in an aromatic pot plant, and when Octavius appeared to inspect her dead body it leaped out of the bush and bit him too. He died next day (so much for Augustan Rome), having first composed 'some verses, in Romish language, on the accident that had befallen him and the history of his rival', verses which Al-Masūdī claims were still well known in the tenth century.[12] The image of the beneficent scholar Cleopatra is quite possibly as much of an imaginary construct as the Roman one of the temptress Cleopatra. All the same, the contrast between the two is illuminating – a salutary reminder that every story has, at the very least, two sides.

Interestingly, a Roman who knew and (by his own account) hated Cleopatra, Cicero, confirms that she had bookish interests. He appears to have felt that she let him down in some way but, as he wrote to a friend, despite salacious rumours arising from her reputation in Rome, 'Her promises were all things that had to do with learning, and not derogatory to my dignity, so I could have mentioned them even in a public speech.'[13] There was evidently at least some truth in the notion of her erudition. Appian asserts that in Egypt Antony 'went out only to the temples, the schools, and the discussions of the learned', choosing these high-brow pastimes 'out of deference to Cleopatra, to whom his sojourn in Alexandria was wholly devoted'.[14] Perhaps so, but Cleopatra's supposed scholarship was soon to assume fabulous dimensions. Plutarch ascribes to her prodigious linguistic attainments.

It was a delight merely to hear the sound of her voice, with which, like an instrument of many strings, she could pass from one language to another, so that in her interviews with barbarians she seldom required an interpreter, but conversed with them quite unaided, whether they were Ethiopians, Troglodytes, Hebrews, Arabians, Syrians, Medes or Parthians. In fact [at this point in the catalogue of her attainments Plutarch's own credulity seems to have been uncomfortably stretched] she is said to have become familiar with the speech of many other peoples besides.[15]

In the two centuries after her death Alexandrians ascribed several literary works to Cleopatra. These attributions should not necessarily be taken to mean that she wrote the books in question, but they do indicate what these ancient scholars supposed her interests to have been. It is no surprise to find that a work on cosmetics was said to be from her hand,[16] but her special knowledge was not imagined to begin and end with the craft of self-adornment. She was also believed to be the author of a work on weights, measures and coinage, one on gynaecology and another on alchemy.[17] In the first century AD it was said that she had been taught by the sage Comarius, and had learnt from him the mysteries of the philosopher's stone.[18] An unknown author assigned her a leading role in a fictitious *Dialogue Between Cleopatra and the Philosophers*,[19] and around the turn of the first century AD Flavius Philostratus described her as 'deriving a positively sensuous pleasure from literature'.[20] To Al-Masūdī (who, in common with most Arabs of her period, lamented Greece and disregarded Rome) she, the last great Hellenistic ruler, was 'a princess well versed in the sciences, disposed to the study of philosophy and counting scholars among her intimate friends. She was the author of works on medicine, charms and other divisions of the natural sciences. These books bear her name and are well known among men conversant with art and medicine.' It was not in order to display her in his Triumph that Al-Masūdī's Octavius wanted to capture her alive, but because he wished to learn from her 'the precious secrets she possessed' as the last surviving exponent of ancient Greek wisdom.[21]

Cleopatra was also believed to have been a public benefactor, designing and commissioning many of the great engineering projects which had enabled Alexandria to prosper. This aspect of her posthumous reputation may have some foundation in fact. It is known that she could command the resources and the expertise required to drag ships across the desert from the Nile to the Red Sea. It is also known that she built a monument for herself massive enough to do duty as both bank vault and fortress. But again the claims made on her behalf by later writers are evidently fantastic. In the fourth century the Syrian Ammianus Marcellinus and the Byzantine chronicler John Malalas credited her with having built the lighthouse of Pharos, one of the Seven Wonders of the World, and the causeway connecting it with the mainland.[22] (In fact both structures were complete two hundred years before she was born.) Other writers asserted, equally erroneously, that she had constructed the canal which brought water to Alexandria.[23] John of Nikiu united all these traditions in his chronicle, adding that she had built a palace 'and all that saw it admired it, for there was not the like in all the world. . . . And she executed all these works in vigilant care for the well-being of the city.'[24]

This image of Cleopatra as philosopher and heroine of the public works department forms a clear and pleasing contrast with the barbaric voluptuary of the Roman imagination. But it is possible to discern yet a third image, one infinitely grander and more charismatic than either of the others. It is the image of Cleopatra as depicted in her own propaganda, the image of a mighty queen who was also a messiah, the long-awaited liberator of Asia, a goddess and an immortal.

All public figures are fictional. In our own time it is possible to feel that we know certain television personalities or politicians as intimately as we know our own friends, but what we know in such cases are not people but representations of people. They are characters constructed, just as the characters in a novel are, by reference to archetypal models, by illustrative anecdote, by the use of rhetoric and of visual imagery, and by the semiology of clothing, physiognomy and gesture. When politicians appear in public every detail of their speech, dress and behaviour can be read as part of a complex message about power and their fitness to wield it, about the institutions they represent and about the values that those institutions endorse. Astute celebrities take an active part in formulating and transmitting that message, inventing (or employing others to invent) new selves for themselves. But even those innocents who refrain from deliberately writing themselves will all the same be read. A president, a princess, the host of a television chat show, are all of them imaginary beings (although each one resembles, possibly quite closely, the flesh-and-blood person of whom he or she is an image). Hence the odd, incredulous shock common to anyone who for the first time meets someone famous. To shake a president or rock star by the hand is as disorientating as it would be to see a ghost or a vision. As image and actuality collide the word is, bewilderingly, made flesh.

None of this is peculiar to the television age. The art of public relations is a very ancient one. Cleopatra, Antony and Octavius all conducted themselves in public as actors in a drama of which the symbolic code was thoroughly familiar to themselves and to their audience. Through the accounts that have survived it is possible to see how they treated the events in which they participated as the raw material of propaganda and myth, and to trace the strategies whereby they struggled to turn the tale to their own various advantages. Moment by moment they were writing, directing and performing in their own legends, even in the act of living out their lives.

Cleopatra was as adroit as Octavius in shaping the public perception of her own actions. Like him, she deliberately imposed on them an imaginary meaning designed to enhance her perceived image, to justify her policies and to further her cause. Unlike him she did not use words, which were inaccessible to the illiterate majority (or if she did, her speeches and writings have been erased from the historical record), but the language of drama and spectacle. Between the lines of the ancient accounts of her career one can watch a fantastic pageant being performed, a pageant which is simultaneously a sequence of real events and the symbolic and immensely exaggerated representation of them.

Rulers of the period commonly advertised themselves and

their world views by means of ceremonial spectacle, while simultaneously entertaining a grateful people. The Roman tradition of the Triumph provided the military leaders and, later, the emperors with a perfect medium for self-glorification. These were far from being mere military parades. When Julius Caesar celebrated his Triumph after the Alexandrian war, so Lucius Florus records, the procession included not only Cleopatra's sister, the Princess Arsinoe, in chains but also huge tableaux borne on floats, representations of the Nile and of the famous lighthouse of Alexandria, with 'very life-like flames' apparently darting from it.[25] The provision of such a show was considered virtuous. Roman emperors boasted of their games as being among their finest achievements. Octavius, summing up his life, placed among his conquests and his benefactions eight gladiatorial shows involving ten thousand fighting men (a large proportion of whom would have died for the amusement of the Roman people), five athletic displays, twenty-seven separate festivals of Games and twenty-six 'hunting spectacles', in the course of which three thousand five hundred African wild animals were killed. He was also proud to have mounted 'an exhibition of a naval battle' (almost certainly a re-enactment of his victory at Actium), in which thirty ships, a number of smaller vessels and three thousand sailors took part.[26]

Cleopatra's spectacles were less gross than those of Rome, using the language of religious symbolism rather than that of warfare, but, like Octavius's massacres and mock battles, they were designed to impress spectators with the power and glory of their originator. The surviving accounts of her life contain descriptions of several such staged occasions, the last of which was her own death.

The legend of Cleopatra begins with the story, first narrated by Plutarch,[27] of her unorthodox entry into the besieged palace at Alexandria, hidden in a roll of bedding and smuggled into Julius Caesar's presence by her loyal supporter, Apollodorus. The anecdote is picturesque and titillating, and yet it may be true; it is not obvious who would have had anything to gain by inventing it. It evokes a character consistent with what is known of Cleopatra's later career. The princess who had herself bundled up in rugs was desperate and audacious. In daring to enter the palace, heavily guarded by Pothinus's troops, she was risking her life. This first vignette of the teenage Cleopatra is swashbuckling, comical even, but it demonstrates considerable courage and resourcefulness. It also, most significantly, suggests that she had already developed the sense of theatre which was to distinguish other crucial events of her life. Her throne, and possibly her survival, depended on her impressing Caesar. To make such an entrance into his private apartments would ensure that he would at least take notice of her. Ptolemy XIII, for one, understood that this sudden appearance was a great deal more than a frivolous erotic escapade. According to Dio Cassius, 'the sight of his sister within the palace was so unexpected that the boy was filled with wrath and rushed out among the people crying that he was being betrayed, and at last he tore the diadem from his head and cast it away'.[28]

Her throne secured and peace restored, Cleopatra staged a more elaborate show, this time for the benefit of her newly subdued subjects. She and Julius Caesar, according to Suetonius, 'would have sailed together in her state barge nearly to Ethiopia had his soldiers consented to follow him'.[29] The suggestion that Caesar was so besotted with her as to risk provoking a mutiny is highly questionable. But some sort of river-trip probably did take place. It would not have been the sybaritic private cruise about which later writers were to enjoy fantasizing, but a procession charged with political meaning. The new Queen, who had so lately been deposed and in exile, travelled up the Nile (not a holiday resort but her kingdom's main thoroughfare) with all possible pomp and splendour, and at her side sat the man who had recently become Rome's undisputed ruler. Thus, in a kind of investiture-*cum*-summit meeting, she paraded before her people her newly confirmed monarchy and her alliance with a mighty protector.[30] Her barge may have been faced with ebony, trimmed with gold and hung with purple silk, as story-tellers were later to assert; if it was, its splendour was designed not for Cleopatra's own sensual pleasure but as a symbol of her royal magnificence.

Seven years later she was to stage a waterborne spectacle of even greater brilliance. Most of the ancient historians (Appian being an exception) ignore the fact that Antony and she must already have known each other well by 41 BC. It was recognized that the meeting on the Cydnus was, in all senses but that of literal fact, the beginning of their association, and therefore the beginning of the story about them. In this the historians were not exercising their independent editorial judgement, but recording a legend whose structure and significance had been carefully planned by the chief performers in it. Cleopatra did not so much arrive on the Cydnus as make an entrance there. If historians have perceived that encounter as the beginning of the Antony and Cleopatra story, that is largely because one, and possibly both, of the principals intended them to do so. The manner of Cleopatra's arrival was calculated to impress all beholders as the inception of an indomitable partnership and the inauguration of a new era.

A consummate actress, she paid due attention to timing. She ignored Antony's often-repeated invitation which might, coming from the overlord of Asia, seem humiliatingly like a summons. She arrived in Asia Minor by her own route and in her own time. She was properly prepared. Later writers no doubt exaggerated the luxury of her entourage; but she put on a gorgeous show. Plutarch's excited description conveys some of the splendour of the scene. She sailed up the river in a barge embellished with all the conventional accessories of wealth and power: gold, silver, purple cloth, music, clouds of perfume, beautiful boys and girls. At the centre of this dazzling tableau 'Cleopatra herself reclined beneath a canopy of cloth of gold'. Crowds gathered, perhaps rounded up by Cleopatra's people under orders to ensure that this spectacle was not wasted, and followed her along the bank, both impressed by, and by their attendance adding impressiveness to, her progress. The rumour of her coming spread into Tarsus (again probably carried there by her agents).

People spilled out of the city to see her, thereby thwarting what must have been Antony's intention, that she should make her first appearance in a properly subordinate role, paying homage to him in the marketplace.[31]

This spectacle had several themes. The first, and most obvious, was opulence. Heads of state have always visited each other with as much pomp as they have been able to muster, the richness of the ruler's turn-out being a sure index of a nation's economic strength. Cleopatra's and Egypt's security depended on Antony's recognizing her value as an ally, and that value would be primarily financial. At Tarsus she took the opportunity of parading it.

Subsequent events bear out the ancient authors' view that this pageant was also, at least in part, a piece of erotic display. Cleopatra's youthful experience with Julius Caesar had taught her how sex can cement an alliance. Very likely she did come to Cydnus with the intention of seducing Antony, but her motives for wishing to do so would have been far more complex than the 'lechery' of which the Augustan poets accuse her. When they became lovers their sexual congress was itself part of the performance she was staging for a watching world. Their coupling was a divine union, a heavenly marriage (though never legally an earthly one).

For her progress up the river Cleopatra was, says Plutarch, 'dressed in the character of Venus (or Aphrodite), as we see her in paintings, while on either side to complete the picture stood boys costumed as Cupids, who cooled her with their fans'.[32] This is not just an indirect way of comparing Cleopatra's beauty with that of images of Venus, as Shakespeare's Enobarbus does. It is a precise and literal description. Just as a poet could make use of the personages of legend and mythology as units of meaning in a widely understood symbolic language, so too could monarchs and commanders. Cleopatra and Antony were both adept in the use of this numinous vocabulary.

In the eyes of her subjects Cleopatra was a goddess. While her father was still alive the Alexandrians dedicated a temple precinct to him and his children as 'Our Lords and Greatest

Gods'.[33] Already a deity as a princess, as ruling queen she was doubly divine. The Ptolemies inherited their godhead from Dionysus via Alexander the Great, who claimed to be a descendant of the god and who himself became the focus of a cult after his death, and also from the Pharaohs, the ancient Egyptian god-kings whom they had supplanted.

As Queen, Cleopatra was automatically identified with Isis, the supreme goddess of Egypt whose cult, by the first century BC, was widespread throughout the Hellenistic world. This was a useful association for her, bridging the gap between the culture of her Greek-speaking court and that of her native Egyptian subjects. Isis was already a great deity in early Pharaonic times. By linking themselves with her and invoking her sanction to rule, Ptolemaic queens like Cleopatra were able to give a semblance of legitimacy and venerability to the power of their dynasty, still perceived by many Egyptians as one of foreign usurpers.

At the end of her life, in one last desperate attempt to raise an army and reverse the defeat of Actium, Cleopatra was to seize treasure belonging to sacred shrines, or so Dio Cassius alleged.[34] But later authors were wrong to deduce from this accusation that she was lacking in reverence for the gods. An inscription from Hermonthis (modern Armant) records that in 51 BC, the first year of Cleopatra's reign, 'the queen, the Lady of the Two Lands, the goddess who loves her father, rowed the Bull in the barge of Amon to Hermonthis'. This bull was the incarnation of the bull-god Buchis, just as Cleopatra was the incarnation of Isis. A previous bull had died, and the replacement had to be escorted up the Nile from Thebes in one of the great waterborne processions which formed an essential part of Egyptian ceremonial life. Most historians agree that the queen-goddess who accompanied it must have been Cleopatra.[35] At a distance of more than four hundred miles from her capital, in the ancient and sacred heartland of Egypt, she made what must have been one of her first formal appearances as Queen on an occasion which made it plain that she intended to take her sacred role seriously. The gesture must have done much to ensure the loyalty

106

of the denizens of Upper Egypt, who had launched numerous nationalist revolts against Cleopatra's forebears.

The cult of Isis was known to Rome. In 50 BC a consul decreed that all the shrines of Isis should be torn down, but no labourer could be found willing to carry out the order. Finally the consul himself had to take up an axe and begin the demolition.[36] The story illustrates both the respect in which the goddess was held by the lower classes, and the suspicion that her cult accordingly aroused among the authorities. Her worshippers must have included many slaves and other immigrants from the Hellenistic east, and the cult was therefore perceived as a focus for disaffection. But this was only one part of the picture. Isis counted among her devotees many Roman women of the highest class. Propertius complains bitterly that his beloved Cynthia has banished him from her bed for ten nights because she is keeping a vigil in honour of Isis.[37] Juvenal, writing a century later, testifies even more resentfully to the typical Roman lady's devotion to Isis. 'If some Egyptian goddess instructs her to make a pilgrimage to the Nile, she'll leave at once, follow the river to its source, and return with a phial of sacred water to sprinkle on the temple. She actually believes that Isis speaks to her! As if any god would bother to talk to such a fool!'[38] Roman propaganda had made of Cleopatra the alien and the distillation of all that was worst in womankind. By a pleasing reversal she herself had assumed the persona of the goddess known in Rome as protector of foreigners, and of those Romans who were themselves outsiders in the patriarchal state – women.

Rome assimilated the religions of its Asian dependencies, just as it assimilated the pantheon of the Greeks. In the process the new deities often became merged with familiar ones by the simple change of a name. This assimilation was facilitated by the fact that images played such a central part in the religions of the period. A mother with a baby could be Venus with Cupid, Aphrodite with Eros or Isis with Horus. Later this same, ever-popular iconographical tradition was smoothly, and with supreme success, taken over by yet another religion, according to which the figures were dubbed Mary and Jesus. The change of names was easy, so long as the essential nature of the deity remained the same.

Isis was an especially adaptable goddess, combining within herself a multiplicity of divine characters. Her portmanteau nature is celebrated in an Egyptian hymn of the first century BC: 'for thou art, and thou alone, all of the goddesses which divers people call by divers names'.[39] The novelist Apuleius, writing in Madaura, a Roman colony in Africa, in the second century AD, described a vision of Isis in *The Golden Ass*. The narrator, Lucius, who has been turned into an ass, prays to 'The Queen of Heaven', the moon. He does not know her name, but begs her to help him regain his human shape, whether she be Ceres, Proserpine, Venus, Artemis or some other. The goddess appears to him in a dream, not in the least put out by his haziness as to her identity. 'Though I am worshipped in many aspects, known by countless names, and propitiated with all manner of different rites, yet the whole round earth venerates me.' Only the Egyptians 'who excel in ancient learning and worship me with ceremonies proper to my godhead, call me by my true name, namely, Queen Isis'.[40]

When Caesar returned to Rome after the Alexandrian war he set up a golden image of Cleopatra, Isis's earthly representative, in the temple of Venus Genetrix, Venus the Mother.[41] The action was important to Cleopatra, for it was the nearest Caesar ever came to acknowledging Caesarion as his son. It also suggests that he understood the links between Cleopatra, Isis and Venus. Cleopatra herself certainly did.

On public occasions, so Plutarch tells us, she customarily wore 'the robe which is sacred to Isis, and she was addressed as the New Isis'.[42] Apuleius's description of Lucius's vision suggests how she must have looked when so attired.

[Isis's] long thick hair fell in tapering ringlets on her lovely neck, and was crowned with an intricate chaplet in which was woven every kind of flower. Just above her brow shone a round disc, like a mirror, or like the bright face of the moon, which told me who she was. Vipers rising from the left-hand and right-hand parting of her hair supported this

108

disc, with ears of corn bristling beside them. Her many-coloured robe was of finest linen; part was glistening white, part crocus-yellow, part glowing red and along the entire hem a woven bordure of flowers and fruit clung swaying in the breeze. But what caught and held my eye more than anything else was the deep black lustre of her mantle. She wore it slung across her body from the right hip to the left shoulder, where it was caught in a knot resembling the boss of a shield; but part of it hung in innumerable folds, the tasselled fringe quivering. It was embroidered with glittering stars on the hem and everywhere else, and in the middle beamed a full and fiery moon.[43]

Fancifully sumptuous though this description is, it is not the poet's invention. The design of the Egyptian royal crown incorporated the devices of the serpents sacred to the supreme god, Ra, and the crescent moon, emblem of Isis. The red, white and yellow dress was also conventional. Plutarch notes that 'the robes of Isis are variegated in their colours, for her power is concerned with matter which becomes everything and receives everything, light and darkness, day and night, fire and water, life and death'.[44] Robes of many colours and black silk-fringed shawls woven with golden stars would not have been beyond the skill of Alexandrian dressmakers. When Cleopatra sat in state her appearance would have closely resembled that of the goddess as described by Apuleius.

In this guise she would have seemed to her subjects an immensely attractive figure, to be loved as well as revered. Isis was all-powerful. Although her male fellow-deities, Osiris, Horus and Amon-Ra, played important roles in her myth, her cult seems to have come close to monotheism. A hymn has survived from Hellenistic times which makes plain the extent of her power: 'I divided the Earth from the Heaven. I showed the Path of the Stars. I ordered the Course of Sun and Moon. I devised the activities of the Sea. . . . I created walls of cities. I am called the lawgiver. I brought up islands out of the depths into the light. I am lord of rainstorms. I overcome fate. Fate hearkens to me. . . .'[45]

Isis was awesome, but she was also kind. She was the special protector of women, but her beneficence was universal. She effected miraculous cures[46] and she was a goddess of plenty. Herodotus, writing in the fifth century BC, roundly declared that she was one and the same as the Greek goddess Demeter.[47] The identification is a natural one, for both are goddesses of the earth and of fruitfulness, and both number the ear of wheat among their emblems. Diodorus Siculus, a Sicilian writer who visited Egypt while Cleopatra was a child, witnessed Festivals of Isis when stalks of wheat and barley were carried in processions and heard labourers give thanks to the goddess at harvest time: 'Standing beside the sheaf they strike themselves and call upon Isis, by this act rendering honour to the goddess for the fruits which she discovered.'[48] It was easy for Romans to appreciate her in this role, for much of Rome's grain supply came from Egypt. It would have seemed equally appropriate to Egyptians, for Isis presided over the annual rising of the Nile, which rendered their country fertile.

She was also a mother, a wife and a sister, and in each relationship exemplary for her affection, her fidelity and her devoted self-sacrifice. According to the myth, of which the earliest surviving account is given by Plutarch, she and her twin brother Osiris are the progeny of the Sky and the Earth. Before they are even born they fall in love and 'consort together in the darkness of the womb'. Once mature, Osiris travels over the world and subdues all nations 'without arms but with persuasive discourse, song and music'. This virtuous and successful mission arouses the jealousy of his brother Seth (or Typhon). Seth kills Osiris and divides his body into fourteen pieces. Isis, consumed with sorrow, searches hither and thither until she has found all the parts but one, the phallus. She pieces them together and so bestows on Osiris eternal life. Magically making amends for the absence of Osiris's genitals she contrives to conceive and gives birth to Horus, who is both Osiris's child and a reincarnation of Osiris himself.[49]

Plutarch interprets this myth as a parable of the annual

110

rise and fall of the Nile, and the cyclical fertility of the soil of Egypt (Isis) which sprouts anew when the river (Osiris) returns.[50] Certainly Osiris is one of the vegetation gods, whose fate it is to die and to come again repeatedly. But it is Isis's devoted quest for his body, and her miraculous restoration of his life, which made the myth resonant for her devotees.

'I made man strong. I brought together woman and man. I appointed to women to bring their infants to birth in the tenth month. I ordained that parents should be loved by children. I laid punishments on those without natural affection towards their parents.' So proclaims the Hymn to Isis.[51] Cleopatra, imagined by the Romans as a wanton sensualist, was the earthly representative of a goddess whose special attraction was that of 'the kind, warm-hearted wife, sister and mother, nursing her child at home'.[52] Horus's magical conception left Isis pure, for in an ancient Hymn to Osiris she is addressed as 'the Great Virgin'.[53] The Greeks associated her with Artemis, the chaste goddess of childbirth. She has even more in common with the virgin mother of Christianity. The milk of life flowed from her breasts[54] and with it she joyously fed the infant god Horus, who, like Jesus, was one with his father. Figurines and paintings depicting her in this, her most characteristic pose, are indistinguishable from representations of the Madonna and child.[55] Early Christians saw, and happily made use of, the resemblance. Next to the temple of Isis at Philae the Coptic bishop Theodore built a church to Mary, Mother of God. His congregation must have worshipped this new avatar of Isis Myrionymos (Isis whose names cannot be numbered) with the ease of familiarity.[56]

The idea that Cleopatra, known to us, as she was to her Roman contemporaries, as the profligate libertine, could have any link with the Virgin Mary seems almost laughable. In the imaginary museum of Western culture they have been placed in opposite corners. Yet to her subjects she must have embodied just those qualities of self-denying love, fidelity and compassion which the Virgin Mary shares with Isis. Isis the Great Mother was her favourite role model. When she appeared in public at her moment of greatest (if illusory) triumph, the Donations of Alexandria, her children were on the silver dais beside her, each one, even two-year-old Ptolemy Philadelphus, seated on a child-sized throne.

In Cleopatra's society, as in ours, the image of the mother was a positive and attractive one. But she had other, more specific reasons for wishing to associate herself with Isis's maternal aspect. Isis was the mother of a son who was also a god. Shortly after Caesarion was born Cleopatra issued coins showing herself as Isis, suckling an infant.[57] This image was expanded and its meaning made explicit in a temple at Dendera decorated with reliefs celebrating her son's birth and depicting herself and Caesarion in the guise of Isis and Horus.

Such representations would have acquired a new meaning after the Ides of March, 44 BC. When Cleopatra first identified Caesarion with Horus on her coinage she was claiming divinity for him and presenting him as the boy who could bring new prosperity to Egypt. In the ancient text *Lamentation of Isis for Osiris* Isis proclaims: 'Thy son Horus is ruler of the lands.'[58] As a god, and son of a god, Horus/Caesarion was fit heir to the Egyptian empire, and perhaps to that of Rome as well. In publicly emphasizing his identity with the god, Cleopatra was stressing that he was indeed the true son of his divine father, Julius Caesar, who was known after his death as 'the deified'. She knew her country's ancient myths; she also knew how to shape them to her own political ends.

There was a place in those myths for Antony and her association with him. If Julius Caesar was the Osiris who died, and whom she mourned devotedly, Antony was the resurrected Osiris whom she brought home, rejoicing, to Egypt. Dio Cassius records that Antony and Cleopatra posed for double portraits as Isis and Osiris. 'This, more than anything,' says Dio, 'made him seem to have been bewitched by her through some enchantment.'[59] On the contrary, it suggests that Antony had noted with clear eyes how subtle and effective was Cleopatra's public relations programme. He would have had no cause to object at being identified with a god who, as Diodorus Siculus records, was 'of a beneficent turn of mind and eager for glory', and had travelled 'as far as India and the limits of the inhabited world' establishing agriculture, founding cities and receiving the homage of grateful nations.[60]

Cleopatra's arrival at Tarsus by water was appropriate to her divine persona. Isis was the inventor of seafaring and the protector of sailors. Apuleius's Lucius describes the Navigium Isidis, the festival celebrating the beginning of the summer sailing season. A procession of comedians in fancy dress, women crowned with flowers, choirboys and musicians, priests and effigies of the Egyptian gods, makes its way to the seashore. 'There with solemn prayers the chaste-lipped priest consecrated and dedicated to the Goddess a beautifully built ship, with Egyptian hieroglyphics painted over the entire hull; we admired the gilded prow shaped like the neck of Isis's sacred goose, and the long, highly polished keel cut from a solid trunk of citrus wood.' The ship was loaded with aromatics and other offerings, the cables were cut and, unmanned but in the keeping of the goddess, she sailed out to sea.[61]

Legends about the journeys of the gods frequently reflect the spread of their cults. The Navigium Isidis festival was the symbol of the extension of the goddess's power beyond Egypt. Isis Pelagia (Isis of the Sea) was known and worshipped all over the Near East from Byblos to Ephesus, where St Paul was to encounter her.[62]

In Tarsus especially, where Cleopatra arrived to meet Antony in her barge with its poop of gold and purple sails, Isis was honoured. The heroine of the *Ephesiaca*, a novel written by the Ephesian Xenophon in the third century AD, visits Tarsus in order to make offerings to Isis. Archaeological finds demonstrate that the cult was established there well before the Christian era.[63] When Cleopatra, the Queen of Egypt and thus Isis's human representative, came sailing up the River Cydnus with all possible pomp and circumstance the people of Tarsus would have had no hesitation in identifying her as the goddess who is frequently depicted on coins standing on the deck of a ship in front of a billowing sail, emblem of the Breath of Life.[64] No wonder they flocked to see her, leaving Antony alone in the marketplace. This was no ordinary state visit – it was for them the epiphany of the supreme goddess.

Plutarch had heard a different story. In the accounts which he had read, Cleopatra's claim to divinity had been translated into terms which would have been more familiar and acceptable to Antony's European companions. He records that she came in the character of Aphrodite.

By the first century BC Isis and Aphrodite had been closely identified for at least two hundred years. Cleopatra's ancestress, Berenice I, had been deified as Aphrodite (although as an Egyptian queen she was already, as a matter of course, Isis) in the third century BC, and her daughter-in-law, Arsinoe, was worshipped simultaneously as Isis and Aphrodite.[65] Cleopatra's Cyprus coinage celebrating Caesarion's birth bore Aphrodite's symbols as well as those of Isis. Such melding was not unusual. Statuettes of a figure bearing the names and attributes of both goddesses have been found all over the eastern Mediterranean.

Isis Pelagia, like Aphrodite, was born 'on the gleaming waves of the sea'[66] and, like Aphrodite, she presided over sexual love. The goddess who 'brought together man and woman' smiled kindly on the pleasures of the marriage bed. It is true that in Rome prurient rumours circulated about goings-on in her temple, but since no such scandal attached to the worshippers of Venus it must be assumed that they were motivated by the racist equation of foreign women with promiscuity (the same equation from which Cleopatra's own reputation was to suffer in Rome) rather than by any disapproval of goddesses of love in general. An early Christian writer was to allege that Isis had been a prostitute in Tyre for ten years. Josephus recounts a scandal in the time of Tiberius, when a noble lady was seduced in the temple of Isis by a man disguised as dog-headed Anubis. Juvenal calls Isis 'a bawd'. Ovid, in his *Ars Amatoria*, warns a girl's guardian: 'Don't ask what can happen in the Temple of linen-clad Isis!' His innuendo suggests that the temple was used for clandestine meetings. Certainly in Pompeii the shrine of Isis stands next to the brothel.[67] These somewhat insalubrious associations are the underside (as perceived by those who were suspicious of foreign cults) of one aspect of Isis's nature, that which made her identical with Aphrodite and Venus.

So when Cleopatra sailed up the Cydnus 'dressed in the character of Aphrodite', she was impersonating both Isis and the Graeco-Roman goddess.

> Her rowers caressed the water with oars of silver which dipped in time to the music of the flute, accompanied by pipes and lutes. . . . Instead of a crew the barge was lined with the most beautiful of her waiting women attired as Nereids and Graces, some at the rudders, others at the tackles of the sails, and all the while an indescribably rich perfume, exhaled from innumerable censers, was wafted from the vessel to the river banks.[68]

To many of the spectators this apparition would suggest Isis Pelagia, but others would have been reminded of Venus as the greatest painter of antiquity, Apelles, had depicted her, rising from the waves. The clouds of incense would have confirmed the identification, for as an anonymous Elizabethan writer was to note, 'Venus (as the Greek poets affirm) never departed from any place not leaving an exquisite perfume and odorous smell behind her in token of her presence.'[69] Cleopatra's progress would, for the spectators, have recalled Venus's sea journeys, one of which is described by Apuleius.

> The Nereids were there, singing a part song. . . . After these came troops of Tritons swimming about in all directions, one blowing softly on his conch-shell, another protecting Venus from sunburn with a silk parasol, a third holding a mirror for her to admire herself, and a whole team of them yoked two and two, harnessed to her car.[70]

The spectacle was a success. Plutarch confirms that the point Cleopatra wished to make by it was taken and understood. Tarsus had been known since the fifth century BC as the site of a meeting between the goddess of love and the god who ruled the east.[71] Now the goddess was come again, to unite herself once more with the same divine partner. 'The word spread on every side that Aphrodite had come to revel with Dionysus for the happiness of Asia.'[72]

Antony was as well aware as Cleopatra of the importance of appearances. In Parthia, after a crushing defeat, he debated carefully what he should wear to address his troops. 'At first he called for a dark robe, as he wanted to make this speech as moving as possible. His friends opposed this idea, and so he appeared in a general's scarlet cloak and spoke to the army.'[73] This is the same Antony, orator and showman, who turned the political current in Rome with one speech in the forum on the day of Julius Caesar's funeral, an occasion which, as the detail of its stage management makes clear, was not nearly as spontaneous as it was designed to seem. J. M. Carter paraphrases Appian's description of it:

> A dirge-like chant paralysed the crowd's weakening self-control, then someone near the bier cried out the line of the old poet Pacuvius so that Caesar himself seemed to speak:
>   'Saved I these men that they should undo me?'
>   The breaking point was reached when a wax effigy of the dead man was raised by unseen hands and rotated above the heads of the crowd, showing the twenty-three wounds and mutilated face.[74]

Antony directed and took the lead in that performance. In his later career he continued to show a lively sense of the political efficacy of histrionics.

Antony modelled himself variously on Alexander the Great, Hercules and Dionysus. As a would-be lord of the East, he inevitably saw himself (like so many others, from Pyrrhus to Napoleon)[75] as Alexander's successor. He stressed the comparison by dramatic actions. Plutarch tells us that at Philippi he 'threw his own scarlet cloak, which was of great value, over Brutus's body and commanded one of his

116

freedmen to make himself responsible for its burial'.[76] Just so had Alexander shown respect for Darius's corpse. Just so had he covered the Persian king's body with his cloak. Antony thus proclaimed himself Alexander's worthy heir, and some of the charisma of the conqueror of all Asia attached itself to him by association.

If Antony flattered himself that his career would resemble that of the great Alexander, his personality, so he would have the world believe, was Herculean. He claimed descent from the legendary hero. 'There was an ancient tradition that the blood of the Heracleidae ran in Antony's family,' says Plutarch, 'and Antony liked to believe that his own physique lent force to the legend.'[77] Ancient families in whom the blood of the Heracleidae ran seem to have been as numerous as the beds in which Queen Elizabeth I of England is said to have slept. Aristides Rhetor records that 'many kings and peoples traced their origins to him'.[78] It was an association which lent glamour and virtue to those who could claim it.

Plutarch tells us that Antony had 'a certain bold and masculine look, which is found in the statues and portraits of Hercules'. Two millennia later the modern tourist in Rome cannot but be struck by the multiplicity of those statues and portraits. On sarcophagi and vases, in reliefs and sculptural groups, the image of Hercules recurs, distinguished always by his lionskin and his club, insignia of brute strength and male potency. Hercules was a simply admirable figure, who devoted his prowess to humanity's service; no wonder Antony took pains to stress the identification of himself with this popular prototype. 'He deliberately cultivated it in his choice of dress,' writes Plutarch, 'for whenever he was going to appear before a large number of people, he wore his tunic belted low over the hips, a large sword at his side, and a heavy cloak.'[79] This was the costume of the hero. When later his enemies taunted him as Hercules humiliated by Omphale they were twisting to their own advantage an image which Antony himself had first fostered.

Hercules's adventures took him from one end of the Mediterranean world to the other, from the Straits of Gibraltar (where he set up the Pillars of Hercules) and Tangier, where he slew a giant, to the Caucasus, where he freed Prometheus. In Egypt he had wrestled with King Busiris.[80] He was known and revered throughout the regions of Asia and north Africa which Antony hoped to dominate. Like Alexander (who also claimed descent from him) he was an appropriate patron for the ruler of the East.

Dionysus was an even better one. His cult was a late introduction to the Mediterranean world. In his myth, as the Greeks knew it, he was recognized as the god who was already obeyed and adored by all the peoples of Asia. He came from over the sea and far away, trailing clouds of glory from his Oriental triumphs, bringing exuberant vitality, a dangerous but sublime ecstasy and, above all, wine.

In 41 BC, shortly before he met Cleopatra on the Cydnus, Antony entered Ephesus as the new overlord of the Roman East. 'Women dressed as Bacchantes and men and boys as satyrs and Pans marched in procession before him. The city was filled with wreaths of ivy and thyrsus wands, the air resounded with the music of harps, pipes and flutes, and the people hailed him as Dionysus the Benefactor and the Bringer of Joy.'[81]

This was probably not the first time Antony had appeared in such a guise. Plutarch reports that several years earlier, when he was officiating as Julius Caesar's master of horse, Antony was already notorious for his extravagances.

> People were scandalised, for example, at the sight of the golden drinking cups which were carried before him when he left the city, as if they were part of some religious procession; at the pavilions which were set up on his journeys; at the lavish meals which were spread in groves or on the banks of rivers; at his chariots drawn by lions and at his habit of billeting courtesans and sambuca-players in the homes of honest men and women.[82]

These journeys may indeed very well have been religious processions, transformed in the popular memory into frivolous and licentious outings only by the prejudices of Antony's enemies, reinforced by the Roman establishment's distrust of Dionysiac cults. The second-century Syrian writer Lucian describes Dionysus riding 'in a car behind a team of panthers',[83] and the lion was another animal regularly associated with the god. The presence of 'courtesans and sambuca-players' could be put down simply to Antony's often-reported preference for permissive, bohemian company, but they may have represented Maenads or Bacchantes, following in the train of Antony/Dionysus.

Here Antony's propaganda dovetailed neatly with Cleopatra's, for Dionysus was her ancestor, the legendary progenitor of the Ptolemies and the particular patron of the Egyptian royal house. In the third century BC Ptolemy II Philadelphus introduced a great four-yearly festival, the Ptolemaia. An effigy of Dionysus so vast that eighty men were needed to bear it was carried in the culminating procession. It was followed by exotic beasts, and tableaux depicting the god as conqueror of the world and master of all creatures, animal or human. Ptolemy IV Philopator had the Dionysiac emblem, the ivy-leaf, tattooed on his own body.[84] Cleopatra's father, Ptolemy Auletes, adopted as one of his titles the name of the New Dionysus. The Greek rulers of Egypt had claimed the god for their own.

Such a claim was the more acceptable to Egyptians because Dionysus could so easily be assimilated to Osiris. Both were gods who travelled widely, bringing the benefits of civilization and agriculture wherever they went. Both gods had a sexually equivocal nature. 'You are the Father and Mother of Men,' proclaimed an Egyptian hymn addressed to Osiris.[85] Similarly there are hints that Dionysus was in fact hermaphrodite, a god of life who was able to reproduce life without the participation of a female.[86] Both were torn apart by their enemies: just as Osiris had been dismembered by his brother, Seth, so Dionysus, while still a child, was cut into seven pieces by the Titans. Both were brought back to life by earth-goddesses: Demeter reconstituted and resurrected Dionysus, just as Isis did Osiris. Both, having died, achieved immortal life. Diodorus Siculus bluntly declared 'Osiris when translated is Dionysus'.[87] Plutarch agreed, citing 'many Greek authors' as authorities.[88] By the second century AD the merging of one god with another was so complete that Apuleius describes the priests of Osiris 'with fir-wands and ivy-chaplets',[89] the insignia of Dionysus.

By casting himself in the role of the New Dionysus, Antony could well have been considered to be slighting the house of the Ptolemies, who had made that title their own. But Cleopatra did not take offence; instead she fastened on this aspect of Antony's public image and incorporated it into the politico-religious myth which she was elaborating, and which was given expression in the marvellous spectacle on the Cydnus. Antony, as Dionysus/Osiris, might be the Heaven-appointed conqueror of all Asia – but was not she, as Isis/Aphrodite, his fellow-deity and equal partner, his sister and his wife?

The image of Cleopatra, enthroned resplendent in her barge, has entered the popular imagination and stayed there for two millennia. But its meaning, played down by hostile historians, has been forgotten. This was, in reality, an occasion for far more than sexual and economic display. It was a carefully planned pageant, replete with symbolic and religious significance, whose multi-layered meanings were cunningly interwoven by Cleopatra for her own aggrandizement. Far from reclining passively as a tempting object to be taken or rejected, she was the author of this shimmering show, in which she had laid out for Antony the promise of a glorious future. She was Aphrodite and, if he chose, he could revel with her for the happiness of Asia; in other words he could join with her in dominating the Oriental world, in his capacity as self-appointed representative of the divine patron of life and culture, Dionysus, the world ruler from the East.

The East was ready for such rulers. The Hellenistic peoples of the eastern Mediterranean were far from content as subjects to Rome: they were looking for a champion and a liberator. Dionysus, Isis and Osiris were gods whom they could call their own. Livy relates the story of the discovery of a Dionysiac cult which 'spread to Rome like a disease' in the second century BC, brought there by a Greek immigrant. Its festival, the Bacchanalia, he describes as a 'factory of all corruptions' where 'men mingling with women and the freedom of darkness added, no form of crime, no sort of wrong-doing was left untried', but the consul of the day, whose speech Livy reports, clearly has stronger reasons for objecting to the cult than prim disapproval of sexual licence. 'Daily the evil grows and creeps abroad. . . . Its objective is the control of the state.' More than seven thousand worshippers of Dionysus are accused of being involved in the 'conspiracy' and many are killed. 'Your ancestors,' explains the consul to those who might feel inclined to protest at such Draconian and intolerant measures, 'did not wish that you should assemble casually and without reason.' The worship of 'those gods who would drive our enthralled minds with vile and alien rites, as by the scourge of the Furies, to every crime and every lust' was clearly perceived to have a subversive political function.[90]

The worshippers of Dionysus in Rome, like those of Isis, were predominantly female. Initially, according to Livy, men were excluded from the rituals. Those who were later admitted would have tended to be Greeks and Asians, slaves or ex-slaves (although Livy asserts that they included 'men of higher rank' as well). The worship of the Oriental gods in Rome was essentially oppositional, a focus for discontent and an emotional outlet for those who felt themselves unprotected and undervalued by the state which denied them the first-class citizenship exclusively reserved for the native-born Roman male. In the eastern Mediterranean it carried an equally subversive, but more positive, political charge: religious devotion mingled with revolutionary enthusiasm, with the resentment and ecstatic hopes of those who longed to free themselves from Rome.

This rumbling resistance movement was an underground, clandestine culture; it has left few relics, but fragments of its literature have survived, mainly in the form of prophecies, writings which were as much utopias, expressions of desire, as they were divinations of the real future. The Prophecy of the Mad Praetor, written before 100 BC, foretold that an army would march out of the sunrise to subdue Rome. A somewhat later prophecy, ascribed (probably fictitiously) to a Persian sage called Hystaspes, made a similar prediction: in Rome the reading of it was banned on pain of death.[91] The largest collection of such prophecies is that of the Sibylline Books. The oracles assembled in these anthologies originated in Syria and elsewhere in the Hellenized East, and circulated widely. In Rome they were carefully expurgated (by Octavius, among others). Anonymous, only approximately dateable, clearly gathered together in fragmentary form from many sources, they provide a fascinating if tantalizing glimpse into the political fantasies of an otherwise silenced and subjected group. The furious resentment that Rome's rule provoked speaks clearly through them:

> Though Rome received
> Tribute of Asia, thrice as many goods
> Shall Asia back again receive from Rome
> And savage insolence return to her. . . .[92]

In some of these oracular verses it is foretold that a woman will lead Asia to freedom and revenge: 'O delicate golden virgin of Rome, drunk with thy weddings with many wooers . . . a mistress is shearing thy locks again and again, and she will do justice and hurl thee down from heaven to earth.'[93] All of these passages could be taken to refer to Cleopatra. 'For of the land beside the streams of the Nile . . . she shall be Queen.'[4] Some of them were clearly written with her in mind:

> And while Rome will be hesitating over
> the conquest of Egypt, then the mighty Queen
> of the Immortal King will appear among men. . . .
> Three will subdue Rome with a pitiful fate. . . .
> The Holy Lord, wielding the whole earth's sceptre
> will come to rule for all the ages to come.[95]

These verses clearly belong in the tradition of apocalyptic literature, so much of which has found its way into the Old and New Testaments. Under Roman rule the Jews awaited a

Messiah who would be a nationalist leader, King of the Jews as well as the Son of God. So the Sibylline oracles express fantasies about a great leader and liberator. But among the images of generalized yearning some precise historical details can be detected. A triumvirate in Rome, an Egyptian queen: a real situation is being described here. These prophecies must have been written in Cleopatra's lifetime, with the intention of identifying her with the mysterious woman who would save the world and usher in the Golden Age.

> And then the whole wide world under a woman's hand
> ruled and obeying everywhere shall stand . . .
> the Widow shall be queen of the whole wide world.[96]

When Cleopatra came to Cydnus her brother/husbands were both already dead. Ignoring convention, she had not married again. She was the Widow, the focus of Asia's hopes, the promised liberator. Her arrival in glory at Tarsus may have been a charade, but it was a solemn and momentous one. She was not inviting Antony to join her in a pretty game of dressing up. She was suggesting that just as she was the Widow, and the mighty Queen, it was open to Antony to assume the role of the Holy Lord, the Immortal King, and to share with her power over all the world.

Antony was the New Dionysus and Cleopatra was his consort Isis/Aphrodite: Octavius, meanwhile, identified himself with Apollo. According to stories which were probably circulated by his parents in an attempt to interest Julius Caesar in him, he had been Apollo's protégé, perhaps even Apollo himself, from the moment of his conception. Suetonius repeats the fable: 'Augustus's mother, Atia . . . once attended a solemn midnight service at the Temple of Apollo, where she had her litter set down, and presently fell asleep as the others also did. Suddenly a serpent glided up, entered her, and then glided away again.' When she awoke she found an indelible serpent-shaped mark on her body 'and the birth of Augustus nine months later suggested a divine paternity'. Similarly

Octavius's father is said to have dreamt that the sun rose from between Atia's thighs: in other words that she would give birth to an avatar of the sun-god.[97] Taking a cue from his parents, the adult Octavius set up an image of Apollo in Rome and built a temple to him on the Palatine Hill.[98] It seems that, like Antony, he even appeared in public in the guise of his chosen deity. At 'a feast of the divine twelve', according to a hostile lampoon,

> Apollo's part was lewdly played
> By impious Caesar.[99]

It was to Apollo that Octavius dedicated a temple on a hill above the gulf of Actium after his victory there, and he erected a shrine to the god on the spot where his own tent had stood.[100] In the poems with which his admirers celebrate the battle, his name is repeatedly linked with that of his divine protector. 'Apollo shall tell how the line was turned,' declares Propertius.[101] Virgil writes:

> Actian Apollo
> Began to pull his bow.
> Wild at the sight,
> All Egypt, Indians, Arabians, all
> Sabeans put about in flight. . . .[102]

Returned triumphant to Rome, Virgil's Octavius is imagined receiving the tribute of the nations of the earth 'Seated at shining Apollo's snow-white threshold'.[103] Romans might profess to be scandalized that Cleopatra and Antony had had themselves depicted in the personae of Isis and Osiris, but Octavius, who claimed to be representative of Rome, was not above claiming divine sponsorship himself.

On the one hand Octavius/Apollo, masculine god of moderation, of light, of intellectual order; on the other Cleopatra and her consort Antony/Dionysus, androgynous god of exuberance, of abandon, of vegetable life. This opposition between the two deities, an interpretation of the struggle between Octavius and Antony which both the principal parties endorsed, has dropped out of later accounts of their story.

124

Contemporaries, bent on trivializing and mocking Antony's claim to divinity, mention it only in passing: in the Christian era it was forgotten. During the Middle Ages, when understanding of Graeco-Roman mythology was in general so hazy that Sir Lancelot, Hercules and Julius Caesar could be referred to generically as 'knights of old',[104] it would have been meaningless. The Renaissance failed to revive it. Shakespeare, dramatizing the moment when music under the earth signals Dionysus's desertion of Antony, changed the name of the departing patron: "Tis the god Hercules, whom Antony loved.'[105] It is only comparatively recently, since psychoanalysis has called for a closer scrutiny of ancient myths in general, and since Nietzsche reimagined those of Dionysus and Apollo in particular (his insights were subsequently confirmed and elaborated by archaeologists and mythographers), that the intellectual climate in which this opposition could have any potency of meaning has come once more to exist. Even now, no retelling of the story of Antony, Cleopatra and Octavius has made full use of it.

Nietzsche described two ways of coming to terms with the inevitability of death. The way of Apollo is through the exaltation of the individual, through order and beauty. The Apollonian man achieves serenity by discipline and refinement of the self; he cultivates those aspects of his personality which are least carnal, least obviously a part of the dying animal which is his body. Thus he separates himself from the rest of biological life and transcends his wretchedness. The Dionysiac way leads in the opposite direction. It is the way of self-abandonment. Freed from the mortal isolation of his own subjectivity, a person can become reconciled with the certainty of individual death as he merges in spirit with all animal and vegetable life, and feels himself to be a part of an indestructibly vital cycle of generation and regeneration.[106]

To what extent Cleopatra and Antony developed these ideas explicitly we can only guess. But it is clear that, their partnership established, the Dionysiac theme continued to figure largely in their self-glorifying spectacles. Athenaeus relates that in Athens Antony entertained visitors in an artificial 'cave' with a canopy of green boughs, like those customarily erected for Bacchic revels: 'on this he hung tambourines and fawnskins and other Dionysiac trinkets'.[107] After his victory over Armenia in 34 BC he led the King Artavasdes back captive to Alexandria. He entered the city with great ceremony – ceremony which Octavius deliberately misrepresented, claiming that he was slighting Rome by celebrating a Roman Triumph, 'the honourable and solemn rites of his own country', in an alien capital.[108] In fact he was doing no such thing. Velleius Paterculus describes the occasion in detail. 'He commanded himself to be called the new Liber Pater [one of Dionysus's Latin names]; and being adorned with ivy and bound with a golden crown', wearing buskins and carrying a fir-wand, he rode into the city 'in a chariot like Bacchus'.[109] This was no Roman Triumph; it was a Dionysiac procession, of a kind familiar to the people of Alexandria from the Ptolemaia festivals. Like the god, Antony came victorious from out of the East, to be welcomed by Cleopatra/Isis/Aphrodite, his divine sister/wife.

At the end of his life, Antony's god was said to have deserted him. Plutarch describes the night before his final defeat and death. Octavius's army was camped just outside Alexandria. Within the palace, 'it is said', Antony's slaves wept as they filled his cup, for he had told them, all too credibly, 'no man could say whether on the next day they would be waiting on him or serving other masters, while he himself would be lying dead, a mummy and a nothing'. On that fateful night

> about the hour of midnight when all was hushed and a mood of dejection and fear of its impending fate brooded over the whole city, suddenly a marvellous sound of music was heard, which seemed to come from a consort of instruments of every kind, and voices chanting in harmony, and at the same time the shouting of a crowd in which the cry of Bacchanals and the ecstatic leaping of satyrs were mingled, as if a troop of revellers were leaving the city, shouting and singing as they went.

The sounds were heard passing through the outer gate in the

direction of Octavius's camp. 'Those who tried to discover a meaning for this prodigy concluded that the god Dionysus, with whom Antony claimed kinship and whom he had sought above all to imitate, was now abandoning him.'[110]

The gods forsook their altars and shrines in Troy the night before that city fell. Athens and Jerusalem were similarly abandoned in dire straits, and Minerva appeared to the Emperor Domitian in a dream just before his assassination to warn him that she was withdrawing her protection.[111] The classical gods were known for their rat-like habit of leaving a loser. The story that Dionysus, Antony's divine alter ego, the patron of Cleopatra's dynasty, had gone from Alexandria, could have originated either with their enemies (it would have boded well for Octavius, who liked to boast that fate and the gods fought on his side) or with the friends who later mourned their defeat and remembered the great days when Aphrodite revelled with Dionysus 'for the good of Asia'. Whoever first told it, though, the story vividly illustrates the extent to which Dionysus was identified with Antony, and with the imperial endeavour on which he and Cleopatra had embarked.

Dionysiac elements are also clearly detectable in the distorting mirror held up to Cleopatra and her partner by Octavius's propaganda. Roman writers laboured the point that both she and Antony were drunkards. When Octavius defeated her at Actium, wrote Horace, he

> ... dragged back to fearful reality
> Her mind swimming in Mareotic [wine].[112]

The slur was so often repeated and so offensive that Antony was finally moved to refute it in a pamphlet, *De sua ebrietate* (On His Drunkenness).[113] These allegations of debauchery could have arisen from deliberately garbled reports of solemn rituals. 'Antony and Cleopatra gathered around them a company of friends whom they called the Inimitable Livers,' writes Plutarch, 'and each day they gave banquets for one another of an almost incredible extravagance.' Modern scholars have suggested that that 'company of friends' may have been a circle of Dionysiac initiates, and that the 'banquets' were not occasions for irresponsible self-indulgence but sacred ceremonies. Cleopatra used to wear an amethyst ring on which a figure of the goddess of drunkenness was engraved. The amethyst is the stone of sobriety, and the ring signified that on Cleopatra's hand Drunkenness herself was sober. The pretty paradox in turn evoked the mystical concept of *sobria ebrietas*, the state of frenzied self-transcendence by means of which the Bacchante attained wisdom and serenity.[114] For in the rites of Dionysus alcoholic intoxication was used both to facilitate, and as a metaphor for, the dissolution of consciousness in religious ecstasy. The legend of Cleopatra's banquet contains within it traces of sacred observance, memories of the ritualized orgies of the Bacchanalia.

The recurrent Roman taunt that Cleopatra had emasculated Antony may also be connected with his Dionysiac character, for Dionysus's sexual identity was equivocal.[115] It is appropriate that he should have been represented by a dyad in which the female partner, Cleopatra, was as powerful and charismatic as her mate. Unusually among the Greek gods he was nearly always depicted in long robes. His attendant satyrs were often spectacularly ithyphallic but his own genital organization was a mystery. The myths relate that he was reared by women, nymphs who hid him in a cave and fed him on honey. In this all-female environment the god grew girlish, being dressed, like Antony/Hercules in thrall to Omphale/Cleopatra, in women's clothes.[116] In later life he travelled the world accompanied by an entourage of female followers, Maenads or Bacchantes, who ran wild on the mountain-tops or followed their lord and master with music and singing. And just as Dionysus was surrounded by women in his myths, so his cult was always popular with women. When Octavius characterized Alexandria as a site of effeminacy he may well have been alluding to the fact that Dionysus was much venerated there. He described Antony as surrounded by women and eunuchs, a scornful description which mirrored in an unflattering light the markedly feminist character of the cult of Dionysus. In claiming contemptuously that Antony had lost his manhood he was belittling and bending to his own use Antony and Cleopatra's devotion to the god whose exuberant creativity derived from his essentially androgynous nature.

Just as the difference between one gender and another is lost in the ambiguous figure of Dionysus, so are all orders and hierarchies. Dionysiacs, in seeking through frenzy to become one with all life, menace the orderly models which identify humankind as the crown of creation. Similarly they undermine all social and political structures. In Nietzsche's words, 'The state and society and, quite generally, the gulfs between man and man give way to an overwhelming feeling of unity leading back to the very heart of nature.'[117] This anarchic aspect of Dionysus-worship relates to another recurrent theme of Octavius's partisan historians: that Antony, Aeneas's opposite, had neglected all his responsibilities, ceasing to function as a political being once he reached the Never-Never land of Alexandria. 'Straightway [after meeting Cleopatra]' records Appian, 'Antony's former interest in public affairs began to dwindle.'[118] In Plutarch's account he gave himself up, with his new mistress, to 'the diversions of a young man with all his future before him'.[119] For all that they were both quite evidently ambitious and energetic workers in government and politics, Cleopatra and her lover, in their Dionysiac association, are imagined to have slipped the net of social duty. This is what makes them seem so threatening, so abominable to the Apollonian Roman, a type of which Octavius proudly proclaimed himself the prime example. It is also what made their story so attractive. For the dutiful, well-regulated Apollonian, limiting himself to 'moderation in all things', must always feel a fleeting envy of the Dionysiac, whose way seems so easy, so self-indulgent, even though it leads in the end to what is, for the Apollonian, the ultimate horror, the annihilation of the self.

The theme has been submerged, but not entirely hidden. Octavius, his power once established, burnt two thousand documents. In this bonfire of books he may have incinerated

129

his enemies' written propaganda, but he could not erase a mythical connection which, albeit accidentally (Cleopatra and Antony, who no doubt hoped for long and glorious lives, cannot be supposed to have deliberately identified themselves with Dionysus's tragic, dying aspect), proved so resonantly appropriate.

Cleopatra's myth-making embraced not only her partner but also her children. At the Donations of Alexandria her propaganda exercise was further refined and enriched. On this occasion, according to Plutarch, a great multitude were assembled in the athletics arena. Cleopatra, dressed as Isis, and Antony sat on golden thrones, raised on a dais of silver, with their children, also enthroned, beside them. As Antony proclaimed his son Alexander King of Armenia and Media he presented him to the people. The nine-year-old boy was dressed in a miniature version of the costume of the Median kings and he wore the imperial tiara, with its peacock-feather crest, on his head. This vision was equalled by the one which followed, as Antony presented the youngest child of his union with Cleopatra, Ptolemy Philadelphus. This boy, who had yet to celebrate his second birthday, wore the Macedonian royal outfit of 'boots, a short cloak, and a broad-brimmed hat encircled by a diadem'.[120] It was at this ceremony that Cleopatra was first proclaimed 'Queen of Kings', a title which would have been given considerable extra resonance by the tableau with which she illustrated it. In the robe and therefore the persona of Isis she was indeed queen over mere mortal monarchs. Her newly regal children, disposed around her larger throne, illustrated the subordination of earthly kingdoms to the reign of Heaven as vividly as any Renaissance painting in which the princely donor kneels to present a scale model of his palace or city to the Christ child. Romans were scandalized by the arrogance with which Cleopatra claimed the divine role for herself, but they did not mistake her meaning.

Her children's names lent extra point to the spectacle.

130

When she rejoined Antony in the autumn of 37 BC he acknowledged their three-year-old twins for the first time, and both they and the new-born baby were named – or, in the case of the twins, probably renamed. It was at this juncture that Antony granted to Cleopatra valuable territories in Phoenicia and Asia Minor, thus going a long way towards restoring the ancient empire of the Ptolemies. That empire had been at its most extensive and glorious in the third century BC, and Ptolemy II, known as Philadelphus, was remembered as being its most illustrious ruler; it was after him that Cleopatra named her baby. As the little boy, splendid in his toddler-sized version of the purple cloak of a Macedonian king, was held up to the crowd on the occasion of the Donations, everyone there would have remembered his ancestor and rejoiced that the great days of the Ptolemies were come again.

The twins' names were even more suggestive – though perhaps more vaguely so. In 37 BC they had been dubbed Cleopatra Selene (the Moon) and Alexander Helios (the Sun). The girl's name was conventional: her mother was already the seventh Ptolemaic queen to bear the name Cleopatra. But given its literal meaning, Glory of Her Father, and given the fact that Antony had not openly acknowledged paternity of the twins until her third year, it did in this case carry a refreshed pertinency. Selene, the Moon, was also a family name, but one with numinous associations. If little Cleopatra Selene was the Moon, then, like her mother, she must be an earthly representative of Isis, the Moon goddess.

So much was conventional and, for a princess of the Ptolemaic dynasty, not unusual. Nor was it strange for a Ptolemaic prince to be named after the Sun, for all Egyptian kings were children of Ra, the Sun-god. But when the Moon princess acquired a brother named after the Sun further layers of possible meaning attached themselves to the names, for in the Greek tradition the Sun and Moon were, like these terrestrial children, twins, and when so represented they became the associates of Victory.[121] This looked auspicious for Antony, who had not yet abandoned his ambition of conquering

Parthia. Furthermore, the king of Parthia was entitled 'Brother of the Sun and Moon'.[122] At the Donations of Alexandria, Antony made Alexander Helios overlord of all the territory east of the River Euphrates as far as India – in other words, overlord of the Parthian empire. The Brother of the Sun was to be dispossessed by Helios, the Sun himself.

But the glamour of young Alexander Helios's names went beyond the considerations of territorial ambition. Alexander the Great was not only the model for all those who dreamed of marching eastward from the Mediterranean to make themselves masters of the world. He had also propounded a vision of universal concord, of a blessed time when Europe and Asia would coexist in peace, when East and West would meet to their mutual enrichment and, as the wars of conquest and reconquest ceased, a Golden Age would dawn, the Age of the Sun. It would have been presided over (had he only lived to see the day) by Alexander himself – not the Alexander of forced marches and ceaseless strife, but a new, pacific and benign Alexander, the smiling prince as whose successor Antony and Cleopatra cast their child, Alexander of the Sun, Alexander Helios.

This dream of universal concord was still current in Cleopatra's lifetime. The Sibylline oracles do not only testify to discontent. Through their anger these anonymous prophets, Greek-speaking Oriental subjects of Rome, could envisage an Age of the Sun, when oppressor and oppressed might live in mutual harmony and prosperity:

And peace all gentle will come upon Asia, and Europe happy will be.
And the air shall grant long life and strength, and food and nourishment too,
And the birds and the beasts of the earth shall increase and never know storm or hail.
O blessed the man, and blessed the woman, who live to set eyes on that time!
Like peasants who've not seen a palace before, struck dumb at the riches displayed.[123]

This longed-for new age was to be the Age of the Sun. In

132

the third century BC a Greek named Iambulus had sailed to Ethiopia and then on to an archipelago known as the Islands of the Sun, intending to found there a communist Utopia to be known as the Sun State.[124] The Potter's Oracle, a prophecy translated from demotic Egyptian into Greek and probably dating from the third century BC, declares that a king will come from the Sun, that Isis will establish him on his throne and that he will be a giver of good things and usher in an Age of Gold. Annual Sun festivals were celebrated all over Europe and Asia throughout antiquity, and it is known that a particularly splendid one was held in Alexandria during the first century BC on 25 December, a favourite date for the earthly birth of the king of Heaven. In Italy the Sibyl of Cumae predicted an age of happiness to come once the rule of the Sun had been established.[125] These are scattered traces of a potent and widely disseminated belief. The Sun did not only confer warmth and light. It was also the presiding deity of a future characterized by ease, prosperity, and, most signally, by universal amity.

Such visions are often the product of political oppression. The Children of Israel, in their captivity, sang of a land of milk and honey. So Rome's subject races dreamt of a better place and better order. Cleopatra and Antony, in their propaganda and in their actual policies, seemed to be promising to make that dream come true.

Antony ruled Asia through Asian monarchs. Amyntas, Polemon, Archelaus, Herod and Cleopatra herself were his deputies, or clients, or subjects, or allies: the relationship was vague and flexible. When Antony needed support – financial, military or political – they gave it to him, but his power over them, which rested primarily on his commanding the largest military force in the region, did not extend to interference in their internal affairs. These were not Roman colonies ruled by Roman governors; they were Hellenistic Asian kingdoms ruled by Hellenistic Asian monarchs.[126] The distinction may seem over-subtle given Antony's ascendancy, but it is an indication of the kind of future that Antony and Cleopatra offered the world. Unlike Virgil's Anchises, they did not believe Romans to be the only people capable of good government. Their empire, had it ever come into being, would have been a federation of mutually dependent states within which Occidentality would have been no guarantee of superior status or power.

Little Alexander Helios, destined to be lord of much of Asia, seemed to promise, by his very name, that this even-handed policy would allow the inception of the Golden Age of which the Sibyl spoke, when 'poverty, necessity, anger, envy, lawlessness, madness, strife, murder and envy and every evil thing shall quit the earth, and in their stead shall come the rule of love, justice from heaven, and friendship towards the stranger'.[127]

When Cleopatra made Antony her partner and sat enthroned beside him in Alexandria she placed herself at the centre of a tableau that illustrated this universal accord. For the second time in her life she, Queen of Egypt and Queen of Kings, had taken as her consort a Roman leader through whom and with whom she hoped to rule over a newly reconciled world. The dream remained a dream. We cannot know whether Cleopatra would, or could, ever have realized it. We cannot even be sure how sincerely she herself entertained it. But the prophecies of the Golden Age of the Sun would certainly have been familiar to her, and in naming the eldest son of her union with Antony Alexander Helios she made the boy into the dream's emblem and its future hope. Thus she touched on a body of belief and fantasy which was of great emotive significance for all the peoples of the East, and she held out a prospect, as brilliant as it was vague, of a better life. That prospect is hard to discern distinctly now. But in its internationalism, its tolerance, its emphasis on constructive co-operation rather than on competitive warfare, it seems both more attractive and potentially more creative than Aeneas's sad and cramping code of loyalty to the tribe.

Cleopatra's ceremonies, dramatic enactments of her politics, were not reserved for times of peace. In the spring of 32 BC, with war imminent, she sailed with Antony to the island of Samos and there, like Alexander before them, they held a Dionysiac festival in order to call down a blessing on their campaign and, incidentally, to impress both their allies and their opponents with their grandeur. The festival was magnificent. To the Romans, as we have seen, it was yet another proof of Cleopatra's depravity. To others it was an awe-inspiring demonstration of ascendancy and wealth. Plutarch writes:

> The theatres were packed and choirs competed with one another. Every city sent an ox for sacrifice, and the kings who accompanied Antony vied with one another in the magnificence of their gifts and entertainments, until the word went round 'If these people spend so much on festivals just to prepare for a war, what will the conquerors do to celebrate a victory?'[128]

That question was never answered: Cleopatra had no victory to celebrate. But after her defeat at Actium she turned once more to ceremony and spectacle in an attempt to revive her supporters' morale. Once Antony had recovered from his depression they 'plunged the city into a round of banquets, drinking-parties, and lavish distributions of gifts'.[129] They marked the comings-of-age of Caesarion and Antony's son by Fulvia, Antyllus, with a splendid ceremony. If the arrival at Cydnus inaugurated Cleopatra's partnership with Antony and the Donations marked its apogee, then this celebration for the two boys was its last hectic flash. Defeated and friendless, hemmed into Egypt by Octavius's allies, Antony and Cleopatra made it the occasion for a defiant demonstration of their magnificence, a demonstration designed to put heart into their own forces and perhaps to persuade potential allies that their cause was not yet a lost one. Caesarion, destined to be an Hellenistic King of Kings, was enrolled, as was the Greek custom, in the list of *ephebes* or young male citizens. Antyllus's accession to manhood, on the other hand, was celebrated with Roman rites, for he was to be heir to

Antony's Italian estates; he was given the purple-hemmed *toga virilis*. Thus Cleopatra's project of reconciling Europe with Asia and ruling over both was vividly illustrated. As usual, the point was emphasized with memorably lavish expenditure: 'The entertainments, banquets and revels which were given to celebrate these honours engaged the whole city for days on end.'[130]

Cleopatra and Antony founded a new society, successor to the Order of Inimitables, their drinking club of happier days. The new association was named the Order of the Inseparable in Death. Its title was lugubrious, but its founding was a way of romanticizing the wretched situation. Slovenliness and gloom are signs of defeat. Cleopatra held them at bay, maintaining her supporters' spirits with febrile but stylish gestures. She celebrated Antony's birthday with a party so extravagant that 'many of the guests came to the banquet as paupers and went away rich men'.[131]

Cleopatra shaped and embellished facts. On occasion both she and Antony went further, presenting a version of events so far removed from reality as to be downright mendacious. After his catastrophic Parthian campaign Antony sent dispatches to Rome reporting that he had won a great victory. Octavius, who would undoubtedly have had independent reports to the contrary, politely pretended to believe him. Truth mattered less to him than policy, and he was not then ready to challenge Antony openly. Similarly, after Actium, Cleopatra sailed into Alexandria having 'crowned her prows with garlands as if she had actually won a victory, and had songs of triumph chanted to the accompaniment of flute-players'.[132]

So Cleopatra rewrote her life as she went along. Even more remarkably, when death was inevitable she proved her ingenuity and her coolness by making of that inexorable reality another flattering show.

Plutarch had read the memoirs (of which no other trace remains) of Cleopatra's private physician, Olympus. Presumably because he was drawing on a source so close to her, his account of her last days is intimate, almost painfully vivid, and strikingly different from those of the hostile writers who portray her as an unprincipled seductress to the last. He describes Antony, his suicide botched, writhing in pain and bellowing for help while his terrified attendants run from the house. Eventually he is conveyed to the monument in which Cleopatra has taken refuge.

> Those who were present say that there was never a more pitiable sight than the spectacle of Antony, covered with blood, struggling in his death agonies and stretching out his hands towards Cleopatra as he swung helplessly in the air. The task was almost beyond a woman's strength, and it was only with great difficulty that Cleopatra, clinging with both hands to the rope and with the muscles of her face distorted by the strain, was able to haul him up, while those on the ground encouraged her with their cries and shared her agony.

Once she has winched him up she tears her dress to make a covering for him, lacerates her breast in her frantic grief and smears her face with his blood. Antony asks for wine 'either because he was thirsty or because he hoped it might hasten his death'. Shortly afterwards he dies.

Cleopatra speaks through the door to Octavius's men. The second time she does so one of them sets a ladder against the monument, climbs in and surprises her as she stands, still talking at the door. She tries to stab herself, but her captor flings both his arms around her, seizes her dagger and shakes out her dress to check that she has no more weapons hidden about her.[133]

Now a captive, she falls ill. Her breast, which she has scratched and beaten, becomes infected. She refuses all food until Octavius, by threatening her children, coerces her into abandoning her hunger strike. When he comes to visit her she is lying on a pallet bed dressed only in a tunic, her hair unkempt. She flings herself at his feet (a far cry this, from the image Dio Cassius presents, of her cunningly adorning herself to seduce her conqueror). She begs to be allowed to pour libations at Antony's grave. There she makes a sorrowful and dignified speech, concluding with the plea: 'Hide me and let me be buried here with you, for I know now that the thousand griefs I have suffered are as nothing beside the few days that I have lived without you.'[134] Returning to her prison she prepares, and gallantly meets, her own death.

There is some doubt about the exact manner of that death. Plutarch relates the story of the asp brought to her in a basket of figs but he allows room for other possible versions. 'The real truth nobody knows, for there is another story that she carried poison about with her in a hollow comb, which she kept hidden in her hair.'[135] The real truth is, indeed, unverifiable, for by all accounts neither of the two witnesses to her death outlived her long enough to tell the tale. Plutarch relates that, having bathed and dined, 'she dismissed all her attendants except for two faithful waiting women and closed the doors'. By the time Octavius's messengers arrived on the scene she was dead and both the waiting women, Iras and Charmian, were dying.

What greeted those messengers' eyes was the last and perhaps most wonderful of all Cleopatra's spectacles. The Queen of Egypt, already dead, lay on a golden couch. Exhausted, starved and self-mutilated as she was, she had still found the will to adorn herself for death. She was wearing all her royal robes, and as the messengers burst in they found Charmian, already tottering, arranging her mistress's crown. Cleopatra's robes for solemn occasion were, as we have seen already, those of Isis. In the guise of the goddess, crowned and ceremonially dressed, she met her death in the full panoply of her divine monarchy.[136]

The death-instrument she is believed to have chosen completed the symbolic picture she had staged. Earlier, according to Plutarch, the guards at her door had stopped an Egyptian peasant carrying a basket. When challenged he had 'stripped away the leaves at the top and showed them that it was full of figs'. The guards commented on the figs' unusual size, and the peasant invited them to try some.[137] 'According to one account,' said Plutarch carefully, 'the asp . . . lay hidden under the leaves in the basket.' The forensic evidence found afterwards was scant.

The asp was never discovered inside the monument, although some marks which might have been its trail are said to have been noticed on the beach on that side where the windows of the chamber looked towards the sea. Some people also say that two faint, barely visible punctures were found on Cleopatra's arms, and Octavius Caesar himself seems to have believed this, for when he celebrated his triumph he had a figure of Cleopatra with the asp clinging to her carried in procession.[138]

'Asp' is a zoologically imprecise term which has been applied to several different varieties of north African viper. *Cerastes vipera* is commonly known as 'Cleopatra's Asp'. The word is also used of *Vipera berus, Vipera aspis* and the horned viper, *Cerastes cornutus*.[139] In fact it is unlikely that any of these was Cleopatra's executioner. The venom of vipers is a blood poison. It tends to cause intense burning pain which spreads rapidly from the site of the bite. The person bitten feels giddy, nauseous and acutely thirsty. Blood clots soon form, covering the affected limb with disfiguring purple blotches and swellings. The victim may be seized by fits of vomiting, and urinate and defecate incontinently before losing consciousness.[140] Such a death would be horribly different from the dignified and tranquil end which Cleopatra would surely have sought, and which she is believed to have found.

The venom secreted by cobras, on the other hand, is a nerve poison. It does not cause any damage to the tissue of the bitten limb, so, although the victim may feel a certain amount of local pain, the only marks visible on him or her are the twin punctures of the cobra's fangs. The venom induces drowsiness combined with a sense of intoxication. The bitten person's eyelids droop, apparently in sleep, in fact in a paralysis which gradually immobilizes the whole body, culminating in coma and then death.[141] This, surely, is the humane death which Cleopatra would have chosen for herself. The 'asp' which killed her must then have been *Naja haja*, the Egyptian cobra or *uraeus*. Paintings which show her with a dainty little serpent a few inches long on her breast or arm are misleading, as Sir Thomas Browne pointed out in his essay 'Of Many Things Questionable Which Are Found in Pictures'.[142] To have secreted enough venom to have killed her and her two women the cobra would need to have been around six foot long. On the other hand, more than one snake may have been involved (Propertius, Horace and Virgil all appear to have believed that there were at least two.)[143] The smallest *Naja haja* capable of killing a human being is four foot long. The peasant whom she guards saw pass by them was not only the bearer of outsize figs; he must also have been carrying an outsize basket.

The Egyptian cobra, or *uraeus*, was the distinctive emblem of the royal house of Egypt. It was the sacred beast of the goddess Wadjet and it sat on the monarch's brow, hood inflated, ready to spit flame at his or her enemies.[144] Wadjet, a goddess of the Lower Nile whose cult had come down from prehistory, was assimilated with Isis, and images of the *uraeus* inscribed with the name of Isis have been found in the Valley of the Kings. By Cleopatra's day the *uraeus* was widely recognized as being Isis's own sacred beast. It not only twined around her crown; in a wall painting at Pompeii the goddess holds it in her hand as its tail twists about her wrist. Her priestesses imitated her: a sarcophagus dating from the second century AD shows a priestess with her forearm extended and a snake coiled round it.[145]

When the Roman messengers reached Cleopatra's death chamber they saw her robed and crowned in the guise of Isis. Very likely she wore a bracelet (such as are still widely sold to tourists all over the eastern Mediterranean) in the form of a coiled snake, emblematic of Isis's familiar creature. Later, when craftsmen were instructed to prepare the 'effigy of Cleopatra dead on her couch' which Dio Cassius tells us was carried in Octavius's Egyptian Triumph, they would have represented her as she had been found, in the regalia of Isis. Michael Grant has suggested, intriguingly, that the effigy may have misled both its first viewers and posterity.[146] Roman women like Propertius's Cynthia, who were devotees of Isis, would have readily understood the sacred significance of the snake on Cleopatra's arm, but it was men who were to compile the historical records, and men like Propertius, who was so impatient of his lover's devotions, may have been less perspicacious.

> I saw your arms all bitten by sacred adders,
> And limbs draw torpor in by secret paths.

These lines in Propertius's poem, the similar ones in Horace's Ode XXXVII:

> with fortitude
> she handled fierce snakes, her corporeal
> frame drank in their venom

and Virgil's reference in the *Aeneid* to 'twin snakes of death' dogging Cleopatra at Actium are the only contemporary accounts of the manner of Cleopatra's death.[147] They may have been based on a misunderstanding. When Propertius writes 'I saw' he can only mean that he saw the effigy carried in the Triumph. He saw, but not being well versed in the iconography of Egyptian religion he did not know what he saw. He took the image of a goddess for a Madame Tussaud-style representation of a death scene. If Grant is right, his ignorance gave rise to a fallacious story which has been believed and repeated from that day to this.

There are, however, equally good reasons for accepting the traditional account of Cleopatra's death. It would not have been an unusual way to die. The Greek medical writer Galen records that death by snakebite was a familiar form of capital punishment in ancient Alexandria, and was considered an exceptionally humane one.[148] Besides, Cleopatra – assuming that she did intend to choose such a death – was displaying her usual flair for the eloquent gesture. Not only was the cobra the favoured creature of the goddess whose earthly representative she was, it was in itself replete with symbolic meaning. To die of its bite would be to make of her inescapable end a defiant and hopeful declaration.

In an eccentric study, unpublished but lodged in the British Library, a scholar of the 1920s, A. J. Bethell – whose erudition cannot be disputed but whose common sense perhaps should be – sets out to demonstrate that Cleopatra did not die in Alexandria in 30 BC. He points out that her tomb has never been found, and he maintains that the asp's trail on the beach, to which Plutarch refers, should be understood to mean the traces of her own escape by sea. By some wild flights of numerological fancy Bethell 'proves' that Cleopatra survived to enjoy two more important careers. First, under the name Thea Mousa she married both King Phraates of Parthia and her own son by him, Phraataces. Subsequently, and somewhat bewilderingly, she assumed yet another identity, that of the Virgin Mary, and gave birth to Christ.

Bethell, whose primary aim seems to be that of demonstrating that Jesus Christ was not really Jewish, should not be taken too seriously. But his speculations serve to highlight the mysterious nature of Cleopatra's end. Wild theories take root only where chinks in the historical record allow them space to do so. In any case Bethell, apparently unwittingly, believed exactly what Cleopatra would have wished him to believe. Her Egyptian subjects, hearing of her death by snakebite, would have immediately understood that, far from dying, she had attained immortal life, and that she would come again.

The *uraeus* was the emblem of royalty, and the protector of the monarchs of Egypt. The Greeks, who believed that it could kill with a look, called it 'basilisk', or little king, thus acknowledging its royal nature. In ancient Egyptian wall paintings it is seen guarding the groves of Paradise: the firebreathing dragons who held the gates of the gardens of Hesperides may have derived from it.[149] Besides, in the Egyptian *Book of the Dead* it is said that the snake, which sloughs its skin only to appear revitalized, is the symbol of everlasting life.[150] The single fragmentary page which is all that remains of the alchemical treatise traditionally attributed to Cleopatra shows, among other symbols, the *orobouros*, the snake which swallows its own tail to become a perfect circle and the signifier of eternity[151] (whether or not Cleopatra had anything to do with this text, she would certainly have understood its symbolism). Twined around a pole, the *uraeus* becomes an Egyptian standard – one which represented exuberant and indestructible life, and which was the precursor of the caduceus carried by Mercury, by Asclepius, the Greek god of healing, by Hermes Trismegistus, the inventor of medicine, and by Moses, who made a serpent of brass and put it upon a pole as a talisman to protect the Children of Israel.[152] Cleopatra, who was Isis, was already in a sense immortal, but by embracing the *uraeus* in death she ensured for herself a particularly vital after-life. The Egyptians, wrote Plutarch, compare the asp 'to the planet of the sun, because it doth never age and wax old'.[153] Like the Sun, the emblem of the Golden Age Cleopatra had envisioned, it was an immortal being who died only to be everlastingly renewed. In submitting to its bite Cleopatra proclaimed (in the language of spectacle in which she had always been so fluent) that she had escaped from Octavius's petty, temporal power and that she and Egypt, far from being crushingly defeated, were indestructible.

The Roman poets were generous in their acknowledgement of Cleopatra's fortitude. 'Resolved for death,' wrote Horace, 'she was brave indeed.'[154] If the traditional story of the asp is true, then her suicide shows more than courage. In her closely guarded apartment, physically weakened and surrounded by enemies, she not only planned her own death with resolute coolness, but brought to it as well a grand sense of theatre and a hubristic but splendid vision of her own destiny. If the Cleopatra whom we know from picture and story is superhuman, an artificial construct, a being who looms far larger than any mere person ever could, then she herself must be given some of the credit for that image's creation. She brought to her life not only intelligence and subtlety but also an imaginative vision which encompassed both Europe and Asia, both Heaven and Earth. She allotted herself, and grandly played, a role which was as attractive in its externals as it was substantial in its essence. That vision never left her. Even in the face of her own imminent death, she did not cease to edit and embellish her own story.

# PART TWO

# 4

# THE SUICIDE

CLEOPATRA DIED; HER name did not. She aspired to immortality and she won at least the kind that lasting fame affords. But that fame was to have a curiously chameleon-like character. A mirror rather than a portrait, her image has passed through as many changes as it has had spectators, for those who have tried to see her, to reimagine and reproduce her image, have instead seen and displayed themselves in her.

In the period of Rome's decline she was remembered as a figure of luxuriant sensuality and of the sin with which the pleasures of the senses, under the influence of Christianity, were increasingly associated. But in medieval and early Renaissance Europe another interpretation of her legend gained currency, one which is strikingly at odds with the ancient fantasy of the depraved but lovely temptress. To Geoffrey Chaucer, writing in 1380, and to a host of poets and dramatists both before and in the two hundred years after him, Cleopatra was a paradigm of female goodness, a heroine who proved her virtue by committing the one act capable of absolving a woman from the baseness inherent in her gender, that of killing herself for love of a man. All her other personae were subsumed into that of the suicide, and in this guise she won approval. But the approval has a cutting edge. A virtuous woman who takes her own life, wrote St Augustine, can no longer be counted virtuous, for she has murdered an innocent person.[1] Yet Cleopatra's self-destruction was generally applauded. As the killer she was acclaimed as a good woman. Behind the acclamation lies the suspicion

147

that the person she killed – herself – was, like all sexually active women, bad.

'*Incipit legenda Cleopatrie, Martiris*' – 'Here begins the legend of Cleopatra the Martyr.'[2] Thus Geoffrey Chaucer opens her story in his *Legend of Good Women*. The poem, so Chaucer explains in his Prologue, was composed at the command of the God of Love with the express intention of celebrating illustrious exemplars of feminine virtue, 'clean maidens' and 'true wives', Critics have suggested that in giving Cleopatra first place in it Chaucer was making an ironical joke,[3] but such an opinion is anachronistic. In the songs of the Middle Ages Cleopatra is repeatedly proposed as a pattern of virtue. Like Penelope, Griselda, Lucretia and Dido she is judged to be patient, self-denying and true in love, the evidence of that truth being her willingness to kill herself. John Gower, Chaucer's contemporary, describes her in his *Confessio Amantis* (A Lover's Confession) as

> the woefull queen
> Cleopatras, which in a cave
> With serpents hath herself begrave
> All quick, and so she was totore,
> For sorrow of that she had lore,
> Antony, which her love hath be.[4]

For all the drama of Cleopatra's life, for all her power, for all her vigorous and ambitious statescraft, she was interesting to Gower, to Chaucer and to a host of other authors for one reason only – that she was fallaciously believed to have died for love.

The tradition outlived the medieval era. In the subsequent two centuries more and more ancient texts were found, translated and adapted to a new audience's taste. In 1551 Giulio Landi drew on Plutarch to write *La Vita di Cleopatra Reina d'Egitto*. In 1559 Jacques Amyot translated Plutarch's *Parallel Lives* into French, and twenty years later Sir Thomas North translated Amyot's version into English. But even before these vernacular sources were available playwrights had begun to recognize in the story of Cleopatra a plot perfectly suited to the newly fashionable dramatic form of tragedy. During the latter half of the sixteenth century a flock of Cleopatras took the stage. In Italy Cesare de' Cesari and Giovanni Battista Giraldi Cinthio, in France Estienne Jodelle, Nicolas de Montreux and Robert Garnier, in Germany Hans Sachs and in England Mary Sidney (translating Garnier), Samuel Daniel and Samuel Brandon all wrote tragedies of Cleopatra during the sixty years before Shakespeare turned his hand to the task. Diverse as these plays are in their morals, their sympathies and their artistic merits, they have one thing in common, one partly dictated by the demands of the tragic form. In all of them, as in the works of the medieval poets, the nub of Cleopatra's story lies in its ending.

'I cannot live now that my lord is dead,' declares Giraldi Cinthio's Cleopatra. 'He was my life: without him life is death.'[5] The sentiment is touching, but cruelly reductive. If Cleopatra's only identity is that of Antony's lover then indeed she might as well be buried or burnt with him, as though she were his favourite sword or pair of boots, objects incapable of purposeful independent existence. Similarly the heroines of Chaucer's *Legend of Good Women* have, and wish for, no life outside their love relationships. It is their self-abasement, their readiness to live entirely through their men, that constitutes their goodness. Dido, pathetic rather than tragic in this version, leaps on to the sacrificial pyre when she finds herself left lone and lorn. Thisbe smites herself to the heart rather than be separated from her Pyramus. Most praiseworthy of all is Cleopatra. In a dutiful and devoted speech by Antony's tomb she declares that

> since that blissful hour
> That I swore to have been all freely your

she has never ceased to think of him. Then she leaps, stark naked, 'with full good heart' into a pit full of serpents. Chaucer contemplates this perversely titillating tableau with approval:

> Let see now what man that lover be,
> Will doon so strong a pain for love as she.[6]

149

To die for love, as Cleopatra was supposed to have done, was a fate accounted estimable within the conventions of courtly love. A true knight of the chivalric romances was expected to demonstrate his devotion by submitting to arduous trials and to be prepared to risk his life over and over again for his lady's sake (whether she requited his love or no). Amorous suicide was also lent a reflected virtue by spuriously sacred associations. If the *Legend of Good Women* reads at times less like a pantheon of virtue than a catalogue of corpses it is largely because Chaucer was modelling it explicitly on the martyrologies or Lives of the Saints which served an important dual purpose in medieval culture, being both morally improving and thrillingly horrid. In adapting a Christian form to the courtly and secular religion of the God of Love, he was following a fashionable literary practice of his era. Gower's *Confession*, in which Cleopatra appears among a host of Love's saints on a green lawn reminiscent of the fields of Heaven, was another example of a curious genre in which blasphemy and piety alternate in a fascinating ironical shimmer, a genre which included a Ten Commandments of Love, matins and lauds of love sung by birds, paternosters and credos of love and masses to Venus.[7] In an illustration to a late fifteenth-century French manuscript Antony and Cleopatra stand side by side in a pleasant wooded landscape. He, fully clad, plunges a sword as thick as his arm into his abdomen. She, her furred gown pulled down to her waist but her wimple still prettily in place, holds a pair of asps to her nipples (Plate 26). The image has an edgy eroticism which makes it comically disturbing to the modern eye, but it would have fitted easily among the paintings of the period in which the half-naked saints proffer, as identifying marks and emblems of virtue, the instruments of their own torture.

Cleopatra's name was associated with the cult of the martyrs from an early stage. Towards the end of the second century AD the Carthaginian Christian apologist Tertullian wrote to a group of the persecuted and imprisoned faithful, exhorting them to submit to martyrdom, if it should be their lot, with fortitude, following the example of heroic pagans. Even if they should be thrown to the lions, he urges them, they must be resolute, bearing in mind that 'Woman has voluntarily sought the wild beasts, and even asps, those serpents worse than bear or bull, which Cleopatra applied to herself, that she might not fall into the hands of her enemy.'[8] Tertullian, who believed that 'the best thing for a man is not to touch a woman: and accordingly the virgin's is the principal sanctity',[9] blithely overlooked Cleopatra's fabled promiscuity when he proposed her as a model of courage and honourable behaviour. The dead, even dead women, cannot but be chaste.

In stressing the physical courage common to those who kill themselves and those who submit to being killed, Tertullian diverted attention from the important ethical difference between suicide and martyrdom. He thus glided over an obstacle which was to exercise generations of subsequent Christian thinkers, as indeed it had perplexed their pagan predecessors. The philosophers of ancient Greece and Rome anxiously debated the ethics of suicide. Plato considered it permissible to kill oneself in order to escape incurable and painful illness or intolerable shame, or at the command of the state (as in Socrates's case), but in general, he asserted, suicides improperly arrogate to themselves powers of life and death which by rights belong to the gods. Aristotle considered it a dereliction of the citizen's civic duty. And Pythagoras, according to Cicero, 'forbade men to depart from their guard or station in life without the order of their commander, that is, of God.[10] In Rome both Julius Caesar and Ovid were to argue that truer courage is shown in enduring adversity than in avoiding it by suicide,[11] and Virgil, in the *Aeneid*, imagines a wretched after-life in a 'drear hateful swamp' for

> those sad souls, benighted, who contrived
> Their own destruction, and as they hated daylight,
> Cast their lives away.[12]

These careful and moderate voices, though, have always been opposed by those exhilarated by the physical courage involved in suicide, and the moral absolutism displayed by those who die for a principle or for honour. 'Either Reason or the Rope,' is the alternative the Cynic philosopher Diogenes is said to have proposed for himself.[13] Such a formulation speaks of uncompromising integrity. It has the allure of simplicity, of extremism and of high-minded swagger. Those who reject life, paradoxically, often sound more vigorous, more exciting than those who embrace it.

For the Stoics, suicide had in addition a political dimension. In choosing the time and manner of their deaths, asserted the Roman dramatist Seneca, suicides make themselves free both of capricious fate and of human tyranny. Seneca himself, who held the dangerously exalted post of tutor to the Emperor Nero, was finally obliged to slit his wrists. Had he done so before falling from imperial favour he might more convincingly have illustrated his own conception of voluntary death as the touchstone of freedom. 'See you that precipice? Down that is the way to liberty. See you that sea, that river, that well? There sits liberty at the bottom. Do you ask what is the highway to liberty? Any vein in your body,'[14] Seneca's gruesome tragedies were much admired and imitated by Renaissance dramatists. It is largely to his influence that we owe the set of values to which Spenser refers when he alludes respectfully, in *The Faerie Queene*, to

> High-minded Cleopatra, that with stroke
> Of asps' sting herself did stoutly kill[15]

or which Shakespeare's Cleopatra invokes when she says

> what's brave, what's noble,
> Let's do it after the high Roman fashion,
> And make death proud to take us.[16]

It is a value system which the Christian Church early rejected. Tertullian, writing around 200 AD, might seek to encourage the martyrs by the example of famous suicides but two centuries later St Augustine was declaring roundly, 'Certainly a suicide is also a homicide'. Christian thinking had transformed the terms of the debate. Classical models of heroism like Lucretia, raped by Tarquin, or Cato, defeated at Utica, killed themselves in order to preserve their honour in the eyes of the world. Thus, wrote Augustine, they proved themselves 'too greedy of praise'. The Christian, by contrast, should care nothing for the 'stupid opinion of the mob', hearkening only to the voice of conscience; and if that told him that he had sinned then he must trust to God's mercy rather than lapsing, Judas-like, into the heinous sin of despair. To Augustine, Cato displayed only 'weakness unable to bear adversity'. The pattern of Christian courage was Job, who submitted patiently to all his trials. This was a major intellectual and moral shift. Subsequent centuries were to accept Augustine's opinion as orthodoxy but to many of his first readers it must have seemed strange, even repellent, for he felt it necessary to discuss it at length in his *magnum opus*, and to make his point with the most emphatic solemnity. 'This we say, this we declare, this we by all means endorse, that no man inflict on himself a voluntary death, thinking to escape temporary ills, least he find himself among ills that are unending.'[17]

Augustine's case was accepted by all subsequent Christian writers. In *The Anatomy of Melancholy*, Robert Burton lists Cleopatra among those who 'voluntarily died to avoid a greater mischief, to free themselves from misery, to save their honour, or vindicate their good name'. Such 'honour' is worthless, he thunders: 'These are false and pagan positions, profane Stoical paradoxes, wicked examples.'[18] In similar vein John Sym, a seventeenth-century English pamphleteer, included Cleopatra among his 'woefull examples' of 'self murderers', heathens who took their own lives prompted by the fallacious 'wisdom of flesh and blood, of corrupt nature and carnal reason'.[19]

Yet the history of attitudes to suicide demonstrates with startling clarity the human capacity to think one thing while feeling another. For most of the last fifteen hundred years 'self-murder' has been accounted both a crime and a sin, but, as Christian writers repeatedly warn, wicked pride is more glamorous than virtuous humility and impudent bravery more lovable than patient self-abnegation. Repeatedly, in discussing suicide, writers have distinguished between goodness and 'greatness', an epithet which covers a complex of attributes – high social class, courage, integrity and self-esteem. St Augustine himself equivocated: 'Those who have laid violent hands on themselves are perhaps to be admired for the greatness of their souls, but not to be praised for the soundness of their wisdom.'[20] Twelve hundred years later the English cleric Jeremy Taylor was equally torn: 'The case is indeed very hard: and every one in this is apt not only to excuse but to magnify the fresh and glorious minds of those who to preserve their honour despised their life.' Taylor does not flinch from rectitude: 'yet this does not conclude it lawful'.[21] But though legality and goodness have preoccupied the theologians, the poets have tended to see only the greatness and the glory. Cleopatra, the asp at her breast, became a fit heroine for tragedy and a pattern of steadfastness. The commission of a Christian-defined sin made her, in the supposedly Christian culture of medieval and Renaissance Europe, the object of general admiration.

'Will she fear her fate who, but for death, must see her glory die?' asks Eras (Iras) in Estienne Jodelle's tragedy of 1553, *Cléopâtre Captive*. 'No, no,' replies Cleopatra. 'Let us die! Let us die and let us snatch a victory even though Caesar has overcome us.'[22] Her resolve accomplished, the chorus applauds her, declaring that she will be remembered from the lands of the sunrise to those of its setting for having preferred death to humiliation, and having thus given evidence of *'un coeur plus que d'homme'*,[23] a more than manly heart. In Samuel Daniel's *Tragedy of Cleopatra*, first published in 1594, it is Honour personified who urges Cleopatra to do away with herself. In Robert Garnier's *Marc-Antoine* both lovers gladly embrace death. For this, says the chorus, they are more to be envied than the victorious Octavius.

O Antony with they dear mate
Both in misfortunes fortunate!

Not only will they, in killing themselves, escape their enemy.

They will also be redeemed. 'Die, die I must:' declares
Antony.

> I must a noble death,
> A glorious death unto my succour call:
> . . . that my last day
> By mine own hand my spots may wash away.[24]

Antony, in choosing death, gives evidence of courage and
pride. So does Cleopatra, but in a woman's case suicide
almost always carries, in legend or literature, another, sexual
meaning. Cleopatra's death has been understood to demonstrate, as nothing else could, that she was no harlot, but true
in love.

The ideal of the good woman whose love was stronger
than death is an ancient one. When Seneca was ordered to
die, his wife Paulina declared that she would cut her wrists
as well rather than outlive him – a resolution which Seneca,
predictably, approved.[25] Pliny the Younger relates the story
of a woman who, discovering that her husband was fatally
ill, 'gave up hope, and tying herself to her husband she
plunged with him into the lake'. When, in the first century
AD, a senator was found to be implicated in a conspiracy,
his wife, Arria, declared that she would die with him. Her
stern resolve made her a by-word for marital devotion.[26]

Pagan Rome prized the loyal wife. Christianity added to
this esteem a veneration for the chaste woman in which
pragmatic morality merges with mysticism. When Tertullian
praised the firmness of pagan suicides like Dido and Lucretia
he was also impressed by the impulse which led them to
prefer death to sexual infidelity. In his *Exhortation to Chastity* he declares that 'second marriage will have to be termed
no other than a species of fornication'.[27] Women who chose
to die with their husbands were therefore to be praised above
all for having demonstrated beyond the possibility of doubt
that they would never allow themselves to be tempted to seek
a second mate. Thus Dido was to be admired as well as
pitied. Tertullian knew an older version of her story than
that which Virgil narrates, one in which Aeneas has no part.

St Jerome, who also considered her an admirable exemplar of chastity, relates it: 'When her hand was sought in marriage by Iarbas, king of Libya, she deferred the marriage for a while until her country was settled. Not long after, having raised a funeral pyre to the memory of her former husband Sichaeus, she preferred to "burn rather than marry".'[28]

This valorization of those who died rather than be unfaithful to a dead husband overlaps in the writings of the Early Fathers of the Christian Church with the cult of those numerous female martyrs who killed themselves rather than allow their chastity to be compromised. Eusebius tells of one Domnina, a Christian of Antioch captured with her two daughters during the Diocletian persecutions. Fearing that their captors intended to rape them, Domnina took her daughters by the hand and all three leapt into the river 'and so sank unsullied in the wave'. The fifteen-year-old St Pelagia, when captured by rude and lascivious soldiers, asked permission to go alone to her room to change her clothes. From there she climbed on to the roof and threw herself to her death.[29] Even St Augustine did not condemn such suicides outright. After all, in so resolutely preserving their status as virgins or faithful wives, women at least proved themselves pure. 'Who so lacks human sympathy as to refuse to pardon them?'[30]

Such cases seem to have only the most tenuous relevance to the story of Cleopatra, a ruler who killed herself after a crushing defeat had left her no political future, a twice-widowed woman and probable murderer of one of her husbands, whose four children had all been born out of wedlock. But, however incongruously, this is the context in which her story was placed, and in which it became, so surprisingly, a parable of womanly virtue. Chaucer described Cleopatra as a martyr, not because he believed she had been persecuted for her religious beliefs, but because, as he understood her story, she had laid down her life for the sake of an abstraction – not the Roman ideal of honour, but the Christian one of chastity. The form of the *Legend of Good Women* precisely recalls that of a martyrology, and the submissive wives and loyal lovers whose histories it contains are thus associated

156

with the spotless martyrs, for the chastity of a faithful wife is second in virtue only to virginity itself. So Cleopatra's liaison with Julius Caesar was forgotten or ignored and her imagined lechery erased from the collective imagination. In following Antony to the grave she was understood to have given evidence of the virtues considered most proper to women, fidelity and sexual restraint, the only evidence which, given the notorious fickleness of women, could be considered conclusive.

The cult of those who die for love has had a long life. In a popular biography of Cleopatra written at the end of the nineteenth century the American author John Lloyd asks: 'As for her – this selfish, heartless sorceress, gifted and beautiful as she was – what does she do when she sees her lover dead – dying for her? Does she share his fate? Not she. What selfish woman ever killed herself for love?'[32] In R. H. Case's preface to the Arden edition of Shakespeare's play, written in 1906 but still widely used in Britain by students and general readers alike, Cleopatra's 'unwillingness to outlive Antony' is unquestioningly equated with virtue.[33] The woman who cannot live without her beloved, who pines away and dies of consumption or simply of a broken heart, rather than seek happiness alone or with another man, is still a popular stereotype. Familiarity lends the appearance of normality. The remarkable implications of this aspect of Cleopatra's legend can be more clearly understood if it is juxtaposed with a phenomenon which is, to the Western understanding, apparently alien – the Indian practice (outlawed since 1829 but not yet defunct) of widow-burning, known as suttee.

The word suttee is an anglicized form of *sati*, a word common to both Hindi and Urdu and deriving from Sanskrit. Its literal meaning is 'good and faithful wife': its etymological root is *sat*, which means, simply, 'good'. For the orthodox Hindu, just as for Chaucer, a woman's claim to 'goodness' depended on her being willing to subsume her own existence into her man's and to end her life with his.

British administrators in the eighteenth and nineteenth centuries were shocked by suttee, seeing in it evidence of the cruelty, fatalism and disregard for the sanctity of human life which they considered typical of the Oriental character. But Europeans of an earlier era had known about suttee, and heartily approved of it. In the first century BC Propertius complained of Roman girls' self-indulgence and prayed:

> Prosper the law of eastern husbands' pyres! . . .
> For when the last torch is thrown on the corpse's bier,
> His dutiful wives stand gathered, flowing hair,
> And compete for death, who shall follow alive
> Wedlock: their shame is not to be allowed to die.[34]

Propertius may be suspected of teasing: not so St Jerome, who took up the theme four hundred years later in a treatise on the immorality of widows who take a second husband.

> It is a law with them [Indians] that the favourite wife must be burned with her dead husband. The wives therefore vie with one another for the husband's love, and the highest ambition of the rivals, and the proof of chastity, is to be considered worthy of death. So then she that is victorious, having put on her former dress and ornaments, lies down beside the corpse, embracing and kissing it, and to the glory of chastity despises the flames which are burning beneath her.[35]

The image Jerome evokes has its parallels in the literature of Cleopatra. Garnier's Cleopatra calls upon her women to weep for the dead Antony on her behalf. She herself has no more tears: they have been dried by the heat rising from her breast as though from the glowing coals of a furnace. While the women weep, beat their breasts and tear their hair at her behest, she lays herself down by her lover's corpse. 'My body joined with thine, my mouth with thine', and showers him with a hundred thousand kisses until, finally,

> in this office weak my limbs may grow,
> Fainting on you, and forth my soul may flow.[36]

Thus in an ecstasy of self-sacrifice she dies, apparently by spontaneous combustion, consumed by the ardour of her own passionate heart.

Garnier's is one of a long line of imagined Cleopatras transfigured by death. His account is only exceptional in that the erotic nature of Cleopatra's self-sacrifice is so clearly delineated in it. Swooning to death in Antony's arms – immolating herself, as it were, on his funeral pyre – this Cleopatra proves her love true and her virtue intact, just as an Indian widow does in the act of suttee.

The proof is drastic, one that few women would wish to give unless under duress or in despair. As early as the eleventh century the Islamic scholar Al-Biruni had noted that, although a Hindu widow was nominally free to choose whether or not she wished to die, the choice was an empty one for 'as a widow she is ill-treated as long as she lives'.[37] The nineteenth-century reformer Rajah Ram Mohan Roy quotes reports of women 'forced upon the pyre and there bound with ropes and pressed with green bamboos until consumed by the flames'.[38] It is now widely accepted that the plight of a Hindu widow was (and in some conservative circles still is) so wretched, and the social pressures which impelled a widow to commit suttee so ineluctable that the women who threw themselves on their dead husbands' funeral pyres, or in more recent years have drenched themselves with paraffin and burned to death in their own kitchens, were not and are not making a free choice. So much Westerners, viewing suttee with detachment, can see. And having seen it, it is easier to turn back to Western culture and note the points at which the cult of those who die for love, which suffuses so much of Western art and literature, overlaps with this 'barbaric' practice.

In Jodelle's *Cléopâtre Captive* the ghost of Antony announces that he has appeared to Cleopatra, 'that murderous serpent', in a dream and ordered her to follow him into the underworld, not because he longs to be with her (on the contrary, he yearns for Octavia, 'honour of all ladies') but because it is her duty 'to be companion to my pain and sadness'.[39] Many Cleopatras are of the same mind. Chaucer's declares that she has resolved to share all that may befall Antony, 'well or woe . . . life or death', and thus honour the requirements of 'wifehood'.[40] (Those authors who depict Cleopatra as a good woman generally award her, in defiance of the facts, married status.) Giraldi Cinthio's asserts that

> since I had become his wife, I should
> Have been devoid of honesty and justice
> Had I not wished to share in common with him
> All happiness and griefs, all good and evil.[41]

Daniel's apologizes for not having killed herself immediately on receiving the news of his death:

> My heart blood should the purple flowers have been,
> Which here upon thy tomb to thee are offered

and promises to remedy her omission as soon as she can obtain a weapon.[42] Garnier's assures her mate that

> Dead and alive, Antony, thou shalt see
> Thy princess follow thee.

If she were to refuse to share his fate,

> Not light, inconstant, faithless should I be,
> But vile, forsworn, of treacherous cruelty.[43]

The code of proper wifely conduct to which all these Cleopatras refer seems to coincide at every point with that which authorizes suttee.

The radical feminist Mary Daly has called suttee 'the ultimate consummation of marriage' and pointed out that 'the widows' sexual purity is "safe-guarded" by ritual murder'.[44] Like St Jerome, she perceives that chastity is the heart of the matter. So do the 'good' Cleopatras. Garnier's heroine explains to her women why she must kill herself. If she fails to do so,

> the after-livers justly might report
> That I him only for his empire loved
> And high estates: and that in hard estate
> I for another did him lewdly leave.[45]

In Samuel Daniel's *Tragedy of Cleopatra* she declares that

the world believes that once Antony is dead she will seek another man:

> I have no means to undeceive their minds
> But to bring in the witness of my blood.

The messenger who subsequently reports her death describes how she reaches out for the asp

> And so receives the deadly poisoning touch
> That touch that tried the gold of her love, pure,
> And hath confirmed her honour to be such,
> As must a wonder to all worlds endure.[46]

So notorious was feminine inconstancy that had she lived on she would have been forever under suspicion, not of treachery to Antony, her ally (for in this period she is defined solely as a sexual being), but of infidelity to Antony, her lover.

The marital anxiety which can only be assuaged by suttee, or its Western equivalent, is the anxiety of the owner, for a woman is the property of her man. As Chaucer's Parson explains, an adulterous woman is a thief. 'Certes, this is the foulest theft that may be, when a woman stealeth her body from her husband, and giveth it to her holour [lover] to defoulen her.'[47] Just as a man going on a long journey will lock up his house, so the wives of the Middle Ages were confined and supervised. And just as the dying owner of a valuable estate seeks to ensure that his heirs will respect his wishes and refrain from altering his decorations, cutting down his trees or selling the property to a stranger who cares nothing for his memory, so a dying lover or husband longs to take his woman with him, to prevent her giving herself, his possession, to someone new. In a tragedy by the eighteenth-century Italian Cardinal Delfino, Cleopatra is about to embark on a promising love affair with a gallant and devoted Augusto (Octavius) when the ghost of Antony intervenes. Ardently as he still loves Cleopatra, he would rather have her dead than happy with another. He borrows two of the Gorgon Megaera's snaky locks and sends them down to

161

earth as asps to ensure 'his' woman's fidelity by ending her life.[48]

The insecurity of the male partner/proprietor was compounded in medieval Europe by the belief that women were by nature promiscuous. Cleopatra is frequently mentioned in lyrics from the fourteenth, fifteenth and early sixteenth centuries. In all of them she appears as a pattern of virtue, as one of the 'worshipfullest ladies' because, as one fifteenth-century lyric has it, after Antony's death

> thee list no longer dure
> For in a pit with serpents to take
> Thou went all naked so thy death to make.[49]

These songs harp always on the same note, the fickleness of women. It is as an exception to the general rule that Cleopatra is mentioned in them. In a heavily ironic ballad, John Lydgate suggests that 'Cleopatra's faithfulness' might seem to prove all women true, but he himself is not convinced: 'Yet aye beware of doubleness.'[50] George Turberville's song in 'Dispraise of women that allure and love not' compares contemporary women, who weep crocodile tears and sing like mermaids to lure men to their doom, unfavourably with the 'modest matrons' of the past, Cleopatra among them.[51] Leonard Gybson exhorted women to

> Leave lightly love, ladies, for fear of ill name
> And true love embrace ye, to purchase your fame

but he had little hope of being heeded, for, the women of his own time having fallen from ancient standards of virtue, 'Not one Cleopatra, I doubt, doth remain'.[52] In the face of such widespread prejudice a woman's innocence could only be proved by the severest trials. Just as a Hindu woman is only entitled to the name of *sati*, 'faithful wife', after having immolated herself, so nothing but her death could have attested the gold of Cleopatra's love pure.

There is a further correspondence between these imaginary versions of Cleopatra's suicide and suttee. According to some interpreters, the burning of the Hindu widow was as much

162

a punishment as a sacrifice. A man's death could be caused by the bad *karma* attending his wife as a result of her sins in a previous life: his misfortune was called down by, and was therefore evidence of, something morally or spiritually wrong with her. His death was her fault.[53] It was only fitting, therefore, that she should die too. Similarly, one after another of the early Renaissance Cleopatras admits her responsibility for Antony's downfall. He has been foolish, mistaken, even sinful, but he is not to blame, any more than Adam was for eating the apple, Odysseus for lingering with Circe or Aeneas for allowing himself to be seduced by Dido. Once more the old theme of male innocence emerges. Only women are accountable, and unforgivable. The ancient prejudices on which Octavius played when first promulgating the story of Cleopatra have proved as tenacious of life as has that story itself.

Jodelle's Cleopatra proclaims her guilt on her first appearance. She is, she says, the murderess of a great man.

> Ah gods, if I could but pluck
> From my heart the wrong that I have done him!

She was the cause of his defeat in Parthia and of

> A thousand, thousand thousand other things
> to which love of me had closed his eyes.

The war with Rome, the defeat at Actium, Antony's own suicide – all are her fault.[54] Giraldi Cinthio's Octavius agrees that it is with Cleopatra that all his enemies' villainy originates.

> How true the saying is that woman is
> The breeding place of lying and the nest of all deceits.[55]

Garnier's Antony bewails his own degradation at Cleopatra's hands: 'In her allurements caught ... I honour have despised.' He accepts no responsibility, for his will is no longer free. His flight from Actium and his subsequent defeat, so Garnier's furiously self-disgusted Cleopatra declares, was 'not his offence, but mine'. Antony dead, she mourns him in terms which make her acceptance of culpability explicit. She is the destroyer

> Of you whom I have plagued, whom I have made
> With bloody hand a guest of mouldy tomb:
> Of you whom I destroyed, of you, dear Lord,
> Whom I of empire, honour, life have spoiled.[56]

Samuel Daniel's Cleopatra declares that she is to blame both for Antony's fall and for her country's defeat.[57] Like the Indian widow whose husband's death is evidence of her lack of virtue, so Cleopatra must die to atone for the death of her man – of which, for reasons which are only vaguely posited, she is judged guilty.

The very imprecision of this verdict of guilt is terrifying. But two things are plain: that Cleopatra's culpability is primarily sexual, and that it is connected with greed. Dead, she has proved her selflessness; but alive she is suspected of harbouring desires, both for sexual pleasure and for worldly power, and worse still, of having wished to gratify those desires rather than devote herself whole-heartedly to Antony's service. These suspicions become explicit accusations in those versions of Cleopatra's story which, during the period that produced Chaucer's good woman and the tragic heroine of the Renaissance dramatists, perpetuated the hostile image of Cleopatra the harlot queen.

Cleopatra's rehabilitation was never absolute. The malleability of stories does not only allow for their meaning to change over a period of time; it also permits them to be told, and read, in contrary ways within the same chronological period. Dante placed Cleopatra in the second circle of his *Inferno*, characterizing her only by the epithet *lussoriosa* (lustful).[58] John Lydgate condemned her avarice and her 'lusts foul and abominable'.[59] In Spenser's *The Faerie Queene* both she and Antony are confined in the dungeons of the House of Pride, fit punishment for their 'wasteful Pride and wanton Riotise'.[60] Most hostile of all is Giovanni Boccaccio's depiction of her in *De Claris Mulieribus* and *De Casibus Illustrium Virorum*. Boccaccio's Cleopatra 'was known throughout the

164

world for her greed, cruelty and lustfulness'. With her shining eyes and her seductive eloquence she draws Caesar into lascivious ways. Subsequently, 'she gave herself to her pleasures', becoming 'almost the prostitute of oriental kings'. Avid for gold and jewels, she uses her wiles to strip her lovers of all their treasures and, still unsatisfied, loots the ancient temples of Egypt. She captivates Antony and then uses her power over him to demand the kingdoms of Syria and Arabia. She attempts to seduce Herod in the hope that she can thus purloin his kingdom. 'To bring the covetous Cleopatra to his embraces' Antony gives her King Artavasdes, with his silver chains and his fabulous treasures. 'The greedy woman, happy at the gifts, embraced the ardent man so seductively that he made her his wife.' Boccaccio recounts with relish the tale of the dissolving pearl before proceeding to his climax. 'As the insatiable woman's craving for kingdoms grew day by day, to grasp everything at once she asked Antony for the Roman empire ... Good lord, how great was the audacity of the woman who requested this!' At last she slits her veins and places asps in the wounds, thus putting an end to 'her avarice, her lasciviousness and her life'.[61]

The account contains much that is familiar from the ancient sources, but Boccaccio has given the story a new focus, one which marks him as a man of his time. In his depiction of Cleopatra his contemporaries would immediately have recognized a personification of the deadly sins of Avaritia and Lascivia, sins which, as Chaucer's Parson explains, are closely allied, for 'Avarice ... is a likerousness [lecherousness] in heart to have earthly things.'[62] These are precisely the sins which good Cleopatras abjure. The contrast between Boccaccio's wicked seductress and Chaucer's Good Woman is striking, but, opposite though they are, they lie one on each side of the same moral axis. Both authors subscribe to the same definition of feminine virtue. Boccaccio's Cleopatra is distinguished by her greed – greed for sex and greed for money. Chaucer's Good Women – Cleopatra among them – are good precisely because they have no such appetites. Asking nothing of themselves, they give their all, even their lives, for their beloved men.

That women are grasping and will take every opportunity to wheedle presents from the men over whom sex has given them power has always been a commonplace of bawdy comedy. What the wiser proponents of this old joke make plain is that in doing so women are not so much proving themselves childishly acquisitive as shrewdly earning a living in the only way that is open to them. Traditionally denied financial independence, relegated willy-nilly to parasitism, women have inevitably seemed to the men struggling to support them, or to win their favour, deplorably mercenary.

Money-greed and sex-greed go together, and were the more easily ascribed to women because the Christian male authors of the Middle Ages, like the men of ancient Rome, laid the responsibility for passions which shamed them not on the guilty subjects, themselves, but on the passive objects, the women who aroused them. They repudiated their own sexual nature, exteriorized it, called it Woman and condemned it to damnation. 'The sirens have the faces of women,' wrote Pope Gregory the Great, 'because nothing so estranges men from God as the love of women.'[63] In the twelfth century the French scholar Peter Abelard rejoiced in his castration, which 'cut me off from the slough of filth in which I had been wholly immersed in mind as in body. Only thus could I become more fit to approach the holy altars ... free from the heavy yoke of carnal desire.'[64] 'Always hot desire and wantonness precede lust,' wrote Pope Innocent III, 'stench and filth accompany it, sorrow and repentance follow it.'[65] Were it not for the existence of women, men would never have been so degraded and bestialized. Sacred scriptures, wrote Hugh St Victor, signify the soul by the man and sex and flesh by the woman.[66] Thus man made woman the scapegoat and proxy for his own blameworthy flesh; and women, piteously to the modern mind, accepted their guilt. 'Is it the general lot of women to bring total ruin on great men?' asked Eloise in a letter to her lover Abelard, and gave herself the answer yes, quoting Ecclesiastes: 'I find woman more bitter than death; she is a snare, her heart a net, her arms are chains.' Eve, Delilah, Job's wife: scripture provided her with plenty of precedents for her guilt,[67] and so she accepted sole responsibility for the misfortunes of Abelard, a man who had, by his own admission, repeatedly forced her to have sex with him against her will.

It is for sexuality – not her own, but man's – that woman must be punished. Garnier's Eras, wondering at the rigour of Cleopatra's self-condemnation, seeks clarification: 'Are you therefore cause of his [Antony's] overthrow?' Cleopatra replies with devastating lucidity: 'I am sole cause: I did it, only I.'[68] Sole cause – of a series of events in which she has played an entirely passive part. 'I did it,' she says, but it was Antony who loved her immoderately, Antony who preferred her to military honour, Antony who broke the battle line to follow her. But she will stand proxy for Antony because what he has done was motivated by sexual feeling; and sexuality, as Octavius and his Roman contemporaries asserted, and as posterity has agreed, is a female responsibility. 'If we enquire, we find that nearly all the kingdoms of the world have been overthrown by women,' assert the authors of the witch-hunters' manual, the *Malleus Maleficorum*, adducing in support of their theory the examples of Helen, the kidnap victim who has always been so illogically blamed for the war occasioned by her abduction, and Cleopatra 'the worst of women'.[69] The psychoanalyst and critic Catherine Clément has demonstrated how, in the Freudian game of transferred meaning and misdirected drives, it is always, when the music stops, the woman who is left holding the parcel of sexual guilt.[70] So Cleopatra is to blame for Antony's love, the love which supposedly destroyed him. Her guilt is not related to any willed action. If he had seduced her, even if he had raped her, she would still be culpable. Garnier's Antony declares himself deprived of all power of volition, 'a slave become unto her feeble face'. His Cleopatra concurs, 'My face too lovely caused our wretched case.'[71] She has done nothing; she is not an agent but a helpless catalyst. Spenser notes that the 'warlike Antony' neglected

167

The whole world's rule for Cleopatra's sight,
Such wondrous power hath women's fair aspect
To captive men, and make them all the world reject.[72]

Cleopatra's physical existence, her face, her 'aspect', is all the evidence required to find her guilty.

That guilt can only be cancelled when the body that contains it is done away with. The body of the Hindu widow, the woman who, alive, caused her husband's death, must be immolated. The charred corpse becomes *sati*, a faithful wife, something no living woman can be. So Cleopatra, in a succession of poems and plays, achieves virtue by destroying herself. Her suicide wins her love, pity and admiration. She is 'fair as is the rose in May', says Chaucer. She is truly repentant, says Jodelle. She is dutiful and true, says Giraldi Cinthio. She is a tender-hearted mother and a sweet mistress, says Garnier. Her lips are of coral, her skin of alabaster, and her hair of fine, flaming gold: 'Naught lives so fair'. She is queenly and courageous, says Daniel.[73] She has become a good woman, but she has had to pay for her redeemed reputation with her life. For the only good woman is a chaste woman, and the only chaste woman is a dead one.

# 5

# THE LOVER

'GIVE ME A kiss,' says Shakespeare's Antony to his Cleopatra. 'Even this repays me.' The Battle of Actium has ended in shameful defeat for them, kingdoms and provinces are forfeit, Antony's honour is irremediably compromised – and yet in his Egyptian mistress's arms he can still assert that one of her tears

> rates
> All that is won and lost.[1]

Modern audiences weep for love of such a reckless lover. Many of Shakespeare's contemporaries, by contrast, would have sat heartstruck and horrified to hear a once great man give voice to such dangerous folly.

'Cleopatra has in her heart the all-purifying flame: she loves.' Thus the critic François-Victor Hugo in 1868.[2] 'This is what redeems Antony's memory,' wrote William Tarn in 1934, 'that at the end he did lose half the world for love.'[3] So the post-Romantic reader tends to conclude, but such reverence for the holiness of the heart's affections is comparatively modern. Love may have been 'the all-purifying flame' to Hugo, but to Petrarch in the fourteenth century it was the 'unworthy fire' which, far from ennobling Cleopatra, had burnt her cruelly.[4]

To the thinkers of the Renaissance passionate love was a personal calamity commensurate with disease or madness and, like those afflictions, undignified and dehumanizing. Physicians prescribed for it as for any other kind of mental and physical distress. Wits mocked it: nothing could be more laughable, wrote the dramatist Thomas Heywood, than 'foolish enamorates who spend their ages, their spirits, nay themselves, in the servile and ridiculous employments of their mistresses'.[5] Philosophers pitied it: 'He that runs headlong from the top of a rock,' wrote Robert Burton, 'is not in so bad a case as he that falls into the gulf of love.'[6] The word 'passion' derives from the Latin verb meaning to suffer, an etymological connection which most writers of the sixteenth and seventeenth centuries would have found perfectly appropriate. Just as Virgil had described Dido, afflicted with love, as 'Luckless, already given over to ruin',[7] so, in the era which saw the revival of classical learning, thinkers concurred with the classical repudiation of violent emotion. To Shakespeare and his contemporaries Cleopatra's primary identity is that of the lover, and her story is a parable of the spiritual and actual perils attendant on immoderate feeling. Jodelle's Antony considers himself 'a hundred times wretched' because in the frenzy of his love for Cleopatra he has trampled his own reputation underfoot, abandoned his wife and children and taken to his breast a 'murderous serpent'. He calls his love a wound, a madness, a poison, a cruel fire, a divine punishment inflicted on him by jealous gods determined that his life should end in pain and dishonour.[8]

> Poor Cleopatra! to what hour of grief
> Have you been led.

So Giraldi Cinthio's heroine bewails her fate, wishing that the day she first saw Antony had never dawned, for then it was that her 'miserable ruin' was begun.[9]

Shakespeare's *Antony and Cleopatra* dramatizes the conflict between reason, the wise person's prop and guide, and its adversary, sexual love. Shakespeare allows passion to speak eloquently for itself. He pictures it gorgeous and seductive, generous and brilliant – but he does not, finally, give it his endorsement. The critic Franklin Dickey has pointed out that he exhibits Antony and Cleopatra, not for our admiration, but 'gravely and sadly as patterns to pity but to shun'.[10] So intoxicating is the verse in which he allows them to hymn their own passion that the modern reader – accustomed to the Romantic notion that love ennobles the lover – tends to accept their own valuation of themselves and their relationship and is therefore frequently disappointed or startled to notice how ignoble, in fact, they are. Few people in Shakespeare's first audience would have been thus surprised.

In the first scene of the play Antony, embracing Cleopatra, declares

> The nobleness of life
> Is to do thus.[11]

To Shakespeare's contemporaries such a sentiment would have been quite obviously mistaken: many of them would have considered it morally reprehensible; all of them would have known it to be incorrect. It is possible to recapture something approximating to their understanding of it if one imagines the protagonist of a modern play uttering the same words while injecting himself with heroin. In the hands of a latter-day Shakespeare (or Baudelaire, or Rimbaud) the addict could be a charming, even an heroic, character. His self-destructive habit could assume the glamour of a defiant refusal to compromise with the banality of life. His plight could move an audience to love and to pity. Given sufficient eloquence he could make them understand, if against their better judgements, how the moments of ecstasy and self-transcendence the drug afforded him could be (or could at least seem to be) worth more to him than all the sum of tedious day-to-day experience. But nearly everyone hearing him would feel certain that he had made a grave mistake, and that his story could only end (unless he changed his ways) in wretchedness. So seventeenth-century theatre-goers would have understood Antony's words. The grand absolutism of his declaration of love must certainly have thrilled them, as it thrills us still, but they would not have wished to emulate it. For them such extreme feeling could be, at best, the object of compassion.

It was strong emotion, not sexual pairing, that Renaissance

171

thinkers perceived as being dangerous. Marriage, an alliance motivated in this period mainly by economic self-interest (the bridegroom's or his father-in-law's), the urge to reproduce and (in more fortunate cases) a desire for domestic security and affectionate companionship, could safely be approved. It is marriage rather than passion which underlies the happy-ever-aftering of Shakespearean comedies – Venus and Eros are excluded from the wedding masque in *The Tempest* – and if it is sometimes evident in the plays that partners have been paired purely for narrative convenience, regardless of their emotional or sexual compatibility, well, that is not so different from the way marriages were in reality arranged. Marriage helped to knit together the fabric of the state. A homilist sponsored by Elizabeth I saw the matrimonial bond as one of the links which held society together. 'Kings and . . . Subjects, Priests and Laymen, Masters and Servants, Fathers and Children, Husbands and Wives, Rich and Poor; and every one hath need of other: so that in all things is to be lauded and praised the goodly order of God.'[12] But if marriage was among the ties which held together the great net of social order, passion threatened to unravel it. 'What plague infernal worse than this?' asks the wise and virtuous Octavia in Samuel Brandon's *Letter From Octavia to Antonius*,

> What multitudes of souls are lost!
> What cities overthrown!
> What kingdoms by licentious lust
> With ruin overgrown![13]

This flinching from sexual ardour was distinct, in Shakespeare's day, from any moral or social condemnation of extra-marital sex. The modest matron and the harlot agreed in wishing to be spared the torments of excessive feeling. 'Amorous love,' wrote Margaret, Duchess of Newcastle, a generation after Shakespeare's play was first published, 'is a disease or a passion, or both, I know only by relation.' Another seventeenth-century lady, Dorothy Osborne, who had married against her family's wishes and whose feelings for her husband were of the tenderest, could still write disapprovingly of 'this senseless passion; that whereso'ever it comes destroys all that entertain it'.[14] Their condemnation of it transcended any notions of sexual propriety. In his 'tragicomoedia' *The Virtuous Octavia*, Samuel Brandon introduces as a foil to Antony's morally flawless wife 'a licentious woman', Silvia, who is equally thankful to be impervious to Cupid's arrows.

> Affection, no, I know not such a thought,
> That were a way to make myself a slave.

It is loss of self-control in passion, and therefore loss of independence and free will, that Silvia dreads. Licentious as she may be, in this she is of one mind with the virtuous. In the same play the chorus sadly condemns Antony for giving rein to his love for Cleopatra and thus failing to overcome that 'monster' and 'savage beast' which

> doth all our senses overthrow
> and reason undermineth.[15]

To the thinkers of the Renaissance reason, moderation and self-control were the cornerstones of culture; intemperate emotion threatened to dislodge them. True, the conventions of courtly love had decreed that the lover was uplifted by his feelings, just as a religious devotee is purified by his adoration of God, but the 'love' of the knight for his lady – reverent, obedient and unconsummated – was a far cry from the 'love' that Shakespeare's Antony and Cleopatra boast of enjoying in the soft beds of Alexandria. 'Of *donnoi* [chivalric honour] he knows truly nothing who wants fully to possess his lady.' So a court of love, one of the (possibly imaginary) twelfth-century tribunals of Provençal lords and ladies from whose decrees the laws of courtly love were derived, is said to have ruled. 'Whatever turns into reality is no longer love.'[16]

Any discussion of historical attitudes to sexuality and emotion is bedevilled by the vagueness and instability of language. The same word is used to describe a multitude of feelings, from the hot-blooded yearnings of Romeo to the selfless, all-embracing love of God. Numerous attempts have been made

173

over the centuries to distinguish between 'true', praiseworthy love and those other less respectable impulses – lust, possessiveness, self-delusion and jealousy – which are so inextricably mingled with it. Plato's Diotima proposed an ideal love so refined as to have altogether transcended the sexual desire in which it has its origin. In the Provençal courts of love desire was condoned as a motive but only so long as it remained unconsummated. The medieval cleric Bernardus Silvestris wrote that there are two goddesses of love, the gracious Venus who is 'worldly music, that is, the equal proportion of worldly things, which some call Astraea', and 'the shameful Venus, the goddess of sensuality . . . the mother of all fornication'.[17]

Renaissance thinkers wrestled with the distinction between Agape and Eros, between unselfish benevolence, the *caritas* which 'seeketh not her own'[18] and *cupiditas*, the sexual love which craves physical gratification. The wonder is that the two concepts – so apparently diverse – have been so universally acknowledged to be connected, hard though it may be to define that connection. Sigmund Freud was endorsing a two-thousand-year-old intuition when he concluded, though with much self-questioning, that they were one and the same – that Eros, the pleasure principle, was the motive force behind not only sexual activity but also all creative social achievement. 'Civilisation,' he wrote, 'is a process in the service of Eros, whose purpose is to combine single human individuals, and after that families, then races, peoples and nations, in one great unity, the unity of mankind.'[19] Renaissance philosophers would have recognized that definition of sacred love, the universal reconciler that St Thomas Aquinas had called the *virtus unitiva*, but they were at pains to distinguish between it and the selfish violence of profane passion. '*Amor* is the bond and chain which joins together all things in the universe in an ineffable friendship and an insoluble unity,' John Duns Scotus had written in the thirteenth century. The humanist scholar Vives agreed: 'Nothing else is able to bind together spiritual things, nothing is able to make one out of many, except love.'[20] But such abstract, impersonal

174

love is a world away from the passionate desire which renders those possessed by it

> perjured, murderous, bloody, full of blame,
> Savage, extreme, rude, cruel, not to trust

and which culminates, in Shakespeare's resonant phrase, in 'The expense of spirit in a waste of shame'.[21]

Passionate sexual love destroyed judgement, and if judgement lapsed then calamity, both personal and general, was likely to ensue. A bizarre and discomforting engraving by the seventeenth-century French artist Gaspar Isaac shows Cleopatra with Helen and Lucretia, all three toothless and wrinkled (Plate 7). Lucretia's breasts hang flaccidly; a drip falls from Helen's nose. A caption reads:

> Rome would not have suffered the scourge of Tarquin
> Nor Egypt buried Antony and his empire
> Nor Priam watched the flames reduce Troy to ashes
> If, in your youth, you had had such ugly mugs.

The engraving graphically illustrates the point that Blaise Pascal was to make.

> He who would fully comprehend man's folly has only to consider the causes and effects of love. The cause is a *'je ne sais quoi'*, and the effects are terrible. This *'je ne sais quoi'*, this thing so trifling that one can scarce perceive it, can make the earth, princes, armies, the whole world shake. Had Cleopatra's nose been shorter, the face of the world would have changed.[22]

Pascal cannot have seen any of Cleopatra's coins: in fact an abbreviation of her nose would not have detracted from her beauty – rather the reverse. But he gave memorable expression to the assessment of love which underlies most Renaissance treatments of her story. To him passionate love is both absurd, inspired as it is by such an ephemeral and insignificant thing as physical beauty, and awesomely dangerous, capable of disrupting destiny.

Erotic love was the enemy of reason. In 1598 John Marston wrote:

The bright gloss of our intellectual
Is foully soiled. The wanton wallowing
In fond delights, and amorous dallying,
Has dusked the fairest splendour of our soul.[23]

The pleasures of sex, wrote the humanist scholar Marsilio Ficino, 'are so impetuous and irrational that they jar the mind from its stability and unbalance a man'.[24] Stability and balance were qualities to be prized. Audiences might enjoy the emotional turbulence of Senecan tragedy, but such psychic violence, gruesomely interesting thought it might be, was to be deplored, not admired. The eighteenth-century cult of sensibility was still far off; so was the Romantic hero with his tumultuous experience of pain and passion and his ever-vulnerable heart. Stability, whether personal or political, was considered rare, hard to attain and always precarious. It followed, therefore, that the best kind of person was one who was not prey to unmasterable desires.

> Give me that man
> That is not passion's slave,

says Hamlet,

> And I will wear him
> In my heart's core. . . .[25]

The preference of Hamlet's may strike a modern audience as neurotic, as evidence of his own incapacity to deal with strong emotion, but to his first hearers it would have seemed commonplace and perfectly proper. To Renaissance Europeans, as to Augustan Romans, it would have been clear that only such a man was safe from the anti-social, disintegrative power of irrational feeling. Only such a man could be trusted to behave himself decently and with due consideration for the rights of others. Only under the guardianship of such men could the hard-won culture of western Europe be conserved for succeeding generations. Only such a man (or woman – provided, like Queen Elizabeth I, that she had a masculine soul) was fit to govern, for, as Giraldi Cinthio declares in the Prologue to his *Cleopatra*,

176

He alone can reign for long and well
Who, taking light of reason for his guide,
Knows to command and rule over himself.[26]

Over himself and over his heart. Shakespeare's Bottom sums it up succinctly: 'Reason and love keep little company together nowadays.'[27]

Each generation craves what it has not got. The scholars and poets who so lauded stability and reason inhabited a greedy, volatile world. Robert Garnier, before Shakespeare the most considerable playwright to make Cleopatra the heroine of a tragedy, wrote his *Marc-Antoine* in a France traumatized by civil war. The play was first performed in 1574, just two years after the officially sanctioned wholesale massacre of Huguenots on St Bartholomew's Day. By the time it was published in 1578 the fighting had begun again; it was not an era in which the abdication of political responsibility for passion's sake was likely to be much admired. Garnier, an official servant of the Valois, had frequent opportunity to contemplate the real-life horrors which ensued when princes allowed themselves to be swayed by private desires. His master, Henri III, who took the throne in the year *Marc-Antoine* was first published, was rumoured to be moody, vain and sexually perverted. According to his opponents, his extravagant and voluptuous habits made him unfit to be king.[28] He was assassinated at the age of thirty-eight. Such was the actual context in which Garnier has Antony bitterly regret having allowed personal emotion, his love for Cleopatra, to take precedence over public duty:

As the fatted swine in filthy mire
With glutted heart I wallowed in delights,
All thoughts of honour trodden under foot.
So I me lost. . . .

He lost himself: he also lost his share of worldly power.

The wolf is not so hurtful for the fold,
Frost to the grapes, to ripened fruits the rain:
As pleasure is to princes full of pain.[29]

177

A ruler in love was an unworthy ruler. 'He is no prince that subject is, and subject unto sin,' writes Samuel Brandon's Octavia to her Antony, reproving him for his dishonourable devotion to Cleopatra.[30] Sir Fulke Greville, Shakespeare's contemporary, wrote a tragedy of Antony and Cleopatra, but burnt the manuscript in fear that its chief characters, 'having some childish wantonness in them', might be identified with Elizabeth I and her rejected favourite, the Earl of Essex. Essex was in disgrace, and the Queen was sensitive to any criticism; it was no time, Greville judged, to publish a play censuring a ruler for 'forsaking empire to follow sensuality'.[31] No sixteenth-century monarch would have considered it to her credit that her heart could be touched. There are practical reasons for this. While a 'fond Prince himself in pleasures drowns', unscrupulous usurpers seize their chance:

> Crimes without fear and outrages are done.
> Then mutinous Rebellion shows her face.[32]

But these arguments are beside the main point, which is that immoderate love was felt to attack the social order at a symbolic level. The indulgence of sensual desire militates against discipline and order. Kingdoms have been undone, wrote John Lydgate, 'for sin of princes that were lecherous'. For when a prince – the ruler and the personification of a country – becomes prey to the lusts of the flesh, according to the anonymous author of *A Mirror for Magistrates*, 'The land decays, disorder sprouts and springs abroad'.[33]

The lover's rejection of pragmatism and idolization of the beloved undermine hierarchies and rob political institutions of their value. Emotional absolutism, especially when it leads to a rejection of materialism and rational self-interest, must be anathema to any secular power. 'Kingdoms are clay,'[34] declares Shakespeare's Antony, and his seventeenth-century hearers must have felt a lurch of political vertigo as they listened. It was for proclaiming that 'kingdoms are clay' that the early Christians had been so ruthlessly persecuted and, once the Church had reneged on that first pure rejection and had itself become a secular power, it was for a similar denial

178

of worldliness that it had expelled the Franciscan 'Spiri-tuals'.[35] The sentiment has the power to terrify. It is both a proclamation of anarchy and a curse. Lovers annihilate themselves: to make love, in seventeenth-century English slang, was 'to be naught'.[36] And in the black hole of their deliriously willed self-loss society sees the possibility of its own engulfment. As Angela Carter has written in an oblique reference to Cleopatra, 'The pornographer, in spite of him-self, becomes a metaphysician when he states that the friction of penis in orifice is the supreme matter of the world, for which the world is well lost: as he says so, the world van-ishes.'[37]

The link between sexual licence and political subversion was clearly understood in Shakespeare's era, and it forms a theme of many of the versions of the Cleopatra story written in this period.

> Far greater war against imperial rule
> Is made by pleasures and delights beyond
> The customary rule of human reason
> Than many squadrons of armed enemies.[38]

So wrote Giraldi Cinthio in his *Cleopatra*. This connection has been elucidated in the twentieth century by the French surrealist philosopher Georges Bataille, who links erotic pas-sion with the 'extravagance' of nature which brings into being so many living things, only to allow them to die. This exuberant, excessive production, argues Bataille, is abhorrent to the human mind because it underlines the insignificance of individual beings and demands the death of one generation as a precondition for the existence of the next. In sexual intercourse (despite contraception, an essentially repro-ductive act), the human being thus connives at his or her own death. But the reluctance to die is at least as strong a motive as the urge to make love, and this craving for indi-vidual survival has led to the creation of human society, what Bataille calls the 'world of work'. This work-world – ordered, effortful, economically productive – opposes the wastefulness of nature and endows the individual person with importance.

179

It must therefore exclude, by means of taboos, the dual violence of death and sex. 'Nature asks [all living things] to go crashing headlong to their own ruin. Humanity became possible at the instant when, seized by an insurmountable dizziness, man tried to answer "No".'[39] Tried, but failed, for eroticism is fascinating and death inevitable. Human society, according to Bataille's formulation, is based on the exclusion of the unexcludable, hence the anxiety with which governments throughout history have attempted to regulate and contain sexual behaviour. Those who succumb to passion are felt to have opened a breach in the wall that society builds around itself. Political order is disrupted. The world of work crumbles. In the throes of sexual passion, so Bataille argues, we ignore politics and defy economics, spending rather than getting. 'We want a world turned upside down and inside out. The truth of eroticism is treason.'[40]

The majority of Shakespeare's contemporaries would have readily comprehended Bataille's theory (although they would not have approved of his anti-authoritarian conclusions). 'Nature', agree a group of ladies in Samuel Brandon's play, may have tempted Antony to fall in love with Cleopatra, but his social and religious duty was to have resisted, for

> This is true, that God un-natured all
> And gave us wisdom to suppress our will.
> He gave us perfect reason to recall
> Affection's scouts from following what is ill.[41]

Those who refuse to make use of the divine gift of reason, following instead the beckonings of 'nature' and 'affection', not only call down ruin on themselves but unleash it on those around them. Samuel Daniel's chorus of Egyptians identifies the 'riot' of Cleopatra's court as the cause of their defeat and maliciously invites the Romans to

> Fill full your hands and carry home
> Enough from us to ruin Rome.[42]

Thus sexual rapture is imagined as a kind of political contagion capable of destroying a state.

Shakespeare's Rome is precisely the world of work that Bataille describes. The talk at Octavius's court is of conflicts and treaties, council meetings and civic duties. Relationships are edgy and competitive, for one man's promotion spells another's failure. Much value is attached to status and reputation. Lepidus begs Octavius, in vain, to allow him access to information. Sextus Pompeius is ready to go to war because due thanks have not been given for a favour he rendered to Antony. In this atmosphere loss of face is a calamity, for advancement depends on perceived power. Rome is a vast office, where people may be colleagues or rivals but never really friends, where their relationships are defined by their places in a hierarchy and their energy is all channelled into work.

There is no place in this setting for emotion or sensuality. When Octavius wishes to praise Antony, he recalls how once he endured famine, eating the bark of trees, and drinking 'the stale of horses'.[43] In Rome physical deprivation is accounted virtuous. The pleasures of soft beds and delicate cookery are scorned there, and there is a void where sexuality might be. None of the Roman men, apart from Antony, has wives, let alone lovers. Octavia, the only visible Roman woman, is a sister/chattel, of 'holy, cold and still conversation'.[44] She seldom speaks, and when she does her words are all of duty, and of loyalty to her male masters, her brother and her husband. Even homoeroticism is absent: none of Shakespeare's Romans loves one another. The Rome of his play is a man's world, and an absolutely asexual one.

Shakespeare's Alexandria, by contrast, is Bataille's 'world turned upside down'. A thriftless, disorderly, topsy-turvy realm where, as Enobarbus tells his friends back in Rome, the night is for waking and the day for sleep.[45] It is a place where the impossible can happen. In the first scene of the play Antony proclaims his immeasurable love for Cleopatra. To contain it, he says 'must thou needs find out new heaven, new earth'.[46] And so he has done, for Alexandria does not obey the rules of terrestrial reason. As Catherine Clément writes, 'Madmen, deviants, neurotics, women, drifters,

181

jugglers, tumblers . . . carry out in the Imaginary, figures that are impossible at the present time. . . .'⁴⁷ This Cleopatra's court is a forum for such misfits, a feminine place unhampered by Roman ideas of order and limit, inhabited by soothsayers, clowns, eunuchs and women who ceaselessly prattle and pun, tease, disguise themselves and lie.

If Shakespeare's Rome is an office, his Alexandria is a boudoir. It is beautiful, sensual, idle and, above all, anarchic, for women, excluded from the office-world of men's work and men's politics, are alarmingly free of the hierarchies by which men plot their place in the world. In Alexandria a ruler may liken herself to a milkmaid or allow herself to be kissed by a mere messenger without any loss of dignity. Order is breached and catastrophe does not ensue because the state is not founded, as Rome is, on order. It is founded, instead, on the bewildering power of sex. It is a place of phallic serpents and fertile slime, where women's talk is all lascivious and men lose their sense of their own individuality in the deathly ecstasies of love-making. Identities waver and blur in this setting. A lover, naked and yearning, ceases to be a commander. Brothels make good hiding places and nudity is the best disguise. In Alexandria, harem city, a man is no longer what other men, his colleagues, believed him to be.

Rome and Alexandria: manly effort and womanly self-indulgence. Shakespeare re-creates the polarized version of the Antony and Cleopatra story that Octavius had invented, the story that he had found in Sir Thomas North's translation of *Plutarch's Lives*. In his hands it becomes an infinitely subtler, less censorious thing than Roman propaganda and prejudice had made it, but it is full of echoes of the ancient themes. In the Egypt of Shakespeare's Cleopatra people drift, the mud of the Nile providing no sure footing for their sense of purpose and identity. Octavius had suggested that Antony lost his manhood, his self, for Cleopatra's love. Shakespeare develops the idea. Slippery and volatile, his Alexandria and its people seem alarming to those who have chosen to live by Rome's rules. Emotion, sexuality, susceptibility to change: all menace the tidy hardness of the 'Romans' ancient and modern. 'I love unbroken people: men,' wrote an officer in the proto-Nazi German Freikorps in the 1920s. 'The kind who have no problems: the kind who are self-contained, powerful, calm.'[48] In Shakespeare's Alexandria there are no such people.

> . . . I
> Have lost my way for ever[49]

mourns Antony after Actium. Long before that defeat he lost himself. Rigid identities which deny the waverings of emotion cannot survive transplantation to this fluid world.

It is a commonplace of twentieth-century thought that a 'character' is largely an artificial construct, the product of circumstances, conditioning and expectations. Shakespeare demonstrates the idea dramatically. The nineteenth-century German Romantic Heinrich Heine wrote of the Romans, 'They were not great men, but through their position they were greater than the other children of earth, for they stood on Rome. Immediately they came down from the Seven Hills they were small.'[50] But the disintegration of Shakespeare's Antony is due to more than the disorientation of an imperialist who has strayed outside his empire into alien territory where the natives do not accord him the deference to which he is accustomed. It is a kind of absolute melt-down in which political function is erased, gender becomes blurred and the outline separating a person from that which is not himself wavers. Antony, in Alexandria, no longer 'is Antony'. A babble of doubting voices, his own and others', articulate the fear that he is ceasing to be 'himself'. His predicament illustrates the precariousness of an identity which depends for its coherence on a social context. 'I am Antony yet,' he says with pathetic assertiveness, only to admit, humbled by yet another defeat,

> Here I am Antony,
> Yet cannot hold this visible shape.[51]

He who was once noted for his tolerance of hardship now indulges himself in a round of feasts. The famous battle-winner has become a loser. In Rome, Antony was Antony, the hero, the man of steel. He knew what were the proper virtues for a man and he knew that he possessed them. Transplanted to a place where the Roman concepts of manhood, of honour, of success have no validity, he can no longer tell who he is.

In the floating world which is this Cleopatra's realm, men become dissolute. The ambiguity of the word is telling, for Antony is both licentious and dislimned 'as water is in water'.[52] Sex is the solvent in which he is melted down. This loss of self is both fearful and delicious. If Antony's identity is lost when he leaves Rome, then so are his responsibilities, his exhausting work. In Alexandria, the city of women, he forgets 'Roman thoughts'. He disguises himself to walk the streets at night. Thus he becomes someone else, or no one. He is no longer the husband who owes loyalty to Fulvia, or, later, Octavia. He is not the commander on whose judgement the safety of the army and the might of Rome depends. He has no duties. He is not answerable to anyone. Even his fishing is innocuous and dream-like: the salt-fish attached to his hook was not killed by him. With Cleopatra he enjoys a relationship with no social context and no consequences. (Their political alliance has no place in this play; nor do their three children.) It is hard to be a 'Roman', to be serious, adult, responsible. Life in the world is difficult and frustrating. Only in the sexual sphere, and best of all in sexual fantasy or that kind of dream-like, no-strings-attached promiscuous sex that most resembles fantasy, can the weary subject let go of self and others, and take a vacation from the complexities of life. This is what Shakespeare's Antony does, and that is one of the keys to the abiding fascination of his story. He realizes the dream of all those millions of modern tourists who cram the beaches of the world each summer. In Alexandria with Cleopatra he enjoys the world's best-ever holiday romance.

Cleopatra, the queen of infinite variety, whom everything becomes, in whom vilest things become themselves, is fit mistress of Alexandria, this shifting world which is not-world. Wayward, vacillating, guileful, not to be pinned down, she is the quintessence of womanhood as traditionally defined. For as Garnier's Octavius says, repeating received opinion,

> By nature women wavering are,
> Each moment changing and rechanging minds.[53]

In her realm, where everything shimmers and nothing is stable, masculine and feminine dissolve into each other. Again an old tradition is revived. 'Here comes Antony,' says Enobarbus. Charmian corrects him, 'Not he, the Queen.'[54] The lovers have become indistinguishable, or rather Antony, who was once so monolithic, an armour-plated colossus, has become as chameleon-like as Cleopatra. In mingling bodies lovers also mingle souls, declared Hermes Trismegistus, the mythical Egyptian god-sage whose writings were highly prized by Renaissance scholars; in the act of love the genders merge: 'The female acquires masculine vigour, and the male is relaxed in feminine languor.'[55] So Cleopatra absorbs and negates Antony's virility. 'Though he be painted one way like a Gorgon,' she says of him, 'the other way's a Mars.'[56] Mars is Antony's Roman-hero identity, but his other, the snake-haired Gorgon who turns men to stone, is female, an image of womanly potency and castration which has always struck terror into male hearts. For sex (and here again is the theme that the real Octavius adumbrated more than sixteen hundred years before) makes a woman of a man. Antony the lover has, in Garnier's play, 'Fallen from a soldier to a chamberer', an idle loiterer in ladies' bedrooms.[57] 'Base female Antony,' rails the Bonus Genius in the anonymous tragedy, *Caesar's Revenge*, 'thou woman's soldier, fit for night's assaults.'[58] As Shakespeare's attendant lords have it, 'the triple-pillar of the world' – tough, militaristic, all-male – has been transformed by desire into 'a strumpet's fool', a feminine toy. In Alexandria, scoffs Octavius, he

> is not more manlike
> Than Cleopatra; nor the queen of Ptolemy
> More womanly than he.

Cleopatra delights in recalling how she has dressed him in her clothes, while strapping on herself his 'sword Philippan', the token of his manhood[59] (Freud named, but did not invent, phallic symbols). Gender roles have no validity in Alexandria, where the supreme ruler is a woman.

Antony's loss of maleness is deplorable partly, of course, because to be female is to be inferior. Shakespeare sets up two poles of experience, following a conventional demarcation of that which belongs properly to the male and the female spheres which is at least as old as the story of Cleopatra. The dismay with which Antony's defection to Alexandria and consequent feminization is greeted by other characters is in part fuelled by the same simple misogyny as that on which Octavius depended when he first ridiculed his opponent's imagined effeminacy. But it has as well a more complex motive. The change that Shakespeare's Cleopatra effects in Antony calls into question not only what it is to be a man but also what it is to be a human being.

Sexual difference is abolished at society's peril. The anthropologist Mary Douglas has written eloquently about the apparently universal human horror of the anomalous. In her dissection of the Book of Leviticus she concludes: 'Holiness requires that individuals shall conform to the class to which they belong. And holiness requires that different classes of things shall not be confused.'[60] The animals which are described as 'abominations' in Leviticus, and which the Children of Israel were forbidden to eat, are those which cannot be fitted into the three great divisions of created beings – feathered birds, scaly fish and furred, four-footed mammals. Pigs, snakes, mice (whose forepaws look like hands), 'anything in the seas that has not fins and scales' – anything, in short, which is neither flesh nor fowl nor good red herring – is unclean. The proscription of these abominations (which include many creatures still the object of common phobias) is a powerful expression of a human fear of the uncategorizable, of that which is betwixt and between.[61]

This fear underlies the hostility, more complex than other forms of racism, which people of mixed race encounter. It also explains why sexual indeterminacy is felt to be so threatening. Hence the homophobia which has repeatedly surfaced throughout human history, and hence the superstitious dread which hermaphrodites have traditionally inspired. 'The woman shall not wear that which pertaineth unto a man, neither shall a man put on a woman's garment: for all that do so are abomination unto the Lord thy God,' thunders Deuteronomy.[62] The masculine woman and the feminine man both seem to menace human order at a fundamental level. They are disgusting. Disgust is a response to dirt, and dirt, as Mary Douglas points out (quoting an old adage), is something in the wrong place. The androgyne, who refuses to stay put in either the male or the female category, seems to offer an affront to the symbolic order on which civilization is based.

Shakespeare, an intellectual adventurer, played gleefully with gender: his plays are full of cross-dressing, of boys dressed as girls dressed as boys. He grew up in a realm where an elderly queen teased and spoiled young male favourites; by the time *Antony and Cleopatra* was written, England and Scotland were ruled by a brazenly homosexual, but married, king. Shakespeare was not the only person to take pleasure in the sexual slipperiness of the age. In 1587 William Harrison noted in his *Description of England* that unisex fashion had reached such extremes among some 'trulls ... that it hath passed my skill to discern whether they were men or women'. Thirty years later James I found it necessary to instruct the clergy 'to inveigh vehemently against the insolency of our women, and their wearing of broad-brimmed hats, pointed doublets, their hair cut short or shorn and some of them stilettos or poniards'. These 'man-women' were matched by 'woman-men'. The Elizabethan playwright Barnaby Rich was as puzzled and angered by the younger generation's clothes as any father of the 1960s:

From whence cometh this wearing and embroidering of long locks, this curiosity that is used amongst men in frizzling and curling of their hair? This gentlewoman-like starched bands, so be-edged and be-laced, fitter for Maid Marian in a Morris dance than for him that hath either the spirit or courage that should be in a gentleman?[63]

Those ready to make forays across the border dividing one sex from another were not wanting, but nor were scandalized voices denouncing them. Women in men's attire, wrote the puritan Philip Stubbes in 1583, were 'stinking before the face of God, offensive to man, but also pointeth out to the whole world the venereous inclination of their corrupt conversation'.[64] The rebellion serves to illuminate the orthodoxy, and the shock felt by these upholders of propriety was not only the expression of their own conservatism. They were voicing a profound and universal anxiety, as Marina Warner has pointed out in discussing Joan of Arc's imagined androgyny. 'A Freudian would see this state as analogous to death, not life, because in seeking to cancel sexual difference, it seeks to arrest time and to deny the mutability to which all flesh is heir.'[65]

Antony and Cleopatra, so bound together by sexual passion that they have surrendered their separate selves, have indeed, if with only partial success, defied mutability. Lucan, describing Cleopatra's banquet, had written of wines brought to maturity with prodigious speed and of guests garlanded with never-fading roses.[66] Shakespeare takes up the theme. His Alexandria is a Never-Never Land where time stands still. 'Age cannot wither her,' says Enobarbus of Cleopatra. Empowered by love, she draws Antony outside time. In their rapture, 'eternity was in our lips and eyes'.[67] This is their transfiguration; it is also the root cause of their frivolity. Life in this Alexandria, exempt from linear time, is also exempt from the laws of causation. Nothing of consequence is, or can be, done there.

Asked once where he would most like to live, Charles Baudelaire gave a characteristically Romantic reply: 'Anywhere, anywhere, provided that it is outside the world.'[68] Cleopatra's court is such a place, but Shakespeare does not share Baudelaire's rejection of terrestrial life. The sole exit from this world, as he suggests, is through the grim gate of death. 'Age cannot wither her'; only of a corpse could that truly be said. The words of Enobarbus's famous encomium to Cleopatra's beauty are echoed, not wholly incongruously, in Laurence Binyon's poem 'For the Fallen 1914–1918':

> They shall not grow old as we that are left grow old;
> Age shall not weary them, nor the years condemn.

To live is to change. The supernatural changelessness of Shakespeare's imagined Alexandria, where youth is eternal, gender interchangeable, politics irrelevant and the laws of cause and effect in suspension is a mirror image of the stasis of death.

According to Plutarch, Cleopatra and Antony called their last drinking club 'the order of those who are going to die together'.[69] In Shakespeare's vision of them that is precisely what they always are. The climax of their story, as he and many others understood it, is their double suicide. It is that which gives significance and purpose to their lives; it is also that which condemns them. The affinity between sexual ecstasy and death is perceived in our era as being both heroic and titillating. 'There is not a libertine some little way gone in vice who does not know what a hold murder has on the senses,' wrote the Marquis de Sade,[70] inaugurating an erotic fashion which persists to this day. But Shakespeare is neither so morbid nor so romantic. His Rome, loveless and ruled by reason, may be frigid; but his Alexandria, ruled by passion, is sterile. In turning their backs on human society, Antony and Cleopatra deny their own humanity. In demonstrating the deathliness of excessive passionate love Shakespeare makes clear that he considers such love, thrilling and grand though it may be, to be inimical to life.

'All's but naught,' declares Cleopatra.

> Then is it sin
> To rush into the secret house of death,
> Ere death dare come to us?[71]

Inevitably she decides that the answer must be no, for suicide is only the formal confirmation of a decision made when the couple weighed the world in the balance against their love and found it 'naught'. Besides, death protects passionate love from its enemy, reason. It is in the nature of a holiday romance, an anti-social passion like Antony and Cleopatra's, to be evanescent. Infatuation must burn bright and then burn out before the real world has time to dim it. But Shakespeare does not permit his lovers, alive, any refuge. Reality, in the shape of Octavius, pursues them even into Cleopatra's enchanted realm. The ecstasy they seek in each other is repeatedly frustrated. They are frequently apart, and even when they are together on stage the distracting clash of their rival needs and the intrusion of mundane events disrupt their love-making. But there is one kind of consummation which doesn't disappoint. Death is welcome to Cleopatra because it 'shackles accidents and bolts up change';[72] it will allow her permanent residence in her domain of timelessness and futility. By dying she and Antony ensure, as they could not have done by any other means, that their holiday will never end. They can stay for ever in their enchanted world, playing till doomsday.

Death is the treacherous happy ending demanded by their love fantasy. Their own nihilism calls it down on them. 'Let Rome in Tiber melt,' prayed Antony in Scene I, but Rome, the real world, is too tough to be wished away. It is Antony who becomes insubstantial. 'O, see, my women:' cries Cleopatra, unconsciously echoing his own words as she watches him breathe his last, 'The crown o' the earth doth melt.'[73] Under her spell he has rejected Rome, the work-world, the world-as-it-is. Then, having nowhere left to live, he can only die. For the world-as-it-is cannot accommodate such a rebellion. As the feminist critic Hélène Cixous has written of this play, Shakespeare imagines absolute sexual and emotional rapture only to deny its possibility. 'After it's over, as soon as the magistrates' courts are back in place, someone must pay; immediate and bloody death for these uncontrollable elements.'[74]

As Queen of Love this Cleopatra is also, inevitably, Queen

of Death. Enobarbus claims to have seen her die twenty times: 'I do think there is mettle in death, which commits some loving act upon her'.[75] The Nile mud breeds life as a corpse breeds maggots and Cleopatra, the Serpent of old Nile, is close relation to the deadly worm, the asp that kills her. Like the reptilian females who haunt folklore and mythology, the mermaids and the Gorgons, she is fatal to the man who loves her. Sexually ambiguous, the familiar of phallic snakes, she has a doubled, hermaphroditic potency which threatens to turn men to stone, to castrate or kill them. In *Marcantonio e Cleopatra*, a tragedy by Don Celso Pistorelli of Verona first published in 1576, Antony has a dream in which Cleopatra turns into a snake and twines herself around him so insinuatingly that his servant cannot kill her without wounding him as well.[76] Michelangelo drew her clothed in serpents, with snaky ringlets and braids of hair, with a twining and writhing headdress and an asp which encircles her shoulders like a stole. In a later painting (possibly by Vasari) based on his drawing, Cleopatra has become a Lamia – part woman, part snake, part vampire. The asp bites viciously but she, unmoved, lifts her strange, vacant eyes in a backward glance, as though enticing some hapless victim to follow her to his ruin. The Renaissance temptress prefigures the Romantic and Decadent *belles dames sans merci*. The nineteenth-century Danish critic Georg Brandes wrote of Shakespeare's play, 'Everything sank, everything fell – character and will, dominions and principalities, men and women. Everything was worm-eaten, serpent-bitten, poisoned by sensuality, everything tottered and collapsed.'[77] Strong words – the sexual revulsion they express is Brandes's own – but in them he identifies a theme which is certainly present in Shakespeare's play. His Cleopatra is, in the most terrifyingly precise sense, a *femme fatale*.

The stereotype of the *femme fatale* is conventionally used to load women with guilt which properly belongs to men, but Shakespeare does not employ his vision of Cleopatra as death's ally to excuse Antony. Instead it becomes the focus for his exploration of the essentially self-destructive nature of passion – woman's passion as well as man's.

> Come gentle, cunning thief
> That from ourselves so steals our selves away.

So Samuel Daniel's Cleopatra welcomes her own end.

> And here I sacrifice these arms to Death
> That lust late dedicated to delight.[78]

Self-abandonment was already a theme of the Cleopatra story when Shakespeare took it up, and so was the equivalence of erotic pleasure to dying. Boccaccio had described how her 'body, softened with the greatest delicacies, used to the most tender embraces, was at last embraced by serpents'.[79] The correlation tends to be more evident in the paintings of the period than in the comparatively reticent written sources. Plutarch clearly states that the Egyptian queen dressed herself for death, donning her crown and all her royal robes. The dramatists of the Renaissance were well aware of this detail and many, Shakespeare among them, used it to heighten the theatricality of their plays' dénouements. It is all the more remarkable, then, that of the scores of representations of Cleopatra's death in painting and sculpture the overwhelming majority show her more or less naked.

In sixteenth-century depictions of the theme from Italy, the Netherlands and France she appears nude, in an idealized landscape and attended by the death-dealing snake – a composition which inevitably evokes the parallel between her and that other temptress and ruination of men, Eve. A sensuous painting by an unknown artist of the School of Fontainebleau is representative of many. In it Cleopatra lies on her side, her eyes closed, her lovely alabaster-pale body totally exposed. Her head rests tenderly on the arm which the asp encircles. Drapery hung over a tree-trunk encloses the scene, concentrating its intimacy. Absorbed in her own deathly pleasure, offering herself passively to the viewer's lascivious gaze, this dying Cleopatra is an unequivocally erotic object.

Yet another departure from the historical descriptions of Cleopatra's suicide had the effect of further enhancing the pornographic potential of her death scene. Plutarch and Dio Cassius both mention that it was on her arm that the marks, which could have been those of an asp's bite, were found. A fifteenth-century illustration which shows Cleopatra fully dressed, but with her sleeves rolled up to allow two curiously mouse-eared asps to nibble her arms, may therefore – for all its zoological oddity and sartorial anachronism (Cleopatra wears an elaborate late medieval headdress) – be more historically accurate than most subsequent depictions. By the middle of the next century the Florentine Petrus Victorius, was complaining, correctly, that contemporary artists invariably depicted Cleopatra 'applying the asp to her paps'. In 1638 the English writer Dr Primrose listed the notion that Cleopatra had been bitten on the breast among *Popular Errors in Medicine*.[80] To no avail. In painting after painting history and medicine alike are disregarded. Cleopatra, nude or at best in *déshabillé*, exposes her upper torso to the viewer, while an asp writhes across her milk-white breasts to bury its fangs in her nipple. The pose is covertly blasphemous: Cleopatra with the asp becomes an anti-type of the Madonna and child. More obviously, it makes Cleopatra the voluntary object, not only of the viewer's salacious scrutiny, but of a metaphorical ravishment. Giacomo Francia's lovely drawing, in which a luscious-bodied Cleopatra, wreathed in a flutter of hair and drapery, holds up a helpless hand as though to ward off an assailant, is one of many depictions of the dying Cleopatra as sexual prey.

Shakespeare develops this erotic theme to make of Antony and Cleopatra's double suicide a joyous marriage. Death for both of them is a relief. 'This resolute living towards death,' writes the critic Terry Eagleton, 'is the last word in political irresponsibility.'[81] Quite so. Irresponsibility is precisely what Shakespeare's lovers desire: freedom from social duties, from the consequences of their actions, from anything which deters them from rapturous oblivion.

Antony strips himself for death. As he tears off his armour, the casing of his former self, he dismantles for good and all the man of steel he once was while simultaneously undressing himself for love (the page who shows him how to die is fittingly named Eros).

> A bridegroom in my death I will be, and run into't
> As to a lover's bed.[82]

Cleopatra, preparing in her turn to die, has an equivalently bridal pride and eagerness. 'Husband, I come,' she calls. Dressed in her royal robes, she is

> . . . again for Cydnus
> To meet Mark Antony.[83]

Her death comes to her as a serpent concealed in a basket of figs – an exuberantly sexual form, for, as Plutarch noted long before D. H. Lawrence, the fig 'seemeth naturally to resemble the member of generation'.[84] Its pain feels to her as gentle as a lover's pinch, 'which hurts and is desir'd'. With the asp at her breast she is radiantly happy. Death feels to her 'as sweet as balm, as soft as air, as gentle', but her description of it is interrupted by the involuntary exclamation that marks a lover's climax: 'O Antony!'[85] Of all Shakespeare's tragedies, this one has the happiest ending. Alone together at last (as they never are in the play), the couple are free of all the encroaching realities which threatened their amorous castle in the air.

There is something splendidly exhilarating about their *Liebestod*. It is gallant and grand. It is both exciting – the absoluteness of death provides orgasmic satisfaction – and easy. Rather as two contending nations will turn almost with relief from the intricacies of diplomacy to the kill-or-be-killed simplicity of warfare, so Antony and Cleopatra, rushing together into the loving arms of death, escape the anxious, responsible work that living requires. In doing so they are greatly to be envied. Keats, longing to be ruined by his latter-day Charmian, was craving just such a letting-go. A man ruined is no longer accountable for his folly. He need no longer think. He can be cruel and silly, greedy and craven.

The Temple of Hathor at Dendera in Upper Egypt. The reliefs, in anachronistically archaic style, show Cleopatra and her son Caesarion as Isis and Horus. In stressing his position as her divine heir Cleopatra gave Caesarion an important role in her personal myth. *Donald McLeish Collection*

Coin showing the head of Cleopatra. The representation seems to bear out Plutarch's assertion that, charming though Cleopatra may have been, she was no beauty. *British Museum*

Roman relief depicting a procession in honour of Isis. The leading priestess, like Isis herself in conventional representations, has a snake twined about her arm. Cleopatra's suicide by asp-bite stressed her identification with the goddess. *Alinari*

Drawing by Giacomo Francia: one of numerous representations in which Cleopatra, nude and flustered, looks less like someone dying deliberately of snake-bite than like the victim of a sexual assault. *Art Museum, Princeton*

LA BELLE HELENA | CLEOPATRE | LVCRECE

ROME NEVST DE TARQVIN SENTI LES DVRS FLÉAVX
NI L'EGIPTE ENTERRÉ ANTHOINE ET SON EMPIRE
NI PRIAM VEV LES FEVX TROYE EN CENDRE REDVIRE
SI IEVNES, NOVS EVSSIONS PORTÉ DE TELS MVSEAVX.

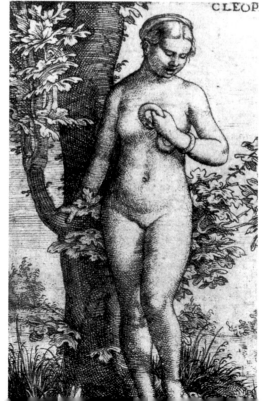

CLEOP

Caricature by the seventeenth-century French artist Gaspard Isaac of Helen, Cleopatra and Lucretia as they might have been in old age. The caption reads:

Rome would not have suffered the scourge of Tarquin
Nor Egypt buried Antony and his empire
Nor Priam watched the flames reduce Troy to ashes
If, in your youth, you had had such ugly mugs
*Warburg Institute*

Sixteenth-century Flemish engraving, one of many in which Cleopatra, discovered naked beneath a tree with a serpent, is assimilated to the image of another legendary temptress, Eve. *Warburg Institute*

Illumination from a fifteenth-century French manuscript. Like martyred saints, Cleopatra and Antony are pictured dying and identified by the instruments of death. *British Library*

Cleopatra before Octavius, by Anton Mengs. Cleopatra demostrates her womanly weakness by kneeling before her male conqueror. *National Trust Photgraphic Library*

Sixteenth-century painting by an artist of the School of Fontainebleau. The vast majority of artists eroticise Cleopatra's suicide by stripping her naked, despite the fact that all the ancient accounts stress that she met her death dressed in her royal robes. *National Gallery*

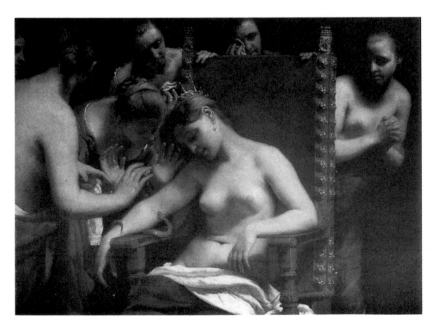

Weakness multiplied. In Cagnacci's *The Death of Cleopatra* the queen's own inert and lovely body is replicated by those of her half-naked attendants. *Kunsthistorisches Museum*

Cleopatra before Octavius, by Guercino. Seventeenth-century artists repeatedly depicted Cleopatra (who killed herself rather than face public humiliation) in this posture of submission. *Museo Capitolino*

In Guido Reni's painting Cleopatra succumbs to her death as to a masterful lover. With the asp at her breast she is also a covertly blasphemous figure, an anti-type of the Virgin with Child. *Collection Her Majesty the Queen*

Giambattista Tiepolo's frescos in the Palazzo Labia, Venice, show Cleopatra haughty, magnificent and surrounded by appurtenances of inherited power. The spindly pyramid in the background is a perfunctory acknowledgement of her non-European home. Still, in the late eighteenth century, Cleopatra appears consistently as a blonde, nordic beauty. *Scala*

He can be innocent and destructive as a child, and most adults at some time or other long for such a release. In Shakespeare's play Cleopatra allows Antony to achieve it. So, apparently unconsciously, Shakespeare revived an ancient tradition. His masculine gender called into question, his duty to Rome forgotten, his reason subordinated to sexual passion, Antony reappears in his submerged character of Dionysus, master of holy mania, androgynous lord among women, whose devotees sought to exceed the limits of their individual selves and merge with the unconscious life of nature.

Shakespeare makes us feel the allure of this self-abandonment, but Shakespeare is no Dionysiac. Since the Romantic era Westerners have been inclined to believe that intense passion frees the spirit and ennobles the mind. But as Shakespeare portrays it it is limiting, claustrophobic, spiritually ugly. Cleopatra is jealous and shrewish. Shakespeare's (few) additions to the story he found in Plutarch all tend to show her in an unflattering light. The scene in which she interrogates a messenger about Octavia's looks is his invention: it shows her small-minded and stupid. Her jealous tantrum, when she threatens to have the same wretched messenger tortured, and then actually draws a knife on him, is another Shakespearean addition. Its violence demonstrates that the frenzy of passion is accompanied in her by a less pleasing loss of control. Antony blaming her after Actium for his own disgrace and then sinking into a fit of childishly self-dramatizing sulks is no more admirable. Passion, we are invited to conclude, brings its own punishment in the form of moral deterioration and erosion of the will. In his *Inferno* Dante placed Cleopatra among the lovers 'who subject reason to desire' and whose punishment it is to be tossed and turned for ever by contrary winds.[86] Shakespeare shows us both the lovers similarly wretched, prey to each emotional wind that blows.

The Alexandria of this play is a cramped and enervating place, a gilded cage. The real Cleopatra's court must have been a bustling place, the centre of an elaborate and efficient bureaucracy, and the real Cleopatra, scholar and administrator, would have had little time for mooning over love letters; but Shakespeare imagines her palace as a site of irrationality from which politics and work have been banished. When Antony is away, and she is left there with her women and her eunuchs, with nothing to do but amuse herself, a terrible *ennui* overcomes her. Alexandria, when no feast is toward, is as boring as a brothel with no customers. Only passion can bring it to life, but even passion is solipsistic, non-productive, as ultimately wearisome as an everlasting holiday. 'The soul of a man in love smells of the closed-up room of a sick man,' wrote the Spanish philosopher Ortega y Gasset. 'Its confined atmosphere is filled with stale breath.'[87]

To Shakespeare intemperate love is barren. It is also absurd. Repeatedly in his comedies he mocked the exalted language of love. Real-life sex, homely and undignified as it often is, makes a fine joke when juxtaposed with such rhetoric, a joke of which he never tired. In *Antony and Cleopatra* he constantly stresses this comical mismatching. The play is full of exalted love poetry which describes Cleopatra, Antony and their mutual passion in ecstatically hyperbolical terms. Yet on stage we watch two all-too-ordinary human beings behaving as foolishly and pettily as human beings habitually do behave. Their relationship appears to be sadly quarrelsome, and the sexual rapture which they are said to enjoy together is conspicuous mostly by its absence. Romantic love story and robust realist comedy at one and the same time: it is this double vision which gives the play its elusive, shimmering feel.

Post-Romantic critics and audiences have frequently been disconcerted by this ambivalence. George Bernard Shaw, in the preface to his own version of the Cleopatra story (of which more later) wrote,

Shakespeare's *Antony and Cleopatra* must needs be vaguely distressing to the ordinary healthy citizen, because after giving a faithful picture of the soldier broken down by debauchery, and the typical wanton in whose arms such men perish, Shakespeare finally strains all his huge command of rhetoric

196

and stage pathos to give a theatrical sublimity to the wretched end of the business, and to persuade foolish spectators that the world was well lost by the twain. Such falsehood is not to be borne![88]

Shaw's diagnosis of the disjunction at the heart of the play is correct, but he dismisses Shakespeare too summarily. Janet Adelman, the American critic, is more perceptive. She writes of the play: 'It is essentially a tragic experience embedded in a comic structure. In that sense it is as treacherous and painful as life itself.'[89] In demonstrating the gap between the enormous cravings of erotic fantasy and the banal pleasures of which human beings are actually capable, Shakespeare makes a subtle and compassionate comment on love itself.

After Antony's death Cleopatra remembers him as a figure in a dream, colossal and god-like. 'His face was as the heavens . . . His legs bestrid the oceans . . . Realms and islands were as plates dropp'd from his pocket.' She asks Dolabella:

> Think you there was, or might be, such a man
> As this I dreamed of?

He replies simply, 'Gentle madam, no.'[90] It is true. There is no such Antony, even in the imaginary world of the play. The Antony we see on stage is tetchy, wilful, dishonest – attractive certainly, but a colossus never. There is the same gap between the Cleopatra imagined by the other characters and the Cleopatra we see and hear. As the actress Ellen Terry astutely remarked, 'If she is represented as a great woman . . . the part does not hang together.'[91] Enorbarbus describes a regal figure, voluptuous but grand; we see a flirtatious, nervous, moody woman. Samuel Johnson found her all too expert in 'low feminine arts'. Another eighteenth-century critic, Joseph Hopkinson, called her 'a repulsive termagant'.[92] Audiences, watching her making trouble for her servants, bullying a messenger or boasting like a callow teenager about her sexual conquests, have often agreed with him. She is replete with human weakness, yet Enobarbus ascribes to her divine powers:

197

> Other women cloy
> The appetites they feed, but she makes hungry
> Where most she satisfies.[93]

There is no such a woman. There is no such appetite. Cleopatra the character Shakespeare shows us (rather than Cleopatra the figment of the other characters' imaginations) is under no illusions about her sexual power. We see her anxiously discussing with Charmian whether she should indulge Antony or inflame his passion by playing hard to get. Far from being 'cunning past man's thought'[94] she sounds often like a woman at the end of her emotional and intellectual tether. The fact that this role is, of all others, the one that actresses most aspire to play is an indication of the paucity of genuinely admirable models offered to women in dramatic literature. Bad-tempered, capricious and, in her sunny moods, playful, Shakespeare's Cleopatra is in fact more comic coquette than grand tragic lover.

The love that binds these two is as flawed as they are. Audiences are promised sublimity, a passion radiant enough to outshine all the glories of the world, but the promise is only fulfilled when they die – for the death of a loved one sets the lover free to love entirely on the imaginative plane, where total union, total rapture is possible as it is not in life. The perfection and intensity of their love are legendary, yet we hardly ever see them when they are not bickering. Antony carps. Cleopatra teases. Antony cynically abandons Cleopatra to marry another woman. Cleopatra interrupts Antony's protestations of passion to suggest they attend to more important business. For all their celebration of it, neither of them actually seems capable of an emotion so intense that it would cause them to forget their worldly affairs. Practical considerations attendant on their high offices repeatedly intrude. It is no wonder that those who come to see the play hoping for high romance go away disappointed.

Between a lover's imagined object of desire and the person on to whom that image is projected there is, always and inevitably, a mismatching. 'To make love, as the term indicates, is poetry. Only there is a world between poetry and the act' – thus the psychoanalyst Jacques Lacan.[95] Those medieval poets who elaborated a religion of love were following a correct intuition. Both the religious devotee and the lover perform an act of faith, vowing adoration to a being whose perfections cannot be seen with the eye of the body. The Antony Cleopatra loves and the Cleopatra loved by Antony are both constructs of the imagination, as romantic love-objects always are. Real people can feel real fondness for each other. Real sex can afford real pleasure. But the kind of passionate, world-denying love that Shakespeare is examining in this play cannot be consummated in the real world.

Freud wrote: 'We must reckon with the possibility that something in the nature of the sexual instinct itself is unfavourable to the realisation of complete satisfaction.'[96] Desire depends for its existence on the absence or unattainability of the desired object. It is self-cancelling. When it has what it wants it must cease, by definition, to want it (for 'want' means to lack, as well as to wish for). When she is with Antony, Cleopatra teases and nags. Only when he is leaving, or dying, does she address him in the language of love. Besides, although desire is normally manifested as sexual craving it encompasses far more than that. It is a craving for ecstasy, for union, for a consummation as permanently uncloying as that which Enobarbus claims Cleopatra can provide. But she cannot, and no more can any human lover. In *The Meaning of the Phallus*, Lacan discusses this 'gap' in desire and concludes: 'To disguise this gap by relying on the virtue of the "genital" to resolve it through the maturation of tenderness (that is by recourse to the Other solely as reality), however piously intended, is nonetheless a fraud.'[97]

But we do not have recourse to Cleopatra 'solely as reality'. Shakespeare gives us a kind of reality, in the person of the stage character of Cleopatra, but he also gives us, through the medium of his poetry, a superhuman being. The hyperbolical terms in which Cleopatra is described by the other characters, in which she herself describes Antony (especially after his death) and in which she and others refer to their rapturous union, do not actually describe her, Antony, or their love affair. Instead the verse creates, on another plane of perception, an ideal pair of lovers and an ideal love affair which promises the loss of self in a perpetual swoon of bliss. The structure of the play, in which this ideal is contained alongside bathetic reality, thus reproduces both the seductive excitement of excessive love, and the disappointment inseparable from it. Shakespeare presents passion to us, allows us to feel its attraction, but asks us to reject it. As Prospero drowned his book, left his enchanted isle and took ship for the mainland, so Shakespeare kills his Cleopatra, and obliges his audience to return from their holiday on the wilder shores of love to become once more full citizens of the humdrum, workaday but, for all that, vital and creative world.

Many have refused to make that voyage home. Bringing to the play an anachronistic sensibility, they have listened only to the love-rhetoric of which Shakespeare himself reveals the emptiness, and, ignoring the soberer, more robust vision presented to them on stage, they have insisted on finding in this play only what the poet Algernon Swinburne found, 'The greatest love-poem of all time'.[98] Shakespeare was writing in an era when eroticism was perceived as a peril. Voluptuousness, wrote his contemporary, La Primaudaye, is a cruel beast which binds men with diamond chains. From Love, wrote Robert Burton, proceed 'dotage, they lose themselves, their wits, and make shipwreck of their fortunes altogether: madness, to make away with themselves and others: violent death'.[99] The nineteenth- and twentieth-century Romantics who have thrilled to Cleopatra's attractions would have agreed with Burton's description of love's destructiveness, but they would have quarrelled with his conclusion – that it is therefore something to be shunned. The Marquis de Sade, Swinburne, Bataille, even rock singers inviting their imagined beloveds to 'Let our love become a funeral pyre'[100] all, like Keats, are intoxicated by the prospect of their own ruin. Dotage, madness, violent death – such is the stuff of modern dreams.

To be alive, sane and free is to be burdened with responsibilities. Freedom, writes the American critic Morse Peckham, 'is the condition of experience, of actually engaging the world . . . yet it is exhausting, tension-laden and frustrating, and it cannot even exist without restraint, restraint by others, restraint of others, and restraint of oneself'. It is this exhaustion, suggests Peckham, that impels people to seek easier, more ecstatic modes of being. Political extremism for instance, which offers 'negative freedom'; 'the freedom of submitting to the state' on the far Right; 'the freedom of destroying the state' on the far Left.[102] Or eroticism. The Romantic imagines that a lover, intoxicated by passion, can abdicate all democratic responsibility, all moral accountability. Actual sexual experience may not bear out this fantasy, but the fantasy is almost universal. Shakespeare's Cleopatra has frequently been made its heroine. 'Here indeed was the woman who could intoxicate and undo a man, even the greatest,' wrote Brandes in 1898. She could 'uplift him to such happiness as he had never known before, and then plunge him into perdition'.[103] Happiness and perdition; perdition and happiness. To Shakespeare they were mutually exclusive conditions. When Cleopatra leads Antony so far astray that he is lost for ever, then for a seventeenth-century audience his wretchedness was clear. Not so nowadays. To a Romantic a man lost is a man free, high, heroically defiant of convention, of niggling duties. In our fantasies, our pornography, our escapist fiction, even if not in our laws or our actual social behaviour, Romanticism is still a potent force. And so we consistently misread Shakespeare and his contemporaries. Galen, the second-century scientist, wrote of 'love-madness' that it was 'an irrational power within us which refuses to obey reason' and promised that, like other 'errors of the soul' it could be cured.[104] The writers and thinkers of the European Renaissance, who stood intellectually closer to the newly rediscovered ancient world than they do to us, took an equally cool and reductive view of the since-sanctified frenzies of sexual passion. Like Virgil's Aeneas, they tended to conclude that, sad though its loss might be, it had to be

201

abjured for the sake of social order and mental stability. In a world in which the wildernesses are dwindling and it is almost impossible to escape the surveillance of governments and the wearisome demands of community, modern Westerners are tempted to court chaos. Four hundred years ago our ancestors, on the contrary, preferred to cherish civilization, a construct they felt to be fragile, precious and forever at risk.

# 6

# THE WOMAN

> Nature meant me
> A wife; a silly harmless household dove,
> Fond without art, and kind without deceit.

Thus John Dryden's Cleopatra, heroine of his tragedy *All for Love*, first performed in 1678, bewails her lack of a husband and her sweetly girlish inability to do without one.

> Fortune, that has made a mistress of me,
> Has thrust me out to the wide world, unfurnished
> Of falsehood to be happy.[1]

So the double bind which held women is neatly summarized. In the century and a half following the first performance of Shakespeare's *Antony and Cleopatra* scores of representations of the Egyptian Queen appeared. In England, France, Germany and Italy new plays based on her story were produced. Painters, especially those of northern Italy and the Netherlands, seized on the erotic and spectacular opportunities that the theme afforded. Cleopatra was the primary heroine of an internationally best-selling historical novel, arguably the first of the genre. Tapestries depicting her hung in banqueting rooms from Bohemia to Scotland. Bronze figures of her adorned the Palace of Versailles and the gardens of Hampton Court. Porcelain ornaments, vases, milk jugs, even snuff-boxes bore her image. And from one after another of this plethora of representations two discouraging morals can be drawn: that good women are, or should at least appear to be, weak, and that those whose energy and talents prevent them from conforming to the ideal of feminine feebleness are, of necessity, 'false' – wily, self-serving and unchaste.

That female weakness is largely a fantasy is made evident, not only by the achievements of twentieth-century women newly permitted, thanks to the efforts of the women's movement, to work, wield power, study and test their own physical strength, but also by the recorded experiences of the women of the seventeenth and eighteenth centuries. In the very period that the myth of female fragility, a myth that was eventually to confine women to the *chaise longue* and the hobble skirt, was being most enthusiastically elaborated, many real women were proving themselves to be intellectually vigorous and practically competent, canny and brave. Dryden had numerous female contemporaries who were neither silly nor false, and who, when the times required, proved themselves capable of stepping outside the household, laying aside their dove-like docility and confidently engaging with the 'wide world'. 'In these late times,' wrote Basua Makins in 1673, not only did women 'play the soldier with prudence and valour', they also 'appeared before committees and pleaded their own causes like men'.[2] In *The Weaker Vessel*, her encyclopaedic study of seventeenth-century English women, Antonia Fraser chronicles the exploits of many of these women. Great ladies, like the Countess of Derby who held Lathom House against the parliamentary army even when its turrets were crumbling under the besiegers' fire, and Lady Bankes who led the defence of Corfe Castle, heaving stones and hot embers over the battlements (assisted by her maidservants), showed themselves as courageous as any of their menfolk. So did the lesser 'she-soldiers' who assumed male dress and went to war, whether to be near a beloved man or simply to earn a living.[3] Such women certainly did not consider themselves frail, and their actions demonstrate that they were free of any real or affected timidity.

The strength of seventeenth- and eighteenth-century women was not only put to use in warfare. Women succeeded as merchants, like the Dutch businesswoman Margaret Philipse who died in 1690 having made her fortune trading between Holland and North America, as pioneers, as scientists and as scholars. Even in government they proved themselves formidable. Queen Christina of Sweden and Catherine the Great of Russia ruled in their own names. Princess Orsini, according to David Hume, 'ruled Spain unchecked' in the name of Philip V,[4] while in eighteenth-century France, so Montesquieu averred, women 'are a new state, as it were, within a state; and a man at court, in Paris or in the Provinces, who observes ministers, magistrates and prelates perform their duties, unless he knows the women who govern them, is comparable to the man who sees a machine in play quite clearly but who knows nothing about its springs'.[5] Women were also capable of Quixotic bravery. In 1657 Mary Fisher, a Yorkshire Quaker, walked alone from the Mediterranean coast of Turkey to Adrianople, where she was granted an audience by the Sultan. Another English (male) observer considered this Sultan, a deformed teenager with a passion for hunting, 'a monster of a man . . . cruel, fierce as to his aspect', but Mary Fisher, undaunted, spoke to him of true and false prophets and then, firmly refusing his offer of an escort back to Constantinople, set off on foot for home.[6]

Such women surprised observers, who described them as 'manlike', possessed of courage or other qualities 'above their sex'. But there were enough of them, and their exploits and achievements were sufficiently well known, for it to be strange and remarkable that seventeenth- and eighteenth-century authors and artists so persistently characterize Cleopatra as being first and foremost female and therefore, by definition, weak. In this period, for reasons which have little to do with external reality, earlier visions of Cleopatra as subtle politician, heroic suicide or inexorable seductress are replaced by the image of a feeble, fluttering creature, a timid dove searching anxiously for a manly bosom in which to nestle.

The fantasy of feminine weakness has complex origins, but the seventeenth- and eighteenth-century paintings of Cleopatra make it abundantly clear that among the motives which inspired it (and still inspire it, for it is by no means defunct) the most potent are erotic. The ancient queen, who ruled a rich empire alone and who killed herself rather than be seen to surrender, was repeatedly depicted by baroque and neo-classical artists in situations expressive of helplessness and self-abasement. Her interview with Octavius after Antony's death was a favourite subject: the encounter between a male conqueror and a defenceless woman fascinated both artists and writers. The painting by Guercino is a fine example, typical of many others. Octavius stands half turned away from the viewer; his face, in profile, is impassive. He gazes down at Cleopatra, who has descended from her throne and kneels before him. Both her small, childish hands are at the front of her dress, which she has pulled down to lay bare a broad expanse of full white bosom. She gazes imploringly up at her captor. He is armed, erect, his body encased in dark, shiny metal. She is all bends and curves. She yields to his judgement, with a gesture in which seduction and submission exactly coincide. Exposing her soft flesh to him, she invites his sexual interest while simultaneously demonstrating her vulnerability, her unquestioning acceptance of his dominance. His hand rests ostentatiously on his sword. He can either stab her or rape her. In neither case could she or would she resist.

In the paintings of Cleopatra's suicide this vision of her as sexual victim is even more explicit. The real Cleopatra, according to the ancient historians, took care to die in the character of a great ruler, her vulnerable body concealed beneath the trappings of monarchy. The artists who stripped her bare deny her the majestic impersonality she sought and, incidentally, the immortality to which, as a representative of royalty, she could lay claim. Thus she is reduced to the persona of a weak and mortal woman, and her death is identified as a moment of erotic violation or surrender. The phallic symbolism of the asp hardly needs stressing, but stressed it was, in a host of titillating images. Guido Reni's plump Cleopatra, whose loose gown has slipped right off her shoulders and bosom, leans back, a posture of submission. Her face is childishly rounded. Her eyes are rolled heavenward, her rosy mouth slightly open. A tiny asp caresses her right nipple with its flickering tongue. This Cleopatra is over-powered by death as by a masterful lover. In pictures like this the motives that lie behind the literary representations of Cleopatra as a sweet, dependent, timid creature are lucidly revealed. A woman who, like Dryden's Cleopatra, can make her first appearance asking distractedly: 'What shall I do, or whither shall I turn?'[7] can be easily prevailed upon to do exactly what her husband or lover demands, at all times and in all places, including the bedroom.

Reni's Cleopatra is swooning. Other painters preferred to depict her already dead. Pietro Ricci showes her naked, her body arched, her belly and pubic mound thrust towards the viewer while the asp writhes upwards towards her breast (Plate 12). In Laurent de la Hire's depiction she sprawls across a bed in a just-raped posture while Iras's corpse, slump-ped in the foreground, adds to the sum of helplessly available female flesh.[8] In Guido Cagnacci's painting (c 1659) Cleopa-tra, though dead, sits still upright in a chair. Her nudity is tenderly presented: her body is that of a very young girl. The painting is all softness and feminine uncertainty. The vulnerability of Cleopatra's lovely inert body is multiplied by those of her women, no fewer than six of whom cluster around her chair, all of them, for no good narrative reason, stripped to the waist. Naked, spineless, dying or dead, these Cleopatras put up no resistance to the viewer who contemplates them. They are pornographic models, puppets invented for the gratification of the voyeur's desire. If Guercino's Cleopatra seemed to say to Octavius, 'Take me!', these prone bodies are beyond saying anything at all. They have already been taken, used and possessed, by Antony, by death, and by the viewer's mastering gaze.

Sadism – the fundamental sadism which is the will to power as well as the urge to inflict pain which is its most readily identifiable form of expression – is unmistakably pres-ent in these paintings. Had it been confined to them, it would be no more than a bizarre curiosity. Sexual fantasy, *per se*, may be harmless. But fantasies shape the world as humans

207

perceive it, and if reality does not accord with that perception it can all too readily be adjusted until it does. Dreaming of meek and yielding women, men of the seventeenth and eighteenth centuries ignored the real strength of their female contemporaries and drafted laws, formulated educational programmes and organized their households with these wilting fantasy-figures in mind. And women (themselves not immune to the sado-masochistic complex of emotions) felt the attraction of the ideal of the feeble female, and set about conforming to it.

Many of them may have been grateful for the privileges that weakness won them. Dependency can be pleasant: it is, after all, not such a hardship to be forbidden to do strenuous work. Besides, the will-to-power often wears a sweet and gentle face. In Handel's opera *Giulio Cesare* (with a libretto by Nicola Haym) Cleopatra, having assured herself of Julius Caesar's love, sings happily:

> Safe to harbour now I'm sailing
> To the crown of all desire.

Her Caesar may have wider ambitions:

> A world is waiting to be won!
> Waiting for the man
> Who dares accept its challenge.

But she asks for no greater happiness than that of knowing herself his beloved protégée.[9] The desire to dominate includes the wish to protect and cherish. The kindly husband, anxious to shield his precious flower of a wife from chill winds, and incidentally from the rigours, responsibilities and satisfactions of adult life, is both a lovable figure and an insidious temptation. Many women did, and do to this day, gratefully accept the offered ease, and so consent to remain for ever childish.

Less innocent women have perceived that weakness, cunningly used, confers power. Sir Charles Sedley's Cleopatra, heroine of his 1677 tragedy, considers her own impotence to be a fine defence against Octavius's revenge. Surely, she reasons, she is too piteous an object to arouse his anger.

> Caesar with pity on a queen must look
> Defenceless too. Winds unopposed give o'er
> And but 'mongst trees and solid buildings roar.[10]

It took women who had honourably refrained from advancing this plea of weakness to expose its disingenuousness. The female novelists of the nineteenth century were to describe with bitter clarity the tyranny exercised by those of their sex who had chosen to make use of the weapon of ostensible incapacity. Jane Austen's Lady Bertram, enjoying a painless and tranquil martyrdom on her sofa while others less elegantly exhausted run her household for her, or George Eliot's Rosamond, using her charming empty-headedness and dependency to get her own way with her husband, clearly demonstrate the way a selfish strategist can rely on weakness to gain the upper hand in personal relationships.

Most cogently of all, the desire to be desirable argues on the side of succumbing and conforming to sexual fantasy, however reductive a form that fantasy may take. The docile girl believed herself to be as silly and incompetent as the united voices of her society told her she was; the bolder and more intelligent woman recognized her own strength but dissembled it in order to attract men. Handel's delectably seductive Cleopatra disguises herself as one of her own waiting-women when she sets out to charm Caesar, and presents herself first kneeling before him, describing herself pathetically as 'Grieving, afflicted and in tears'. Her strategy succeeds. Caesar falls instantly in love, then leaves her alone on stage to sing an aria celebrating her own ingenuity and invincible beauty: 'Everything is possible for a pretty woman.'[11] She subsequently contrives first that Caesar should overhear her bewailing her helpless love for him – 'Lamenting, complaining of Caesar's disdaining, no comfort obtaining, I languish and die' – and subsequently that he should come across her feigning sleep in her bedchamber.[12] At each step in their relationship it is she who is taking the lead, and yet she contrives to appear before Caesar always in a deliciously feeble posture, her monarchy concealed, her bold courtship disguised as passive yearning and her sprightliness veiled by the acquiescent languor of sleep.

In 1757 Sarah Fielding became the first woman to relate her own version of the story of Cleopatra in a pair of fictionalized autobiographies, *The Lives of Cleopatra and Octavia*. Fielding, who corresponded regularly with Samuel Richardson and lived on companionable terms with her brother, the author of *Tom Jones*, certainly knew that women could be as clever as men. But she was also aware that her contemporaries found female competence at best unattractive, at worst morally suspect. Her Cleopatra, a sophisticate who well knows the way to a man's heart, pretends to stumble as she descends from her throne to greet Antony in Tarsus.

> Anthony flew to raise me: and as soon as it might be thought I could recover the fright, which I affected to be in at my fall, I thanked him, and said, I hope this accident, at our first interview, was a good omen, that by his strength he would support a woman's weakness . . . He little imagined how this was in reality an omen, that by tricks and deceit I should rule him for the remainder of his life.[13]

If to be feeble was both charming and commendable, then the strong, independent woman must of necessity conceal her true nature. As Dryden's Cleopatra had suggested eighty years earlier, she could not but be 'false'.

It is an essential concomitant of the notion of feminine weakness that their relationships with men should become the centre of women's lives. Sedley's Agrippa, who deplores Cleopatra's unladylike insistence on ruling her own country, says,

> Women should sit like idle passengers,
> While the tall ship some able seaman steers.[14]

In other words a woman, poor helpless creature, needs a male protector as a snail needs a shell. The getting of such a protector is judged to be her chief, if not her only, business. The question asked about Cleopatra by the majority of the seventeenth- and eighteenth-century writers who treated her story, by Daniel von Lohenstein, Jean Mairet, Isaac de Benserade and La Calprenède, by John Fletcher, Thomas May, Henry Brooke, Sedley, Dryden and Fielding, is a purely sentimental one: 'Can Cleopatra be true in love?' The nub of her drama – the drama of a woman who challenged Rome in a bid to rule the larger part of the known world – is perceived as being variously her anguish when Antony accuses her of flirting with Octavius's messenger or her dilemma after Antony's death – will she try to seduce Octavius, or will she die faithful to her defeated lover?

'What tell'st though me of Egypt?' asks Dryden's Cleopatra. Her Antony has declared his intention of returning to Octavia. Her grief consumes her: she has no political ambition, no conception of her royal responsibility, no interest in the business of her country. In proper feminine fashion, she is obsessed with love affairs. 'My life, my soul is lost! . . . My kisses, my embraces now are hers!'[15] In the plays of the period the men, Antony and Octavius, Maecenas and Agrippa, Ventidius and Dolabella, gravely dispute political ethics or fight each other for mastery of the world, but Cleopatra's preoccupations are all personal. In a play by Henry Brooke (1703–83) she shows herself a typically giddy female, interested – like the imaginary reader at whom women's magainzes were, until very recently, exclusively aimed – in frocks and recipes but not in politics. Dispatches arrive from the outposts of her empire: 'with these she curls her hair, or sends them in hampers to her cooks, to put under the pies, and keep the venison from scorching'.[16] In *All for Love* she sends Antony a bracelet of rubies set in a design of bleeding hearts. Affairs of the heart are all that interest her, and loving and suffering are her only *métiers*.

The two go together. As an exclusively erotic being Cleopatra is, inevitably, a victim. She lives to love, and when Antony deserts her, as he temporarily does in Dryden's play, or dies, as the story requires that he always must, she is left helpless and redundant. What power she has is sexual and emotional, and it amounts to little. Sedley's Agrippa scoffs at the contention that even gods have been enslaved by love.

> The god that loved, what nymph yet ever ruled?
> He was again a god, his lust once cooled.[17]

It is Antony's downfall that he fails to be a god again, but perversely chooses to dawdle in the empty little world of women. It is Cleopatra's that her gender condemns her to eternal residence there. In Colley Cibber's play *Caesar in Aegypt*, first performed in 1736, she finds that her attractions cannot win her much of her lover's attention. She complains petulantly of Caesar: 'His heart is all ambition! Beauty has only charms for useless hours!'[18] Too true: women of her kind are leisure-time diversions, toys of quickly exhaustible interest, all too frequently cast callously aside when playtime ends.

Politically and practically incompetent, preoccupied with finding and keeping a man, the Cleopatras of the seventeenth- and eighteenth-century dramas frequently act ignobly, for women's weakness can manifest itself as a moral deficiency. Dryden excuses himself for portraying Cleopatra and Octavia engaged in an undignified cat-fight over Antony, 'for after all, though one were a Roman and the other a Queen, they were both women'.[19] Octavia's frequent appearances in these plays mark their authors' new preoccupations. In the Middle Ages she had no part in the story, but as women's nature and proper role came to be a part of that story's meaning she was reintroduced into it, as an alternative model to that represented by Cleopatra and as a touchstone of feminine virtue.

The historical Octavia was a great lady and an intelligent patron. Maecenas and Vitruvius, two of the cleverest men in Rome, were among her friends and protégés. This aspect of her character is completely ignored by the post-Renaissance dramatists, who make her a model woman along the lines sketched by an anonymous seventeenth-century verse:

> Those virtues that in woman merit praise
> Are sober shows without, chaste thoughts within

212

True faith and due obedience to their mate
And of their children honest care to take.[20]

The imaginary Octavias are certainly chaste. In Brandon's play Octavia's sexual innocence is such that she can hardly be brought to believe that Antony could be unfaithful to her. 'Did not he swear on our nupital day . . . ?'[21] In Sedley's she attempts to commit suicide after Maecenas has declared his love for her (Sedley's imagination makes of the traditional story a love-tangle as absurdly complicated as any operetta's). Blameless though she is, she does not wish to go on living after having so much as 'heard of love in my Antonius' wrong'.[22]

Octavia's sexual propriety is matched by her unquestioning loyalty to her husband. Samuel Brandon describes her as 'one that knew not how to disobey'.[23] In Jean Mairet's tragedy, *Le Marc-Antoine ou La Cléopâtre*, published in Paris in 1637, Octavia, 'a heroic soul, a beauty without reproach', comes to Alexandria disguised (appropriately to her modest spirit) as a slave. Antony receives her, only to inform her that he will never leave Cleopatra. Octavia, undeterred in her beneficence, declares that although she will love him until her dying day she expects no return. Like Brandon's Octavia, who is wrung by pity at the thought that her beloved husband will burn in Hell, she only wishes to save him. She embraces Antony's knees as she assures him that since he cast her off she has done nothing that could possibly offend him. She obeys his commands without a murmur. She has always been careful, despite the terrible pain in her heart, not to blame Cleopatra, for she would not wish to anger her husband by speaking ill of one whom he holds so dear. For this devotion, she says, she deserves no praise or reward. It was her simple duty 'which the laws of Hymen impose on a well-born wife'.[24] In the face of such self-abnegation the modern reader is likely to have some sympathy with Sedley's Octavius, who demonstrates his lack of fine feeling by mocking Octavia's 'fawning' determination to

213

Fulsomely pursue
The Man with kindness, who despises you.

Octavia soon sets him right.

> Wives . . .
> To husbands, though unjust, long patience owe:
> They were for Freedom made, Obedience we,
> Courage their virtue, ours is Chastity.[25]

Cleopatra, though never a paragon like Octavia, is equally
aware of her dependent status and the debt of obedience and
fidelity that she owes to her man. In paintings of Antony's
death (for instance those by Domenico Maria Muratori,
Pompeo Batoni and Nathaniel Dance) she is all womanly
solicitude, bending anxiously over her prostrate lover. In
Henry Brooke's play she is touchingly dependent. 'Have I
another lord to guard my weakness?' she protests when
Antony announces his intention of returning to Rome.
Throwing herself to her knees and clutching at his robe she
pleads brokenly: 'I could not bear it – You will not – must
not – cannot!'[26] Cleopatras of this kind are as soft and doting
as their equivalent Octavias. De Benserade's Cleopatra is full
of womanly anxiety over the dangers Antony runs in battle.
As a mere woman she cannot, of course, understand the
honour, the *gloire*, that is so precious to his masculine soul.
This she has in common with Mairet's Cleopatra, who confesses to a 'timid heart' and who cares nothing for victory or
defeat, so long as Antony is safe and loves her still. When he
accuses her of treachery towards him she is distraught. To
lose his trust is 'the most insupportable of all her afflictions'.
In a transport of wronged innocence she cries out that to
regain his affection she will pour out not only teardrops but
even her heart's blood.[27] Sedley's Cleopatra sacrifices herself
with even more alacrity, and less good reason. Her Antony,
dying, advises her to make her peace with Octavius. She
refuses, declaring that she will follow him even into death.
He is too faint to argue the matter further, but subsequently
she takes her life on the mere suspicion that it might please
him: 'When I named Death, speechless my hand he pressed.'[28]

These Cleopatras, no less than the Octavias, recognize that their men have an absolute right to demand of them not only their loves, but their lives as well. 'Will he be kind?' asks Dryden's Cleopatra, the most abject of lovers.

> And will he not forsake me?
> Am I to live, or die? – nay, do I live?
> Or am I dead? For when he gave his answer,
> Fate took the word, and then I lived or died.[29]

Women like these, so passive and biddable, such easy prey for any man that passes, need the protection of law and convention. In the seventeenth century a new theme enters the legend of Cleopatra, that of marriage, and its corollary, adultery. Three possible characters are proposed for Cleopatra in the seventeenth- and eighteenth-century versions of her story: the wife, the failed or would-be wife, and the brazen whore. One is weak and virtuous, one weak and pathetic and the third bad and strong. All, including the last, have in common their lack of autonomy: they are defined entirely by the nature of their relationships with men.

In *Cléopâtre*, La Calprenède's prodigiously popular twelve-volume romance published in instalments between 1647 and 1658, and promptly translated into English by Richard Loveday, Julius Caesar is captivated by the diamantine brightness of Cleopatra's eyes. Staying with her in her palace, he has 'much ado to hinder his amorous fever from breaking out into the hottest proofs', but the prudent Cleopatra allows him only such favours as she can grant him 'without offending virtue'. Caesar becomes desperate. One day when he is kneeling by her bedside kissing her hands (as is his wont) he cries out: 'I die, fair queen!' He beseeches her to have mercy, but she is coy as ever. Lowering her eyes, she begs him to understand her position. A queen's reputation must be spotless. She cannot yield to him 'except in the way of virtue'. Caesar, who fears a royal marriage may damage his prospects in republican Rome, assures her he would marry her if he could but he can't. Cleopatra resorts to sexual blackmail: 'After that she lived with him in a fashion more reserved than formerly.' No more bedside hand-kissing sessions. Caesar capitulates. They are married before six witnesses (but no priest). At last Caesar enjoys 'those admirable beauties envied of all the Princes of Asia'. This story is told, so La Calprenède's narrator informs us, to 'defend the memory of that great Queen who doubtless hath been foully blotted by the ignorance of those that knew not of her marriage'.[30]

Knew not, or cared not. La Calprenède's preoccupation with legal marriage would have seemed strange to most earlier interpreters. The medieval poets referred to Cleopatra as Antony's (or Caesar's) 'wife', the word then signifying simply that she was his sexual partner – 'wife' meaning any mature woman, as the equivalent words in French and German still do. Dryden noted, in the Preface to *All for Love*, that he was by no means the first English 'wit' to tackle the theme. 'I doubt not,' he went on, 'but the same motive has prevailed with all of us in this attempt; I mean the excellency of the moral: for the chief persons represented were famous patterns of unlawful love; and their end accordingly was unfortunate.'[31] He would have been wiser to doubt such a conclusion. The end of Shakespeare's lovers was 'unfortunate' not because their passion was adulterous but, quite simply, because it was passion. It was not until the seventeenth century that the illegitimacy of Cleopatra's love affairs began to exercise those who related her story.

In medieval and early modern England marriage, for people of property, entailed five distinct steps: a financial contract between the two families, a formal exchange of vows known as 'spousals', the proclamation of banns, the wedding in church and the sexual consummation. It was by no means clear at which point in this process the couple were actually wed. Equally confusing law obtained elsewhere in Europe, and it was everywhere true that only the possession and sharing of property rendered such formal, legally enforceable agreements desirable. For the lower classes financial contracts were unnecessary and church weddings discouragingly expensive. Marriage, for the majority, was, in Laurence Stone's words, 'a private contract between two individuals, enforced by the community sense of what was right'. Once a man had taken a 'wife' to bed, so long as both were free of other ties, they became an acknowledged couple, respectably married in their own eyes and those of their neighbours. Whether such a union would be endorsed by Church and State few either knew or cared.[32]

This vagueness about matrimony's definition did not lead to mass promiscuity. A medieval 'wife' belonged to her man and could expect to be sternly punished for infidelity. It did, however, mean that the distinction between virtuous marriage and the more casual cohabitation which would later be known as living in sin was meaningless. It also made polygamy, or rather serial monogamy, easier. The fact that Antony was legally married to Fulvia and to Octavia but not to Cleopatra would have seemed a point of little importance to those few medieval readers of this story who even knew it. He lived with Cleopatra for seven years. They were lovers and the mutual parents of three children. So he was her 'husband', the male head of her household, and she was his 'wife'. As late as 1595 Robert Garnier has Cleopatra invoke the dead Antony in the name of

> Our holy marriage, and the tender ruth
> Of our dear babes, knot of our amity.[33]

The image of the mistress, the woman who, by indulging in extra-marital sex, either ruins herself or proves herself depraved, has yet to appear.

It was the Reformation which brought it to birth. While Garnier still made no distinction between mistress and legally married wife, in Protestant England Samuel Brandon, writing only four years later, celebrated 'The Virtuous Octavia' and contrasted her with Cleopatra, 'She that taught him [Antony] first to sin'.[34] In French or Italian versions of the story, even those dating from well into the seventeenth century, the irregularity of Cleopatra's relationship with Antony seldom carries any particular stigma. De Benserade's heroine dies bitterly bewailing the fact that she has lost her honour, because, instead of being faithful to the dead Antony, she has hoped to attract Octavius. English Cleopatras, by contrast, know that their honour is forfeit as soon as they embark on a love affair not sanctioned by marriage. The cultural difference has proved to be long-lasting. French and Italian commentators are, to this day, astonished by the importance attached by the British and American press and public to the marital fidelity of politicians.

The Protestants' condemnation of extra-marital sex followed naturally from a new-fangled valorization of marriage. Luther, and Calvin after him, extolled the state of wedlock, insisting that monogamy was as 'chaste' as virginity. The English Puritans whole-heartedly endorsed these doctrines. In 1609 William Perkins, the author of an influential Puritan manual, declared that marriage was 'a state in itself far more excellent than the condition of single life'. This was arrant heresy. Perkins's contemporary, Cardinal Bellarmine, expresses the opposite and more venerable view. 'Marriage is a thing humane: virginity is angelical.'[35] The Catholic Church had always taught that sexual relations of any kind were tainted with sin. Monogamous marriage was a lesser evil than promiscuity, but an evil it none the less was. 'It is laws which seem to make the difference between marriage and fornication: through diversity of illicitness, not through the nature of the thing itself,' wrote Tertullian in the second century AD.[36] It was not until the Protestants insisted on the clergy's right to take wives that the ideal of the chaste marriage could develop, and the relationship between husband and wife be idealized as being inherently virtuous, creative, even holy.

Samuel Brandon's Octavia, Antony's lawfully wedded wife, is acclaimed 'Earth's glory' and 'the heaven's beloved bride', while Cleopatra, partner in his adultery, is notable only for her 'gilded baits of sin'.[37] Apparently married women, at least, benefited from this division of female humanity into good wives and scheming mistresses. But, as the many versions of Cleopatra's story make plain, the fictional Octavias, as well as the Cleopatras (and all of the real-life women whose predicament they jointly represented) lost

218

by the polarization. Octavia is praised for her patience, her constancy, her obedience – in other words for her acquiescence in an outrageous double standard of sexual propriety and for her self-denying readiness to devote her life to the promotion of her neglectful husband's interests. Such virtue is scarcely to be envied, nor is the sexlessness attendant on it. Before marriage could be fully approved it had to be purged of all voluptuousness, all erotic excitement. When Dryden's Cleopatra boasts of her 'charms' Octavia retorts primly:

> Far be their knowledge from a Roman lady,
> Far from a modest wife![38]

Thus married women are doomed to frigidity and frustration. The spiciness attendant on unsanctioned love is imagined to be entirely missing from the pure and decorous marriage bed. Even Dryden's timid Cleopatra claims that her outlaw passions are more ardent than those of a wife,

> That dull insipid lump, without desires,
> And without power to give them.[39]

The good wife's virtue, by a cruel catch, wins her a reputation for prudishness, as Samuel Brandon's poor wronged Octavia knows.

> Is chastity so loathsome then,
> Unto a wanton ear
> That beauty is no beauty where
> Such chaste desires appear?[40]

The question expected the answer yes, and continued to receive it for centuries.

Once more, it took a female writer to expose the wretched truth behind the conventional simplicities. In Delphine de Girardin's *Cléopâtre*, first performed in 1847, Octavia proudly asserts that she cares nothing for Cleopatra, or any other of Antony's mistresses. 'It is I whom he will respect, and it is I who should be envied.' Cleopatra, the libertine, may enjoy his laurels with him, but it will be for her, the honoured wife, to cherish his white hairs. So, poignantly, she

219

tries to preserve her dignity in public, but once alone she breaks down and confesses that, in truth, the good wife's lot is a dismal one. This Octavia would trade all she has – rank, fortune, reputation – 'for the shameful happiness of a mistress who is beloved'.[41]

The wife was denied pleasure; the mistress was denied respect. Unhusbanded, but no virgin, Cleopatra was, to the Protestant and most particularly to the bourgeois English mind, in a state of lamentable sin. This troubled the dramatists, who liked their protagonists to be not only great but good. To pass as a presentable heroine Cleopatra had to be brought more closely in line with the ideal of feminine virtue.

Dryden's Cleopatra repeatedly assures the audience that she longs to marry Antony, and is by no means a light-hearted sinner. La Calprenède was not the only author to go further, to make an honest woman of her by discovering that she had been married, unbeknown'st to history, all along. In a novel by Charlotte Lennox published in 1752 the heroine asserts that Cleopatra was 'ravished'. 'Cleopatra was a whore, was she not, Madam?' asks another character nastily. 'Hold thy peace, unworthy Man, said Arabella; and profane not the memory of that fair and glorious Queen by such injurious language.' Another gentleman joins the debate: 'Sir . . . you were in the wrong to cast such reflections upon that great Queen . . . For all the world, pursued he, knows she was married.'[42] 'Is it certain that your emperor is married to this wonder?' asked Henry Brooke's Agrippa. 'As sure as an Egyptian priest can fetter him,' replies Enobarbus. In Brooke's play the conquered Armenian King, Artavasdes, turns out to be none other than Cleopatra's long-lost elder brother. He has not made himself known to her while he believed her to be 'harlot to Antony'.

> While thy fame was doubtful
> I long disdained to claim alliance with thee.

When Cleopatra assures him that he has heard a foul Roman rumour and that she is in fact Antony's 'wedded wife' he is overjoyed at 'the redemption of thy fame'.[43]

This Cleopatra, unusually, has visible children. Brooke brings on the twins, Alexander and Cleopatra Selene – her 'sweet lambs', 'prattlers', 'precious little ones' – who address each other, in playful, domestic style, as 'Ally' and 'Patty'.[44] As an honorary wife, this Cleopatra can be credited with the attributes of a good woman, motherhood being one of them. The perfect Octavia is repeatedly presented as a quintessentially maternal being. At the climax of Brandon's play she is seen being evicted from Antony's house, surrounded by children, her own and Fulvia's. In Dryden's version she comes to Alexandria with her two little daughters: it is as their mother that she temporarily wins back Antony's love. Cleopatra's offspring, by contrast, are invisible in nearly all of the plays in which she is unmarried. The respectable charms of maternity are the exclusive prerogative of the good wife. The pretty tableau of a mother playing with her children is only pleasing when it can be read as the representation of a family headed by and belonging to a man.

Those seventeenth- and eighteenth-century Cleopatras denied honorary wifehood are frequently pathetic beings – not so much mistresses as failed wives, sad, frustrated creatures yearning in vain for the respectable security symbolized by a wedding ring. Dryden's Cleopatra has all the right womanly virtues but no context, no marriage, in which to display them. In versions of her story in which she is so portrayed Cleopatra's single status does not represent any kind of libertarian or feminist rebellion against conventional morality – on the contrary, it can be read as evidence of her proper feminine self-abasement. Dryden's Cleopatra welcomes the shame of being a fallen woman: it is one of the trials she gladly undergoes in order to prove her devotion to her lord and master.

> The world condemns poor me.
> For I have lost my honour, lost my fame,
> And stained the glory of my royal house,
> And all to bear the branded name of mistress.[45]

This kind of mistress is as eager as a wife to prove her

self-effacing devotion to her man. Dryden's Antony, after deciding to abandon Cleopatra, demands that she should remain celibate for the rest of her days,

> For, though 'tis past, I would not that the world
> Should tax my former choice, that I loved one
> Of so light note.

Cleopatra, piteously, acquiesces, sighing not because the demands he makes on her are so exorbitant, but because she cannot bear him to think her capable of any trespass against absolute fidelity.[46]

Such wives and would-be wives alike make dull companions. While idealizing women who made their menfolk the centre of their existence, men in practice recoiled from them. The clinging, adoring spouse begins after a while to feel like a devitalizing parasite, and love-talk must eventually pall if one of the partners has no other kind of conversation. A chilling boredom speaks through the startlingly effusive scene in *All for Love* in which Antony welcomes his male friend Dolabella to Alexandria.

> Art thou returned at last, my better half?
> Come, give me all myself![47]

Antony's evident relief makes it uncomfortably plain that, for all his passion for Cleopatra, she is not sufficiently his equal to be his friend. Until Dolabella came he lay in his mistress's arms and felt, along with his rapture, loneliness and tedium.

'Some men are of that humour,' wrote the Duchess of Newcastle in 1664, 'as they hate honest, chaste women ... they love the company and conversation of wanton and free women.'[48] It is only when Cleopatra appears in the guise of a bold adventuress or a bare-faced whore that she and Antony can be friends. In Jan Steen's painting of her banquet Antony takes his ease on the floor while Cleopatra lolls tipsily in her throne. The setting is indeterminate – the palace at Alexandria here looks much like the interior of a tavern, perhaps even a brothel. The picture space is crowded with

222

dogs, melons, colourful carpets and buxom serving wenches. The atmosphere is festive and richly carnal. Paintings like this one (of which there are several – the theme was popular with Dutch and Flemish artists) bear out the view that Canidius expresses in Thomas May's *Tragedie of Cleopatra* (1654) when he asserts that 'the love of ladies' is 'a merry occasion'.[49] When Cleopatra appears in the guise of a strumpet Antony's relations with her need not only afford him lacerating extremes of passion; he can actually have fun.

The whore is more dangerous than the wife, and stronger. She is financially independent. Her sexuality is her own, to sell or to enjoy, not to be meekly offered for the enjoyment of others. She is clever and 'false'. She does not die for love because, manlike, she believes life has more to offer than romantic sentiment. With access to many masculine advantages she makes men feel at ease, and she knows how to benefit from her popularity with them. The bourgeois Protestant cultures that spawned the pitiful wife, as though recognizing that such a pallid stereotype could not encompass the diversity and energy of womankind, also invented her sister-opposite, the jolly adventuress. During the sixteenth and seventeenth centuries in numerous Dutch and Flemish paintings, and in plays from England and Germany, a new kind of Cleopatra makes her appearance – shameless, shrewd and hedonistic.

The harlot-Cleopatras are cold-hearted, but hot-blooded. They are brazenly sexual beings, taking or bartering pleasure without guilt. Samuel Daniel's libertine Cleopatra confesses that she never loved Antony until after his death:

> My lascivious court
> Fertile in ever-fresh and new-choice pleasure,
> Afforded me so bountiful disport
> That I to stay on love had never leisure.[50]

This robust capacity for enjoyment gives Cleopatra an allure which, when presented as a wife or a failed wife, she tends to lack.

The playwrights were aided in their representations of Cleopatra as enticingly depraved woman by the fact that the actresses who played her shared that reputation. In 1629 a troupe of French performers were hissed off the London stage for being 'notorious whores'.[51] When, after the Restoration, Englishwomen were permitted to act they were immediately assumed to be sexually available to the highest bidder. As the satirist Tom Brown wrote, "'Tis as hard a matter for a pretty woman to keep herself honest in the theatre, as 'tis for an apothecary to keep his treacle from the flies in hot weather, for every libertine in the audience will be buzzing about her honeypot.'[52] Mrs Barry, a leading lady whose private life was famously irregular, was commonly known as Cleopatra, although she does not appear ever to have played the role – an appropriate nickname, according to a contemporary satirist, because the original was 'so unfortunate to Antony as the other has been to many an honest country gentleman'.[53] Thus the Cleopatras of Sedley, Dryden, Cibber or Brooke brought traces of scandal from the dressing rooms on stage with them, a sauciness which the playwrights could usefully exploit.

A harlot-Cleopatra may be a simple pleasure-seeker, a good-time girl. More frequently she is a professional courtesan, using her sexuality as a bargaining counter or a weapon. Thomas May's Canidius describes Cleopatra as

> ordained by fate
> To be possessed by them that rule the world

thus suggesting that she is a passive property, a glorified callgirl provided for the enjoyment of visiting heads of state; but when she herself comes on stage we realize that she is managing her own meretricious career with considerable adroitness. With Antony she flatters and coaxes. When his fortunes fail she offers herself to Octavius. It is only when he has proved indifferent to her charms that she resolves to kill herself.[54] In *The False One*, written by John Fletcher, possibly in collaboration with Philip Massinger, and first performed around 1620, the young Cleopatra resolves to seduce Julius Caesar in order to further her own political interest.

> Though I purchase
> His grace with loss of my virginity,
> It skills not, if it bring home Majesty.

She persuades Sceva, a 'plain speaker', to carry her to Caesar's apartment wrapped in the usual roll of bedding. Caesar is immediately captivated, but throughout the ensuing love scene Sceva keeps up a wry commentary which makes its effect bawdily comical.

> She brings her bed along too, she'll lose no time,
> Carries her litter to lie soft, do you see that?

The cynic has assessed Cleopatra correctly. She is coolly prostituting herself in order to gull Caesar. 'He is my conquest now,' she tells the audience in an aside, 'and so I'll work him.'[55]

These harlot-Cleopatras are as devious as they are unchaste. In Daniel von Lohenstein's *Kleopatra*, first performed in Nuremberg in 1661, the heroine is both a lusty mistress and a scheming manipulator. The heartiness with which she enjoys her liaison with Antony in the first half of the play is complemented by the subterfuges to which she resorts in order to preserve her safety in the second. She pretends to commit suicide, a piece of play-acting deliberately staged in the hope that Antony will kill himself, leaving the way open for her to come to terms with Octavius. (Lohenstein was the first dramatist to place such a construction on her misleading message.) That ruse successful, she tries to win Octavius's favour by acting as though afire with love with him. 'I burn! I burn!'[56] It is only when he proves himself her equal in guile that she gives up hope and dies. Colley Cibber's Photinus describes how the Queen, though supposedly in love with Caesar, contrives to make sure of Antony's heart as well, 'With all the blandishments of glancing beauty', affecting a 'seeming woe' and shedding pretty tears 'Like dew-drops trickling o'er the bloom of roses'.[57] Duplicity and promiscuity are closely linked. To say of a woman in this period that she was 'honest' meant that she was either a virgin or a faithful wife. To say that she had 'deceived' her husband meant, as it still does, that she had had sexual relations with someone else. Truth, in a woman, is sexually defined.

The assumption that the sexually promiscuous woman is by nature mendacious seems to spring from a suspicion that she withholds some essential part of herself in sexual intercourse. Love-making ought to involve absolute self-surrender, but the 'dishonest' woman may be using it to pursue her own selfish ends, to gain pleasure for herself, to win favours from a man, even to earn a living. Besides, a woman who had only one sexual partner could be assumed to be transparent to that partner's view, but a woman who had had several lovers was not fully to be reached or understood by any one of them. Her life had areas of privacy, controlled by no one but herself. She had knowledge other than that which her husband had imparted to her. She could not be seen through. She was not as malleable, as weak, as a woman ought to be. She was not 'honest'.

Artifice and unchastity are therefore equated, and Cleopatra's skill in self-presentation is a symptom of her moral looseness. This is an ancient theme. Maecenas, the historical Octavia's friend, praised her 'natural' coiffure, while it was rumoured in Rome that Cleopatra wore a wig.[58] Cosmetics, false hair, womanly wiles, contrivances of any kind were the marks of the strumpet; simplicity that of the good wife. In 1608 the English traveller Thomas Coryat described a Venetian courtesan 'decked with many chains of gold and orient pearl like a second Cleopatra . . . divers gold rings beautified with diamonds and other costly stones, jewels in her ears of great worth'.[59] Ostentatious self-adornment – which suggests that the woman who practises it is actively in pursuit of a lover, rather than waiting meekly, as a good woman should, to be chosen by a husband – is the mark of a harlot-Cleopatra. 'The great art of pleasing,' noted Mary Wollstonecraft in 1792, '. . . is only useful to a mistress. The chaste wife and serious mother should only consider her power to please as the polish of her virtues.'[60] Heavy make-up is, to this day, read as a signal of sexual availability, the livery of the tart.

A deceiver has power over the one deceived. 'Everyone

In Lawrence Alma-Tadema's painting, Cleopatra, passive and mysterious as the Orient was supposed to be, awaits the arrival of Antony, the vigorous European dicoverer. *Vern Swanson*

In *The Arrival of Cleopatra* by
William Etty the queen comes
from the sea like a second Venus,
attended by water-nymphs in
a tidal wave of diaphanous
femininity. *Walker Art Gallery*

Frederick Sandys's drawing shows
Cleopatra as the exotic *femme
fatale*. 'She sees the heart of death
made bare', wrote Swinburne of
this image. *Cornhill Magazine*

In the painting by the orientalist Jean-Louis Gérôme Cleopatra stands before Julius
Caesar like a slave before a purchaser. *Mansell Collection*

Gustave Moreau's painting of the Cleopatra of the decadent imagination who, in Arthur Symons's words, could 'draw the stars out of the sky with love' because she had looked into the heart of death. *The Louvre*

Theda Bara, Hollywood's original vamp and the last of the Romantic killer-Cleopatras in the film of 1917.

Minnie Stevens of Boston, one of three Cleopatras at a fancy dress ball given by the Duchess of Devonshire for Queen Victoria's Diamond Jubilee. Her dress, made by Worth, was encrusted with diamonds, rubies and emeralds. *Devonshire Collections*

In 1951 Charles Bestegui gave a ball, the most glittering Europe had seen since the war, at the Palazzo Labia. Lady Diana Cooper, dressed as Tiepolo's Cleopatra posed beneath the original. Subsequently she used Cecil Beaton's photograph of her in costume in her passport. *Sotheby's*

(*Facing page*) Vivien Leigh plays Bernard Shaw's ambiguous Cleopatra – flirting like an adult, sulking like a child – in the film made in 1945. *Kobal Collection*

Cleopatra as bimbo. Amanda Barrie, in *Carry on Cleo*, with Sid James as Mark Antony.
She: 'I've been thinking.' He: 'You do??!!' *Kobal Collection*

Parodies of the Burton/Taylor Cleopatra abound. In *Asterix and Cleopatra* the queen
makes her idea of a discreet entrance, remarking, 'I didn't even stop to change.'

around me was born to be my slave,' boasts Sarah Fielding's megalomaniac Cleopatra. Throughout her affair with Antony this Cleopatra is play-acting: 'thus did I contrive to heighten his passion by every trifling incident chance threw in my way'. Her pleasure in hoodwinking him becomes an addiction: it makes her 'greater than the greatest hero', and the relishing of that power is more piquant to her than any amorous pleasure. Fielding's estimable Octavia, on the other hand, loves truth beyond all other forms of goodness. She never needs to use any guile with men because 'I have never once dreamed of superiority over my husband.'[61] Fielding (who never married) clearly grasped the link between the ideal of the loyal 'honest' wife and the subordination of women in marriage. As Silvia, the 'licentious woman' of Samuel Brandon's play, observes, constancy, the much-vaunted virtue of the ideal wife, is

> the thing that works all woman's fall
> It . . . gives men scope to use us as they list.[62]

The harlot-Cleopatra, repudiating constancy and 'falsely' considering her own interests before those of her man, has some independence, but nothing can entirely free her from the weakness congenital to her sex. To seventeenth- and eighteenth-century interpreters she is only ever as powerful as men's favour can make her. Seduction is her only talent, and male indifference can render its potency null. In Fletcher's *The False One* Cleopatra is much put out to find that Caesar, when feasting with her, is more interested in the golden dinner service and the 'mine of treasures' than he is in her person.

> How?
> Am I grown old o'the sudden, Caesar? . . .
> A little dross betray me?[63]

In H. Govaerts's painting of her banquet she is richly and titillatingly dressed – both her pearly breasts are exposed – but Antony slumps sideways in his chair in the foreground, his gaze wandering towards the ample backside of the maid kneeling by the fireplace. The harlot-Cleopatra puts herself up for sale in a buyers' market. Thus she is open to humiliation, for many punters may prefer the buxom maid to the glacially grand mistress. Colley Cibber's Cleopatra invites the love-smitten Caesar to come dally with her in her bower. There a thousand gurgling fountains fill a lake on which float silver swans. Slaves pass to and fro on a golden drawbridge. Silken pavilions provide shade, and while the lovers feast they are entertained by 'bands of mimic masters', dancing Gauls, 'melodious virgins' and 'warbling eunuchs'.[64] To no avail. When the curtain rises on this lavish scene it is to reveal Cleopatra sitting neglected while Caesar reads his letters, as careless of the spectacle mustered for his pleasure as any bourgeois husband ignoring the pretty fol-de-rols in his wife's drawing room when absorbed in business. The seventeenth-century dramatist Aphra Behn called the courtesan 'that glorious insolent thing, that makes mankind such slaves'.[65] But the slaves have only to look the other way and the courtesan's glory collapses like a house of cards. The kind of power that the harlot-Cleopatras command depends on their beauty, and beauty, as Sedley's Cleopatra conventionally but truly remarks, is 'a fair but fading flower'.[66] It is ephemeral; it is also without any autonomous existence. The beholder, in whose eye it lies, can cancel it by a simple denial. The women who had access to no more substantial kind of influence were still weak.

When Cleopatra became the *femme fatale* of the nineteenth-century imagination she temporarily escaped this weakness, but the sexual morality which ensured that women's perceived nature should be determined by their relationship with men was to remain a perennial part of her story. She is wife or not-wife, good or bad, her virtue dependent on whether or not a man has taken her under his protection. In the Epilogue to *Caesar in Aegypt* Colley Cibber challenged the 'Prim prudes' who 'urge that lawless fire', like the extra-marital love enjoyed by Cleopatra and Julius Caesar, 'in death and desolation should expire'. He asks: 'Would belles and beaux refuse the joy from terror?'[67] and merrily concludes that they would not, but he cannot banish the question from his mind. Never again would Cleopatra, the unmarried lover, be, as she was for the Senecan dramatists of the Renaissance, fully respectable. In an early nineteenth-century cartoon by James Gillray, Sir William Hamilton contemplates his art collection, including a pair of portraits labelled *Cleopatra* and *Antony* but actually depicting Hamilton's wife Emma and her lover, Lord Nelson.[68] Cleopatra's name had become synonymous with adultery. Coleridge disapproved of her. He wrote, somewhat tortuously, of Shakespeare's heroine, 'The sense of criminality in her passion is lessened by our insight into its depth and energy, at the very moment that we cannot but perceive that the passion itself springs out of the habitual craving of a licentious nature.'[69] In 1813 Mrs Siddons declined to take the part of Cleopatra, saying that she would hate herself if she had played the role 'as it ought to be played'.[70]

Marriage and transgression against it tinted all nineteenth-century understandings of Cleopatra's story. In Shakespeare's play 'from beginning to end', wrote an anonymous contributor to *Fraser's Magazine* in 1849, 'Cleopatra's mind is haunted and humiliated by the consciousness that she is not Antony's wife'. Such a startlingly unfounded reading could only spring from a widespread intellectual and moral bias. François-Victor Hugo, writing in 1868 about the same play, was taken aback to notice that when 'an outraged wife disputes her rights with a courtesan, it is not the wife who moves us, it is the courtesan!'[71] Wife or courtesan, courtesan or wife. These are the two roles between which a woman, in her imagined weakness, is obliged to choose. In order to find a place for herself in society, in order to survive at all, she must win men's favour. The price of that favour is her own natural strength, for men have tended to deplore toughness in a female. Cleopatra's personality, wrote the popular historian Jacob Abbott in 1852, is greatly improved by her (apparently asexual) relationship with Julius Caesar. 'The sprightliness and vivacity of her character, which became at later periods of her life boldness and eccentricity, now being softened and restrained within proper limits by the respectful regard with which she looked upon Caesar, made her an enchanting companion.' Marriage, according to Abbot, often has a similarly salutary effect, for

> It is the characteristic of pure and lawful love to soften and subdue the heart, and infuse a gentle and quiet spirit into all its action; while that [like Cleopatra's for Antony] which breaks over the barriers that God and nature have marked out for it tends to make a woman masculine and bold, to indurate her sensibilities and to destroy that gentleness and timidity of demeanour which have so great an influence in heightening her charms.[72]

In 1853 Charlotte Brontë placed the heroine of *Villette*, Lucy Snowe, before a typical academic painting of Cleopatra. Lucy reflects upon it in characteristically sardonic style: 'She lay half-reclined on a couch: why, it would be difficult to say; broad daylight blazed around her; . . . She had no business to lounge away the noon on a sofa . . . out of abundance of material – seven and twenty yards, I should say, of drapery – she managed to make very inefficient raiment.' This Cleopatra is both weak and wicked, a passive temptress invented for the gratification of the tempted. Monsieur Paul, Lucy's irascible beloved-to-be, is shocked when he finds her looking at such a picture, whose subject he judges to be a woman '*je ne voudrais ni pour femme, ni pour fille, ni pour soeur*' – a woman whom he would not want as a wife, daughter or sister. He bustles Lucy off to a dim corner and orders her to remain there in contemplation of a set of four genre paintings entitled *La Vie d'une Femme*. The first shows a young girl, 'her dress very prim, her eyes cast down, her mouth pursed up – the image of a most villainous little precocious she-hypocrite', the second a bride, the third a mother and the last a widow by her husband's tomb. 'All these four "*Anges*" were grim and gray as burglars, and cold and vapid as ghosts. What women to live with! insincere, ill-humoured, bloodless, brainless nonentities! As bad in their way as the indolent gypsy-giantess, the Cleopatra, in hers.'[73]

So at last a trenchant female intelligence confronts the two stereotypical weak women, the selfless dependent wife and the soliciting whore, between whom the story of Cleopatra has oscillated since the Reformation. Despite her virginity, Lucy Snowe has much in common with the seventeenth-century harlot-Cleopatras. Like them she is economically self-reliant. Like them she is impatient of mincing, ladylike morality. But unlike them she is good. Brontë, through her, refused the either/or imposed on women. Lucy Snowe is not yet free of weakness. Emotional and sexual deprivation is the price of her virtue, and her dogged pursuit of independence exposes her to the particularly feminine perils of hysteria. But she is intellectually prepared for strength. She has rejected the example of the good wife and she has mocked the fantasy of the alluringly bad mistress. So she has cleared an imaginative space in which to be herself, to develop her own potential without reference to reductive models. It is significant that Cleopatra should play a part in the scene which illustrates that readiness. The vicissitudes of her character, presented variously as the pseudo-wife, the failed wife, the prostitute and the mistress, have, since the Reformation, vividly demonstrated the paucity of choice allowed to women. Just as Lucy found the domestic angels and the gypsy-giantess equally ill matched to her own sense of herself, so none of the writers or artists who represented Cleopatra in the seventeenth and eighteenth centuries could create a mould grand and flexible enough to contain a just image of her, of the lover who was also a ruthless stateswoman, of the unmarried mother who was also a scholar-queen.

# 7
# THE QUEEN

THOMAS MAY'S *TRAGEDIE of Cleopatra* opens, conventionally enough, with a scene in which a group of attendant lords discuss the deleterious effect that Antony's infatuation with Cleopatra is having on his character and reputation, and the immorality of deserting a lawful wife for the sake of such a love affair. The sentiments are commonplace, the course of the conversation predictable, until, abruptly, Canidius interrupts:

> 'Is it become a care worthy of us
> What woman Antonius enjoys?'[1]

Cleopatra and her waiting-women may be obsessed, in their feminine way, with love, true or false, but men have more important things to talk about – things like tyranny and freedom, the duties of a prince, the rights of a citizen and the constitution most proper to a well-ordered state. During the two centuries which saw the foundation of republics in England, America and France, Cleopatra and her *amours* are frequently no more than a decorative fringe on the dramas that bear her name, their real narrative and ideological centre being a political debate conducted by the menfolk.

Among those practices 'that weaken, or tend to the dissolution of a commonwealth' wrote the political philosopher Thomas Hobbes in 1651, is the reading of 'histories of the ancient Greeks and Romans'. Such histories spread a contagion as dreadful, in Hobbes's estimation, as rabies, for they can persuade 'young men, and all others that are unprovided of the antidote of solid reason' that 'the subjects in a popular commonwealth enjoy liberty; but that in a monarchy they are all slaves'.[2] Hobbes was writing as an exile in Paris; there he was mathematics tutor to the young Charles Stuart, whose father, King Charles I, had recently lost his head. In England the regicides were in the ascendant. In France Mazarin's regency was shaken by the successive revolts of the Fronde. Hobbes may have been confusing causation with synchronicity, but in one respect his observation is undoubtedly correct. The revival of classical learning in Europe coincided with the reopening of an argument that Cleopatra's adversary had temporarily closed when he called himself Augustus and, assuming absolute power, brought centralized autocratic government to Rome.

That argument, from the Reformation to the French Revolution and beyond, was customarily conducted with reference to ancient examples. In his commentaries on Livy, Niccolò Machiavelli proposed the Roman republic as the model of wise government, praising Brutus the liberator and condemning Julius Caesar the would-be tyrant. The authoritarian political philosopher Jean Bodin, writing in France in 1576, answered him and those who, like him, 'praise the Roman republic to the skies', counselling them to remember 'the discords and evil commotions to which it was prey'.[3] The English monarchist Sir Robert Filmer echoed him in *Patriarcha*, written in the 1630s but not published until after the Restoration. 'Popular government is more bloody than a tyranny ... this was the height of Roman liberty ... any man might be killed that would. A favour not fit to be granted under a royal government.'[4] For these thinkers, and for the political theorists who followed them, the city states of ancient Greece and, to an even greater extent, Rome were the touchstones and exemplars *par excellence*. La Calprenède, in his *Cléopâtre*, calls on 'all that wield sceptres' to join forces against republican Romans, who are the 'enemies of mankind' in general and especially of kings.[5] Every rebel was a Brutus, every military dictator a Pompey. Julius Caesar's assassination illustrated numerous debates on the propriety of tyrannicide. And every absolute ruler, of course, was a successor to Cleopatra's arch-enemy, Octavius/Augustus.

To a democrat Octavius was thus the personification of all that was detestable. Montesquieu called him a 'crafty tyrant'. Voltaire went further: 'a man without shame, without faith, without honour, without probity, false, ungrateful, avaricious, bloody, tranquil in the commission of crime, a man who, in a well-policed republic, would have been put to death for any one of his misdeeds'.[6] To a courtier, by contrast, he was the epitome of monarchical glory. Charles Perrault declared that one could justly compare the age of Louis XIV of France to the *'beau siècle d' Auguste'*. No doubt the King savoured the comparison. It was one he himself suggested when he assumed the persona of Apollo, as Octavius had done so many centuries before, rode to the Fête de Versailles in a gold chariot and had himself painted by Jean Nocret in the character of the god, clad in periwig and classical drapery.[7]

Both the love stories which made up Cleopatra's legend were politically charged. When Julius Caesar came to Alexandria he had just defeated his greatest rival. His liaison with a royal princess coincided with, and seemed neatly to illustrate, his progress towards an hereditary dictatorship on the monarchical model. And although the rivalry between Antony and Octavius was primarily a power struggle between ambitious individuals, hindsight inevitably lent it the character of a political watershed: behind it the republic, before it the empire. 'The Heavens are astonished at the greatness of your power!'[8] de Benserade's Agrippa tells Octavius. Cleopatra's death has opened the way for an unprecedented absolutism. To many of the writers of the *ancien régime* this was the chief significance of her story.

The moral to be drawn from that story varied according to the standpoint of the writer and also according to the sources he or she was using. The fullest ancient account of Caesar's sojourn in Alexandria was Lucan's *Pharsalia*, a source on which Fletcher, May, Cibber and Pierre Corneille all drew. In spite of having been for a while a member of

Nero's entourage, Lucan was a passionate anti-imperialist. He was obliged to commit suicide at the age of twenty-five after becoming implicated in Piso's conspiracy, 'ranting publicly about how glorious it was to murder a tyrant and even offering to present his friends with Nero's head'.[9] A speech he places in the mouth of Pothinus, the eunuch guardian of Ptolemy XIII, makes clear his views on monarchy: 'Once kings begin to think in terms of abstract justice their power wanes, and down go their fortresses. . . . The palace is no place for an upright man; nor is virtue consonant with monarchy.'[10]

After a millennium and a half such doctrines were still being debated. 'Our forefathers did not without reason coin the phrase "a bad man makes a good king",' wrote Jean Bodin, advocating stern government.[11] Machiavelli, with somewhat different intent, came to similar conclusions. A prince should be ever ready to break his promises, to betray his allies and put his subjects to death, for 'he who has best known to play the fox has ever been the most successful'.[12] John Fletcher has his Pothinus faithfully repeat Lucan's sentiments in the 1620s:

> The stars are not more distant from the earth
> Than profit is from honesty. . . . Let him leave
> The sceptre, that strives only to be good.[13]

The intrinsic immorality of kingship was, in Stuart England, a topic of lively contemporary interest.

A contrary and far more favourable view of autocracy is to be found in another important source for Cleopatra's legend, the history of Dio Cassius. Dio imagines Octavius asking Maecenas and Agrippa for advice as to how he should administer Rome. Agrippa advises him to resign his power, thus allowing the Senate to resume its proper constitutional function, and goes on to rehearse the conventional arguments in praise of democracy. But Maecenas, in a far longer and more considered speech, argues that to allow the people power is 'putting a sword into the hand of a child or a madman' and urges Octavius to continue to rule, aided only by 'the other citizens among us who are best qualified'.[14] In one after another of the seventeenth- and eighteenth-century Cleopatra plays, echoes of Dio Cassius's imagined debate can be heard. Agrippa (who, as far as is known, was a loyal supporter of Octavius's and never questioned the rectitude of his assumption of supreme power) repeatedly appears as a spokesman for the oppressed plebs, and Maecenas's arguments are paraded almost verbatim. The debate had not lost its urgency. All over Europe the rival merits of autocracy, oligarchy and democracy were still being disputed, with swords as well as with pens.

In the pursuance of that debate writers and artists imposed their own ideologies on Cleopatra's image. Some seventeenth- and eighteenth-century interpreters took their political cues from the ancient sources. The majority of them, though, adapted her story to suit their own and their audience's convictions. Corneille based his *Pompée* on Lucan's *Pharsalia*, and yet from that essentially republican and egalitarian text he drew a tragedy in which the natural superiority of the high-born, and particularly of the royal, person is a central theme. Sir Charles Sedley, writing after the Restoration of the Stuart monarchy but for a middle-class audience which remembered the execution of one king and was shortly to witness the deposition of another, portrays Octavius as a calculating megalomaniac, intent on 'universal empire', who intimidates and bribes the Senate. Wiser characters shake their heads over his gluttony for power, and Agrippa sorrowfully notes that while the first Romans bought freedom, 'the god-like treasure', with their blood when they deposed the ancient kings,

> We their vile issues in our chains delight
> And, born to freedom, for our tyrants fight.[15]

By contrast, in Marmontel's *Cléopâtre*, which was performed for the first time before a courtly audience by the Comédiens Français Ordinaires du Roi in 1750, the advantages of one-man rule are exhaustively discussed and Octavius, though conceding that liberty might once have been a desirable commodity, explains regretfully that

> The people are no longer worthy of it. Slaves by nature, whether we like it or not, they would sell liberty in the market place in their greed for gold.

A strong leader is required to remedy their weaknesses and to protect them from unprincipled pedagogues. Generously, for their own good, he has consented to be their dictator and thus to bring them repose, plenty and the happy condition of 'peaceful slavery'.[16]

However he is judged, Octavius's role is, on the whole, plain. Cleopatra's political function is more variable. When viewed on her own she represents hereditary monarchy, a variation on the autocratic theme personified by Octavius. When taken in tandem with Antony she stands for oligarchy in general and for the feudal and quasi-feudal aristocracy which, in seventeenth- and eighteenth-century Europe, was being progressively pushed aside by monarchs intent on establishing strong central governments with the aid of bourgeois meritocrats. Terry Eagleton has likened Shakepeare's *Antony and Cleopatra* to W. B. Yeats's celebration of a declining Anglo-Irish aristocracy, their 'swaggering defiance' contrasted with 'the niggardly calculations of the middle classes'.[17] In later dramas the theme was to be made explicit. In a tragedy by Giovanni Capponi, first published in Bologna in 1628, Cleopatra describes Octavius, with a detectable trace of snobbery, as being 'astute' and 'double-tongued'. She, as the descendant of an ancient and glorious house, is distinguished, in contrast, by the more glamorous qualities of 'noble constancy [and] intrepid ardour'.[18] Like the constitutional monarchs of post-1688 England, like the alliance of Louis XIV with Colbert and the pen-pushing lawyers and officials who made up the newly powerful *noblesse de robe*, Octavius represents a more efficient but less romantic new order. Cleopatra and Antony, meanwhile, in plays which elaborate this theme, are arrogant and noble, not so much born to rule as born not to be ruled; they are as proud as the independent princelings and ungovernable great nobles of feudal Europe. Sedley's Antony refuses to accept peace terms which would make him answerable to Rome; he was not made to be a 'drudge of state'.[19] Capponi's Cleopatra is furiously impatient of Octavius's insistence that he must decide her fate in consultation with 'the fathers in the Senate'. To treat with him, a leader of men, she could bear; to be judged by an assembly of commoners is intolerable to her.[20] Aristocrats of this temper are as unpopular with dictators as they are with democrats, and in seventeenth- and eighteenth-century Europe, as in imperial Rome, they were a dwindling but still substantial menace to central government. In Alexandre Soumet's tragedy *Cléopâtre*, Octavius proclaims his intention to bring order to chaos by imposing his uniform rule over petty domains, 'all these peoples, these kings shaking their chains'.[21] Dio Cassius's Maecenas advised Augustus to 'bring in men of the noblest descent, the highest qualities and the greatest wealth' and keep them close to him. 'In this way you will enlist many helpers for yourself, and you will have in safe keeping the leading figures from all the provinces. Because these regions will henceforth be without their recognised leaders they will not start any rebellions.'[22] Shrewd advice, followed (albeit probably unconsciously) by Louis XIV when he persuaded the aristocracy of France to join him at Versailles.

In the plays where Cleopatra and Antony are perceived thus, as disaffected aristocrats, the common arguments in favour of monarchy are used against them. These arguments vary from the strictly practical to the religious, the latter generally being felt to carry most weight. Robert Filmer quoted St Chrysostom, 'God made all mankind of one man, that he might teach the world to be governed by a King, and not by a multitude.'[23] It is by God's will, declared Jacques-Bénigne Bossuet, that kings reign, for the children of Israel prayed in the wilderness: 'May the Lord . . . provide a man that may be over this multitude . . . lest the people of the Lord be as sheep without a shepherd.'[24] An even more illustrious precedent for one-man rule than the leadership of Moses is

238

provided by the constitution of Heaven itself. Garnier's
Agrippa points the moral:

> As of heav'n one only lord we know
> One only lord should rule this earth below.[25]

Cleopatra, in trying to obstruct Octavius's attempt at world
domination, is not only seditious but heretical as well, impi-
ously challenging monotheism. 'He who contemns his sovereign prince,' wrote Bodin, 'contemns God whose image he
is.'[26]

The religious justification for monarchy is close to, and
often mingles with, the argument from nature. As well as his
*Marc-Antoine* Garnier wrote a *Hymne de la Monarchie* in
which he likens a kingdom to a beehive, a well-organized
community whose inmates are all devoted to their queen and
industrious in working for her – and therefore indirectly for
their own – benefit.[27] In Capponi's play one of Cleopatra's
servants likens the greatness of princes to the sun, which
gives warmth, and to a great oak tree, which gives shelter
and which, if uprooted, brings down many smaller plants
with it.[28] Most symbolically potent of all the models from
'nature' adduced for monarchy was that of the patriarchal
human family. 'Do we not find', wrote Filmer, 'that in every
family the government of one alone is natural?' Adam, the
first father, was, in Filmer's view, the first king. After the
Flood, when the people were dispersed over the face of the
Earth, each group had its patriarch, and it is from those
patriarchs that all modern kings were descended. 'There is,
and always shall be continued to the end of the world, a
natural right of supreme father over every multitude.'[29]

In flouting Octavius's authority Cleopatra and Antony are
thus rebel children, in revolt both against a would-be patriarch (the historical Octavius, having defeated them, was
accorded the honorary title of 'Father of the Roman People')
and against the sacred institution of the family, paradigm of
the state. Adulterous and apparently childless (only rarely is
their parenthood acknowledged by writers or painters), they
fit this role well. Philosophers and politicians from Aristotle

to Margaret Thatcher have perceived the affinity between the hierarchical family and centralized government. Cleopatra, the marriage-breaker, and Antony, the unfaithful spouse, raise a rebellion at a point where sexual and constitutional politics intersect. When Octavius claims, as he frequently does in the plays, that he has gone to war in order to avenge the insult to his wronged sister Octavia, the assertion is not always hypocritical. In refusing to take his place in a patriarchally structured family, and choosing instead to ally himself with the alarmingly family-less Cleopatra, Antony has offended not only against Octavius's personal pride but also against his political creed, for, as Bodin pointed out, the family, which 'has only one head', is 'the true image'[30] of the autocratic state.

If Octavius (and Cleopatra in her character as Queen) represent monarchy and Antony (and Cleopatra in her character as his partner) represent aristocratic oligarchy, it is left to subsidiary characters in the plays about them to speak for the third option recognized by political theorists – democracy. Sedley's Caesar (Octavius) declares:

> To set all right I must be absolute
> My last commands none daring to dispute[31]

while Antony is a Coriolanus-like tyrant in the making. When an attendant lord reminds him:

> 'Tis ill to discontent whom we must use
> And men fight best when they their party chose

he replies testily: 'Maxims too popular you still maintain. . . . The rabble is a thing below my hate.'[32]

Cleopatra, Julius Caesar, Octavius and Antony all in their different ways embodied forms of power unacceptable to seventeenth- and eighteenth-century egalitarians. The voice of democracy in the plays that tell their story is a humble and often a defeated one. Significantly, it is often given to Egyptians. In Sedley's play, and in Dryden's *All for Love*, it is members of the subjected race who speak out against

240

tyranny. The rights of the individual in a democratic state and the right of nations to self-determination are thus juxtaposed.

> Had I my wish, these tyrants of all nature,
> Who lord it o'er mankind, should perish, – perish,
> Each by the other's sword[33]

Thus Dryden's Alexas. In May's play two Egyptians discuss the Roman civil wars and agree that they are just retribution for Roman empire-building. Rome's attempt to conquer the world has 'dyed all regions with their native's blood'.[34] Thus, in a few fleeting conversations between minor characters, the ethics of imperialism are introduced into Cleopatra's legend.

In none of these discussions does Cleopatra herself participate. Neither a silly household dove nor a pleasure-bent whore can be expected to take an interest in political theory. The Cleopatra who was believed to have conducted her own diplomacy in nine languages, and whom the Alexandrian philosophers deemed a worthy disputant, had been replaced by a pretty fool who used state documents as curling papers. But although Cleopatra is not judged capable of comprehending abstractions, she can represent one. Whether perceived, with Antony, as an aristocrat or, on her own, as a monarch, she embodies the principle of heredity, and thus stands squarely at the centre of the political argument which runs through so many of the versions of her story.

Of the few remarks relating to Cleopatra's story that Plutarch reports, none has been so often repeated as Charmian's comment on her mistress's suicide, 'It is well done, and fitting for a princess descended of so many royal kings.'[35] Cleopatra, as representative of a venerable dynasty, is 'noble', a word which means primarily 'illustrious by rank, title or birth' but which, from the beginning of the sixteenth century, had begun to acquire the secondary meaning 'having high moral qualities or ideals; of a great or lofty character'.[36] The newer usage marks not a new snobbery, but rather a new awareness and questioning of a very ancient one. Throughout the Middle Ages to say that someone was 'illustrious by rank, title or birth' was automatically to suggest that he or she was possessed of 'a great or lofty character' – there was no separation between the two concepts. La Calprenède's prose fiction, *Cléopâtre*, is a doubly anachronistic work. It is both a very early novel and a very late romance, and it preserves values typical of the chivalric period. After describing the love of Cleopatra and Julius Caesar, La Calprenède goes on to tell the story of Britomarus, a young man of peerless beauty and exquisitely refined manners, a bold horseman, invincible in the jousting ring, tenderly respectful of ladies. This paragon, being apparently humbly born, is not permitted to fight a duel with the prince or to marry the princess, much though he loves her. At no point is it suggested that there is any injustice involved in describing such an admirable person as 'base' or 'vile' because of an accident of birth. Britomarus's only misfortune is that the other characters are all too obtuse to realize that a young man of such sterling qualities must, of course, be a prince in disguise. Such is the stuff of romance. Of such, also, is a tragedy made. Cleopatra's high social class makes her a fit tragic heroine, for all her sins. For tragedy, according to Aristotle and his Renaissance imitators, requires a central character whose exalted position will render his or her fall (like that of Capponi's oak tree) pitiable and terrifying.

So two of the dominant forms of European literature helped to preserve an anachronistic value system, that of a pre-Christian warrior-aristocracy, into a culture which only very slowly learnt to criticize it. In 1528 Castiglione asked whether noble birth is not 'Rather a praise of our ancestors than our own?'[37] Over the next two centuries the question was to be repeatedly posed, but not conclusively answered. Corneille's Caesar declares that Roman virtues include 'the hatred of name and the scorn of rank',[38] and Colley Cibber's Caesar tells Cleopatra's brother that he disdains inherited titles, 'What heirs from heirs receive, blind fortune gives',[39] but this apparent egalitarianism is not to be taken seriously. In both plays Cleopatra's exalted spirit is perceived to match, and be consequent upon, her high birth.

Greatness does not always accord with goodness, or with

political rectitude: the hero is not necessarily a saint. Just as the suicide was both condemned and admired, so the arrogance of a great personage can win respect even from a democrat. And as the concept of greatness escapes Christian morality, so it can cancel conventional gender. 'To be a prince,' says Daniel's Octavius, 'is more than be a man.'[40] He is referring to Cleopatra. In the plays in which her royalty is her defining characteristic, Cleopatra is less than usually hampered by womanly weakness. Feminine faults – feebleness, timidity, pettiness and duplicity – are the failings of an under-class. Cleopatra, when identified as a 'prince', is discovered to be free of them – a hint (which none of the playwrights took) that these perceived deficiencies of womankind might be the consequence, rather than the cause, of their inferior social status.

Queenly Cleopatras are brave. 'Think of thy birth,' Fletcher's Cleopatra urges Arsinoe as a terrifying battle rages outside their palace. The royal sisters remain calm, but their servant is distraught with fear:

You that were born
Daughters and sisters until kings, may nourish
Great thoughts which I, that am your humble handmaid
Must not presume to rival.

When Ptolemy's copse is brought in Arsinoe weeps at the sight, to Cleopatra's displeasure. 'Common people do so. . . . Study to die nobly.'[41]

The high-born Cleopatras' courage is linked to what Corneille's Charmian calls 'A noble and proper pride'.[42] A great Cleopatra will never abdicate.

To one who was born to rule, the servile life
Is more abhorrent than death[43]

says Cleopatra's councillor in Capponi's play. Daniel, de Benserade, Sedley, Marmontel and Delfino all assure us, through a variety of spokespeople, that Cleopatra is too well-born to think of resigning her kingdom and, sure enough, in play after play, she dies rather than do so, often for no

243

better reason than that to surrender would be 'vile'. This intransigence firmly identifies her with her constitutional function. Her personal greatness, her honour, has no autonomous, absolute existence: it depends entirely on her retaining her high social and political place. Sedley's Antony insists: 'Princes have no retirement but their graves.'[44] 'No one', declares Cardinal Delfino's Cleopatra, 'will ever see this head, accustomed to wear a crown, bow to any lesser power than death.'[45] Born rulers cannot consent to be governed by another, like any ordinary mortal; they cannot admit themselves to be in the wrong or the foundation of their power to be unjust. Thus insisting on a royal role long after it has become practically untenable, these Cleopatras give evidence of pride, that deadly sin that has always, in secular circles, been inordinately admired.

Their pride obliges these royal Cleopatras to be true to themselves and to their rank. It also requires them to be true, within a clearly prescribed code of honour, to those around them. In particular they are meticulous in their observation of the laws of hospitality. Mairet's Cleopatra explains to Octavius, who accepts her explanation, that she could not but support Antony while he was with her in Egypt. It was her duty as hostess to lend him every assistance. Corneille's Cleopatra is aghast when she hears that her brother Ptolemy is intending to kill Pompey, a guest in their country. Such a treacherous and ignoble plan cannot, she is sure, have originated with him: 'Everything in princes is illustrious, when they trust their own judgement.' Young Ptolemy must reject the evil counsels of his base-born regents Achillas and Photinus, and trust instead to

> That lofty virtue with which the heavens and our blood
> Always fill the heart of those of our rank.[46]

Physical courage, an inflexible insistence on hierarchical rank, open-handed hospitality – 'greatness', as it was understood in the seventeenth- and eighteenth-centuries and as it is still largely understood today – is a quintessentially masculine and military form of virtue, defined by a primitive and immeasurably ancient code. Homer's Achilles, sulking in his tent because Agamemnon had slighted him, was 'great' in much the same way as the Cleopatras who will lay down their lives (and, incidentally, those of their servants and supporters) rather than be less than queen. The romantic and tragic literature that has perpetuated this ideal of greatness has preserved in Western culture a code of conduct and morality evolved by nomadic warrior peoples, whose cohesion depended on loyalty to chiefs, for whom physical courage and prowess at arms were prerequisites for survival, and who had repeatedly to trust to the forbearance and generosity of those neighbouring tribes into whose territory they wandered. The notion of honour they evolved, surviving – however quaintly – into modern Western culture, shapes the image of our imaginary heroes. It also, sometimes dangerously, often unfairly, affects our political institutions.

Cleopatra, as a royal personage, is set apart from others: the blood royal flinches from contact with any that is less blue. Fletcher's Pothinus proposes marriage to Cleopatra, only to be indignantly dismissed as a 'sea of rudeness... baser than thy birth'.[47] In Capponi's play Dolabella presumes to believe that Cleopatra is attracted to him. She mocks him for his risible failure to understand that she will never stoop to a plebeian love.[48] Sedley's Cleopatra is equally plagued by an impertinent commoner, Thyreus, whose declaration of love she sharply snubs: 'Romans but ill the heart of monarchs know.'[49] Like the real Cleopatra's forebears, who disdained to marry any but their own siblings, these imaginary Cleopatras feel themselves to belong to a race apart. The Great are a separate species: they cannot cross-breed with humans of ordinary stock.

The idea that those not royally or nobly born are essentially, not just circumstantially, different from their so-called betters has obvious political ramifications. And it is in this context that Cleopatra, in the plays of the seventeenth and eighteenth centuries, frequently bears silent witness to a crucial argument in the debate between democrats and authoritarians. Aristotle believed humanity to be divided into those who were 'by nature ruler and by nature master' and those who were 'by nature slave'.[50] Bodin went much further. 'The bad and vicious, who are the great majority' must, he wrote, be denied advancement. 'The ability to command cannot be made equal, as the citizens of popular states desire, for we all know that some have no more judgement than brute beasts, while in others the illumination of divine reason is such that they seem angels rather than men.'[51] The imaginary Cleopatras, who, because their blood is royal, are so much braver, prouder and more punctiliously honourable than a commoner could be, demonstrate that inequality. Thus Cleopatra is made tacitly to endorse the widespread belief that certain qualities are class-determined and hereditarily transmitted, and that therefore the government of a country can only safely be entrusted to members of the already-ruling class.

The 'lofty virtue' of which Corneille's Cleopatra spoke is always attendant on royalty, but it is not quite royalty's exclusive prerogative. Military and political success can confer it when enhanced by wealth. It is possible for a commoner to be great – provided, that is, he has a private income. 'Base mercenary souls who fight for pay,'[52] as Sedley's Cleopatra remarks, are not to be trusted: the self-interest necessary to earn a living makes them suspect. But the grandees of Rome, Julius Caesar, Antony and Octavius, can be understood to meet Cleopatra on equal terms, for the freemasonry of enormous power transcends distinctions between monarchy and aristocracy. Corneille's Caesar may declare his hatred of titles and his abhorrence of rank, and Colley Cibber's proclaim his republicanism, but in both plays Cleopatra is quite right in supposing that, like her, Caesar will be noble enough to condemn the murder of Pompey. Greatness can be gained by conquest as well as by inheritance. In this it resembles wealth, and indeed the two concepts overlap both in actuality (money confers power, power can command money) and in symbolic representation. The ancient tradition of the great lord as dispenser of munificent hospitality neatly illustrates that association; so does the story of Cleopatra's banquet, where she demonstrated both her vast wealth and her aristocratic carelessness by drinking her pearl.

Cleopatra's banquet was an immensely popular subject for painters throughout the two hundred years that preceded the French Revolution. In sequences of tapestries designed to be hung in palatial banqueting halls and to set the mood for real-life feasts the theme is elaborated with gusto and splendour. A Flemish tapestry of the seventeenth century shows a pretty, if vacuous-looking, fair-haired Cleopatra entertaining Antony *al fresco* beneath a tasselled canopy hoisted between blossoming trees.[53] The table, and the ground beneath it, are scattered with roses and carnations. Merry pages bring bowls of apples and pears. The whole composition is framed in a garland of fruit and flowers, emblematic of pleasure and plenty. This straightforward celebration of sensuous enjoyment, though, was only one aspect of Cleopatra's banquet. Entertaining and ostentation have always gone hand in hand. A feast is a fine occasion for the parade of wealth, and Cleopatra's fabulously expensive meal is as deliberate a piece of conspicuous waste as that of the millionaire of modern folklore who lights his cigar with hundred-dollar bills.

'Make this capital beautiful,' Dio Cassius's Maecenas advises his Octavius. 'Spare no expense in doing so, and enhance its magnificence with festivals of every kind. It is right for us, who rule over so many peoples, to excel all others in every field of endeavour and even display of this kind tends to implant respect for us in our allies and to strike terror into our enemies.'[54] Power, displayed in the form of wealth, lavish feasts, splendid buildings and gorgeous clothing, inspires awe and thus multiplies itself. Actual power provides the wherewithal for the spectacle of power, and the perception of that spectacular power in turn generates more actual power in a self-fulfilling process exceedingly pleasing to the potentate whose wealth and status are thus simultaneously displayed and augmented. Laura D'Este, one of seventeenth-century Italy's greatest ladies, had herself painted as Cleopatra. She looks out of Baciccio's portrait with a coolly level gaze. Dropping a pearl the size of a quail's egg into a golden bowl, she demonstrates that she is enormously rich. And the crown left negligently on the gilt and marble table beside her confirms the maxim that the whole composition silently asserts, that to be rich is to rule.[55]

The seventeenth- and eighteenth-centuries painted Cleopatras – imagined, nearly all of them, for the benefit of wealthy patrons who liked to see the worldly magnificence in which they themselves had a share so glorified – wear dresses of brocade, silk damask and fine gauze. Their sleeves are trimmed with ermine or deep ruffles of lace. Their hair is bound with pearls, their bodies are suspended on shoulder-straps of gold, their necklines are encrusted with emeralds and rubies. Their sumptuous toilettes, which they are depicted alone, fill the picture space with billowing masses of expensive stuff. Their setting not only proclaims their royal, or aristocratic, grandeur – it also advertises their money. In a number of paintings, of which that by Trevisani is representative, Cleopatra appears surrounded by profuse quantities of gold plate. Walls are hung with gleaming salvers. Ewers and basins stand on the floor, while the table is loaded with chased goblets and massive dishes, all of gold. The golden dinner services of Alexandria still exerted their fascination, and to the wealthy patrons who commissioned or bought these paintings they were esteemed not for their fabulous strangeness, but for the pleasing way in which they duplicated the patron's own possessions.

The Labia family, who commissioned Giambattista Tiepolo to paint a cycle of frescoes on the subject of Cleopatra, were *nouveau riche* textile merchants who had paid a substantial bribe to have their name included in the Golden Book of the Venetian nobility. They were noted for their flamboyance, and also for their bragging. A forebear of Tiepolo's patron gave a fabled dinner party at which guests were served on gold plates, all of which was afterwards thrown into the canal.[56] Tiepolo imagined Cleopatra's table equally laden with precious metal (the sketch now in the National Gallery in London shows a buffet literally heaped with gold dishes). His patron, a widow who, like Cleopatra, was famous for her numerous and fabulously valuable jewels, must have enjoyed entertaining in a room decorated with images which so flatteringly juxtaposed her own munificence with that of the fascinating Egyptian queen.

The story of the royal Cleopatra and her two great lovers was an appropriate theme for courtly entertainment. It was repeatedly set to music, danced, sung or staged in extravagantly grand style. Seventeen 'music-dramas' on the theme are known to have been presented in Europe before the end of the eighteenth century, several of them with accompanying ballets. Some, like Fuzelier's *ballet héroique* performed in the King's apartments at Versailles in 1748, and in which the Duchesse de Brancas took the part of Cleopatra, were designed for a supremely select audience. Others were more popular: in the course of twenty years Antonio Sografi's opera *La Morte di Cleopatra* was staged three times in Venice, twice in London and once apiece in Verona, Trieste, Genoa, Modena, Naples, Parma and Paris. These works were distinguished increasingly by their lavish special effects. A French epigram of the 1750s makes fun of one production which featured a mechanical whistling asp.[57] Fuzelier's ballet, in which Cleopatra arrives on stage by boat, is adorned by dancing Egyptians, Bacchantes, male and female sailors and a twenty-piece orchestra. Henry Brooke's stage directions require Cleopatra to make her first appearance in 'a splendid galley' which sails down to the front of the stage and goes off through the wings to the accompaniment of flutes. When David Garrick revived Shakespeare's tragedy in 1759 a reviewer remarked that it was better not to read the play (which suited ill with English eighteenth-century taste) but to see it in the theatre where 'scenery, dresses and parade strike the eye, and divert one's attention from the poet'.[58]

The parade of wealth and class-defined greatness was unfailingly gratifying to the rich and aristocratic audiences of *ancien régime* Europe. Patrons could take pleasure, as they contemplated Cleopatra's picture on their walls, in the reflection that they, like her, could claim glamorous and laudable virtues as part of their birthright, and that, also like her, they could command the means to exact the deference, and control the destinies, of their economic and social inferiors. Or so they believed. But display, however magnificent, is a representation of political power, not the thing itself, as events from the real Cleopatra's career vividly demonstrate. When Cleopatra sat on a golden throne on a silver dais in the stadium at Alexandria and Antony proclaimed her Queen of Kings they were enacting a kind of magical charade, simulating not what they actually were but what they wished to be. The gold and silver were real enough, but the vast empire they seemed to signify had yet to be conquered. Octavius, less 'great' but in this respect more shrewd, gave his power no outward form. Abjuring the name of king, he made himself infinitely more powerful than any monarch in the empire he ruled. Like a Colbert, unostentatiously controlling France while the great nobles devoted themselves to fêtes and ballets, he was happy to forgo the simulacrum of glory in order to achieve its reality. 'These are not days in which monarchs value themselves upon the title of *great*,' wrote Edmund Burke in 1796. 'They are grown philosophic: they are satisfied to be good.'[59] And so, in the period culminating in the French Revolution, the blue-blooded aristocracy of Europe, the great families, heirs of a long anachronistic warrior élite, were gradually supplanted by humbly born civil servants, bourgeois plutocrats and middle-class intellectuals who perceived the irrationality of their claims to greatness. When Colley Cibber's Achoreus comments on Cleopatra's majestic bearing, her gracious manner and her nobly dauntless spirit, Pothinus's response is sharply cynical:

> All dissembled!
> Train'd up in courts, she knows to mask her malice.[60]

Cibber does not suggest we should pay much attention to the opinion of Pothinus, who is merely a 'vile Egyptian', but he has allowed him to articulate what was, by the middle of the eighteenth century, an increasingly prevalent suspicion — that aristocratic grandeur, and even the very notion of class-

determined greatness, were insubstantial constructions of
tinsel, not of true gold.

# 8

# THE FOREIGNER

WHEN JULIUS CAESAR went to Egypt, so wrote the Romantic historian Jules Michelet in 1831, he 'yearned to penetrate the mute and mysterious world of Upper Asia'. To Michelet Cleopatra embodied that world. The East 'appeared entire in the Queen'.[1] In Cleopatra's own lifetime Octavius had fashioned her story as one of East–West antagonism – of the subjugation of feckless Orientals by a race of divinely appointed imperialists – while also, inadvertently, creating the seductive fantasy of an Elsewhere characterized by luxury and limitless sexual opportunity. Nearly two millennia later, as the Ottoman Empire fragmented and Westerners again turned greedy eyes eastward, that significance of Cleopatra's story acquired fresh currency. In the nineteenth-century European imagination Cleopatra once more comes to signify, first and foremost, the Orient. Mute (for a fantasy can speak only with the voice of its creator), alluringly mysterious, she reclines among cushions or on barges of rich, outlandish workmanship, waiting, like Asia, to be penetrated.

The European writers and artists who reimagined Cleopatra before 1800 were seldom preoccupied with her foreignness. Shakespeare made brilliant dramatic use of the essential difference between her court and that of Rome, but the Orientalist style of most modern productions of his plays is anachronistic. 'Cut my lace,' says his Cleopatra, who would have been dressed in the first production, just like the Roman Octavia, in a farthingale.[2] Some writers puzzled over the conundrum presented by her complexion. No reliable

252

description of the historical Cleopatra's colouring has come down to us – as a Macedonian she may have been quite fair – but a few Western interpreters were haunted by the possibility that, as a north African queen, she might have been as black as Othello the Moor. Robert Greene, writing in 1589, used the fact that Antony was 'enamoured of the black Egyptian Cleopatra' as evidence that 'affection is oft blind and deemeth not rightly, the blackest ebon is brighter than the whitest ivory',[3] for to those Europeans who believed Cleopatra to be dark-skinned it seemed evident that this should make her unattractive.

> Her sun-burnt beauty cannot please his sight
> That hath a mind with any reason fraught[4]

opines Samuel Brandon's Plancus.

> Our Egyptian dames are born too near
> The glowing sun, to boast of Roman luster

says Cibber's Cleopatra, modestly refusing to believe that Caesar can find her beautiful.[5] These remarks signal an obstruction in the way of those who wished to reanimate Cleopatra's legend. Her reputation for beauty, though unsupported by any historical evidence, was unassailable, but it was not consonant with the possibility of her being anything other than a light-skinned European lady, for in fiction beauty (as distinct from sexual magnetism) has traditionally been the prerogative of social and ethnic élites. The problem was insoluble: the vast majority of pre-nineteenth-century writers and artists simply circumvented it by abolishing Cleopatra's foreignness and changing her appearance to suit their own ideals.

In the medieval chronicle *Li Fait des Romains*, Cleopatra, 'the loveliest woman in the world', has long, thick, yellow-gold hair.[6] In Guillaume Belliard's charming sixteenth-century erotic poem, 'Les Delitieuses Amours de Marc Antoine et de Cléopâtre', her whiteness is said to outshine the whitest ivory, the brightness of her yellow hair makes gold seem dark by comparison, her rosy cheeks are more brilliant than all the flowers of spring and her breasts are as round and firm and pale as a pair of ivory billiard balls.[7] Garnier's heroine, that loving and heroic wife, has hair of 'fine flaming gold', and de Benserade's is blessed with a complexion in which the 'rose and the lily mingle'.[8]

The Renaissance and baroque painters, by the same logic (or lack of it), depicted Cleopatra as a beauty of their own times and places. Tiepolo's Cleopatra, in common with dozens of others, has strawberry blonde curls, glass-blue eyes and nacreously glimmering neck and breasts. Her attendants wear headdresses of vaguely Turkish or Jewish character, but this dressing-up is perfunctory. The architectural frame is Renaissance-classical, Cleopatra's clothes are in the height of eighteenth-century Italian fashion, and she herself is almost identical to Tiepolo's depiction of Beatrice of Burgundy in his *Marriage of Frederick Barbarossa*. To the Venetian artist, as to most of his contemporaries, Cleopatra was a great lady much like any other, united in power and wealth to Europeans of the same rank, an exalted being but not a distant one. Such Cleopatras are queens of Egypt, but their non-European home is not much remarked on. It does not make them so different from their Western creators as to be mysterious. It does not automatically endow them with the set of characteristics (cruelty, idleness, sexual voracity) typical of the Orientalist Cleopatras of the post-Romantic period. It neither confers glamour nor arouses suspicion. The exoticism which now seems so inseparable a part of Cleopatra's image has only accrued to it since the beginning of the nineteenth century.

Very rapidly, around the beginning of the last century, Cleopatra and her world receded from Europe, becoming distant and unfathomably strange. The scholars and poets of the eighteenth-century Enlightenment had aimed at a kind of universal philosophical containment, an all-encompassing intellectual system which would make it possible to know and understand all the world and its people; the new Romantic sensibility, on the other hand, seemed bent on discovering difference, on alienating the feeling subject from the world

254

in order to set up a space between them, a space where the imagination might rule. Reality was too confined – some other sphere, quite unlike it, must be found if the free spirit was to find room to move. 'Hell or Heaven, what does it matter?' cried Baudelaire. 'To the depths of the unknown in search of the *new*!'[9] The writers and artists of nineteenth-century Europe sought that novelty in their own dreams, in Heaven, in opium, in a variety of Utopias – and in the East. Above all (for they were mostly male), they sought it in women, the strangers in their midst. Once again Cleopatra and her country come to represent the antithetical domain of the feminine in the fantasies of the West, self-designated sphere of masculinity. As a woman, and as an Oriental, she offers strangeness and the inscrutable vacancy of imagined space. 'Only in the East', proclaims Michelet's Napoleon, 'can one work on a great scale.' The same author's Cleopatra rules an Alexandria which is no longer one of the originating centres of European culture but has become instead 'a caravansery . . . the centre of the Eastern world'; and her story, hitherto part of the body of classical history and legend which formed the proper subject matter for European art, has been transformed into something occult, alien, far off both in space and time: 'the eastern myth of the serpent, which we find in the most ancient traditions of Asia'.[10]

This remarkable shift in the status of Cleopatra's story clearly mirrors a profound alteration in the way that Westerners viewed the East. That change in perception coincides with a change in actual political relations. Recent scholars like Edward Said, Norman Daniel, Alain Grosrichard and Rana Kabbani have traced the intricate connection between the Western art and literature of Orientalism and the Western practice of placing Eastern people under subjection. The period in which Cleopatra ceases to be primarily a great lady and reappears as an exotic alien saw both the burgeoning of the Romantic cult of nationalism and the endeavours of historians and anthropologists like the Comte de Gobineau, C. Meiners and Baldung Niebuhr to evolve a 'progressive' theory which suggested that non-white races were socially, politically and morally retarded by comparison with Westerners.[11] These theories grew up alongside European imperialism. It is not within the scope of this book to explore the complex interplay between theory and policy, to ask to what extent the policy predetermined the theory, and to what extent the theory enabled the policy. But whichever came first, the chicken and the egg were both present by the time Cleopatra became a foreigner. Western suspicion of, and fascination with, the East were by no means brand-new phenomena. Both were already lively in Cleopatra's own lifetime. But the combination of Romantic taste and imperialist politics gave them new prominence. By the second decade of the nineteenth century the countries of the eastern Mediterranean, with whom Europe had long traded, fought and corresponded, from whom Europeans had borrowed their mathematics, their textile design and their religion, had become, in versions of the Cleopatra story, weird and distant places, full of strangers whose differences from the people of the West far outweighed the links of common humanity and a largely common culture.

This cultural phenomenon has been analysed, most notably by Edward Said, in the context of racial and territorial politics. But, as Said recognized, 'Orientalism' is a discourse not only of empire, but also of desire. The imagined East, like an imagined woman, is shaped to satisfy the longings of those who imagine it/her. The nineteenth-century Cleopatra, like the visionary Queen of Sheba who tempts Flaubert's St Antony, is both a woman and a world. Henry Houssaye, attempting to describe Cleopatra in his biography of 1889, invited his readers to 'Imagine Asiatic pomp, Egyptian grandeur, the refinement of Rome, all united in a single woman, sensual and magnificent, madly intent on pleasure and luxury'.[12] To Henri Blaze de Bury, writing in 1875, she was 'the incarnation of the poetry of a world in which all principles were abandoned – all that beauty without reserve, spirit without consciousness of duty, passion without check, can bring forth of brilliance and shadow, of love, of intoxication, and of impurity'.[13] A love affair with such a Cleopatra

256

is sexual possession: it is also, simultaneously, geographical exploration and political conquest. She is the Orient; the Orient is female. In representations of her in this period, as in those Roman ones produced in her own lifetime, there is a ceaseless shimmering as the twin discourses of racial politics and eroticism overlay and alternate with each other. And behind both lies a third layer of meaning. Beautiful woman and exotic country both symbolize a longed-for escape, or exaltation, to a condition of being more passionate, more vivid, more careless than that offered by drab diurnal existence.

The East inhabited by the Cleopatras of Pushkin, Gautier, Swinburne, Victor Hugo, Rider Haggard and a host of other, lesser-known writers, and of painters like Lawrence Alma-Tadema, J. Gérôme and Gustave Moreau, is an imaginary place. Ingres's *Le Bain Turc*, one of the most famous and influential of Orientalist artworks, was painted in Paris by a man who had never left Europe. Gautier became enamoured of the East not after travelling in Asia, but after seeing Prosper Marilhat's picture *La Place de L'Esbekieh au Caire*. 'This painting . . . inspired in me a nostalgia for an Orient in which I have never set foot. I believed that I had just then discovered my true home-land.'[14] The imagined realm which could inspire such yearning was designed precisely to accommodate those who conjured it up. Gustave Flaubert intuitively grasped the European Orientalists' use of the East when he wrote of Egypt, 'it seemed like . . . an immense stage set made expressly for us'.[15] Gérard de Nerval, one of the few Romantic Orientalists who attempted to measure the actuality against the dream by travelling extensively, sadly concluded that the dream and reality were hopelessly mismatched. His often-quoted remark to Gautier contains both realist humour and a sensitive appreciation of the psychological needs which kept the Orientalist fantasy alive: 'For a person who has never seen the Orient . . . a lotus is still a lotus; for me it is only a kind of onion.'[16]

Onion-reality is no substitute for the lotus of the mind. The imagined Orient is fascinating precisely because it is a

257

mirage. It is both pornographic and mystical. It proposes an alternative world where desire can be satisfied and commandments transgressed, where, though experience is intensely sensual, dull materialist cares vanish, a place where rapture is possible. 'What we have to describe,' wrote Théophile Gautier in 1845,

> is a supreme orgy, a feast to make Balthasar's seem pale, a night with Cleopatra. How, in chaste, icily prudish French, can we express that frantic transport, that vast and potent debauch in which the twin purples of wine and blood are fearlessly mingled, those furious surges of ever-yearning pleasure careering on, with all the ardour of a sensuality not yet curbed by the long fast of Christianity, in pursuit of the impossible![17]

Gautier's Cleopatra is an erotic fantasy figure, but the desire that this fantasy articulates is not restricted to a sexual object, it is a quasi-religious craving for something which, being negatively defined, is thrillingly limitless. To Gautier, and to many others like him, Cleopatra and her world represent everything which is not-here, not-us, not-known, not-possible. A remark supposedly overheard at a London performance of Victorien Sardou's play, in which Sarah Bernhardt played Cleopatra, is revealing; the probably apocryphal theatre-goer is said to have commented: 'How unlike – how so unlike – the home life of our own dear Queen!' The remark is smug, it expresses a complacent sense of 'our own' moral superiority, but it also hints that Cleopatra's attraction lies precisely in her unlikeness, in her embodiment of everything that Victorian England (or bourgeois France) denied. The other is not only the adversary. She/he/it is also the promised consummation of all unconsummatable desire.

The other might be a geographical space; it might equally well be a woman, for women, like foreigners, were strange to Western men and the realms of the East, like women, invited penetration and possession. The medal struck to commemorate Napoleon's expedition to Egypt in 1798 shows a Roman general unveiling an Oriental queen.[18] Edward Lane, travelling to Egypt for the first time in the 1830s, noted that, 'As I approached the shore, I felt like an Eastern bridegroom, about to life the veil of his bride, and to see, for the first time, the features that were to charm, or disappoint, or disgust him.'[19] In 1833 Prosper Enfantin, leader of the Utopian socialist St Simonians, arrived in Egypt intent on unifying East and West. This union was to be solemnized when Enfantin, the 'father', married a mysterious 'mother' in the East, and its concrete demonstration would be the building of the Suez Canal which, in rupturing the membrane of land which divided Asia from Europe, would consummate this extraordinary erotico-geographic union. 'Suez is the centre of our life work,' proclaimed Enfantin. 'We shall carry out the act for which the world is waiting to proclaim that we are male!'[20] Such references are legion. The image of an Eastern country as a woman and of a Western male – whether military aggressor, mystic, scholar or tourist – as her heterosexual lover is one so commonplace as to pervade all Western thinking about the East. For nineteenth-century Europeans, as for the Romans of Cleopatra's era, the rhetoric of imperialism and of heterosexuality are inextricably entwined.

In Alfred O'Shaughnessy's poem 'An Epic of Women', Cleopatra tempts Antony by displaying to him

> a splendid pageantry of all her East
> Beauteous and captive.

Amid heaps of jewels, silver dishes and feathered fans stand dark-eyed handmaidens, 'Their captive arms enchained with gold',[21] mute embodiments of the gratification that Cleopatra, monarch of a nation doomed to subjection, offers to those who master her. In Antonio Sografi's libretto *La Morte di Cleopatra* the Queen is brought in chains before her Western conqueror. Octavius, who secretly lusts after her, reminds her that her life, her liberty and her royal splendour are in his hand. 'I have subdued Egypt. Only a woman still stops the course of my glories. She must be conquered.'[22] Cleopatra epitomizes the triumph for which he thirsts. To possess her sexually will confirm and complete his possession of her territory. For spectators the vision of her thus in bondage is a piquant and titillating image of the subjection of Asia by Europe. This is the tableau in which, according to the usual story, Cleopatra died rather than participate. In it an erotic code is used to represent a political reality: the pornographic image of a woman bound and helpless becomes the metaphor for a conquered country.

The use of this erotic discourse represents a kind of wish-fulfilment, for sexual union, even sexual love, is possible in a way that the possession of one civilization by the representatives of another is not, and sexual rapture does offer at least a temporary self-loss. Lovers, as Shakespeare's Antony found, can escape their own identity in a way that travellers cannot. As Horace, Cleopatra's contemporary wrote, 'They change their sky, not their soul, who run across the sea.'[23] States can be, and frequently have been, annexed to empires, but the Western desire to absorb the essence of the imaginary East is as hopeless as an attempt to return to childhood, to Eden, or to last night's dream. Sexuality provides a vocabulary which will give expression to it while apparently offering some possible satisfaction.

The second act of Sardou's *Cléopâtre* opens on a banquet. Antony and his Roman officers recline on red leather cushions while slaves pour wine for them from golden jars. Musicians and acrobats entertain them. 'Enough of these jugglers,' cries Antony petulantly. 'Is there no snake-charmer here?' 'No, no! No snakes!' says Cleopatra, who has obviously had some kind of premonition. 'But rather my Nubian dancing-girls. Let them be called.' 'Reptiles of another sort!' remarks Antony with satisfaction when the dancers appear. 'I can hardly believe the suppleness of their curves.'[24] The interlude, unintentionally comic as it is, recalls a familiar twentieth-century scene, that of a group of tourists watching a self-consciously 'exotic' cabaret. Bored and ill at ease, the tourists fidget through the recitations and performances of regional songs but liven up when the belly dancer appears. So sex appears to provide the key whereby a strange place, whether it be a tourist's destination, a conquered province, or a yearned-after imaginary Erewhon/Nowhere, can be completely known, completely had. By concentrating in Cleopatra's person the essence of all the rich strangeness with which they surrounded her, nineteenth-century interpreters aimed to make it possible for Antony to possess not only herself but also the entire imaginary East in her.

That East, of course, bore little relation to the historical Cleopatra. Nineteenth-century Cleopatras tend to be curiously hybrid figures, Hellenistic queens to whom three anachronistic sets of conventional attributes have become attached. One is that of Pharaonic Egypt, smelling, as Algernon Swinbune has it, of 'that spice of cerecloths',[25] immeasurably old, enigmatic, morbid. Another is that of the Islamic Orient, increasingly accessible during this period to European visitors, whether colonialists or tourists, but still imagined as the realm of the souk and seraglio, full of gorgeous silks and doe-eyed dancing girls, despotic sultans, dark-skinned slaves and princesses under sentence of death sensuously divesting themselves of spangled veils and tinkling anklets (an Arabian Nights setting which would have surprised Cleopatra, a Macedonian who died six hundred years before Mahomet was born). The third, of course, is that of contemporary Europe, for in this period, as in all the others treated in this study, artists and writers depicted Cleopatra using the paints and props to hand in their own time. Nineteenth-century Cleopatras inhabit palaces cluttered with knick-knacks and curios, Turkish rugs and *chaises longues* in the Egyptian Revival style, just as the people who imagined them did. And, like the women of the society which generated them, these Cleopatras live for and through their men. 'Cleopatra's whole character,' wrote William Hazlitt in 1817, 'is the triumph of the voluptuous, of the love of pleasure and the power of giving it, over every other consideration.'[26] Such a Cleopatra may not be good, but she is nothing if not obliging.

'I have already lost, kingdom after kingdom, province after province, the more beautiful half of the universe . . . but it is Egypt that I most regret having driven out of my imagination, now that I have sadly placed it in my memory':[27] so wrote de Nerval of his travels. Egypt has long had a reputation as a garden of sexual delights. The preconceptions on which Octavius played when he attempted to provoke the Romans' disapproval for Cleopatra's supposedly dissolute court were already well entrenched, and they had a long life. An anonymous English traveller, whose account of his visit to Egypt was first published by Hakluyt in 1598, describes the Nile at Cairo in terms which suggest that the image of Cleopatra in her barge may have been in the back of his mind.

> There are innumberable barks rowing to and fro laden with gallant girls and beautiful dames, which with singing, eating, drinking and feasting, take their solace. The women of this country are most beautiful, and go in rich attire bedecked with gold, precious stones, and jewels of great value, but chiefly perfumed with odours, and are very libidinous, and the men likewise.[28]

The author does not name the sources of his information on the Egyptian libido; an observable taste for waterborne pleasure parties hardly seems adequate evidence. Later travellers made similar deductions from equally uncertain premises. In his *Manners and Customs of the Modern Egyptians*, published in 1836, Edward W. Lane notes that 'the women of Egypt have the character of being the most licentious in their feelings of all females who lay any claim to be considered as members of a civilized nation ... most of them are not considered safe unless under lock and key'. Such a 'character' was obviously as alluring as it was disreputable: in Egypt Lane bought, and subsequently married, a female slave.[29]

By the beginning of the nineteenth century Cleopatra's country shared this lascivious reputation in the West with the whole of the Middle East. Rana Kabbani has recently described the gradual eroticization of the West's imaginary Orient, which began with anti-Saracen slanders in the age of the Crusades, proceeded through curious travellers like Jean Chardin, who wrote in 1686 that the Oriental women were lazy and lascivious, given to lying all day long in bed, smoking while little slave girls massaged them,[30] to the first

European publication, in 1704, of *The Thousand and One Nights*. The enormous popular success of the latter propagated the view of the Orient to which Alexander Pope referred when he wrote to Lady Mary Wortley Montagu, then journeying eastward, 'I shall hear how the very first night you lay in Pera you had a vision of Mahomet's Paradise, and happily awaked without a soul. From that blessed instant the beautiful body was at full liberty to perform all the agreeable functions it was made for.'[31] Indolent, shameless, uninhibited by soul or Christian conscience, the stereotypical Oriental woman featured ever more frequently in Western erotic fantasy.

In part the association of the Orient with sexual licence arose from the belief, which is at least as old as Aristotle, that the inhabitants of sunny southern countries are more sensuous and self-indulgent than those reared in the bracing cold of the north. As Byron merrily remarked:

> What men call gallantry, and Gods adultery,
> Is much more common where the climate's sultry.[32]

Nineteenth-century Cleopatras are surrounded by black retainers, living reminders that they come from the passionate south. In Frederick Sandy's drawing of 1866 Cleopatra herself is glimmeringly white but behind her stand three negresses, of whom little can be seen but thick lips and frizzy hair, and at her feet a black male servant crouches. Sardou's Cleopatra explains that she is not like the Romans. 'Daughter of Egypt and Greece I am of another race. The African sun, which has gilded my brow, has kindled flames in my breast.'[33] The heroine of Delphine de Girardin's play, first performed in 1840 with the great Jewish actress Rachel in the title role, is bewilderingly bi-coloured. In the presence of the rosy-cheeked Octavia she is briefly ashamed of her 'burning pallor, sensuality's mark' but she blames the African sun 'which laughs at chastity' and makes blood run hot, which has 'stained my heart and blackened my brow'.[34]

The transcendent sexual pleasure that Cleopatra was supposedly capable of affording has been a part of her legend ever since Octavius derided Antony for preferring it to honour and his share of world power. Nineteenth-century Cleopatras, as sultry and ardent as the torrid countries they inhabit, offer their men ineffable delights. In Jean Cantel's gorgeously decadent romance, *La Reine Cléopâtre*, a scent of amber and cinnamon lingers about her and her breath is as heady as incense. Her lovely golden body palpitates beneath dresses of silver gauze. Her smile is suffused with the exquisite sweetness of every possible caress. Princes travel from the ends of the Earth seeking her love, which, so rumour has it, affords a rapture worth fortunes and kingdoms. A suitor, invited to her bed, approaches, through a succession of sumptuous antechambers, a room which seems to contain the very essence of feminine sensuousness. Three steps of jasper, a curtain of cloth-and-gold and two sleeping Ionian slave girls frame its entrance. When the man finally penetrates the innermost recess he finds himself in an all-white space both soft and dazzling, encircled by opals and alabaster, mother of pearl and polar bear skin, the snowy plumes of white ibis, ivory and diamond-spangled gauze. Opening her arms, the languid Cleopatra draws him down on to her bed, into an embrace which, we are led to understand, is as incomparably marvellous as its setting.[35] To know such transports men will gladly die.

Not only does Cleopatra hold out the promise of sexual rapture; she craves it. Like the seraglio, so fascinating to Western fantasists who pictured it filled with 'libidinous' but sex-starved houris, her court, inhabited chiefly by women and eunuchs, is feverish with frustrated female lust. When Gautier's Cleopatra becomes testy Charmian comments drily, 'It is easy to be seen that the queen has not had a lover . . . for a whole month.'[36] The Cleopatras of Alexander Pushkin's story, *Egyptian Nights*, and of Delphine de Girardin's play are fidgety and febrile when without a man. Sardou's, yearning in the stifling heat of Memphis for Antony, lies sleepless on a vast bronze bed on a terrace high above the town. The tantalizing sound of distant wedding music arouses her sexual envy. She raises herself 'in the attitude of a sphinx' to scan the horizon for a messenger, only to fall back tormented by reminders of her deprivation. 'Nothing, always nothing! As far as my eyes can see. ... Nothing but belated couples walking with slow steps and, with each kiss, calling the stars to witness their love.'[37] In a sonnet by Albert Samain the heaving of Cleopatra's breast, which lifts her heavy golden necklaces, betrays her 'mute fever'. The night is full of velvety enchantment, a rosy sunset touches the ancient monuments and crocodiles can be heard, weeping, in the distance. At last Cleopatra's amorous tension finds release. As she feels the lascivious and delicate touch of the wind, like hands caressing her hair, a great *frisson* seizes her and she sobs out wordless vows. In another of Samain's sonnets the night lies heavy on the Nile, the stars burn. Cleopatra turns abruptly pale, tears her tunic and flaunts her naked body 'swollen with love like a ripe fruit'. She shudders

> uncoiling to the warm
> Devouring wind, a serpent of desire.

And as she spreads the perfume of her flesh, 'dark flower of sex', on the night air, the Sphinx, becalmed on the sands of *ennui*, feels the desert move.[38]

This mood seizes Cleopatra, naturally, only when Antony (or Julius Caesar) is absent. It is when Cleopatra is alone with her exotic followers, with her eunuchs and slaves and vari-coloured waiting-women, when no vigorous Western male has come to satisfy her desire and give purpose to her idleness, that she is at her most voluptuous and abandoned. It is then that the image of her court most closely resembles the seraglio of fantasy – impenetrable, but crying out for penetration. For the East, womanlike, is incapable of looking after herself. Her 'mystery' is closely allied to her irrationality and capriciousness. She is indolent, inefficient and extravagant. Above all, her voracious sexuality makes her unhappy: she is tormented by the craving for an unknown master. If she is Cleopatra, then Cleopatra badly needs her Antony (or Caesar, or Octavius – any Western power will do) to ravish her, reorganize her and annex her to his vigorous, common-sensical empire.

The luxuriant erotic atmosphere of Cleopatra's court is stressed, in Orientalist versions of her story, by the profusion of beautiful and unfamiliar objects with which she is surrounded. In this period her story becomes a spectacle, a show laid on for the delectation of the Western spectator, one in which the pleasures of pornography, window-shopping and tourism are all combined. 'If ever a Shakespearean play called for music, processions and Tadema-like excesses in bathroom marble,' wrote the critic James Agate, '*Antony and Cleopatra* is that play.'[39] Directors have since proved him wrong (Adrian Noble's Royal Shakespeare Company production with Helen Mirren as Cleopatra, one of the most exciting of recent years, was played on a bare, dark stage), but no Romantic interpreter would have disputed his opinion. Hazlitt, in 1817, declared that Cleopatra personified 'Eastern magnificence', and magnificence was to remain a constant feature of her story. In paintings, in Shakespearean productions and in new plays, in poems, novels and operas (of which seventy on the theme are listed in Loewenborg's *Annals of Opera*), even in ostensibly sober historical works, the nineteenth-century Cleopatra appears at the centre of a spectacular tableau cluttered with exotic detail. Pyramids, pylons, obelisks and animal-headed idols surround her. Her furniture, all made of gold, ivory or rare, fragrant wood and encrusted with precious stones, is minutely itemized. Her attendants are ethnically diverse and picturesque: 'beaded women of a yellow Ind',[40] sambuca players, magicians and acrobats who dance naked with golden rattles. Nubile (or Nubian) slaves fan her with plumes of peacock and ostrich. She eats extraordinary delicacies – 'truffles as big as a fist which seemed to have fallen, like meteorites, from the sky', and fish cooked in a sauce of pulverized pearls. Her clothes are gorgeous, outlandish, fabulously expensive. Her rooms are draped with leopard skins or lined with mother-of-pearl. Her barge is built of jasper, lapis lazuli and alabaster. Her thrones are supported by solid gold sphinxes. Her letters are

266

carried by homing ibises. In her gardens tropical flowers exude heady, disturbing perfumes. She attends lion hunts and chariot races in stadia strewn with saffron and goes sailing on lakes of rosewater. Alexandria, her city, is a glittering metropolis, all marble and porphyry, where painted triremes discharge cargoes of spices and silk and where naked negresses dance in the taverns to the beat of the tympanum.[41]

Thus surrounded with things, the nineteenth-century Cleopatra herself is reified. She is presented as a spectacle, something to be viewed and coveted from the other side of a picture frame or proscenium arch. The more gorgeous and exotic her surroundings, the further away from the spectator she seems to move. An object of wonder, not a person to be loved or understood, she becomes both superficial and profoundly mysterious, a surface so dazzling that one cannot think of looking beyond it. So the viewer is absolved of responsibility for her. We need not seek to know what she wants, because she is not of our kind. A foreigner, and a sight for seeing, she is nothing to do with us.

Although she may not be known, she can be had. Just as Lucan reproved Cleopatra in the second century for entertaining Julius Caesar with rash magnificence, as though in parading her wealth and her personal beauty she was issuing an invitation to pillage and rape, so many of the post-Romantic interpreters of her story elided her regal hospitality with that of a prostitute, in which sexual invitation is implicit. Henry Houssaye dedicated his life of her to Alexandre Dumas, because the latter had created her 'avatar' the courtesan Marguerite Gautier, the Lady of the Camellias.[42] Théophile Gautier's Cleopatra is not too queenly to perform a lascivious dance, accompanying herself on castanets.[43] Sardou's promises Julius Caesar 'a coffer containing the most precious of the jewels in the royal treasury'. That jewel is herself, 'half-naked, lowering her great gazelle-like eyes and shivering, with fear perhaps, or perhaps with love'.[44] Later, to amuse Antony, she recites and mimes the story of the nymph Nitocris, who undressed to bathe in the Nile: 'Her tunic slithers down to fall around her feet . . . she twists the

267

silver lotus in her black hair'.[45] The performance amounts to a striptease: Sarah Bernhardt's admirers must have relished it. Gérôme's painting *Cleopatra before Caesar* shows the Queen in provocative dress. A gauzy skirt is split over each thigh to reveal her legs as high as her jewelled girdle. Her belly is bare, and her breasts are displayed by a sort of harness, which titillates by reversing expectation, proffering that which it might be expected to conceal. Caesar, seated at his ease, looks up from his writing as though coolly estimating whether this visitor is sufficiently diverting to justify the interruption to his work. Cleopatra's pose is haughty: but no amount of disdain can disguise the fact that the basic situation is that of a brothel, or of one of the slave markets which were stock subjects for Orientalist painters and about which, as Mark Twain remarked, 'we have all read so much – where tender young girls were stripped for inspection, and criticized, and discussed just as if they were horses at an agricultural fair'.[46] In Gérôme's painting the crouching attendant, swarthy and almost naked, pushes the carpet aside, as though unwrapping his wares for a critical customer. Cleopatra, however proudly and unwillingly, submits to this appraisal. Displayed both to the viewer and to Caesar she waits for approval and, assuming she will be fortunate enough to win favour, for a purchaser.

As a houri/whore, a woman who is both alien and an object to be bought and sold, the Orientalist Cleopatra is, like the imagined Orient, inscrutable. It is easy for the man who dreams of possessing her not to know her, to perceive her as a blank screen on to which his fantasies can be projected. Flaubert, visiting Egypt in 1850, spent a night with a dancing girl.

> Watching that beautiful creature asleep . . . my night was one long, infinitely intense reverie – that was why I stayed. I thought of my nights in Paris brothels – a whole series of old memories came back – and I thought of her, of her dance, of her voice as she sang songs that for me were without meaning and even without distinguishable words.[47]

The notion that the East (like womankind) is mysterious evidently arises from ignorance, an ignorance not easily remedied because those who confess it actually prefer it to knowledge. To attempt to understand foreigners, to learn their languages and study their culture, is to transform the lotus back into an onion. If Flaubert could have spoken to his one-night lover, if Baudelaire, who adored his black mistress's enigmatic stupidity, had taken the trouble to discover her state of mind, the fantasy would have vanished. Cleopatra, beautifully blank, is the more seductive the less you know her. Sardou's Antony is delighted to follow her up the Nile to Memphis: 'Your beauty seems more strange in the shade of these forests of granite or in the dazzling brilliance of burning horizons.' He finds her as intriguingly opaque as her country: 'Your deep eyes your enigmatic smile, your serpentine suppleness – you are truly Egyptian, Isis always veiled in shadows, living enigma, the Sphinx.'[48] In this she is the perfect erotic object. 'No one can ever really know an oriental woman,' wrote Flaubert of his *Salammbo*, 'the pedestal is too big for the statue.'[49] The pedestal was erected by Westerners who, having placed that doubly foreign creature, Asian Woman, on top of it, were free to conclude that intelligent communication was impossible and to sink into the desired sleep of reason, the ecstasy of the senses.

Mysterious Cleopatras are condemned to silence and stillness: any kind of animation would invalidate their promise. In Alma-Tadema's painting Cleopatra lolls on her barge in the dim light of a pavilion hung with silk and garlands of roses. Through the hangings we can see the world of life and sunlight where Antony, eager and curious, approaches. But Cleopatra, beautifully enervated, does not even turn her head. This extreme torpor clings insistently to Cleopatra's image. Incapacitated by a combination of genetic exhaustion and erotic languor, painted Cleopatras recline somnolently on cushions or lie prone on barges. Actresses who played her, from Bernhardt to Theda Bara, chose to be photographed posing in costume on *chaises longues*. In O'Shaughnessy's poem Cleopatra lies on a couch of Tyrian crimson, her

269

loosened vest pinned on one shoulder with a serpent brooch to reveal one white arm and 'half her foamy breast'. Her hair is 'like wine or music or kisses', and as she waits, inert, for Antony she sighs.[50]

The recumbent position suggests both sexual readiness and the state of mind that Sir Richard Burton described as the typically Oriental *kayf*:

> the savouring of animal existence; the passive enjoyment of mere sense; the pleasant langour, the dreamy tranquility, the airy castle-building, which in Asia stand in lieu of the vigorous inten- sive, passionate life of Europe ... it argues a voluptuousness unknown to northern regions, where happiness is placed in the exertion of mental and physical powers.[51]

In Cleopatra's case it is exaggerated both by her sex – for women, by long tradition, are understood to be essentially passive – and the fact that she is not only Oriental, she is Egyptian.

By the beginning of the nineteenth century ancient Egypt had come to be perceived by Westerners as a static, oppress- ively morbid culture. In his fascinating study of racist histori- ography, *Black Athena*, Martin Bernal charts the growth of this negative reputation. During the Renaissance the ancient wisdom of Egypt was venerated: in 1460 Cosimo de' Medici ordered Marsilio Ficino to lay aside his translation of Plato in favour of the more important task of translating the Hermetic Texts, the ancient philosophical and scientific writings ascribed variously to the Egyptian god Thoth and the legen- dary sage Hermes Trismegistus. In the seventeenth century Isaac Newton declared that it was from the ancient Egyptians that the Greeks 'derived their first and soundest notions of philosophy', and he dedicated himself to reconstructing the Egyptian system of measurement, believing that it would enable him to calculate the circumference of the world.[52] In the eighteenth century the freemasons adopted Egyptian symbols and built their lodges in Egyptian style. Finally, in the most extraordinary example of simultaneous actual and cultural conquest, Napoleon went to Egypt in 1798, taking with him not only troops but also a whole academy of historians, topographers, mathematicians and archaeologists in a dramatic attempt to appropriate a whole country, past as well as present, ancient art and science as well as modern wealth and power, to his growing empire.

Napoleon's expedition marked both the climax and the end of Europe's veneration of Egypt. It sparked off a fashion for Egyptian style, but, at the same time as Europeans succumbed to a craze for chairs whose legs were carved sphinxes and for little ornamental obelisks, they began to lose their respect for Egypt as their own culture's intellectual predecessor, or as a political entity. In the Preface to the twenty-three-volume *Description de L'Egypte*, in which the expedition's findings (and takings) were recorded, Jean-Baptiste-Joseph Fourier wrote: 'No considerable power was ever amassed by any nation, whether in the West or in Asia, that did not also turn that nation toward Egypt, which was regarded in some measure as its natural lot.' Egypt is no longer an autonomous and venerable culture to be admired and learnt from, but a passive thing, a prize to be taken. Fourier is thinking of 'Caesar, Mark Antony and Augustus'.[53] There is a tacit admission that the expedition of which he formed part was primarily intended not to study or to conserve Egypt, but to annex it as Octavius had done when he conquered Cleopatra; and just as Octavian propaganda had been designed to downgrade Cleopatra's people to the point where they could be denied full human rights, so the expedition of 1798 initiated a process whereby Egypt, past as well as present, was subtly derogated. Its art came to be viewed as exotica, its religion as superstition, its science as crankiness and conjuring tricks.

The immense age of Egyptian civilization and its artefacts remains a part of Cleopatra's story. In plays, operas and romantic novels she appears surrounded by sages, their robes decorated with indecipherable hieroglyphs, by astronomers bearing instruments of enigmatic purpose, and by priests who speak darkly of omens and sacrifices.[54] An atmosphere of occult knowledge and semi-magical power lingers about her

271

palace, but the content of this knowledge has been degraded. No post-Romantic Cleopatra would be worth keeping alive for the sake of her learning, as Al-Masūdī's was. The ancient wisdom of Egypt and the scholarship of Hellenistic Alexandria is converted, in her story, into aphrodisiac recipes and meretricious expertise. Arthur O'Shaughnessy imagined Cleopatra seducing Antony with the aid of 'soft Egyptian spells'.[55] In a novel published in 1894 Georg Ebers, the German classical scholar, wrote of the 'secret science of the Egyptians' of which Cleopatra's son Caesarion has made use in his amorous adventures. Ebers's Cleopatra holds Antony's love by making him gaze into a magical goblet, and the native quarter of her Alexandria is said to be full of 'wretched magicians and Magians' from whom love philtres can be obtained.[56]

> Have I not learned love
> In Egypt?

asks the heroine of Arthur Symons's play *Cleopatra in Judaea*.

> ... there the wise old mud of the Nile
> Breeds the dark sacred lotus, and the moon
> Brims up its cup with wisdom; I have learned
> The seven charms of Isis, each a charm
> To draw the stars out of the sky with love.[57]

Symons's tumescent lotuses are richly suggestive. The ancient wisdom to which this Cleopatra lays claim has nothing to do with Newtonian mathematics or gnostic philosophy. It is sexual knowledge, the antithesis of youthful innocence, and Cleopatra's possession of it makes her seem old, however smooth her skin and lustrous her hair.

Henry Rider Haggard wrote a popular novel about her in deliberately archaic language – appropriately, since, like the heroine of his better-known *She*, the nineteenth-century Cleopatra combines the attractions of a young woman with freakish longevity. In Théodore de Banville's series of poems, *Les Princesses* (published in 1874), her vast dark palace is like a fearful dream. Black sphinxes stand in the avenues. The ceaseless plaint of the Nile sounds like weeping. Moonlight bathes the monumental staircases, but no living creature is in sight except for Cleopatra, who is discovered naked, asleep, so blindingly beautiful that the bull-headed jasper idol who is her only companion has scorched eyes.[59] Sensuous, melancholy, morbidly erotic, the poem is charged with an atmosphere that Cleopatra borrows from the imagined character of her country and of her Pharaonic forebears. In Hector Berlioz's throbbingly lush setting of a poem by P. A. Vieillard, Cleopatra sings of her impending death. She calls on her royal ancestors, imploring their forgiveness for the disgrace and ruin she has brought on Egypt, and then prepares for suicide, welcoming with heartbroken rapture the end which will reduce her to the same state as her already lifeless country, defeated by men and deserted by the gods.

In 1838 Heinrich Heine described Egypt as 'the stark, silent land of the dead'. The long strip of the Nile reminds him of a coffin, and the whole country conjures up nightmarish images, 'wild grotesque carvings', hideous crocodiles, 'Mummies taking their siestas while the gilded masks protect them from swarms of flies of decay'.[59] Gautier, in a similar vein, imagines Cleopatra oppressed by the 'solemn and mighty sadness' of her country 'which was never aught else than a vast tomb, and in which the living appeared to be solely occupied in the work of burying the dead'. He describes 'monstrosities of Titanic architecture', a dry, desolate landscape, a heavy sky, 'monstrous chimerae and monuments immeasurable', 'interminable hieroglyphs telling, in language unintelligible, of things which are no longer known'.[60] De Girardin's Cleopatra characterizes her kingdom as a 'country of murder and remorse'. Its greatest monuments are tombs. Even the Nile, with its silent ripples and its unknown source, seems to presage some calamity, and the sun that hangs so sullenly in the unchanging sky appears to her 'like a great ever-open eye bleeding above us'.[61]

Historians were infected by the same horror as the poets. Theodor Mommsen, writing in 1854, speaks of 'the wearisome mystical host of the grotesque divinities of Egypt'.[62] As Bernal points out, Condorcet's theory of progress, first articulated in 1793 and enthusiastically taken over by historians, damaged Egypt's reputation.[63] Very ancient cultures came to seem not venerable, but archaic, rigid, sinister. While Heine, Gautier and de Girardin were writing with fascinated disgust of Egypt, Thomas De Quincey was plagued by opium-induced nightmares. 'Thousands of years I lived and was buried in stone coffins, with mummies and sphinxes, in narrow chambers at the heart of eternal pyramids. I was kissed with cancerous kisses, by crocodiles, and was laid, confounded with all unutterable abortions, amongst reeds and Nilotic mud.' He explained his phobia thus: 'The mere antiquity of Asiatic things, of their institutions, histories, above all, of their mythologies, etc., is so impressive, that to me the vast age of the race and name overpowers the sense of youth in the individual.'[64] Cleopatra, denizen of one of these realms of ghastly antiquity, becomes tainted with morbidity. Her story, which begins with her presiding over a realm of death and ends with her dying in person, takes on a kind of fatal languor. In Edward Said's words, 'the very possibility of development, transformation, human movement – in the deepest sense of the word – is denied the Orient and the Oriental'.[65] The Cleopatras of Heine, Gautier, de Girardin and their successors epitomize that imagined stasis: *ennui* possesses them; useful action seems to be forbidden them. Gautier's Cleopatra, her inherited spiritual torpor apparently sapping her physical energy, never walks, but is carried from place to place in a litter borne by naked Nubians and draped with panther skins.

To regard the civilization of Pharaonic Egypt, which endured for over two thousand years and left such a spectacular legacy of monuments to testify to its own vigour, sophistication and originality, as being doomed to failure, spiritually dead from its outset, is strikingly perverse. The political significance of this image of an ancient culture as atrophied, incapable of creative endeavour, is plain to see. De Girardin's Diomède comments on the Egyptians' apathy and superstition: 'One can decimate them or load them with taxes without causing any revolt, but if you kill an ibis in the sacred forest war is declared.'[66] Such a nation is ripe for colonizing. As Martin Bernal has pointed out, by the 1830s Mohammed Ali had reasserted modern Egypt's independence and regenerated its economy, yet Europeans persisted in viewing the country as characterized primarily by deadness.[67] Debilitated, decadent, essentially uncreative societies can be colonized with an easy conscience. Moribund Egypt lies ready, in the Western imagination, for the taking.

That taking could have a sexual, as well as a geopolitical, sense. Again sex and conquest, woman and country, are interchangeable. The extra strangeness, the distance from the modern West not only in space but also in time, which Cleopatra gained by association with ancient Egypt, could be put to pornographic use. In his Introduction to de Girardin's *Cléopâtre*, Gautier asserted that

> Only antiquity . . . could bring to light such tremendous personalities, such colossal lives . . . gigantic natures who carelessly disposed of the gold heaped up by twenty dynasties, the spoils of a hundred different nations, the sacrificed lives of numerous troops of slaves. . . . To these vast means Cleopatra added the attractions of her sex carried to an unprecedented degree.[68]

When exoticism was combined with archaism the poet was removed twice over from drab reality, and doubly free to indulge his erotic fancy and his craving for something more sublime than actual experience.

The distant past was, to the Romantics and the Decadents who followed them, as liberating a site for fantasy as the East. From the Gothic fantasies of Beckford, Keats and Rossetti to the pseudo-classical pornography of Walter Pater, Alma-Tadema and Frederic Leighton the nineteenth century displays a host of fantasies elaborated by people who seemed intent on fleeing backwards across the centuries. Anywhere, any time, appeared lovelier, grander and more free than their own society. It is ironic that possibly the richest of all sources for these dreams of escape from Christian Europe proved to be the Bible, as Flaubert, Oscar Wilde, Gustave Moreau and numerous others availed themselves of its entrancing combination of an Oriental setting and distance in time. Nineteenth-century descriptions of Cleopatra's court, with their catalogue of precious stones and affectedly archaic language, frequently read like pastiche versions of the vision of St John the Divine.

The irony is the greater given that a part of Cleopatra's significance, and of the symbolic force of her antiquity, lay precisely in her not being Christian. Gautier rhapsodized over a sensuality not yet attenuated by Christianity's 'long fast'.[69] John Lloyd, the American author of a collection of biographies entitled *Great Women*, published in 1885, took Cleopatra as his typical example of 'Pagan women' and explained to his readers, whose fastidious sensibilities might otherwise have been affronted by the narration of such a licentious life, that 'that class of women' – courtesans and others who engaged in extra-marital sex – 'who with us are shunned and excluded from society' were 'in pagan times . . . honoured and flattered'.[70] Oscar von Wertheimer, the German historian whose highly coloured biography *Cleopatra: A Royal Voluptuary* was published in 1931 (Romanticism did not die with the nineteenth century), describes the atmosphere of Cleopatra's court: '. . . the open sensuality of Greece was combined with the most feverish eroticism of Egypt and the East . . . In Alexandria love soon acquired a coarse, morbid and decadent character', but goes on to warn his readers they must 'bear in mind that the ancient world was far more primitively sensual and full of vitality than we are today and had no feeling for the delicate sentiments of which we now think so much'.[71] Rana Kabbani has written of imagined Oriental women: 'What the narrator felt himself unable to say about European women, he could unabashedly say about Eastern ones. They were there for his articulation of sex.'[72] Cleopatra, an Oriental woman and an ancient pagan, was doubly suitable for the purpose.

She was also doubly the West's opponent. After her death,

wrote Michelet, Rome 'unites and settles, as if to receive with more collected earnestness the Word of Judaea and of Greece'.[73] Cleopatra was the adversary who had to be defeated before Octavius could establish the earthly empire which, three centuries later, would become the vehicle of Christianity. According to Henri Blaze de Bury she was 'the oriental Circe, alluring and demonic, personification of an age which was irrevocably damned'.[74] Christian Westerners have always, more of less explicitly, identified themselves as Rome's inheritors. Western institutions – the Papacy, the Holy Roman Empire, British consulates, the American Senate, the French republic – borrow the glamour of ancient authority from Rome. Fascists and Jacobins alike have invoked Roman precedent. Military heroes (like the Duke of Marlborough, whose statue stands atop a massive column in the park at Blenheim Palace clad in the tunic and greaves of a Roman centurion), politicians and poets alike have considered that to associate themselves with Rome was to lay claim to a special *gravitas* and special virtue. In the fourteenth century Dante, who believed that his native Florence had been founded by the Romans and was therefore a cradle of Christianity, was proud to be 'of that holy seed'. In the seventeenth Milton modelled *Paradise Lost* on the *Aeneid*, thus identifying the Christian myth of origin with that of Rome. In the nineteenth century, the era of the exotic Cleopatras, every schoolboy (girls, who were not meant to rule, were spared) learnt from Virgil of Rome's special talent for government, while poets like Macaulay who celebrated Horatius's manly stand against the barbarians proposed the heroes of Rome as models for those of the modern empires. Cleopatra, who threatened to conquer Rome, or, worse, to taint its civilization by mingling it with her suspect, effeminate Oriental one, was to the dominant classes of nineteenth-century Europe, just as she had been to those of Augustan Rome, the personification of everything they had rejected in order that their civilisation might flourish.

Cleopatra *had* to be vanquished, the East *had* to be conquered and annexed. To nineteenth-century Western writers it seemed as though Christianity, as yet unborn, had demanded that it should be so, just as later it was to demand that the Western nations should carry the Gospel to every corner of the Earth, acquiring empires as they went. Michelet enunciated the theory most clearly:

> The asp which kills and delivers Cleopatra closes the long dominion of the eastern dragon. This sensual world, this world of the flesh, dies to rise again more pure in Christianity ... The imperceptible serpent of Cleopatra following the triumph of Octavius, the triumph of the West over the East, was a fine figure.[75]

A fine figure indeed, and, like most 'figures', an imaginary construct. In the nineteenth-century literature of Cleopatra a ceaseless struggle between desire and guilt can be observed. Having dubbed the East the 'world of the flesh', Westerners projected their own fantasies on to it – only to recoil from them in self-righteous horror. In Georg Ebers's novel Cleopatra, towards the end of her life, begins to repent of her wild ways and turns for advice to a wise old Greek friend, Archibius, who agrees to undertake her children's education. He will endeavour to quash in them the taste, native to all Easterners, for 'what is monstrous, superhuman, exaggerated', and to foster instead the non-Oriental habits of 'steadfast moral discipline'. Like the denizens of an English or Prussian boys' school, this Cleopatra's children will be encouraged to develop 'character' and to forget their unfortunate appetite for free-thinking and sophisticated entertainment. 'The simple duties of the domestic hearth!' exclaims Ebers's Octavius, arriving to launch a *mission civilisatrice* – 'They are too prosaic for you Alexandrians, who imbibe philosophy with your mother's milk.'[76] We are left in no doubt that this antipathy reflects badly on the Alexandrians, not on the domestic hearth.

Yet the Westerners who imagined them would not have wanted the Alexandrians of their fantasies, or the imaginary Cleopatras who rule over them, any other than they are. Steadfast moral discipline and the domestic hearth are cramping ideals; there is no room, in a society which embraces them too whole-heartedly, for passion, for self-expression or for growth. The fantastic penetration of the East by the West has had real political consequences – consequences which now, at the end of the twentieth century, can be seen to have been generally deplorable. (To the Eastern people who lost their property, their freedom or their lives in the process of this fantasy's realization its pernicious nature was, of course, evident considerably sooner.) But although the Orient of the imagination, in which Cleopatra plays such a glittering rôle, has served to validate and glamorize colonialism, it was not constructed for that purpose. It was invented to gratify its inventors' desire. Passive, mysterious, sexually enticing and palpitating with sexual neediness, atavistic and ahistorical, the Romantic image of the Orient is the image of a woman. And place and woman are not only metaphors for each other (sexual intercourse equals annexation, conquest equals rape), they are also symbolic of something else – of the ill-defined rapture for which the nineteenth-century Romantics felt such vague but vast longings.

Keats described the 'feel' of Cleopatra as 'what I cannot describe . . . somewhat sideways, large, prominent, round and colour'd with magnificence'.[77] It is no coincidence that the language of Orientalist fantasies about Cleopatra so often has a liturgical ring. As the German critic F. Brie has observed, the exoticist has much in common with the mystic:

> The latter projects himself outside the visible world into a transcendental atmosphere where he unites himself with the Divinity; the former transports himself in imagination outside the actualities of time and space, and thinks that he sees in whatever is past and remote from him the ideal atmosphere for the contentment of his own senses.[78]

The contentment of his senses and the liberation of his spirit. The Romantics and their successors dreamt of another world where they would be free of convention, of petty commercial cares, of their own personal limitations, where sex was uninhibited, the material world was brilliant and beautiful, and man (for the dreamers were mostly men) could be grand. The Orientalist vision may be a dangerous one, but like all human visions, religious and otherwise, it is a manifestation of an impulse which can also be creative, the refusal to settle for what lies easily to hand, the craving for a life of risk and fabulous rewards, a life which is larger, more generous and more beautiful than actual experience is ever likely to be.

# 9

# THE KILLER

JEAN CANTEL'S CLEOPATRA, loaded with jewels, sits in
state on a throne supported by the carved figures of crouching, bound captives. In the shadows behind her the squat
silhouettes of her negro torturers can be descried. Before her,
his hands roped together, stands handsome, ardent Arsiesi,
the captain of her guard, who loves her and who has – on
her secret orders – murdered her brother. She watches while
he is interrogated. He refuses to name any accomplice. 'Make
him talk!' commands Cleopatra. The Nubians drive sharp-
ened reeds beneath his fingernails. He pales and bites his lip
but holds his silence. Slaves bring forward a hideous array
of instruments – iron claws, torches, spikes, lashes, copper
basins of boiling oil. Long nails are heated in the fire until
they sizzle against the torturers' heavy leather gauntlets.
Arsiesi never takes his eyes off the Queen. With an impatient
gesture she interrupts the Nubians' preparations. 'Now!
Death.' Arsiesi kneels. A gigantic black man raises an axe.

Then all of a sudden the expression on the Queen's face
changed; her features softened. Across her lips floated a
strange, voluptuous smile, a smile which held the sweetness
of all caresses, a smile imprinted with a mysterious understanding recognisable only to one man among those present.
Arsiesi saw that smile and at once the brow of the condemned
man lit up as his sovereign's face had done. The axe fell and,
his eyes still lifted to the throne, the fool died with a laugh.[1]

Cleopatra has always been sexually potent, and she has

281

frequently been cruel; in the Romantic era her cruelty and her sexuality me···. Shakespeare used her story to illustrate the destructive tendency of passion, but although his Antony and Cleopatra long to annihilate the world and lose themselves they are not intent on killing each other. But after 1825, when Alexander Pushkin revived an ancient but previously neglected story – that Cleopatra would demand a man's life as the price of one night in her bed – she appears repeatedly in the horrific but fascinating guise of the dominatrix, the man-eater, the *femme fatale*. Throughout the nineteenth century, and even as late as the 1920s, when the poet C. E. Ironmonger imagined her decked with rubies 'like drops of living blood' and lying all night with her cheek pressed to that of Antony's corpse,[2] her story is suffused with an atmosphere of eroticized violence.

Those who imagined Cleopatra as a Sadeian heroine were able to draw on the well-established traditions of her ruthlessness, her deceit and her emotional frigidity. During the latter part of the eighteenth century the duplicitous harlot-Cleopatras had become ever blacker-hearted. In 1775 the Italian dramatist Vittorio Alfieri, whose 'fever coldness' would later win Lord Byron's admiration, has her 'lifting a veil to disclose the truth hidden in the deep abyss of a dissimulating heart'. Obsessively ambitious and incapable of love, Alfieri's Cleopatra resolves to kill Antony so that she may the more easily seduce Augustus. Antony escapes her assassin and returns to express his horror at her heart of frozen stone and to wonder that, though even Medea and Megara blushed at their crimes, 'You, O coldly atrocious woman, are unmoved.'[3] In Alexandre Soumet's *Tragédie de Cléopâtre*, performed in 1824, in which she first appears in the gloom of her monument surrounded by instruments of death – a cup of poison, an asp hidden in a bronze basket, a poisoned dagger – Cleopatra murders Octavia and then terrifies her victim's little son by appearing from the horrid shadows brandishing a sword still smoking with his mother's blood.[4] In August von Kotzebue's *Octavia* (1801) she attempts to poison Octavia and to lay the blame on Antony, thus ridding herself of them both. That strategy having failed, she sends the false message about her suicide as a deliberately 'infernal' ploy to precipitate Antony's death. Antony expires in the arms of the faithful and ever-forgiving Octavia while Cleopatra lives on, intent as ever on gratifying her lust, her selfish ambition and her pride.[5]

The wickedness of these melodramatic Cleopatras is unequivocal, but such out-and-out villainesses were gradually to give place to more insidiously menacing figures. The Antonys of Alfieri, Soumet and von Kotzebue have all, by the end of their respective dramas, seen and recoiled in horror from the evil of their Cleopatras. Not so the victims of the killer-Cleopatras who were imagined in the century after Pushkin first tackled the theme. As the passage from Cantel's novel quoted above makes plain, the men seduced, corrupted and killed by the *femmes fatales* of the Romantic imagination are accomplices in their own destruction. Like Keats, they long to be ruined.

It would be grossly simplistic to write off the stereotype of the *femme fatale* as a projection of straightforward misogyny. Misogyny, all the same, shaped it and served to give it credence with the public. 'Be but ware of Woman the Destroyer!'[6] cries a wise counsellor to the hero of Rider Haggard's *Cleopatra*. Arthur O'Shaughnessy, in 'An Epic of Women', propounds the theory that God created woman without a soul:

> . . . this is the reason
> She is so fair to see, so false to love

and draws from his narration of Cleopatra's story a moral which, cliché as it is, is still striking for the bitterness of its sexual paranoia.

> The lot of every one hath been so cast:
> One woman bears and brings him up a man,
> Another woman slays him at the last.[7]

The image of the *femme fatale*, potentially both repellent and absurd, gained acceptance because it was founded on widely

283

held prejudices concerning the character of real-life women. 'For Cleopatra is – a woman,' wrote Heinrich Heine.

> It is a mistake to think that women when they betray us have ceased to love. They only follow their inborn nature: and if they will not empty the forbidden cup, they like at least a sip from it, or lick the brim just to see what poison tastes like. . . . Yes, this Cleopatra is a woman in the blessedest and cursedest sense of the word![8]

Heine saw Cleopatra as resembling those demanding wives 'who torment and bless their titular spouses with love', who are sometimes faithful, but frequently not, and who insist on instant gratification of every one of their 'wild whims'.[9] Later authors, writing with a consciousness of the growing feminist movement, identified her with that even more threatening female type, the virago who asserted her independence from men by refusing to marry. A biographical dictionary published in Paris in 1844 judged that Cleopatra's worst failing was that 'she never learnt to see her own glory in that of the object of her choice; she persisted in placing herself first, before her beloved, and that, in a woman, is a serious fault'.[10] Rider Haggard's Cleopatra, a woman replete with 'every evil', gives evidence of her wickedness by scorning the hero's honourable proposal and delivering a tirade against 'the iron link of enforced, unchanging union'. 'Marriage! *I* to marry! *I* to forget freedom and court the worst slavery of our sex!'[11] In Cantel's novel the King of Ethiopia begs Cleopatra to share his throne. 'No,' she says. 'No bond will ever chain my royal hands.' He offers her fabulous presents: gold, ebony, tame panthers and Ethiopian boys chained by the neck in pairs. 'It is not enough,' says Cleopatra. He must give her all he has – his kingdom, his treasure, his army, his numberless subjects. In return he will be allowed to enjoy her love for a while. 'But, on whatever day I may wish it you will leave without asking for anything back. . . . With my love, you will lose all.' The King agrees; we next see him sitting among the beggars on the palace steps.[12] Cleopatra, a proclaimer of women's rights, is revealed as a conscienceless predator, refusing the duties of marriage in order to despoil men.

Simple sexism, though, provides only a small part of the impetus towards the creation of imaginary *femmes fatales*. For one thing, just as wicked courtesans may be more attractive than good wives, the killer-Cleopatras are ambiguous images. The gusto with which they are painted or described suggests that their creators desired them as much as they feared them. In *Mademoiselle de Maupin* Gautier describes how Cleopatra has each of her lovers killed after one night of love, and then hails her: 'Sublime cruelty! . . . Great sensualist, how well you knew human nature, and what profound wisdom there is in this barbarous act!'[13] Besides, it is often made clear that the most intriguing thing about these terrifying Cleopatras is that they are not really women at all. In Georg Ebers's novel a virtuous young matron meets Cleopatra and finds that the Queen's eyes 'roused an ardent desire to press her lips even on the hem of her robe, but afterwards she felt as if a venomous serpent had crawled out of the most beautiful flower':[14] the image of a woman lifting a dress and being startled by a snake scarcely needs interpretation. Anatole France, with similar blatancy, imagined Cleopatra surrounded by 'gigantic columns topped with human heads or lotus flowers'.[15] In numerous accounts Cleopatra is attended by unmistakably phallic pets. Cantel describes her one day when *ennui*, as so often, oppresses her, lying stretched out on blue leather cushions toying with some serpents which a black dwarf has brought to her in a silver casket. 'She rolled and unrolled their supple spirals; the larger ones wrapped themselves around her waist, the smaller made bracelets for her wrists or climbed up to her neck. . . . She pressed the long, living ribbons to her mouth, to her shoulders, to her breast.'[16] These Cleopatras, provided with surrogate penises, exempted by their viciousness and their power from the curse of feminine weakness, are beings of equivocal gender. 'I have wished to be a woman in order to know new pleasures,'[17] declares one of Gautier's heroes: that wish imposes a complementary sex-change on the object of

285

desire. In an opera by Massenet (with a libretto by Louis Payen) Cleopatra, who is discovered when the curtain rises reclining on a couch with two dead slaves, her most recent victims, lying at her feet, dresses as a man to haunt the taverns of Alexandria in search of dancing boys with supple bodies and lips blooming with the 'purple of desire'.[18] Sigmund Freud noted of his male patients that 'masochistic phantasies . . . place the subject in a characteristically female situation' and suggested that the desire for punishment 'stands very close to the other wish, to have a passive (feminine) sexual relation to [the father]'.[19] The killer-Cleopatra, whose victim is most often a girlish, beardless youth of low social status, stands in for that father. She is frequently recognizable as a man, or at least a part of the male psyche, dressed up in splendid but transparent drag. 'Cleopatra!' exclaims Louis Bouilhet rapturously in his poem 'Melaenis', 'Ageless epitome of grace, and of virility!'[20]

In this period, as in all previous ones, the vast majority of the writers and artists inspired to reanimate Cleopatra were male. (The irritation with which Charlotte Brontë responded to the image of her has already been described.) The most notable nineteenth-century Cleopatra to have been created by a woman is that of the dramatist Delphine de Girardin (although the tone of Victorien Sardou's tragedy, written expressly as a vehicle for Sarah Bernhardt, may owe as much to the star's taste as to the male author's). De Girardin presents a heroine conforming closely to the stereotype of the *femme fatale*, but Théophile Gautier, for one, thought that in this she was writing against the bias of her own gender. He praised her for having produced 'the most male work ever to have come from a woman's hand' and declared that her only original contribution to the theme was in the character of Octavia, a woman torn between pride in her wifely dignity and envy of the mistress who, unlike her, is able to excite passion.[21] Gautier's apparent assumption that sadomasochistic fantasies are distinctively male is highly questionable: the heroes of romantic novels aimed at and avidly read by women, both in his time and in our own, are frequently as cold-hearted, promiscuous and violent as the worst of the *femmes fatales*. All the same it is illuminating that he believed Cleopatra the killer to be, like Cleopatra the foreigner, the object of a specifically masculine antagonism and a specifically masculine desire.

'Cleopatra is bored,' says de Girardin's Ventidius. 'The world is in danger!'[22] He exaggerates hardly at all. While Antony ogles dancing girls, Sardou's Cleopatra amuses herself by tearing the petals off roses.[23] Other Cleopatras relieve their *ennui* by venting their destructiveness more bloodily. That of the Lebanese writer Khalil Saadeh, whose *Caesar and Cleopatra* was published in 1898, spends her nights drawing up lists of those noblemen she intends to put to death and her days savouring the spectacle of their hanged bodies decorating her palace walls with 'swinging hieroglyphics'.[24] Gautier's Cleopatra watches gladiators killed by tigers, or each other. Like the Cleopatras of Rider Haggard and Cantel, she enjoys poisoning slaves, and as the dying men dash their heads and beat their feet in agony on the mosaic and porphyry pavements of her palace she smiles briefly before boredom again engulfs her.[25]

This vicious delight in others' pain is of course compatible with Cleopatra's character as a foreigner, for cruelty was one of the attributes of the imagined Oriental, especially of the Oriental monarch. The framing narrative of the text which was taken by Europeans to encapsulate the Orient, *The Thousand and One Nights*, is that of a king who, like a nineteenth-century Cleopatra, has his sexual partners put to death the morning after he has enjoyed their virgin favours. In Victor Hugo's 1858 poem 'Zim-Zizimi', a Sultan of Egypt disembowels two thieves with his own hands for amusement's sake, 'slowly . . . curious to watch the entrails fall out'. Later a marble sphinx tells Zizimi about Cleopatra, with whom, it is plain, he has much in common: 'Kings died for love, entering her chamber.'[26] Oscar von Wertheimer notes that Cleopatra has cruelty in her genes. 'For although the Lagidae were of Greek origin, their ghastly crimes would have made Oriental princes blush with shame. Could

287

Cleopatra escape the power of this tradition, this unbridled racial force, which mercilessly trampled over the bodies of the slain?'[27] The question expects the answer no.

This voluptuous cruelty is connected with the absolute power of Oriental monarchs like Cleopatra. The fantasy of the cruel Eastern potentate has a thinly disguised sexual significance. The poet who thrills at the thought of being tortured by a tyrant is using a fictional power-relation as a framework for his masochistic fantasies: the imagined despot is an excitingly violent dream lover in fancy dress. But the often-remarked connection between sado-masochism and totalitarianism runs two ways. The fictions in which killer-Cleopatras appear are not only perversely sexual scenarios: they are also wish-fulfilment fantasies of submission to totalitarian power.

Khalil Saadeh's Cleopatra remarks to the republican Brutus (who fears her 'as the tiger quakes before the spring of a boa'): 'People in Rome have got into their stupid heads that all men and women are equal. A more erroneous idea I have never heard in all my life.' However, 'It is not a difficult thing to put up a gallows.' This Cleopatra has skin like jasmine and lips like roses, but it is not until she draws a dagger on him that Caesar falls in love with her.[28] Sardou's Cleopatra deliberately sabotages Antony's battle plans at Actium, knowing that, once defeated, he will never return to Rome and Octavia. When she explains herself he is aghast. 'On the shores of Actium not a wave breaks but it tumbles a corpse! . . . So many brave men have died, and it was you, sorceress, you alone, who sacrificed them to the mad imaginings of your senseless, savage jealousy!' Cleopatra listens to this tirade unmoved. 'As though I had time to count the dead! . . . Are we all-powerful ones to be checked by such things? . . . I had need of a hecatomb, and you expect me to haggle over the quantity of blood!' This Cleopatra has no desire to see her lover happy and successful, nor is she about to relinquish her share in the world for love, as Shakespeare's Antony did. On the contrary, she needs her absolute power to aggrandize her selfish passion. 'Let it be war!' she cries. 'Let the world burn! And let its furnace light our love!'[29]

The modern world, wrote Gautier in *Une Nuit de Cléopâtre*, lacks 'the dazzling spectacle of all-powerful will, the lofty vision of a human spirit whose least desire is translated into unheard-of actions'. That spectacle Cleopatra 'with her gold-pointed diadem and her imperial purples, standing above a nation on their knees' could provide. Like Heliogabalus, Sardanapulus and a clutch of other ancient tyrants noted for their extravagance and contempt for the lives of others, she towers above 'the dark swarm of men' like a Titanic colossus, thus fulfilling by proxy the dark swarm's fantasies of power. 'These prodigious lives were the realisations by day of the dreams which haunted man by night.'[30] That, in Gautier's opinion, is why their terrorized and oppressed subjects tolerated them – a judgement which reveals much about the way politics and desire meshed in nineteenth-century Europe. 'In the world as it used to be', wrote Georges Bataille in his analysis of the Marquis de Sade's work, men 'wanted mankind personified by one of their fellows to escape the bonds to which the masses were subject.' Deprived by democracy's spread of the real-life spectacle of political absolutism, the European imagination filled with images of its erotic equivalent. And the fantasy of absolute sexual power is, invariably, cruel. 'The man subject to no restraints of any kind,' wrote Bataille, a latter-day Romantic, 'falls on his victims with the devouring fury of a vicious hound.'[31]

Quite frankly and knowingly the poets and artists of the post-Romantic period acknowledged the sado-masochism implicit in their Cleopatra fantasies. 'Beaten in the streets of Alexandria, and mocked by Cleopatra,' writes Michelet, 'Antony was in ecstasies.'[32] To love Cleopatra, says one of de Girardin's attendant lords, is 'a pleasure full of anguish, a terror full of charm'. 'May my love be my torment,' prays the slave who has agreed to give his life for a night with her.[33] Swinburne adores his Cleopatra for her callousness.

Shall she not have the heart of us
To shatter, and the loves therein
To shed between her fingers thus?

To him she is 'the whole world's bale and bliss',[34] just as to
de Banville she was 'the delight and executioner of the
world'.[35] Even the degradation consequent on loving her was
to be savoured for its exquisitely pleasurable pain. The Russian poet Valery Yakovlevich Bryusov, writing in 1905,
declares that he envies Antony his ruin at Cleopatra's hands,
apostrophizes Love,

Blessed is he who has known mockery,
And shame, and ruin – for thee!

and prays that he too, one day, may find an opportunity to
abase himself for a woman.[36] 'She had conquered me, she
had robbed me of my honour, and steeped me to the lips in
shame,' confesses Rider Haggard's hero. 'And I, poor fallen,
blinded wretch, I kissed the rod that smote me, and was her
very slave.'[37] The elaborators of these Cleopatras were not
freaks. Swinburne's taste for flagellation is well documented,
but although his erotic practices may have been exceptional,
his erotic fantasies, as the Cleopatra literature demonstrates,
were not. There was, and is, nothing unusual about sado-
masochism.

This perversity found cogent expression in the fantastic
story which, under Romanticism, was to become the essential
Cleopatra plot, all but replacing the approximately historical
narrative of Caesar, Antony, Actium and the asp. In the
fourth century the Latin historian Sextus Aurelius Victor
wrote of Cleopatra, 'She was so lustful that she often prosti-
tuted herself, and so beautiful that many men paid with their
lives for a night with her.'[38] From this single sentence (which,
for all its sensationalism, and despite the fact that the text
was available and several times published, lay ignored for
fifteen hundred years) sprang all the Romantic killer-Cleopatras, of which Pushkin's was the first.

He attempted the theme in poetry, prose or a combination
of the two at least four times; none of the resulting works

was ever finished. The most substantial, the story *Egyptian Nights*, appeared in 1837. Despite its fragmentary state it became an enormously influential text. Thirty years later Dostoevsky has one of the characters in *The Idiot* refer to it when the fatal and self-destructive heroine Nastasya Filippovna appears 'pale as death' and turns great black eyes like burning coals upon the crowd gathered to watch her wedding. ' "For a princess like that I'd sell my soul," cried a clerk. "One night at the price of a life!" he quoted.'[39] Meanwhile in France, England, Italy and America it inspired a host of similar fantasies. The story of a lethally lascivious queen who has each of her lovers put to death the morning after she has enjoyed him is conventional: Diodorus Siculus had told it of Semiramis; Lermontov was to tell it of Queen Tamara of Georgia.[40] But throughout the nineteenth century it is Cleopatra who most frequently figures as its heroine.

Pushkin imagines Cleopatra falling silent in the course of a feast. All luxury, all pleasure is available to her – in an early draft he even provides her with a harem, guarded by eunuchs, of

> . . . handsome slaves for her to choose,
> And bashfully impassioned youths[41]

but still an unsatisfied yearning makes her pensive. Abruptly, to the thrilled but terror-struck crowd of her admirers, she announces her dreadful bargain:

> For sale is now my love divine:
> Who dares to barter in this fashion
> His life against one night of mine?

There is a pause while she waits, scornful and brazen. At last three volunteers present themselves. One is an old soldier:

> His pride resolved to bear no more
> A female's challenge to his mettle.

The next is an Epicurean philosopher, a worshipper of the goddess of love. The last is a nameless boy, as fresh and bashful as a flower budding in springtime:

291

Untasted passion flared and tested
His heart with unaccustomed blaze. . . .
And softly touched, the Queen's eye rested
Upon him with a gentler gaze.[42]

It was this last victim, virginal, powerless, effeminate, a pure lamb fit for the slaughter, who caught the imagination of subsequent writers. Gautier, de Girardin, Sardou, Cantel and Rider Haggard all provided Cleopatra with an innocent young devotee of inferior social class – slave, farmer or huntsman – who adores her and is ready to give his life, his all, for her love. So did the opera librettist d'Arienzo, the makers of films produced in Germany and in Hollywood during the first decade of this century, and Mikhail Fokine, who in 1908 choreographed a version of Gautier's story for the Russian Ballet, a work which was the greatest single success of the ballet's first Paris season under Diaghilev. The scenario at which Aurelius had hinted was enthusiastically expanded and varied: Jean Cantel's novel alone provides over a dozen permutations of it as one after another of his male characters is lured to his death by Cleopatra. But through all these versions the pattern remains essentially the same. A hard-hearted Cleopatra, through boredom, caprice or deliberate cruelty, uses her sexual attractions to procure a man's death and he, enraptured, is glad to succumb, for to die in such circumstances is to know the greatest pleasure that life can offer. As Gautier writes of his Cleopatra's lover-victim, 'were he to live to the age of Nestor or Priam . . . he could never know another new experience – never feel another new pleasure . . . there was nothing in the world left for him to desire'.[43]

The attractions of such a fantasy are subtle, various and sometimes mutually contradictory. Most obviously, to surrender life and all to a tyrannous lover is to escape responsibility; submission to another's will allows a blissful exemption from the need to exercise one's own. Released from what Hegel called 'concrete freedom', the condition in which the free subject is obliged to answer for his or her own

292

actions, the masochistic victim, absolutely overpowered, enters a state of 'negative freedom' in which he or she can indulge desires without consciously condoning them.[44] Masochists (that is most people, at some time or in some moods) are 'only obeying orders'. Freud considered masochism, unlike sadism, to be a great danger.[45] When unacknowledged masochistic desires are permitted political expression pandemonium follows, as this century's history demonstrates only too clearly. But those masochists self-aware enough to confine their lusts to erotic fantasy can be carried away by pleasures to which they could never have allowed themselves deliberately to consent.

A lover who determines to die as soon as he has consummated his love cheats time and change, for death is the only true permanence. Besides, a violent, murderous love promises a kind of intensity inaccessible by means of tenderness. The torture, the poison, the dagger-thrusts become metaphors for the fury of passion, and the orgasm that ends in death promises to be infinitely more rapturous, more transcendent, more deliriously pleasurable, than the safe transitory lovemaking after which a return to normality is possible. 'To die now, at once, in the fullness of life's intoxication, in the fullness of love's pleasure, what a dream that would be!' exclaims Sardou's Cleopatra. 'Ah! how I wish that at the moment of ecstasy your life and mine were suspended from our lips, so that we could snap the thread with a single kiss!'[46] That wish is granted to the victims of the killer-Cleopatras.

But masochism is more complex than a simple craving for irresponsible ecstasy. The critic Bram Dijkstra has called it 'the opiate of the executioner's assistant'. Admiring and yearning after power, but despairing of ever himself (or herself) becoming one of the powerful, the masochist craves at least that intimacy with power granted to the victim. Dijkstra argues that the men of nineteenth-century Europe and America, living in a secular democratic society increasingly dominated by massive commercial conglomerates, where wealth came, if it did come, not from the easily comprehensible sources of land or labour, but from fluctuating investments, came to feel themselves adrift, individually powerless and without any clearly identifiable 'master', whether employer, monarch, or God.[47] Deprived of a power-figure to love, admire and fear, the masochistic male therefore invented one – the *femme fatale* – and sought, through fantasies in which she honoured him with her rage, to establish for himself an intimate relationship with power – albeit one in which he was always the underdog.

Sadism and masochism, the lust for absolute mastery and the lust for absolute submission, lie very close together, and not only because they are complements. The sadist seeks to subdue and punish; so does the masochist. The difference, as Freud pointed out, lies in the fact that the masochist includes his (or her) own ego among the objects to be overcome.[48] Thus the site of erotic excitement in a masochistic fantasy wanders, for the fantasist is both dominator and dominated. In some versions of the killer-Cleopatra's story we are invited to view the Queen, beautiful as she is cruel, as an object of desire. Equally often our attention is directed towards her victim, a flower-like boy, an heroic warrior or a lissom slave with copper-coloured limbs, each described with homoerotic relish. It is the situation which exists between sexual predator and prey which is exciting, not either party in isolation. The violence which permeates Cleopatra's story is as invasive and elusive as a scent. Sometimes she herself is victim as well as perpetrator of it. Isabella Glyn, the actress whose performance as Shakespeare's Cleopatra in 1849 was much admired, died on stage, according to one reviewer, 'in a sort of sleepy ecstasy', a death 'of self-indulgence, not self-sacrifice'.[49] In Walter Savage Landor's *Scenes for the Study* Antony gives Cleopatra a hollow ruby ring filled with almond-scented poison. She kisses it gratefully, exclaiming:

How sweet the flower
Of death.[50]

Cantel's Cleopatra wonders what it would be like to feel an assassin's embrace and when an enemy comes to her private chamber she folds him in her arms, pressing her naked breast

294

to his tigerskin-clad chest, throwing back her head and arch-
ing her supple body 'as though she were tempting him to use
his dagger'.[51] 'In the shadow of death's wing life is at its most
beautiful,' says Payen's Cleopatra, thanking one of her lovers
for attempting to strangle another. Satiated with frenzied
delights, she was beginning to be bored. Violence has restored
a zest to her life: 'You have enriched pleasure by the addition
of fear.'[52] William Wetmore Story's Cleopatra is bruised:

> Here, Charmian, take my bracelets
> They bar with a purple stain
> My arms.[53]

De Banville's is one of a procession of exotic Princesses,
'Their lips opening like bloody flowers'.[54] It is unimportant
whether their mouths are still wet after a vampire feast, or
whether they are bleeding because they have been struck.
Both suggestions are contained in the image. What matters
is that blood, whatever its source, should flow.

The force by which masochists imagine themselves or their
frail representatives (Cleopatra's lover-victims for instance)
being overcome can be defined – simply – as everything they
feel themselves actually unable to control. Killer-Cleopatras
personify those terrifying, anarchic elements, whether in the
environment or in the psyche, by which the writers and
artists who invented them felt most threatened, and by which,
because they could not fully understand and control them,
they felt themselves most irresistibly seduced. The killer-Cleopatra is everything that nineteenth-century Western society
felt itself to lack. She is Orient to its Occident, tyranny to its
democracy, peril to its security, libertinism to its propriety,
woman to its man.

She is also, most emphatically, that old cliché, female
nature to its male culture. 'My lips held fast the mouth o'
the world,' she says in Swinburne's 'Masque of Queen
Bersabe', 'To spoil the strength and speech thereof.'[55] A killer-
Cleopatra is inimical to language and all it represents in the
way of rational thought and social discipline. The instincts
to which she appeals are not those of Freud's Eros, the love

that binds civilization together, but those more atavistic ones which urge a return to a simpler, more passive mode of existence, to Dionysiac orgy or to death. Michelet, who identified Cleopatra with 'the eastern myth of the serpent', interpreted that serpent as signifying 'the magnetic power of nature over man, that invincible fascination which it exercises over him in the East'. In Cleopatra's conflict with Rome Michelet finds an allegory of the defeat of the 'God of nature' by the 'God of the soul'. Civilized, spiritually elevated, self-disciplined Western man confronts snaky, sexual, anarchic woman, 'the tempter serpent, which whispered evil thoughts to the heart of Adam, which unseen swims and crawls and glides'.[56] The killer-Cleopatra represents a 'nature' distinguished, not by innocence or spontaneous goodness, but by amorality, ferocity and ungodliness.

Sardou's Cleopatra summons up a storm. Her people believe it to be a miracle. She reveals to Antony that in fact she was counting more on her meteorological expertise than on magic. 'Already, towards Nubia, the horizon is lost in a copper-coloured haze. . . . Listen. No insect hums, no leaf shivers, no bird cries!' But whether the effect is achieved by sympathetic magic or by equally sympathetic knowledge, the fifth act of the play closes on the spectacle of her surrounded by reverent priests and awestruck Roman legionaries, exulting in the thunder and lightning which roar and flash at her bidding.[57] Blaze de Bury describes Cleopatra as 'light, flame, tempest'.[58] To Oscar von Wertheimer she is not so much a person as a source of energy. Her 'whole nature seemed to be shaken by a perpetual storm. . . . We must remember that in her the life force played a much more important part than any spiritual or moral inhibitions.'[59]

These 'natural' Cleopatras are as foreign to human society as the fierce, beautiful animals with whom they are surrounded and frequently compared. In José-Maria de Hérédia's sonnet 'Le Cydnus', Cleopatra stands upright in the prow of her silver trireme like a great golden hawk marking with its eyes its distant prey. In Arthur Symons's play she feeds unwelcome messengers to lions and snakes:

> My beasts
> Love dearly a man's flesh.

In this she finds them congenial.

> They do my will
> When a man's justice lingers.[60]

In his poem of 1866 Swinburne associates her with a hawk poised to strike and a yawning cat. Blaze de Bury attributes to her 'the elegance and guiltless ferocity which lends such grace to a young tigress toying with her prey'.[61] Wetmore Story has her ordering her women to

> Take her from my chamber
> That stupid little gazelle

lest, in her restless irritability, she snap 'its thin neck in twain'. Falling into a doze, she dreams of a past time when she was a tiger and lived with her

> wild mate . . . fierce in a tyrannous freedom.
> I knew but the law of the woods.

By night her lover stalked her, his yellow eyes flashing.

> Then like a storm he seized me
> With a wild triumphant cry.

She would watch while he fought off rival males, leaving the desert sands soaked with their blood, and then together the feral pair would slink down to the waterhole to lie in wait for antelope:

> We drank their blood and crushed them
> And tore them limb from limb.[62]

Most often, of course, Cleopatra's familiar is a snake. Flaubert called her 'the pale creature with a fiery eye, the viper of the Nile who smothers with an embrace'.[63] Killer-Cleopatras habitually appear clad as Rider Haggard's does in 'a garment that glistened like the scaly covering of a serpent, everywhere sewn with gems'.[64] Snakes are beautiful, stealthy, cold-blooded, poisonous and – as already demonstrated – a

297

gift to poets in search of thinly disguised erotic imagery. 'And she, the Egyptian snake, how she loves her Roman wolf!' exclaims Heine. 'Her betrayals are only the external irrepressible twinings and coils of her evil serpent nature.'[65] Swinburne paid tribute to Gautier, in his verses on the latter's death, as the poet who had allowed Cleopatra to

> ... feed from veins of his,
> Her close red warm snake's mouth, Egyptian-wise.[66]

Swinburne himself wrote repeatedly about Cleopatra, both in poetry and in a passage on Michelangelo's drawing of her, in which he praises

> the subtle and sublime idea which transforms her death by the aspic's bite into a meeting of serpents which recognise and embrace, an encounter between the woman and the worm of the Nile, almost as though this match for death were a monstrous love-match ... so closely do the snake and the queen of snakes caress and cling.... For what indeed [he concludes provocatively] is lovelier or more luxuriously loving than a strong and graceful snake of the nobler kind?[67]

The coupling of Cleopatra and her 'luxuriously loving' snake is a vivid image of the sexuality which pervades the 'nature' she represents. In Rider Haggard's novel the hero, Harmachis, is warned by his wise old uncle that 'Woman, in her weakness, is yet the strongest force upon the earth ... for Nature fights ever on her side.' Harmachis soon learns to abjure that nature. As a priestly acolyte he communes 'with the Invisible' and yearns to become all spirit. 'Oh vile flesh to drag us down!' His mentor tells him that Cleopatra is the incarnation of 'Evil of that greater sort which, fearing nothing and making a mock of laws, has taken empires for its places of play, and, smiling, watered the growth of its desires with the rich blood of men'.[68] This nebulous evil is clearly related to, if not identical with, the 'love of women' which inspires Harmachis to further empurpled meditations (for women, as we have repeatedly seen, are to be held responsible for the sexuality of men). 'What a powerful force love is!' muses Saadeh's Caesar. 'It is as deep as space, subtle as electricity, and irresistible as the tides of the ocean.'[69]

Especially the ocean. In Cantel's novel Cleopatra's bed 'which is mounted pell-mell by slaves and kings, is like the borderless bed of the sea, from whence none return alive'.[70] Ebers's Cleopatra receives guests in a wonderful hall like a marine grotto, completely covered with coral, seashells, starfish and the inlaid figures of Tritons, mermaids and sea monsters.[71] Anatole France remarked that she is 'as charming and terrible as the sea which bore Aphrodite'.[72] Like the goddess of love she comes to men from out of the waves, water-born and waterborne. Antony is imperilled when she floats on her barge up the Cydnus, lures him off the dry land of duty and bears him away with her over the sea to Egypt, land of reeds and floods and sexual licence. There she holds him, with fishing parties and water picnics, in a bewildering swamp of instinctual pleasure. His ruin is finally accomplished when he disregards those reasonable men who advise him to depend upon the solid earth, and, beguiled by Cleopatra, entrusts his fortunes at Actium to the inconstant water.

The mother sea, which ebbs and flows with the moon, is always female. It is man's beloved enemy, image of his unconsciousness and his sexuality. It is the slippery, yielding, deathly element from which Goethe's Faust tried to reclaim land for rationality and masculine culture:

> Hardy knaves, with mastery clever,
> Delved the dykes, the ground to gain,
> Foreshore from the sea to sever,
> Making it their own domain.[73]

Women like Cleopatra threaten that precarious domain and thus threaten man's control over his environment and over himself. 'Where id was, there ego shall be,' wrote Freud, describing the primary task of psychoanalysis. 'It is a work of culture – not unlike the draining of the Zuider Zee.'[74] Cleopatra opposes that work. The 'love of women', says Rider Haggard's Harmachis, thinking of her, 'is a torrent to wash in a flood of ruin across the fields of Hope, bursting in the barriers of design, and bringing to tumbled nothingness the tenement of man's purity and the temples of his faith'.[75] In the sea men drown. José-Maria de Hérédia's Antony, 'the passionate imperator', bends over a swooning Cleopatra and in her wide eyes he sees the image of his destruction: 'a whole vast sea where galleys were in flight'.[76] The English salon painter William Etty (of whose crowds of naked women William Thackeray remarked that a whole curtain of fig leaves would be required to render them decent)[77] painted a *Triumph of Cleopatra* in which the Queen's barge, overflowing with curvaceous semi-nude women, seems to invade the solid ground of Tarsus. In the water around it nymphs gambol lazily, proffering their foam-white breasts to the viewer, while their element – gauzy, luminous and soft-edged as themselves – laps improbably against the angular masses of the temple steps.

The sea is cold as it is wilful, destroying without compunction, and the killer-Cleopatra, like the sea, is oblivious of the carnage for which she is responsible. Sometimes, indeed, she seems barely sentient. 'Still she stands and, blind with love, shoots the shuttle of our fate', thus Rider Haggard on the subject of Woman in general and Cleopatra in particular. His Cleopatra has 'eyes that seemed to sleep and brood on secret things as night broods upon the desert'.[78] In 'Zim-Zizimi' Victor Hugo refers to Cleopatra's 'unfocussed eyes' which exert an attraction as strong as a chain. Swinburne describes her shredding and shattering a string of pearls with 'long sweet sleepy fingers', her eyes glinting 'through shutting lids' while she dreams, unmoved, of death. 'There is no heart in her for sighs.' Cantel's heroine is still and pale as a statue of ivory opening sightless eyes on vacancy.[79] As scapegoats loaded with the desires and censored instincts of the men that imagine them, these Cleopatras have hardly any life of their own.

Bestial, untamed, existing torpidly at some deep, dark level of 'natural' instinct, a killer-Cleopatra is incapable of the civilized human emotions of tenderness and pity. 'No, no, you never loved,' declared Louis Bouilhet, apostrophizing her corpse. 'Your heart is no colder now, under the fragrant wood which covers your mummy, than it was in the time of your beauty! . . . You watched your glorious lovers fall without granting them, in exchange for the world they gave for you, one single tear of love.'[80] Such Cleopatras are as devoid of loving kindness as snakes or tigers or the candle flame into which the lover-moth flies. They use their suitors as sexual objects, feeling no more for them than Gautier's Queen does for the 'Asiatic pages whose beautiful flowing hair served her guests to wipe their hands upon'.[81] Cantel's Cleopatra presides at one of her many banquets; beside her throne kneels a prisoner loaded with chains. 'From time to time she rested on the captive's shoulder an arm wearied by the weight of her rings.'[82] When Ahmosis, one of the many Egyptian nobles who is helplessly in love with her, disguises himself as a slave, enters her service and proceeds to vent his jealousy by poisoning her discarded lovers one by one, she is barely aware of the crimes. Nor does she recognize him, though he was once himself her lover, even when she walks, arm in arm with her new victim the King of Bactria, past the trees to which he has been lashed on her orders so that he may be slowly burnt to death by the Egyptian sun. Her cruelty is capricious, superbly negligent. She orders that a man be torn to pieces by lions, but when the time for the gruesome spectacle comes she is absorbed in a new seduction and cannot even be bothered to watch her previous plaything die. Gautier's Cleopatra feels a momentary relenting (more lustful than compassionate) towards Meiamoun, the virginal young huntsman who has sworn to drink poison after his night of love with her. She would perhaps have released him from his dreadful bargain, but at the crucial moment a fanfare sounds: Antony is approaching. The Queen, distracted, quite forgets about poor Meiamoun, who dies anyway, a futile and disregarded sacrifice.

Without love or morality to give purpose to her existence the killer-Cleopatra is engulfed in boredom. Her *ennui* is immense. It infects her whole world. The hot sky of Egypt seems to press down on her, forbidding change.[83] All stimulus is blocked by 'the lassitude of absolute power, the *ennui* of desires satisfied even before they are formed. . . . "I can desire nothing which I do not already possess; I can wish for nothing which I have not already had and I can feel no joy, experiment with no pleasure which I have not already savoured." '[84] She seeks novelty in sex but her lovers, because she feels nothing for them, are all the same to her. She tries to titillate herself with violence but, invincible, she meets no stimulating challenge. Her beauty disarms opponents. At the sight of her, conspirators drop their daggers and the resolve of a murderer softens like wax in the sun. In a play by Vernon Knott, published in 1904, even Antony, who has commanded her to die with him, is paralysed when she strips herself naked and dares him to stab her. Defeated, he sinks to the floor and allows her to place her foot on his neck.[85] No one can withstand a killer-Cleopatra.

In this too Cleopatra resembles 'nature', from whose monotonous cycle of death and reproduction there is no escape – except in God. Her *ennui* is akin to atheism, or more precisely to the despair of a believer who has lost his or her faith and feels existence to be rendered meaningless by the lack of a judging and rewarding deity. Her cruelty, wrote Blaze de Bury, has its origin in the 'indomitable fury of a nature recognizing the authority neither of morality nor of God'.[86] Amoral as a soulless animal, she leads a life of ceaseless, futile repetition, the very antithesis of the pilgrim's progress that is the paradigm of a good Christian life. Sterile herself (killer-Cleopatras are never mothers), she presides over a realm which teems and swarms with life, but life of a horribly amorphous kind. Swinburne surrounds her with

> . . . asps and water-worms afloat
> Between rush-flowers moist and slack

and 'dank dregs, the scum of pool or clod'.[87] Like the 'slimy things' with which the Ancient Mariner lived when he was outcast from human society, like the hyacinths bred from T. S. Eliot's dead land, this fecundity depends on death. Cleopatra/nature gobbles up men with careless voracity. 'One fair woman's days,' wrote Arthur O'Shaughnessy, 'sufficeth many heroes' loves and lives.'[88] For the biological imperative of exuberant reproduction must always evoke the corresponding imperative of death, unless some physical or religious bulwark is interposed. And Cleopatra, pitiless and promiscuous, is inimical to all things spiritual. Her only deities, according to Swinburne, are

> God-spawn of lizard-footed clans,
> And those dog-headed hulks that trod
> Swart necks of the old Egyptians.[89]

When Khalil Saadeh's Julius Caesar keeps vigil in a temple on the eve of his deification his mind is constantly distracted from solemn thoughts by irredeemably carnal memories of Cleopatra, of her 'dazzling beauty ... seductive eyes ... white, velvety hand'.[90] Cleopatra is ungodly, and she leads men away from God.

At dead of night, in a temple so vast it takes an hour to traverse, Jean Cantel's Cleopatra witnesses the rites of Amoun, the supreme deity. In the first chamber, the largest, she hears priests expound to the ignorant faithful the doctrine of a benign personal god who, with his assistants, bears a marked resemblance to the Christian Trinity: 'To teach us he has sent Thoth, who is his Intelligence; to save, he has sent Osiris, who is his Mercy. From his heavenly palace he watches over men, the children of his love. . . .' In the second chamber initiates celebrate a less comforting deism. 'Nothing exists outside of him ... man is his thought thinking itself . . .' Finally, in the last room, a priest whose face and voice are suffused with a solemn terror enunciates the ultimate truth, bearable only by those who have been arduously prepared:

> Amoun does not exist. The laws of matter and the chance combinations of its elements alone have created all things. When man dies no part of him survives: his body returns to the earth. . . . Nothing watches over man and nothing protects him. Matter, in its never-ending motion, ceaselessly dissolves

and reforms itself. It is blind, senseless, deaf. It and it alone exists.

Pursued by the cries and sobs of the appalled initiates and of the priest who has revealed to them this terrible, despair-inducing truth, Cleopatra, unmoved, passes into the holy of holies. There, in the knowledge that there is no god to censure her, she takes her pleasure with a young priest whose glistening eyes and pale cheeks have caught her fancy. The encounter, of course, is fatal for him. 'If tomorrow,' she reminds him, 'it were to be discovered that a woman had been in this sanctuary – if for instance I left my veil behind here – it would mean torture and death for you.' Then, deliberately, she tosses a wisp of gauze over the Osiris-idol's crown before enveloping her besotted victim in her long black hair and making him drunk on the splendour of her starry-cold eyes.[91]

Those who surrender to the power of a *femme fatale* enter a lonely and terrifying sphere. Cantel's 'matter' resembles a killer-Cleopatra in that it (or she – the French word is feminine in gender) is inexorable, impassive and death-dealing. The scientists of the Enlightenment who had asked themselves whether matter was truly inanimate had been fully aware that the question had broad, and potentially revolutionary and blasphemous, implications. If matter was autonomously active, then it had no need of a divine spark to animate it, nor indeed of a divine creator.[92] The great advances of nineteenth-century physics brought ever closer the vision of the universe as a closed system which 'ceaselessly dissolves and reforms itself' on energy of its own generation. As the German philosopher-scientist Hermann von Helmholtz put it in 1847, 'all that occurs is described by the ebb and flow of the eternally undiminished and unaugmentable energy supply of the world'.[93] Such insights induced considerable anxiety. Where, in such a cosmos, was there room for God? And if God had been displaced, then who cared for humanity? No one and nothing, came the hard answer. In Fokine's ballet of Cleopatra the hapless youth (danced in the first production by Fokine himself, and later

304

by Leonide Massine) who has promised his life to Cleopatra drinks his poison and then, dying, crawls to where she stands. With a great effort he raises himself to his knees, clinging to her body, as though searching for some explanation of his cruel fate. But Cleopatra's costume has a round, mirrored panel covering her stomach. The man searches for comfort and protection, but all he sees, before falling dead at Cleopatra's feet, is his own face.[94] In the universe of the killer-Cleopatra, a universe governed by 'nature', people find themselves unpitied and alone.

Cleopatra, by her very nature, denies God. Sometimes she goes further, deliberately desecrating the sacred. Rider Haggard's Cleopatra persuades her lover, a lapsed priest of the ancient Egyptian religion, to reveal his secrets. Guided by him, she makes her way into the burial chamber at the core of a pyramid. There she opens the tomb of a long-dead Pharaoh and, disregarding the awful curse inscribed on his mummy's chest, exposes his corpse and rips it open with her dagger to reveal the priceless emeralds that she knows are concealed within it. The dead Pharaoh, a great patriarch, is said to be in the care of the goddess Nout, described as the Mother. The pyramid is unmistakably womb-like – Cleopatra and her companion invade it by way of secret doors and passageways so narrow that a person can scarcely squeeze through them. The decoration at the head of the relevant chapter in the first edition of the novel shows a hand rummaging in a remarkably vulvaic wound. So Cleopatra, in an extraordinary portmanteau act of transgression, defies the gods, stabs a father, violates a mother, robs a grave, dismembers a corpse and contaminates sacred things by putting them to sexual use (the stolen emeralds are for her own adornment).[95]

Such a woman, in Swinburne's words, 'treads on gods and god-like things'. In that she is the masochist's ideal accomplice, for masochism, as Freud remarked, 'creates a temptation to perform "sinful" actions, which must then be expiated by the reproaches of the sadistic conscience . . . or by chastisement from the great parental power of Destiny'.[96]

305

To sin so dreadfully calls for courage, resolution and superb defiance. In the portrayals of a killer-Cleopatra goodness and greatness are once more found to be at odds. 'It is utterly dangerous to enter into intimate relations with such a person as Cleopatra,' wrote Heine. 'A hero can go to the devil in this way, but only a hero.'[97]

A hero must be ready to stake his life. The killer-Cleopatra's victims often seem intent, even before meeting her, on pursuing peril. Their fatal encounters with her are explicitly likened to the battles, gladiatorial combats or duels in which they would otherwise have been happy to die. Meiamoun, the beautiful virgin boy who loves Gautier's Cleopatra, steals lion cubs from their mother (thus risking the wrath of a terrible female). He bathes in cataracts (exposing himself to danger from water, Cleopatra's element). For months on end he lives in the desert, fighting with hyenas for food; 'the Abyss called him!'[98] The slave to whom de Girardin's Cleopatra allows one night of love drinks his poison gladly next morning, after singing a hymn to Death, 'Daughter of Night! whom one fears to adore.'[99] All of the young men who, in Cantel's novel, hate and love Cleopatra are equally bent on testing themselves, whether in battle, under torture or in the trials of passion. As a boy, Ahmosis used to be a hunter in the mountains of Libya, chasing antelope and fighting with lions: 'My heart yearned for great battles and the cry of iron greedy for blood.' His friend Hyllos sings in praise of military self-sacrifice: 'It is beautiful to see a brave man, fighting for his country, falling in the first rank. . . . Let each of you, ready one and all to face his destiny, raise his shield, and let him love black death more than he loves the splendour of the sun.' The youths crown themselves with flowers, as sacrificial victims are crowned, and sing: 'We smile with a proud heart at the death to which we have consented.'[100] By the end of the book every one of them has been killed, directly or indirectly, by Cleopatra. The *femme fatale*, terrible as she may be, is also the instrument that will gratify these men's dearest desire. She gives them, in a time of tedious peace, a chance to immolate themselves.

In Pushkin's unfinished story *We Were Spending the Evening at Princess D.'s Dacha*, the protagonist argues that the killer-Cleopatra's love is like a duel, which can give focus and exhilarating purpose to the otherwise diffuse and squalid business of living. 'Just think of it: the first scamp happening by, whom I despise, says something about me that cannot hurt me in any way, yet I expose my forehead to his bullet . . . And you think I would act like a coward when my bliss is at stake? What is life worth if it is poisoned by dejection and unfulfilled desires?'[101] For the hero life is valueless until it is at the point of ending. It is worth recalling that, four years after writing so apparently sceptically about the code of honour, the author himself fought a duel and died.

Pushkin died Romantically in 1837, but during the nineteenth century, as spurs gave way to spats and the values of the archaic warrior élite were eclipsed by those of the bourgeoisie, the arena in which the hero proved himself shifted inward to the moral or the erotic sphere. The heroic sinner, the Byronic or Rimbaud-like adventurer who risks his own redemption in order to explore the deepest and darkest corners of the human psyche, became a familiar type. Such a hero needs a trial, and just as the fictional heroes of an earlier era had searched dark forests or sinister swamps for dragons and rival knights, so these modern heroes ventured in imagination, fearful but exalted, into the terrifying realm of sexuality, there to meet and grapple with the monstrous adversary, the *femme fatale*. Like the dragons of old, such women left heaps of dead warriors behind them. A famous publicity photograph of Theda Bara, who became in 1917 the cinema's last Romantic killer-Cleopatra, shows her gloating over a collection of human bones.

The heroes' motives in undertaking this quest into the wild terrain of eroticism were ascetically self-improving. 'I have neither sought nor given pleasure,' says one of D'Annunzio's Romantic sexual perverts. 'But in my trembling hand I have taken another trembling hand, to descend in search of the bottom of the abyss. . . . Such love disdains happiness for an unknown but infinitely higher good.'[102] That 'good' was

307

higher, not only than happiness, but also than goodness itself. The tamely virtuous who have never risked their souls may win the approval of legislators, but implicit in many of the nineteenth-century versions of the Cleopatra story is the admiration of the audacious sinner which impelled Nietzsche to ask

> What if a symptom of regression were inherent in the 'good', likewise a danger, a seduction, a poison, a narcotic, through which the present was possibly living *at the expense of the future?* . . . So that precisely morality would be to blame if the *highest power and splendour* actually possible to the type man was never in fact attained?[103]

In the dark wood of sexuality that modern knight, the masochist, is challenged and defeated by Cleopatra, *femme fatale*. As her consenting victim he becomes her partner and associate, a gallant transgressor, and because she tramples on godlike things God will, in turn, gratify his covert desire by trampling on him. The guilt and physical revulsion which accompanied the sexual act for so many nineteenth-century Europeans had at least this compensation, that it made the field of eroticism a space in which such dangerous sin, and therefore such punishment, could be found. 'A man has missed something,' said Flaubert, 'if he has never woken up in an anonymous bed beside a face he'll never see again, and if he has never left a brothel at dawn feeling like jumping off a bridge into the river out of sheer disgust with life.'[104] Such a life-enhancing sense of having plumbed the abyss could clearly not be afforded by the guilt-free sex of merry hedonists. 'Ah Lord!' implores Baudelaire in 'Un Voyage à Cythère',

> Give me the strength and the courage
> To contemplate my heart and body without disgust![105]

His prayer does not appear to have been granted – a denial for which he may perhaps have been grateful, for, as he remarked elsewhere, 'the unique and supreme pleasure of love lies in the certainty of doing *evil*'.[106]

The nineteenth-century Cleopatra, the personification of

exorbitant desire, is also, paradoxically, a protector of propriety and culture, just as the Devil, in punishing wrongdoers, does God's work. 'The denunciation of scandal,' wrote Jean Baudrillard, 'always pays homage to the law.'[107] The would-be voluptuary, imagining torture and death as the consequence of his pleasure, reveals his own condemnation of the thing which tempts him. The *femme fatale* is the projection of a profoundly puritanical conscience. 'My breast is home only to fury,' proclaims Alfieri's wicked Cleopatra. 'Heaven created me to castigate the world.'[108] To believe that, one has to believe the world is indeed a dreadful place. And such a belief, to the self-conscious sinners of Romantic Europe, was the token of a superior person. Cleopatra's love, wrote Heine in a curiously revealing passage, is not dangerous for 'the commonplace man' – the man, that is, who can take his pleasures easily; the man who, unlike Baudelaire, can look on his heart and soul without disgust. In Pushkin's story, after Cleopatra's bargain has been discussed, a young woman with 'fiery penetrating eyes' asserts that even in modern St Petersburg there may be women of 'enough pride and spiritual strength' to demand similar sacrifices from their lovers, women who 'value themselves highly'. Pushkin's hero is enraptured, for she is clearly talking about herself.[109] A killer-Cleopatra may be depraved, but she is certainly not cheap. A woman who values her sexuality so highly that a man can only have access to it by dying effectively places an interdiction on it. The sinner's greatness, which both requires heroism of him and confirms him in his heroic role, resides in his repudiation of sex, the sex in which he so nobly and self-destructively indulges.

The killer-Cleopatra is thus both sin and punishment. Her image, like those of the other Romantic and Decadent *femmes fatales* – Salome and Carmen, Mary Stuart and Dolores, the Sphinx and *la belle dame sans merci* – is ambiguous. Its attractions are never quite eclipsed by its horrors. For all the dangers which are imagined to ensue from association with her, it is clear that she is nearly always proposed as an object of desire, a desire which is highly complex, and which has as a necessary condition its own frustration. She is the happiness of those who feel themselves unfit to be happy, the freedom of those who cannot bear to be free, the ecstasy of those to whom only pain is pleasurable.

She is, obviously, evidence of the neuroses of those who imagined her (and the collective neurosis of the society they inhabited) – neuroses which this book has tried to elucidate. But she is also evidence of the anachronistic survival of human aspirations which, when manifested in more seemly times and places, have customarily been admired. The ethical code which takes 'greatness' as its absolute value, that code which, as has repeatedly been shown, coexists with and frequently contradicts that based on 'goodness', posits voluntary self-destruction as the most praiseworthy of possible acts. In the Middle Ages (and often subsequently), Cleopatra became great when she killed herself. In the Romantic era she was valued chiefly for the opportunity she offered men to prove their greatness by allowing themselves to be killed by her. 'Come!' murmurs Payen's Cleopatra as she hands a cup of poison to a besotted slave, 'I am divine Death, the enchantress.'[110] In Fokine's ballet Cleopatra was carried on stage in a sarcophagus from which attendants lifted a mummy-case containing the bandaged body of the Queen. Yards of multicoloured gauze were unwrapped from the mummy until at last Cleopatra, played by Diaghilev's skeletally thin mistress, Ida Rubinstein, was revealed, her face chalk-white, her wig sky-blue and one bony hand resting on the head of a kneeling slave.[111] Arthur Symons makes explicit the promise embodied by such a necrotic Cleopatra:

> I know how to make every hour of life as great,
> Terrible and delicious, as the hour
> When death tells all things.[112]

The killer-Cleopatra's heyday lasted roughly from the defeat of Napoleon to the outbreak of the First World War, an era during which heroism, the willingness of young men to allow themselves to be killed, was at an unprecedentedly low premium in Europe. In time of peace, noted Freud, 'Life is impoverished, it loses in interest, when the highest stake in the game of living, life itself, may not be risked.' Hence the restlessness of the 'civilized' person; hence the proliferation of fictions in which death could be experienced vicariously at the hands of a monster, a villain, a *femme fatale*. But Freud was writing, with the shocking honesty characteristic of him, in 1915, in a world where fictional killers were no longer required. Death was now readily available in actuality; for many it was inescapable, and so 'Life has, indeed, become interesting again; it has recovered its full content.'[113] In the security of faraway Hollywood the killer-Cleopatra was to live on a little longer – but in the shambles of Europe she rapidly came to be seen as a childishness, a dirty story, a joke.

# 10

# THE CHILD

IN 1898 GEORGE Bernard Shaw's anti-Romantic *Caesar and Cleopatra* was given its first performance, inaugurating a fresh phase in the development of Cleopatra's legend. In Shaw's 'play for puritans' she appears in a new guise. No longer is she the exotic man-eater, the belly dancer *sans merci*. Shaw has reclaimed her for modern Western society, desexualized her, infantilized her and made fun of her. The Queen of Egypt – scholar, administrator and empire-builder – enters the twentieth century as a pretty little kitten.

Shaw wrote his play in reaction against the 'deification of love' which he found obnoxious in contemporary drama and which he believed to be the theme of Shakespeare's *Antony and Cleopatra*. Dedicated to the cause of realism and to the eradication of cant and mumbo-jumbo in all their forms, he had no respect for the moral interdictions which had charged the romantic Cleopatras with danger, or sympathy with the mystical aspirations which had dignified them. As for the flight from sordid reality into a transcendental fantasy world, he had no time for it at all. 'The pleasures of the senses I can sympathise with and share; but the substitution of sensuous ecstasy for intellectual activity and honesty is the very devil.' His Caesar is a thoroughly modern hero – clear-headed, pragmatic, always kind (because vindictiveness is futile and generosity productive) but never emotional. Impossible that such a man should allow himself to be swayed by passion. To imagine so is 'folly gone mad erotically'.[1]

Shaw's intention was to be unsentimentally truthful about

312

human nature, but in order to arrive at his 'truth' he found it necessary to tamper extensively with the historical record. The action of his play deviates from the generally accepted facts in a number of significant ways. He makes Cleopatra, who was probably nineteen or twenty when Caesar arrived in Egypt, into an emotionally and intellectually retarded sixteen-year-old who pouts and prattles, squabbling with her little brother and peeping out from behind her nurse like a bashful toddler. Instead of leading one of the rival factions in a civil war, this Cleopatra is living idly in the palace, playing with the sacred cats and only occasionally daring to defy her nurse. Far from being an accomplished linguist and a princess who was already taking an active part in international affairs, she is a silly ignoramus who believes that Romans have long noses like elephants 'and ivory tusks, and little tails, and seven arms with a hundred arrows in each; and they live on human flesh'.[2] She is carried to Caesar in a carpet, but in Shaw's version this episode is understood to be neither a seduction nor a daring and ingenious solution to a difficult problem, but a pointless prank with which she wastes Caesar's time. She is as callous as a thoughtless child. Pothinus is not (as the ancient historians report) executed by Caesar, but dishonourably murdered on Cleopatra's orders because he has embarrassed her by telling the truth about her. ('You scratch, kitten, do you?' asks Caesar.)[3] Julius Caesar does not make love to her, does not leave her pregnant, and does not invite her to join him in Rome. In fact so far is he from being impressed by her, erotically or otherwise, that he all but forgets to say goodbye to her on leaving Alexandria. When he goes he does not trust her to rule Egypt jointly with her brother (she would clearly be incapable of any such responsible work), but appoints a Roman governor. Thus Cleopatra is reduced to conform to Shaw's idea of a real-life young lady – in other words a pretty but rather tiresome infant.

Shaw had set out to strip Cleopatra's story of phoney romance. It seemed that he could find no other way of doing so than by stripping it of sex as well. And that in turn could only be achieved by imagining a world free of mature women. Ftatateeta, Cleopatra's nurse, is a savage, and Cleopatra herself is a child. But the pleasure that adults take in the contemplation of a child's sweet ways can have an erotic dimension. When, in 1946, Gabriel Pascal filmed Shaw's play with Claude Rains and Vivien Leigh as the eponymous pair he stuck closely to the original text, but asked Shaw to make two crucial additions. By his own account Pascal shared with Shaw a weariness of adulthood: 'We knew the secret of the Pied Piper – how to induce genuine children to run away from the boring mediocrity of everyday life.'4 But he knew that cinema-goers looked for romance (as sexual love was popularly termed) and he seems also to have sensed that eroticism is not peculiar to adult life. The Cleopatra of his film is both a little girl and a sexual being. In one of the newly written scenes Ftatateeta tells Cleopatra: 'You are still my child, but to all others you are a grown woman now.' The nurse then congratulates her charge on having 'charmed' Caesar and announces that in future she must take a bath every day. The Queen, babyish as ever, petulantly demands that in that case the bath must be perfumed, and reaches for some cosmetics proffered by one of her maids. Ftatateeta rebukes her. 'Caesar hates perfumes, and if you redden your lips he will not kiss you.' There follows a discreet version – in the polite post-war British style – of the bathroom scene which was by this time *de rigueur* in any film set in the Roman era. Vivien Leigh steps behind a diaphanous curtain and, with her back turned, allows her nightdress to fall to her waist. It is a very ladylike piece of provocation, but it is sufficient to make an important change to the meaning of the play. Caesar has awoken Cleopatra's sexuality: she is 'a grown woman' and she is being groomed to seduce him. For all Shaw's cynicism about 'sexual infatuation', for all his refusal to portray Cleopatra as an adult, his play could still be made to carry a more erotic meaning than any he had originally written into it.

To Shaw's contemporaries (and to some extent to ours) it seemed that a mature woman and a child had, and ought to have, a great deal in common. To infantilize Cleopatra was not necessarily to unsex her. In Pascal's film Vivien Leigh does full justice to the childlike wilfulness and naïvety of Cleopatra's character as written by Shaw, but her performance is none the less unmistakably that of an adult, sexually knowing woman. Her pettishness, her silly prattle and her clinging ways are all forms of flirtation. Kenneth Tynan, no great admirer of hers, wrote of Leigh's stage performance as Cleopatra: 'She picked at the part of Cleopatra with the daintiness of a debutante called upon to dismember a stag.'[5] Quite so: it is precisely this contrived delicacy and helplessness which makes Leigh's screen Cleopatra so ambiguous. In her performance feminine coquetry is almost indistinguishable from childish wheedling. Frivolity, cowardice, ignorance and flightiness – these are the qualities which make Shaw's heroine seem such a baby. They are also – as an examination of some other Cleopatras of the period makes plain – the qualities which mark her most clearly as a typical representative of her sex. And they are by no means undesirable. In beings who are known to be 'weaker', whether by virtue of their age or of their gender, faults which would be deplorable in a man appear charming – pretty reminders that women and children must always defer to the adult male.

From 1864, when the German historian Adolf Stahr published an influential biography in which he set out to vindicate Cleopatra, a series of histories and scholarly historical novels began to appear in which the legend of the wicked Cleopatra was derided and a supposedly more realistic and more acceptable image of her was proposed. In the Preface to his biography of 1914 Arthur Weigall suggests that his Cleopatra is 'a very good average type of womanhood'.[6] That type frequently turns out to be an infantile one.

Over and over again we are told, by historians and novelists alike, that Cleopatra is 'a woman in every sense of the word' and that 'a woman will still be a woman whether her forehead be encircled with a royal diadem or not'.[7] For all their earnest endeavours and their scholarship these writers leave on their reconstructions of Cleopatra's era, just as the poets and painters did, the imprint of their own prejudices. Each of them has to struggle to reconcile the image of Cleopatra as a self-assertive ruler possessed of a powerful creative intelligence – the image which their researches revealed to them – with their limited and limiting notions of female capacity and female goodness. They did much to redeem Cleopatra's reputation. Stahr, and Weigall after him, identified and analysed her vision of a pan-Hellenic empire of the East based on Roman military power and Egyptian wealth. Désiré de Bernath laid stress on her intellectual abilities and took pains to contradict the old legend of her debauchery. When de Bernath's Cleopatra is on her own, her 'mode of living... was as peaceful as it was unpretentious'. No unseemly roistering for this Cleopatra and her Antony; on the contrary, 'together they attended the lectures given at the museum'. But even this serious and well-behaved young woman needs to be taken care of. When it comes to planning her foreign policy she is at a loss without 'the support of a man capable of giving a vigorous turn to the wheel of fortune'.[8]

Cleopatra was very small; so historians concluded from highly questionable evidence, arguing that had she been of normal stature it would have been too difficult for Apollodorus to carry her in the carpet. In version after version of her story we hear about her 'little hands'. Saadeh's Caesar wonders at them, fondly teasing her when she threatens to kill him: ' "Do these tender delicate hands know how to handle a sword?" he asked, smiling at the absurd idea.'[9] Her diminutive form is matched by her personality. Weigall, who repeatedly refers to her, even when she is in her late thirties, as 'the little queen', ascribes to her 'a somewhat naïve and childish manner, a waywardness, an audacity, a capriciousness which enchanted those around her'. He claims that she was wild and liked 'to romp'. 'Her manner was frequently what may be called harum-scarum. . . . Her untutored heart leapt from mirth to sorrow, from comedy to tragedy, with unexpected ease; and with her small hands she tossed about her the fabric of her complex circumstances like a mantle of light and darkness.'[10]

Such a woman belongs in a nursery – her own or her children's. Those writers who sought to rehabilitate Cleopatra were eager to stress her maternity. Georg Ebers's heroine, on arriving in Alexandria, goes straight to the royal nursery where, pushing back her lace veil with 'her little hands', she kisses her babies.[11] Vernon Knott's Cleopatra waxes lyrical about her offspring's 'dimpled fingers like soft tendrils' twining round her heart.[12] Weigall imagines her transfigured by motherhood: 'The happy-go-lucky little Queen of Egypt, now so subdued and so gentle, lay clasping to her breast the newborn Caesar.'[13] The image of a mother can be majestic or dominant, but these doting little Cleopatras are mothers of a different kind. They love their babies, and are seen at their best in their company, because, being childlike themselves, they belong with children.

As a child feels lost without a parent, so a child-woman craves the protection of a man. Weigall accepts Dio Cassius's account of Cleopatra's interview with Octavius, in which she weeps and calls upon Julius Caesar, citing it as evidence that she was 'essentially feminine . . . needing desperately the help and sympathy of others'.[14] The references to Caesar, as Dio understood them, were designed to enhance the guileful Cleopatra's allure in Octavius's eyes and to remind him of her links with his adoptive father and therefore with his party's cause. To Weigall it meant simply that, in her sweet girlish way, she was longing for a strong paternal man to care for her and guide her out of trouble. When de Bernath's Antony leaves Cleopatra in order to marry Octavia she loses all interest in affairs of state and becomes preoccupied with her loneliness and jealousy. She longs only to see Antony again: 'She had no other wish; she had offered up no other prayer to her gods'.[15] This feminine susceptibility is, in the end, the child-Cleopatra's undoing. Incapable of manly independence, she clings too fondly to her adored protector. When she fell in love with Antony, wrote Henri Blaze de Bury, 'the queen vanished, only the woman remained, and it is to the account

317

of the woman's weaknesses that all her political errors should be charged'.[16] 'Had she not been a woman,' opined de Bernath, 'had she not been passionately enamoured of the man who should have been no more than an instrument in her hands, it is probable that her efforts would have been crowned with success.'[17]

She could not have hoped to dispense with such an instrument, for as female ruler she was not only incapable of giving a vigorous spin to the wheel of fortune, she was also incompetent in the essential arts of war. Antony was necessary to her because 'her son Caesarion was too young to fight his own battles,' wrote Weigall, 'and she herself could not lead an army'.[18] Why she could not, Weigall does not deem it necessary to say. To him, and to most of his contemporaries, it was self-evident that a woman could not be considered a serious candidate for the grown-up job of military leadership. Besides, Cleopatra, true to her childish-womanish nature, was easily scared. During the last quarter of the nineteenth century several historians put forward the theory, now generally accepted, that Cleopatra's flight from Actium was a planned withdrawal, a strategy on which she and Antony had agreed beforehand. None the less, the majority of writers still preferred to see it as a manifestation of her feminine timidity. Blaze de Bury clearly feels he has adequately explained it when he says: 'Cleopatra was a woman.' Houssaye, despite acknowledging that some sort of retreat was necessary, still imputes the loss of the battle to Cleopatra's 'nervousness' and describes her fleeing, overcome with fever and anguish, 'harkening only to her fear'. Philip Walsingham Sergeant, writing in 1909, believed that she had a sudden fit of panic, or possibly of seasickness. 'For my part,' declared de Bernath, 'nothing seems to me easier than to explain the flight of Cleopatra as no more than the act of a woman in no way accustomed to the din of battle.' In a verse drama by James MacKereth, published in 1920, Cleopatra laments her own cowardice: 'This is the curse of every woman. . . . To fail by nature not by will.'[19]

Women not only lack the courage and constancy of the

adult male, they are also childlike in their capriciousness and the importance they attach to trivial things. In his *Outline of History*, H. G. Wells declares that if Cleopatra's flight from Actium was not treacherous, then it must have been motivated by 'the sudden whim of a charming woman'[20] – the latter being a phenomenon with which he assumed his readers to be so familiar that it needed no further elaboration. Cleopatra, being female, cannot be expected to act rationally. 'Women's ways are always zig-zag, you know,' says Saadeh's Julius Caesar.[21] When, in Weigall's account, she dissolves her priceless pearl Antony looks on, regretting the waste and pondering 'not without gloom upon the ways of women'.[22]

This female foolishness most frequently manifests itself in the form of personal vanity. Georg Ebers's Cleopatra is pathetically anxious about the signs of ageing on her face. When Antony arrives unexpectedly at her palace at the head of a magnificent procession, and later when Octavius visits her, her first response is to bewail the fact that she does not have time to dress. This Cleopatra flees from Actium because she is running out of make-up and is determined to get back to Egypt before Antony sees her face bare of cosmetics.[23] Few Cleopatras take their vanity to quite such lengths, but several of them choose the asp as an instrument of death solely because, unlike a dagger, it will not spoil their looks.[24]

Ebers's Cleopatra, fussing, even at moments of great danger or high seriousness, about her appearance, is not supposed to be comic or unattractive. A male character in the same novel remarks that he would not wish to be married to a woman whose intellectual capacity matched his own. Her 'stimulating remarks and searching questions . . . would not have permitted him, after his return home, wearied by arduous toil, to find the rest for which he longed'.[25] Clothes and cosmetics may be topics unworthy of a man's interest (it is a sign of the degradation of Ebers's Antony that he dyes his hair and wears gem-encrusted red morocco boots), but they are appropriate preoccupations for a child-woman. Besides, women had good reason to devote themselves so solemnly to frivolity. In the Preface to his biography of

Cleopatra, Oskar von Wertheimer gave succinct expression to a seldom questioned scale of value: 'We judge men by their achievements and women by the love they have inspired.'[26] Which being so, a woman who considers separation from her make-up a greater calamity than a lost battle is not a frivolous ninny but a realist who has correctly identified her prescribed social role and the criteria by which her society will judge her. Coquetry may be child's play, but for a child-woman it is her life's work.

Shaw defended his portrayal of Cleopatra on the grounds that similar 'childishness . . . may be observed in our own climate at the present day in many women of fifty'.[27] No doubt. Once it has become established that a certain type is considered attractive plenty of people will be ready to conform to that type, at least in looks and observable behaviour. Even now many girls adopt a girlish, *faux-naïf* manner for purposes of flirtation. But it is still proper to ask why men wished to believe that their sexual partners were just like children. Shaw declared that Shakespeare's *Antony and Cleopatra* must be 'vaguely distressing to the ordinary healthy citizen'.[28] The same could well be said of his own play, which gives vivid life to an ambiguous and potentially pernicious stereotype, one which sexualizes children at the same time as it infantilizes adult women.

There was much that would evidently be pleasing to the male imagination in the child-Cleopatra. Small, flatteringly dependent, amusingly harum-scarum but ultimately docile, she makes an enchanting pet. Masculine protectiveness, the paternal instinct to defend and cherish, is aroused by the image of her. So are darker desires. The fantasy of the child-woman is tinged by the sadistic will to power. A childish Cleopatra's exquisite little limbs can be easily and pleasurably crushed. Henry Houssaye imagines her embracing Antony when he returned, bloodstained and sweating, from battle. 'She had rediscovered her emperor, her god of war. She threw herself passionately on his bosom, bruising her breast against his cuirass.'[29] In his verse drama published in 1904 Vernon Knott has Cleopatra imagine how after her death graverobbers will break open her tomb and pull her long amber-coloured hair, and shows Antony bruising her with his kisses.

> Ever thou wast for these big hands of mine
> A flower too delicate.[30]

James MacKereth's Cleopatra, preparing for her own death, reminisces about Antony, whom she pictures in battle surrounded by horrors and 'The guttural gurgle of foot-strangled men'. Excited by such memories, she prepares to die, calling to her women to dress her:

> That flaming reptile coil about my arm
> Yea, let it press and pain my tender flesh.

Her belt is fastened:

> Nay tighter, Charmian, tighter till it hurts!
> Have I not felt the thews and thongs of love
> And dumbly lain in sweetest torture captive
> In Marcus's brave embraces? O tighter yet![31]

In C. E. Ironmonger's poem of 1924 Cleopatra clenches her tiny fists until her nails 'called forth a rosy drop from tender palm'. In Antony's arms she is 'half-strangled by the fierce caress'. He bruises her soft cheek as

> Crushing her vivid mouth, more crimson still
> With the protesting blood, he drinks his fill
> From the near fountain of her fragrant lips
> And bites the rosebuds of her fingertips.[32]

The Romantic Agony had not been assuaged when the *femme fatale* lost her power to thrill by terror; it simply found a new focus. The imagined violence directed against the child-Cleopatra suggests that, like the killer-Cleopatra, she is at least in part a projection of men's fear of sexuality, as incarnated in women.

That sexuality can be attacked and punished, or it can simply be wished away. Much as Bernard Shaw deplored the education (or lack of it) and conditioning which reduced women to the status of flowerlike infants, he shied away from imagining an adult, erotically potent female. Rather than do so he cancelled the sexual component of Cleopatra's relationship with Caesar. Historians of the late nineteenth and early twentieth centuries did not have the poetic licence to alter the past quite so drastically, but they were at pains to point out that Cleopatra was by no means the libertine of legend. Weigall sadly admits that she was not 'a particularly exalted type of her sex', as witness the fact that she allowed herself to be seduced by Caesar, but he is most emphatic in his insistence that she was victim, not temptress. At the time they met 'Caesar was an elderly man who had ruined the wives and daughters of an astounding number of his friends', while she was 'an unmarried girl . . . against whose moral character not one shred of trustworthy evidence can be advanced'. To 'attribute the blame to Cleopatra' is therefore entirely unjust.[33] Like de Bernath, Weigall also makes a point of stressing that Cleopatra's regrettable lapse from girlish virtue was by no means as precipitately or easily accomplished as legend would have us believe. True, she has herself delivered to Caesar's quarters in her carpet, but what happens then is perfectly innocent: 'She talked to him through the long hours of the night.' After this *nuit blanche* Cleopatra emerges still very much a 'wild and irresponsible girl . . . we may almost picture her making faces at her brother'. Caesar sets about seducing this *ingénue*, but slowly, over a long period of 'gaiety'.[34] Similarly both Weigall and de Bernath vehemently deny that Cleopatra's relationship with Antony was sexually consummated when they met at Tarsus. De Bernath is even indignant at the suggestion that they might have left there together for Alexandria: 'The Queen's conduct had been far too dignified and reserved to allow of her committing so gross an error on her departure.'[35]

These writers, and others like them, push the word 'married' to the furthest bounds of its possible definition in their attempts to prove that their heroine's love-life was perfectly respectable. A woman who chose her own lovers, who said yes on the first date and who, twice in her life and without any apparent compunction, lived with a man not her husband was not the Cleopatra they wanted. Such independent conduct was far too adult, and too masculine, to fit with their image of the dainty little Queen.

There is a third way of dealing with something fearful. If the first is to attack it and the second is to pretend it doesn't exist, the third, and often the most efficacious, is to laugh at it. Shaw, who used both the latter strategies simultaneously to counter the threat of Cleopatra's sexuality, pronounced that 'I have a technical objection to making sexual infatuation a tragic theme. Experience proves that it is only effective in the comic spirit.'[36] In that he proved himself to be a prescient spokesman for the new century's sensibility. His Romantic predecessors might have exalted love in deadly earnest, but since his day, as a survey of modern Cleopatras demonstrates, the dominant tone of representations of erotic love has been humorous. Self-mocking, archly naughty, punning, farcical, grotesque or downright smutty, the vast majority of modern Cleopatras have a comical ambivalence. They are erotically charged but that charge is neutralized, its meaning scrambled and its threat to order and conventional morality defused by a joke. Shaw's Cleopatra enthuses about Mark Antony's 'round arms', but her carnality is as cosily meaningless as a dressing-up game. She sometimes talks like a woman with adult lusts but she clearly is not one. She has a sexual identity, but it is funny and therefore innocuous.

Half a century before Shaw wrote his play Cleopatra had already been invoked in the mockery of Romantic ideas about the love of women. In *Dombey and Son*, written between 1846 and 1848, Charles Dickens gives the nickname Cleopatra to a seventy-year-old coquette with false curls, false eyebrows, false teeth, a false complexion and a false invalidism which permits her to travel everywhere in the reclining posture which, as we have already seen, was one of Cleopatra's seductive attributes.

> Her attitude in the wheel chair (which she never varied) was one in which she had been taken in a barouche, some fifty years before, by a then fashionable artist who had appended to his published sketch the name of Cleopatra. . . . Mrs Skewton was a beauty then, and bucks threw wine-glasses over

their heads by the dozen in her honour. The beauty and the barouche had both passed away, but she still preserved the attitude.[37]

This caricature of feminine artificiality flirts and connives her way through a seedy demi-monde in which séxual attractiveness in a woman, if genuine, is a marketable commodity and, if fake, a camouflage (for who could suspect such an artlessly girlish septuagenarian as Mrs 'Cleopatra' Skewton of selling her daughter, as in effect she does?). Some twenty years later the Russian playwright Alexander Ostrovsky gave the name Cleopatra to another superannuated coquette in his play *Too Clever by Half*. His intention is more lightly satirical than Dickens's; his Cleopatra is a silly, gullible creature who (wrongly) believes all men to be in love with her − a world away from the calculating Mrs Skewton. But different as their treatments are, both Dickens and Ostrovsky associated Cleopatra with the over-valuation of female beauty, and of the love it was supposed to inspire.

This was the theme Shaw took up. When his Cleopatra, in her self-important vanity, expects Caesar to sacrifice his troops so that she shall not be left alone he gravely explains to her, ' "Of my soldiers who have trusted me there is not one whose hand I shall not hold more sacred than your head" [Cleopatra is overwhelmed. Her eyes fill with tears].'[38] While women are such light-minded, laughable creatures it is clearly absurd to suppose that sexual love can be an important motive in the lives of any but the most idiotic of men.

By the beginning of the twentieth century Cleopatra was established as a stock character in a popular tradition of bawdy comedy. In music halls, cabarets, cartoons, nightclubs, even circuses, images of sexual glamour have always been juxtaposed with the rudest humour − humour which seems, paradoxically, to be aimed at the subversion of that glamour. The girls in tights and sequins are succeeded in the spotlight by clowns or comedians whose very costumes mock physical beauty and romantic pretension. The women signify sex; the men signify the snigger which tells us we do not have to take it seriously (or be seriously afraid of it). Cleopatra has long had a place in this double game. In 1909 she appeared as one of the turns in a show at the Ziegfeld Follies. Impersonated by a showgirl, alongside Carmen, Marguerite and a Gibson bathing girl, she was conjured up by Lucifer to tempt the young hero.[39] In a circus describing itself as 'The Greatest Show on Earth', which came to New York in 1925, the girls riding the elephants were dressed as Cleopatra and her maids.[40] Edmund Wilson describes a piece of vintage New York burlesque of the twenties, given at the Minsky Brothers Follies:

> In the current version of *Antony and Cleopatra*, a perennial classic, Julius Caesar, in a tin helmet, smoking a big cigar, catches Antony (the Jewish comic) on a divan with Cleopatra (the principal strip-tease girl) and wallops him over the bottom with the flat of an enormous sword. 'I'm dying! I'm dying' groans Antony, as he staggers around in a circle and Caesar and Cleopatra, the Roman soldiers and the Egyptian slave-girls break into a rousing shimmy to the refrain of 'He's dying! He's dying!' 'I hear de voices of de angels!' says Antony. 'What do they say?' asks Caesar. 'I don't know: I don't speak Polish.' . . . 'Bring me the wassup,' says Cleopatra, and her slave-girl, kneeling, presents a box, from which Cleopatra takes a huge property phallus. (At some point in the development of the ancient act the word *asp* was evidently confused with *wasp*.) . . . Cleopatra falls prone on her lover's body, and Caesar, with pathetic reverence, places on her posterior a wreath, which he waters with a watering-pot. . . . This curious piece of East Side folk-drama has been popular at Minsky's for years.[41]

In these burlesques Cleopatra is not exactly a child, for her physical maturity is always amply displayed, but the next best thing. She is what is now eloquently known as a bimbo, a luscious young woman whose silliness in no way detracts from her sexual allure – who is in fact preferred precisely because she is so dumb. This is the disreputable but lusty tradition which culminated, in the iconology of Cleopatra, with the British comedy film made in 1963, *Carry on Cleo*.

325

The Carry On team's Cleopatra, played with a lisp and an inviting giggle by the huge-eyed comedienne Amanda Barrie, spends most of her time in an asses' milk bath dressed only in a blue fringed bathing cap (her 'only resemblance to an iceberg is that only one-tenth of her is visible' remarks the narrator) coyly toying with a loofah whose shape proclaims it a direct descendant of Minsky's 'wassup'. Described variously as 'that bird that rules Egypt' and 'the lay of Ancient Rome', she has prodigious sexual energy. '*Puer! O puer! O puer!*' exclaims Sid James as Mark Antony, staggering out of her bedchamber. She is also obliging. When Julius Caesar seems a little bashful ('Oooh, I do feel queer!' quavers Kenneth Williams) she proffers him a love philtre with a lot of breathy laughter and eye-rolling and promises that it'll make him feel 'all sort of . . . well . . . you know . . . *friendly*'. But though she is knowing about sex she is otherwise half-witted. 'I've been thinking . . .' she says to Mark Antony, who is astonished to hear it. 'You do?!'

In the tradition of popular bawdry to which both Minsky's Follies and the Carry On films belong there is no sin, only sauciness. Sex is not sublime and dangerous, but undignified and sweet. Physically magnificent women – the Ziegfeld showgirls or Barrie, who is several inches taller than most of the men in *Carry On Cleo* – are proved to be as deficient in mind as the knock-kneed, comical-looking men around them are in body. The sexual power is made manageable by the fact that the men have the monopoly on power of every other kind. That parity once established, a good time can be had by all. At the end of the Carry On film Antony and Cleopatra, or rather 'Mark and Cleo', are left to enjoy a happy ending of unsullied sexual bliss. 'Life was just one long Saturday night,' says the narrator as Sid James dives, fully dressed and helmeted, into the milk bath where Barrie awaits him, simpering lasciviously. Humour of this kind at least clears an imaginative space in which sex is possible, and friendly, but it does so at a high cost. All the participants must consent to be made foolish and the women, before they can be allowed their share of the jollity, must first sacrifice their claim to be fully grown-up people.

Tod Browning's film *Freaks*, made in 1932 – peculiar as it is – casts a sharp and brilliant light on normal sexual relationships. Its leading female character is called Cleopatra. She is the trapeze artist, and her lover is the strong man, in a travelling circus most of whose other performers are 'freaks' – deformed, mentally deficient or otherwise disabled people. Cleopatra and the strong man, both of whom have sleek, splendid bodies and both of whom are possessed of exceptional physical prowess, are characters of unremitting evil. Cruel, greedy and deceitful, they laugh at the 'freaks' and connive in exploiting them. The wicked Cleopatra marries one of the dwarfs in order to get her hands on his money. There is a wedding party. At its climax a loving-cup is passed and, while another dwarf executes a triumphal dance on the table, the 'freaks' chant the slogan of their fellowship, 'One of us! One of us!', apparently exulting to see that Cleopatra, whose perfect body is so awe-inspiring and so unnervingly desirable, can be brought down to their level.

Browning's film was initially suppressed by queasy distributors, but when it was re-released, after thirty years' oblivion, audiences recognized that his treatment of his disabled cast was acceptably respectful and compassionate. But the hostility the film evinces towards female beauty and female sexual potency remains disturbing. At the end Cleopatra has been bizarrely punished. Her glorious body has been transformed into that of a chicken. Weak and ugly, she has become 'one of us'.

A great deal of popular humour, notably the facetious captions conventionally appended to pornographic photographs, indicate that there are still many people who, like Browning's 'freaks', are intimidated by female beauty and who console themselves, and avenge their own fear, by ridiculing attractive women. In New York in the 1920s Edmund Wilson, going even further downmarket than Minsky's to seek out the burlesque at its most basic, saw shows in which magnificent female bodies paraded before an audience of

327

silent and awestruck men. The women were 'priestesses of Venus', glorious and distant. Between them and the shabby men who watched them there seemed to be a great gulf fixed. This gulf was bridged by male comedians, little stunted men 'like Nibelungen or chimpanzees', who dispelled the reverential mood with jokes of extreme cruelty and coarseness.[42] They were the colleagues of the haughty showgirls, whom they treated with familiarity. From their behaviour the men in the audience were able to grasp that the women, who seemed so proud and majestic, were only bimbos after all.

Cleopatra the bimbo/baby is a woman whom men can encounter without fear. Like all women in our culture, she is understood to be sexuality incarnate, but the awful power that identification gives her is cancelled by her infantilism. The innocuous child-Cleopatras of the turn-of-the-century historians with their little hands and winsome ways, the kittenish Cleopatra of Shaw's play and the dumb-broad Cleopatras of smutty comedy all have this in common, that they are each a bit of a joke. Men laugh at them, and that laughter – whether affectionate, teasing or salacious – proclaims them inferior and the laughers safe.

# 11

# CLEOPATRA WINKS

WHEN CLEOPATRA COMES to Rome in the film made in 1962 by Joseph L. Mankiewicz she comes with the maximum conceivable hullaballoo. Trumpeters, mounted twelve abreast on white horses, gallop through a triumphal arch into the forum. Hurtling chariots criss-cross the screen. Brown-skinned archers let loose volleys of arrows. Crowds of attendants, naked but for pink loincloths, tug aside a heap of shimmering silk to reveal a belly dancer with sequined nipples. The forum is filled first with red and then with yellow smoke. Pole vaulters scatter clouds of glitter. A hollow pyramid opens up to release hundreds of white doves. Dervishes whirl, black dancers stamp and gyrate in tiny beaded bikinis. Girls flap enormous wooden wings. The show goes on, and on. More horsemen come wheeling in, pushing back the excited crowd. Drums roll, cymbals clash, trumpets sound. Three hundred straining slaves appear, tugging behind them a mobile stone Sphinx as high as the Senate House. And there, between its paws, dressed in pleated gold lamé, sits the twentieth century's most celebrated Cleopatra, Elizabeth Taylor. A silence falls as the extraordinary edifice crosses the square. Antony looks awe-struck, Calpurnia dejected and Octavius peevish. Steps are lowered, a red carpet rolled out. Cleopatra, still enthroned, is carried down the monumental steps by black slaves. Caesar rises to greet her. She bows, her breasts looming large around the edges of her deeply cut gold bodice. The crowd roars, and then a remarkable thing happens. The camera stays on Elizabeth Taylor's face, made up in fashionable early sixties' style with heavy eyeliner, false lashes and pale lipstick. And, as she catches Caesar's eye, Cleopatra winks.

Somewhere around the beginning of this century it had begun to be hard to take the idea of Cleopatra seriously. But the joke she embodies can work two ways: as the bimbo-child she became its butt; in other versions she is the joke's perpetrator, and so remains the dominant figure in her own story. Khalil Saadeh's novel about her, published in 1898, frequently slips into absurdity, not only because Saadeh is no great literary artist, but also because, by the end of the nineties, the passionate Romanticism of a Pushkin or a Gautier was no longer tenable. 'I generally write my laws with letters of blood,' Saadeh's Cleopatra tells a shocked Brutus. 'They last longer and, besides, it is a beautiful colour for writing.'[1] The self-parody is knowing. As Romanticism turned Decadent, the wicked Cleopatra turned camp.

Only by doing so could she, or rather her creators, avoid ridicule. One way or another, whether at her or with her, those who interpret Cleopatra's story in this century have got to laugh. If they fail to, they will be laughed at. In 1917 the Fox Studios produced a film called *Cleopatra*, using the plot of Rider Haggard's novel. In surviving stills its star Theda Bara, the actress for whom the word 'vamp' was coined, lounges on thrones or tiger skins, her heavily kohled eyelids drooping over glaring eyes, her numerous costumes leaving much of her flesh exposed. Bara, who looks to the modern eye surprisingly fat and blowsy for a fatal beauty, was the daughter of a Jewish tailor from Cincinnati, but she had been provided by the Fox publicity department with an artificial biography and a persona which made her seem type-cast as the killer-Cleopatra. She was born in Egypt, so ran the story in the publicity handouts, 'in the shadow of the Sphinx'. She was the fruit of a 'guilty union' between an Italian artist (or, in some versions, a dashing Spahi) and an Arabian princess. As an infant she sucked, not milk, but the venom of serpents. Her name was an anagram of 'Arab Death'. An ancient inscription found on the walls of a tomb

330

near Thebes prophesied her birth, predicting: 'She shall seem a snake to most men. She shall lead them to sin and destruction.'[2] In a publicity picture for her *Cleopatra* a pair of enamelled serpents curve around her breasts while she looks daggers at the viewer.

Here was the killer-Cleopatra, as fascinatingly sinful as ever, transplanted to a new medium and presented to a huge new public – but the transplantation was not a success. The public enjoyed Theda Bara's *femme fatale* pose for a while; then they began to mock it. Iconoclastic rumours about her circulated: that dark, burning look owed its intensity only to her extreme myopia; the reason she never spoke to journalists was not that she was as enigmatic as the Sphinx but that she was too stupid to know the answer to its riddle, or to any other question. In 1916 a reviewer reported that in one of her usual vamp roles she was 'so outrageously evil that the audience finds several of the scenes rather amusing'. A year later (the year in which she made *Cleopatra*) they were laughing out loud at her latest 'concoction of sensationalism'.[3] Hollywood's next heroine was Clara Bow, the pertly playful 'It-girl'. A public ready to enjoy her flirty sensuality scoffed at the idea that the wages of sin (or rather of sex) was death. The *femme fatale* survived as a stock cinematic character, but since the downfall of Theda Bara (whose career came to an ignominious end in 1920 – after making over forty films in five years she found her style so unfashionable that she could not get work) she has become either a broadly comical figure of fun, or a more complex and sophisticated creature, capable of deflecting mockery by laughing at herself.

The broad humour of Minsky's Follies or of *Carry On Cleo*, the humour that reduces Cleopatra to a bimbo-child, robs eroticism of its intensity. Tit and bum are inadequate substitutes for a beauty so dazzling that it burns the eye of the beholder, and a little of what you fancy is something of a come-down after the transcendent raptures of a fatal love. T. S. Eliot evokes Cleopatra in *The Waste Land*, only to suggest that the vividness and ardour of which she is emblematic have been leached out of the arid, secular modern world:

331

becomes unattainable when sin ceases to be mortal.[4] The passion and extravagance implicit in Cleopatra's legend are still in demand with her modern public, but they can no longer be taken straight. To retain her allure in a sceptical age Cleopatra has had to camp it up.

Camp, in the words of the critic Philip Core, is 'the disguise that fails . . . the lie that tells the truth'.[5] It provides a discourse within which it is possible both to say and not to say, a discourse in which style is so far paramount that the question of what is or is not true – or real, or morally right – can be dismissed as irrelevant. As Susan Sontag has pointed out, camp 'is alive to a double sense', not to the familiar duality of literal meaning and symbolic meaning, but to 'the difference between the thing as meaning something, anything, and the thing as pure artifice'.[6] Camp-Cleopatras are shaped by the conventions of the Romantic story, but not by the ideology that gave that story meaning, for camp allows images which have lost their validity to keep their vitality. The camp-Cleopatra is a signifier from which the original signified has slid away, leaving an ambiguous carnival character, a two-faced mask. She is a heroine appropriate to an era in Western culture in which moral certainty, though still publicly advocated, has been covertly doubted, an era in which loudly stated principles of sexual and civic propriety have coexisted with a lively sympathy for the Devil. The camp-Cleopatra is an image of duplicity, but she also has a benign aspect as a figure of tolerance presiding over a domain where the impermissible is permitted.

In a contemporary review of the 1954 film *Serpent of the Nile*, which was billed by its publicists as an account of 'the sizzling love-life of history's most notorious siren', Cleopatra, played by Rhonda Fleming, is described as 'a gal who wants to eat her cake and have it too'.[7] An apposite characterization: the most popular twentieth-century Cleopatras have it both ways, morally and aesthetically. They are depraved and immoral, but likeable with it – considerably more amusing than the virtuous wives with whom they are contrasted. They inhabit gorgeous places, dress in exotic costumes, and make their entrances attended by troupes of dancing girls, naked savages and galloping horses, but they contrive to intimate, with a shrug or an arched eyebrow, that they are sophisticated modern women to whom all this masquerading seems a trifle quaint. Their creators have acknowledged and traded on the fact that the bad, whether it be bad taste or moral badness, is often more appealing than its opposite. 'There is a kind of vulgarity which by its own boldness becomes beautiful, and this is it,'[8] wrote Dilys Powell, reviewing Mankiewicz's film. There is also a kind of wrong-doing which seems better (more desirable, enviable, fashionable) than doing good.

'How would you like to be the wickedest woman in history?'[9] Thus, according to one of his publicists, Cecil B. De Mille offered Claudette Colbert the starring role in his film *Cleopatra*. The answer to such a question could only be, by 1934, 'Very much indeed, please.' Wicked women were fast – sexually liberated, sharp-witted and well-dressed – and fast women were fun. The old opposition between goodness and greatness has been replaced by a more cynical dichotomy, that between goodness and success. The good woman may win approval, but the wicked woman gets her man, and – such is the ambivalence of the value system which dubs her wicked while relishing her bad behaviour – she frequently gets away with it.

Even the turn-of-the-century writers who had so emphatically insisted on women's childlike dependence acknowledged that women who conformed too obediently to their ideal were unattractive. Octavia, wrote Désiré de Bernath, was 'a kind, good woman: one of those mild and gentle natures over whom the passions hold no sway, and who are alike incapable of inspiring passion'.[10] Weigall is more emphatic. His Octavia is 'a woman of extreme sweetness, goodness and domesticity' who makes clothes for her menfolk and always does what her lord and master tells her. 'Her invariable good behaviour and meekness must have almost driven Antony crazy. . . . She seems always to have been anxious to bring before his notice, in her sweet way, the charms of old-fashioned, respectable, family life, a condition which absolutely nauseated Antony.'[11] If goodness in a woman sickens and drives crazy the very people who fantasize about it, then a bad Cleopatra, who enjoys power, independence, intellectual activity and pleasurable sex and finds that, besides all these advantages, she is actually more popular than a good woman, can afford to laugh at the morality which so hypocritically condemns her.

Like the foreigner-Cleopatras, the bad-girl Cleopatras of this century are alluring outsiders who reveal, by contrast, the defects of those inside. 'I ought to be bored,' says De Mille's Antony, making the common assumption that a wife's company must be tedious. 'I should be longing to go out drinking with my friends, or to find another woman.' 'And are you?' asks Colbert's Cleopatra, raising her perfect plucked eyebrows. 'No!' cries Antony, kissing her hand ecstatically. 'No! You *are* an Other Woman!'

As the Other Woman, a wicked Cleopatra has the advantage over virtuous wives. Queen in her own country, mistress of her own household, tied to no man, she is in a far stronger position than the Roman matrons. In both De Mille's film and Mankiewicz's her entry into Rome is watched by an apprehensive Calpurnia, who looks physically and emotionally worn out. De Mille's Octavia is a goofy blonde given to making sad, self-deprecating jokes like 'Does any wife know where her husband is?' (she certainly doesn't). 'Oh, hello darling,' says Antony carelessly, coming across her by chance at a party, and looks away. If this vacuous, unloved and unlovable creature is a good woman, then who would not prefer to be bad? With their own political interests to occupy them Cleopatras are less dependent on, and therefore more interesting to, men than their submissive rivals. In Mankiewicz's film Richard Burton's Antony is seen smouldering with boredom and irritation while he dines with Octavia. She tries a little small talk about the food and about a clock whose ticking serves to stress the tedium of their marriage. When a messenger enters she excuses herself. 'When I hear matters of state discussed by men invariably I find myself wondering about why the wine has gone sour.' A very meek, domestic, properly womanly remark, to be sure, and a sad contrast with the exciting evenings Antony has spent discussing the conquest of the East with Caesar and with Cleopatra, whose passion for politics, far from neutering her, seems as intrinsic a part of her sex appeal as Elizabeth Taylor's silver eye-shadow or her tight bodices slashed to the waist.

The good women to whom the camp-Cleopatras are opposed are not only unattractive, small-minded and dull, they are frequently nasty as well. Preoccupied with chastity, their only asset, they are censorious and bitchy. 'Oh, I don't know,' says De Mille's Calpurnia when one of her cronies remarks that, say what you like about Cleopatra, she certainly is lovely. This Cleopatra and her handmaidens arrive in Rome like a troupe of golden-hearted whores or a gaggle of mischievous teenage girls too young to sympathize with the plight of neglected married women. 'The senators' eyes will pop right out of their heads,' says one of the maids, helping Cleopatra into a sheer chiffon dress in which she appears almost nude but for some clusters of bead embroidery. 'Do you know anything about senators, Charmian?' asks Cleopatra. 'We only got here yesterday, Majesty!' comes the reply, and the whole pretty crowd collapse into giggles. These are jolly, generous, good-time girls, ready to offer men the sexual fun which has been banished, as being incompatible with goodness, from the domestic scene. The unfortunate good women are imagined as being implacably, stupidly envious of them. De Mille's Cleopatra is confident of her own abilities to charm the senators; 'It's their fat wives I worry about.' A woman unwise enough to take the ideal of the submissive, dependent wife seriously and to attempt to conform to it not only suffers from the consequent cramping of her own personality and experience, she also makes herself an object of disgust to men and of scorn to the Other Woman, the merry 'man's woman' who, like Cleopatra, bends the rules by the power of her superior sexiness.

The historians who explored Cleopatra's empire-building ambition had prepared the way for these clever, independent, good-bad Cleopatras. Writers as well as film makers seized on the attractively shrewd and sophisticated character that historical research was revealing her to be. In a number of plays and novels written during the first half of the twentieth century Cleopatra appears as a woman wittier, more worldly-wise and, above all, more modern than the men who admire or fear her in such ridiculously outmoded ways. In John Stone's comedy *Great Kleopatra*, published in 1911, the humour all derives from the subversion of Romantic expectations. A poet rhapsodizes about Cleopatra's meeting with Antony: 'Unity in Trinity! Man enveloped in Woman!' only to be interrupted by a group of charwomen who throw a bucket of dirty water over him. Stone's Cleopatra is a professional diplomat who comes in disguise to Tarsus to check on the arrangements for her official entry and is disappointed to note that 'The crowd is not very great.' She informs a dumbfounded Antony: 'Policy, not passion, has been the basis of our union', and when, in the last Act, he bursts into the chamber where she is debating whether green gems are sufficiently becoming for her death scene and declares that he has come to die at her feet, she finds the plan both inconvenient and distasteful. 'No, no, no, no. Don't do anything of that sort here!'[12]

Other unRomantic Cleopatras are equally canny without being quite so hard-bitten. The heroine of Mary Butts's novel, *Scenes from the Life of Cleopatra*, published in 1935, is a lovely woman but a thoughtful one, whose mouth is one of those that 'get kissed and kiss again, but are those that count the kisses, keep them in a box for future reference.'[13] She is a mathematician and a connoisseur, and is capable of discoursing wisely on the political and psychological significance of her divine status. The Cleopatra of Lord Berners's comic novel *The Romance of a Nose*, published in 1941, is a bluestocking and an indefatigable sightseer ('she admired

the great sphinx, but the pyramids she thought vulgar, ostentatious and lacking in Grecian elegance'), capable of running
rings round most of the doltish men who wonder at her. 'I
just fed him up with a lot of high-falutin' stuff,' she says of
the governor of Thebes after she has dazzled him with an
analysis of Plato's politics. 'He's the most gullible old bird
I've ever seen. All the same he's rather a pet. He has promised
to help me get together an army.'[14] In a short play published
in 1934, in which all the dialogue is spoken over the tele-
phone, Maurice Baring imagined an ultra-smart Cleopatra
who warns Caesar against those who would make him monarch. 'Anyone in the world will tell you that to be called
Caesar is dignified, but to be called King Caesar is silly. It
sounds like the name of a pet dog.' In Thornton Wilder's
epistolary novel *The Ides of March*, published in 1948, Cleopatra knows the loading capacity of each of the major whar-
ves of the Nile and has all the details of the royal tax on ivory
at her fingertips. 'Oh, oh, oh,' exclaims Caesar, wondering at
such a combination of beauty with brains. 'I have sat holding
that cat-like bundle on my lap, drumming my fingers on
brown toes, and heard a soft voice from my shoulder asking
me how to prevent banking houses from discouraging the
industry of the people.'[15]

These Cleopatras, coming from elsewhere, have the tang
of unfamiliarity, but they are far from being the bizarre
exotics of Orientalist fantasy. In 1875 Blaze de Bury
described Cleopatra's Alexandria as the 'Paris of the ancient
world', a sophisticated capital where the relatively cloddish
Romans might enjoy *'le high life'*.[16] In similar style, Butts's
Cleopatra is unimpressed by the Romans: 'boors and fighting
farmers and promoted peasants'. Their ceremonial – 'people
in chariots, haranguing . . . and bits displayed of the
deceased' – strikes her as 'curiously common'.[17] Butts compares her sojourn in Rome to that of the Frenchified Mary
Stuart among the Scots, both of them cultured, aristocratic
women obliged to deal with barbarous men. 'I imagine Cleopatra very cosmopolitan,' wrote Anatole France in 1914. 'She
lived in Rome like an American in Paris.'[18] An outsider, but

outcast only by the stuffiest, this kind of Cleopatra is dashing and smart. Like Wallis Simpson in England, like the British-born actresses Vivien Leigh and Elizabeth Taylor in Hollywood (or subsequently Elizabeth Taylor when, thoroughly Americanized, she returned to Europe to star in Mankiewicz's *Cleopatra*), they have the suspect but alluring raciness that clings around the idea of the foreign woman. Rich and chic, they arouse hostility in frumps and prudes, hostility which they counter by displays of elegance and *savoir-faire*. 'The women of the aristocracy of Rome will refuse to be presented to this Egyptian criminal,' writes one of Thornton Wilder's Roman ladies. But once Wilder's Cleopatra arrives in Rome her refined manners win her friends. She comes in a simple blue dress with her hair loose to visit Caesar's wife. She shows pictures of her children to Caesar's aunt, who is touched. She gives marvellous presents – model palaces with moving parts worked by water, and emerald cats. When she invites *le tout Rome* to a party the guests, accustomed only to rowdy games and heavy drinking, are nonplussed by the exquisite pageants, the lion and tiger fights and the lakes full of swimming girls she has conjured up for their pleasure.[19]

Such a Cleopatra makes use of spectacle, but only as a tool. In John Stone's play she apologizes to Antony for being obliged, by political considerations, to appear before him in her Isis outfit, 'gaudy trappings that are so offensive to a refined taste'.[20] Mary Butts's Antony is enraptured, after Cleopatra has made her spectacular arrival on her barge at Tarsus, to realize that, divine and queenly though she is, she yet retains an ironic distance from her role. 'Do you know she gave me the wickedest little smile. Saw through it herself, bless her. . . . It took just that to make her perfect.'[21] Cleopatras like these, playing at being what they are expected to be, provide the precedents for Elizabeth Taylor's wink.

Such a Cleopatra, supremely civilized, is not cruel. Since Theda Bara's downfall Cleopatras have not, on the whole, been killers. When John Stone's Antony, having heard of Cleopatra's legendary bloodthirstiness, offers to stage some executions for her – 'We might possibly order some variation

338

from the routine usual in such cases, if that would amuse you?' – she snubs him sharply, clearly finding this a suggestion in crassly bad taste.[22] In De Mille's movie Claudette Colbert sits sphinx-like on a couch contemplating murder while her pet leopard lies growling beside her, living image of her death-dealing intentions, but in the event this Cleopatra proves soft-hearted. True, she tries out poison on a condemned man, but he thanks her for so mercifully sparing him a protracted death by crucifixion and her aim in these experiments is the humane one of sparing Antony (whom she has been persuaded she must kill) any pain. Elizabeth Taylor's Cleopatra, on hearing the bad news of Antony's marriage to Octavia, does not beat the messenger but slashes at her own bed, more heartbroken than angry.

These Cleopatras' only wickedness (and they would not consider it such) lies in their bold sexuality. 'Oh what timid stuff chastity is!'[23] says the heroine of *Queen Cleopatra*, an historical novel by Talbot Mundy. When Butts's Cleopatra spends the night with Caesar in her palace he worries, in his provincial Roman way, that 'it might be difficult for them to leave the royal bed-chamber together', but she walks unconcernedly out past the guards and he remembers 'that she was something a Roman woman could never be'.[24] Berners's Cleopatra has her devoted Apollodorus initiate her into the mysteries of sex at an early age, a useful experience which she regards in a 'purely academic light'. When Berners's Caesar apologizes in advance for leaving their affair out of his commentaries she smiles suavely. ' "Your wife," she said, "and the Roman ladies . . . I have heard strange things about their private conduct, yet I shouldn't be surprised if they were to take up a high moral line. I'm very unconventional, you know." '[25] These knowing Cleopatras are not doomed, heroic transgressors like the nineteenth-century *femmes fatales* and their victims, but sophisticated modern women who dismiss the notion of sexual sin as being outmoded, oppressive and absurd.

In this they are in tune with their times. For all the rigour of official sexual morality, the wicked woman, in other words

339

the sexually active one, has – at least on the level of fantasy – been more liked, emulated and desired in this century than her prim 'good' sister. The publicists of Hollywood were quick to realize it. Three of the actresses who have played Cleopatra on film, Theda Bara, Vivien Leigh and Elizabeth Taylor, have been notorious for their own (genuine or invented) extra-marital love affairs. Others, like Claudette Colbert, Sophia Loren (in a low-budget Italian sex comedy made in 1954, *Due Notti con Cleopatra*), Rhonda Fleming and Linda Christal (in *Legions of the Nile*, an extravaganza of belly dancing and taut-thighed centurions made in 1960), have deliberately played up the bad-girl raciness of the character of Cleopatra, the wickedest woman in the world, the gal who wants to eat her cake and have it too.

The image-makers of Fox Studios made a vamp of Theda Bara, not only in her performances but also in her own persona. While the actress, under strict orders from the studio never to be seen out in public, lived quietly with her parents and sister the publicists devised for her a career as a heart-breaker. In a handout of 1916 Fox announced that she took exception to being described as 'the woman with the most beautifully wicked face in all the world', the 'Ishmaelite of femininity' or 'the torpedo of domesticity' – all epithets which the studio's copywriters had dreamed up themselves for her glorification. Her 'cursed beauty', so they proclaimed, was capable of bringing 'Suffering and Ruin to Thousands of Sturdy Labourers and Their Families'. She was 'lavender lyddite [a high explosive] in a cut glass torpedo; pink arsenic, violet-scented; a poigniard in a peony; the scent in Cleopatra's last bouquet'.[26] Such wickedness, so the Fox bosses calculated, was a highly marketable commodity.

Bara submitted to being provided with a Cleopatra-like reputation. Vivien Leigh, like Elizabeth Taylor after her, seems actually to have conducted herself much as the camp-Cleopatra, who laughs at her own so-called wickedness, would do. Leigh played Cleopatra in 1945 in Pascal's film, and also on stage, in both Shakespeare's and Shaw's plays, in 1951. She brought to the role not only her acting skills but also an appropriate reputation, for she was known to be an Other Woman who had flouted convention and got away with it.

She and Laurence Olivier had become lovers in 1936 when they were each married to someone else. They lived together in London and – while they were starring in *Gone with the Wind* and *Wuthering Heights* respectively – in Los Angeles. By the standards of Hays-office Hollywood this was scandalous behaviour, but the public, it turned out, were forgiving of wickedness in their fantasy-figures. *Photoplay* magazine reported Leigh and Olivier's illicit relationship in 1939, but, far from deploring their immorality, gushed instead over 'the high tumultuous romance that laughs at careers, hurdles the conventions, loses its head along with its heart and laughs for the exhilarating joy of the wildness'.[27] Film stars, like fictional characters (like Scarlett O'Hara, like Heathcliff), were to be granted a latitude impermissible in 'real' life. Like the Oriental despots of the Romantic imagination, they were licensed to enjoy the pleasures that ordinary folk were forbidden (or forbade themselves), so that through them the public could, at least vicariously, live dangerously. Stranded in Hollywood when the Second World War broke out, Leigh and Olivier did their duty to the Allied cause by playing another pair of adulterous lovers, Nelson and Lady Hamilton, in a movie made at the express wish of Winston Churchill to boost morale on the Home Front.[28] Breaking the normal rules of sexual conduct was not only forgivable; if done with enough dash and style, and in the unreal, consequence-free domain of cinematic fiction (or film-world gossip), it could even be considered positively commendable – an inspirational example of reckless action undertaken without cowardly thought of its cost.

To Elizabeth Taylor 'bad' behaviour brought not cost but profit. By the time she played Cleopatra she was already notorious for her seduction of the singer Eddie Fisher. When their affair began he was already married, and she was only recently widowed. When the scandal broke a photograph of Fisher's wife, the good-girl actress Debbie Reynolds, was

341

widely published. In it Reynolds wore no make-up, her hair was in pigtails and (in stark contrast with the ostentatious jewellery for which Taylor was already famous) a bunch of nappy-pins was clipped to her blouse.[29] Stories circulated about her. As a girl she had worn jumpers knitted by her mother with the initials NN (for No Necking) embroidered on the collar.[30] The press reports presented her as the perfect young wife, sexually null, devoted to her children, free of personal vanity or any other kind of selfishness, caring only for the happiness of her man. Like the child-Cleopatras of the early twentieth century, she was as sweet and harmless as her own babies. This was the ideal to which young women in post-war America and Europe were still supposed to conform, but there are unmistakable signs that by the end of the fifties the ideal's powers of attraction were considerably less potent than those of its antithesis. The takings from the film of *Cat on a Hot Tin Roof*, in which Elizabeth Taylor played a fast woman seducing someone else's husband and which was released soon after her affair with Fisher, were enormously boosted by the scandal. Four years later, after the even greater scandal of her affair with Richard Burton, she had become, in the words of one of her many biographers, the owner of 'the priciest torso on earth'.[31] The market value of a commodity, or of an image, may not be an index of its perceived virtue, but it does indicate the level of public interest in it. Taylor the marriage-breaker who, Cleopatra-like, tempted men away from the nursery innocence of their marital homes, was a figure of almost universal fascination.

'I really find it impossible to distinguish between Cleopatra's vulgar exhibitionism and the sort of disgusting spectacle put on for tourists in the red light district of Corinth; the only difference I can discern is that her show cost more.'[32] Thus the fastidious Octavius, describing Cleopatra's arrival at Tarsus in the recent historical novel *Augustus* by Allan Massie. In his prissiness this Octavius under-rates the subtlety of his opponent, but his words could be accurately applied to the camp-Cleopatra. She is a kind of prostitute, who offers her public, her client, a chance to enjoy pleasures forbidden

342

at home. Like a prostitute she is (in relation to her client anyway) an independent, self-supporting woman who does not make the kind of financial or emotional demands that good wives make. And like a prostitute she plays an exotic role to arouse her punters, conniving with them in a game of make-believe.

She is the wicked Other Woman, but we all know that whatever 'wicked' may mean in the vocabulary of public rectitude, in the euphemistic language of desire (and, incidentally, of current slang) it is a term of approbation. 'You don't really care about that, do you,' murmurs Claudette Colbert's Cleopatra caressingly when Caesar has half-heartedly professed fidelity to his wife. Of course he doesn't. Both the fictional Caesar in the film and the real audience in the cinema are agreed that, in the realm of fantasy, naughty is nice and bad is better (freer, more fun) than good. The twentieth-century Cleopatra's image is founded on hypocrisy and bad faith. It is this insincerity which makes her into a camp joke, and makes that joke enticingly ambivalent. As Susan Sontag has written, 'One is drawn to Camp when one realises that "sincerity" is not enough.'[33]

Winking herself, the camp-Cleopatra pre-empts mockery. Like a prostitute, whose image is pornography, she cannot be laughed away. For pornography, which deals in clichés, is impervious to parody. However grossly it is burlesqued, it retains its essential nature. And so does the display of wealth, an inherently brash exercise which is not made any less potent when its vulgarity is exaggerated to the point of absurdity. A camp-Cleopatra, flashing her thighs and her diamonds with equal flippancy, is in command of the laughs which greet her show. In Mankiewicz's film Elizabeth Taylor's Cleopatra, listening to a recitation of Catullus's poetry, hears that Caesar is approaching. Mischievously, she stages an appropriate reception. 'We must not disappoint our visitor. The Romans tell fabulous tales of my bath and hand-maidens – and my morals.' (So, of course, do the film's public.) By the time Caesar arrives the poetry reading has given way to what looks more like an orgy. Dancing-girls sway suggestively to

343

languid music and Taylor-Cleopatra, now naked but for a small towel, lies stretched out on a daybed. The spectacle is both itself – the voluptuous scene which both the fictional Caesar and the real cinema-goer expects and wants – and a caricature of itself. Later in the film Cleopatra once more receives a Roman emissary, Rufio, in her bathroom. While he stands behind a screen she luxuriates in a pool of white liquid (asses' milk?). This was the scene which the makers of *Carry On Cleo* parodied, without perhaps appreciating quite how comprehensively it parodies itself. The fictional Cleopatra teases the fictional Roman by staging one of her famous bath scenes and by allowing him to come so near, but not to see, her naked body. The real film maker titillates his real audience by giving them what they have come to see, Elizabeth Taylor's flesh, in a scene so clichéd (De Mille's bath scenes were already being laughed at thirty years earlier) that their pleasure in it is as duplicitous as Taylor-Cleopatra's own role. She mocks the crassness of the taste for this kind of pornographic display, yet she displays herself. We make fun of such a corny, contrived scene, and yet we enjoy the opulence of it and we are pleased to glimpse the outlines of Taylor's breasts and hips through the not quite opaque bath water (or bath milk).

Such camp-Cleopatras, presenting their cleavages, their hordes of jewelled slaves, their grossly over-gilded palaces and their salacious reputations with a knowing wink, are doubly subversive. They promise forbidden pleasures, and they refuse to solemnize those pleasures by treating them as dangerous sins. A man who fell for an old-fashioned vamp like Theda Bara's Cleopatra might lose himself body and soul, but he didn't lose his right to take himself and his value system very seriously. But the Cleopatras of later films, teasing and ironic, challenge conventional morality more subtly. Why should anyone respect a man who is so obviously attracted to everything he professes to despise? As Claudette Colbert's Cleopatra waits for Caesar to return from the Senate on the Ides of March her maids amuse themselves imagining her wedding night. She is wearing a wonderful spangled dress. 'Imagine Great Caesar unhooking it!' titters Charmian. At one level, of course, the scene illustrates simply the incurable frivolity of women. But it also serves to undermine Caesar's masculine *gravitas*. For all he values himself and his ambitions so highly he has, in the past, been ready to forget his business in his eagerness to undress Cleopatra. Either he is not truly good or great, or the conventional notions of goodness and greatness may be called into question.

The Cleopatra who has most eloquently embodied that questioning has been Elizabeth Taylor, not so much in her screen performance as in her own legendary person. The *Cleopatra* film in which she starred was only ever of marginal interest to the public (by comparison, that is, with the gossip surrounding it). Seen today it has a certain historical interest, relating to the 1960s rather than to the first century BC. Some of the spectacular set-pieces are impressive, though their style is now highly unfashionable without yet being unfamiliar enough to seem exotic. Mankiewicz's script, based on a novel by Carlo Maria Franzero, represents a praiseworthy attempt to do justice to the historical Cleopatra's political acumen and personal intelligence. There are some witty lines. But it is a pedestrian work, visually bland by comparison with De Mille's glorious art deco vision and oddly lacking in erotic *frissons*. The world's favourite Cleopatra story of the early sixties was not contained in the film: it is about the film's making. Taylor is Cleopatra, and Burton Antony, far more effectively in their off-set personae, in the gossip columns and paparazzi pictures, than they are on the screen.

The extent to which the real Elizabeth Taylor does or does not resemble the real Cleopatra is not at issue here. The 'Elizabeth Taylor' with whom the public is familiar, like the 'Cleopatra' who has been passed down to us across two thousand years and so frequently reshaped, is a fictional figure composed of anecdotes, pictures and quoted remarks, whose character has been at least in part determined by the prejudices and desires of those who have produced and consumed her image. The two figures may at some points resemble the actual individuals, the Hellenistic queen and the twentieth-century actress, whose name they share. It is interesting to note that Elizabeth Taylor appears to have at least consented to, if not actually abetted, the construction as a Cleopatran 'Elizabeth Taylor'. Asked on a recent television chat show to name her favourite hobby, she answered precisely in character: 'I like collecting things . . . [pause] . . . like diamonds.'[34] But it does not necessarily follow that the two Taylors, the real and the imaginary, are identical. The Elizabeth Taylor and the Richard Burton referred to in this chapter are, like the Cleopatra and Antony whom they so strikingly resemble, images not people. Some of the stories told about them may have a basis in fact, while others do not; but in so far as the stories have been published and enjoyed and repeated they are, even if incorrect, part of the history of Taylor-Cleopatra, a figure as potent, and as fictive, as those earlier constructs the killer-Cleopatra, the weakling-Cleopatra, Cleopatra the foreigner and Cleopatra the martyr to love.

Film stars were by no means the first latter-day avatars of Cleopatra. An Elizabethan gentleman, Sir Thomas Gresham, pledged his Queen's health in a cup of wine into which a precious stone had been crushed.

> Here £15,000 at one clap goes
> Instead of sugar; Gresham drinks the pearl
> Unto his queen and mistress. Pledge it; love it!

So wrote the playwright Thomas Heywood in celebration.[35] There have always been women, aristocrats and actresses alike, who enjoyed associating themselves with Cleopatra's beauty, her grandeur and her power over men. Numerous portraits depict seventeenth- and eighteenth-century ladies 'as Cleopatra'. Tiepolo's frescoes in the Palazzo Labia in Venice served, among other things, to flatter the artist's patron, a widowed lady who had a reputation for being '*fort galante*'.[36]

Would-be *femmes fatales* of the late Romantic era (real

ones as well as those invented by Dickens and Ostrovsky) liked to identify themselves with Cleopatra. Sarah Bernhardt wore a ring that was said, improbably, to have belonged to Cleopatra herself. She let it be known that the snakes she used on stage when playing Cleopatra's death scene were live, and she kept them in her own house, adorned with jewelled rings and chains.[37] One of Bernhardt's admirers took his cue from her, even to the point of threatening to usurp her role: Pierre Loti had himself carried in to her, as Cleopatra was carried in to Caesar, wrapped in a carpet. Max Beerbohm used to address Bernhardt's English contemporary, Lillie Langtry, as Cleopatra — a teasing reference to her numerous admirers.[38] When the Duchess of Devonshire gave a fancy dress ball in London in 1897 to celebrate Queen Victoria's Diamond Jubilee no fewer than three of the guests (to each other's chagrin) came as Cleopatra. One, Lady De Grey, was attended by a servant dressed as a Nubian slave in 'real old Egyptian slave's attire'. She was said to have spent $6000 on her costume, to no avail — reporters agreed that she was eclipsed by Mrs Arthur Paget, born Minnie Stevens of Boston, whose dress, made for her by the Paris coutourier Worth, was described by the *New York World* as

A marvellous story in white and gold . . . literally covered in jewels. Nothing like such gems on the American lady's dress were ever seen in London or elsewhere. The costume was simply ablaze with diamonds, rubies and emeralds. When she entered, people accustomed to the greatest displays of jewels the world has ever known, gasped [Plate 44].[39]

In Edith Wharton's novel *The House of Mirth*, published in 1905, the adventuress Lily Bart considers posing as Tiepolo's Cleopatra, thus displaying herself 'in a splendid setting' for a parlour game of *tableaux vivants*.[40] The real-life society beauty Lady Diana Cooper actually did so: she dressed as Tiepolo's Cleopatra for a ball held in the Palazzo Labia in 1951 (Plate 45). Cecil Beaton photographed her in her costume and she used the picture in her passport, crossing

347

modern frontiers in the guise of a baroque vision of an ancient queen.[41]

These women deliberately identified themselves with Cleopatra, enhancing their own glamour by borrowing some of hers. Others have resembled her less designedly. Stories that circulated about Vivien Leigh's affair with Laurence Olivier are oddly reminiscent of the legend of Cleopatra's relationship with Antony. Leigh learnt from Olivier to swear obscenely (as Plutarch's Cleopatra did from Antony). She was demanding and passionately jealous, notably of Greta Garbo. She drank to keep pace with her man and never suffered, as he did, for it. 'She has a body like swansdown and the constitution of a GI on leave,' said Olivier. By 1951, when she played Cleopatra opposite him in London and New York, their marriage was becoming painful, especially for Olivier. It was said that he was wasting his own talent, deliberately playing down in order not to eclipse her. Cleopatra-like, Leigh seemed to be in the process of ruining a great man. Kenneth Tynan, reviewing the Shakespeare production, wrote that Olivier 'climbs down and Cleopatra pats him on the head. A cat can in fact do more than look at a king: she can hypnotise him.'[42] The ancient echoes are uncannily persistent, but they are not just curious coincidences. If Leigh's story resembles Cleopatra's it is not because the Queen of Egypt has been resurrected by some supernatural agency, but because the outlines of the stereotypical Other Woman's character has altered so little since her death. Other Women do all the things that good women do not do – they drink and swear, make sexual demands and obstruct men's ambitions by refusing to suppress their own. Leigh matched the role, just as Cleopatra had done nearly two thousand years earlier.

No other pseudo-Cleopatra, though, embodied the myth as completely as Elizabeth Taylor came to do. Taylor was Hollywood's bad-girl. By 1963 she was already, after a successful career as a child star and three financially advantageous marriages, famously rich (when she arrived late on the *Cleopatra* set one member of the film unit speculated that she must have been 'tired from counting her money').[43] She was also famously libertine. 'What do you expect me to do? Sleep alone?' she is reported to have asked the Hollywood columnist Hedda Hopper, who reproached her for seducing Eddie Fisher.[44] British-born, she was a foreigner in Hollywood. American-reared, she was equally an outsider in Europe. As an actress commanding the biggest fee any star had ever been paid, she had, like Cleopatra, the enormous power and prestige that money can buy. It also bought her an independence unattainable for most women. In Burton she met her Antony, and the story of their affair and subsequent marriages, as copiously reported in the press at the time and subsequently repeated by a stack of biographies, is full of Cleopatran echoes.

He is presented (rightly or wrongly) as a man of enormous talent but weak will, too easily tempted by booze and women. She is a famous seductress, fabulously rich, on the loose (though actually married to Eddie Fisher) after the death of her Caesar, the charismatic film producer Mike Todd. Burton and Taylor's first meeting has a professional function (as did Antony and Cleopatra's at Tarsus), but soon passion seizes them. They drink, they swear, they brazenly flaunt their impropriety. They squander enormous sums on jewels and parties. She is jealous and passionate. In sex, her greed and her energy are both prodigious and so are the pleasures she offers. He is still feebly aware of the call of duty (in the shape of his wife). He tries to leave her and she stages hysterical demonstrations of her love for him, even faking a suicide attempt. They part temporarily. His British (cool, northern, commonsensical) friends attempt to separate him from the seductress from Hollywood – land of heat, luxury and loose morals – but her allure is too potent. They come together again. They fight, reunite, fight, reunite. Their union is glittering, public, shocking, hubristic. Finally he is destroyed by it. Drunken, self-indulgent, his proper, honourable work on the English stage long neglected, he dies, a tragic might-have-been whose huge potential (so the story goes) has been dissipated on a love affair. But this Cleopatra is not destroyed with him. At the time of writing Elizabeth Taylor is still, though fifteen years older than Cleopatra was when she died, trading on her Cleopatra-like reputation. Photographs of her, bare-shouldered and scintillating with diamonds, are widely used to market a perfume ambiguously named Elizabeth Taylor's Passion. When she gave a television interview to chat show host Michael Aspel in February 1988 the hoardings proclaimed 'Cleo meets the Asp'.

What Taylor-Cleopatra enjoys, and offers, is excess. Enough is not as good as a feast to her. Nothing like. Sober common sense may decree that a single small stone on an engagement ring is enough. A salary adequate to one's immediate material needs is enough. Three dresses – one on, one clean, and one in the wash – are enough. One spouse is enough. But Taylor-Cleopatra defies such frugality. As Hélène Cixous wrote in 1975, Cleopatra has 'found the secret of embodying Still More, Still More – *Encore* – Never Enough. . . . At every instant another face, at each breath a passion, flesh struggling with a desire for more love, more life, more pleasure.' She demands to be feasted, she is herself a feast. She is 'more than plenty – running over. . . . She is always capable of more, herself the stir. She is extravagance and abundance. . . . The more you have, the more you give, the more you are, the more you give, the more you have. Life opens up. . . .'[45]

Cixous was writing about Shakespeare's heroine, but her interpretation holds true for the modern Cleopatras. The excess which characterizes Hollywood production strategies and Elizabeth Taylor's taste in diamonds may be crude both in conception and expression by comparison with that of Shakespeare's poetic hyperbole, but both forms of super-abundance answer the same craving. Like Shakespeare's Queen of Passion, like the exotic foreigners of nineteenth-century Romantic versions, the modern Cleopatra, consuming and spending on a monstrously flamboyant scale, inhabits, and invites her public to join her in, a space where the normal rules of financial or emotional economics do not apply.

In 1917 Theda Bara's Cleopatra was advertised as 'The Picture Magnificent – a wonder film of stupendous magnificence'. Stills show sets cluttered with Oriental rugs and ostrich-feather fans and a splendid trireme of a barge afloat. Bara's costumes are complicated by huge bosses of jewellery and panels of metallic embroidery (Plate 25). The Donations of Alexandria are staged, complete with golden dais, silver throne and crowds of blacked-up extras. 'The chief consideration', wrote a reviewer, 'are the vast crowds and settings' and costumes of 'barbaric magnificence and startling design'. All this display was of course designed, at one level, to re-create 'a gorgeous period in the history of the world', but with this film, as with most subsequent cinematic Cleopatras, the legendary splendour which the film is designed to illustrate becomes merged in the publicity material and journalism describing it with the actual extravagance of the film-making project. The 1917 *Cleopatra*, so the Fox Studios proudly boasted, had a cast of five thousand people and two thousand horses, and cost $500,000 to make.[46] Such vast expenditure (by the standards of the day) makes it not just a repetition of Cleopatra's legend, but a part of that legend. The awe in the face of grand waste, which the story of Cleopatra's dissolved pearl inspires, was activated again by the prodigality of the studios. Contemplating the huge budgets spent on Cleopatra films the public felt – and feels – something of the envy, disapproval and excitement that the legendary Queen herself has frequently aroused. When Cleopatra becomes a movie, then frequently the movie becomes a kind of Cleopatra, deplorably but thrillingly spendthrift.

'If Mr De Mille ... had requisitioned the moon for his latest carnival, it would certainly have been put through the petty cash without demur,' wrote a reviewer of the 1934 *Cleopatra*. 'I was mildly surprised to find only one Caesar. Everything else seemed to be by the gross.'[47] De Mille's film is a visually sophisticated work with two excellent performances, from Claudette Colbert and Warren Williams, who plays Julius Caesar, but you would never guess it either from the contemporary reviews or from the publicity material, both of which are solely preoccupied with the production's size. 'Amazing Spectacle . . . Terrific . . . Cast of Thousands,' trumpeted the advertisements. Gossip writers reported that the cast included two thousand female dancers, two thousand Roman legionaries, eight thousand extras in all. The set for the inevitable Baths scene extended over 40,000 square feet. For the battle sequence, involving chariot fights on land and the destruction of a whole fleet of ships at sea, the props department provided armour and helmets weighing a total of 75 tons. The mermaids who are hauled aboard Cleopatra's barge to present Antony with oyster shells full of precious stones were fastened to the side of the vessel with chains of solid gold. For the opening night a cinema was converted into an Egyptian amphitheatre and the attendants dressed as Roman centurions. Girls in 'pagan robes' and jingling exotic jewellery acted as usherettes, and helmeted Roman soldiers manned the box office. The film benefited from the 'biggest exploitation campaign ever mounted by Paramount'.[48]

Some of these pieces of information may be accurate. Many, no doubt, are wildly exaggerated, or even invented (the solid gold chains seem unlikely). True or false, they were put about by the studios, repeated by journalists and enthusiastically consumed by the public, all of whom grasped the principle that this kind of (rumoured or real) extravagance was in keeping with the film maker's purpose, which was to provide the public with something akin to Cixous's 'Still More, *Encore*, Never Enough', an experience unconfined by thrift.

When François Rabelais's giant Pantagruel appoints his servant Panurge warden of the fantastic region of Salmagundia, Panurge

> managed his affairs so well and prudently that in less than a fortnight he had squandered the whole income of his wardenship. . . . He spent it on a thousand little banquets and jolly feasts, open to all comers, especially to all who were good company, all young girls and pretty wenches; on felling his timber and burning the great trunks to sell the ashes; on taking money in advance, buying dear, selling cheap and

352

eating his wheat in the blade. When Pantagruel heard this news he was not in any way indignant, angry or perturbed.[49]

The Rabelaisian spirit informs the tales of Hollywood's excessive Cleopatras. There is a careless gusto in the spectacle of their crazily multiplying costs. Panurge, buying dear and selling cheap, cocks a snook at capitalist parsimony, and so does a film maker who uses solid gold props in a black-and-white film or spends thousands of dollars building a quinquireme only in order to sink it.

> Gold freely given,
> A man's freely shriven.

So reads the inscription over the gate of Rabelais's Abbey of Thélème, in whose first court stands a fountain 'on the top of which were the three Graces with horns of abundance, spouting water from their breasts, mouths, ears, eyes and other physical orifices'.[50]

In the 1954 film *Due Notti con Cleopatra*, Sophia Loren plays the twin roles of Cleopatra and her look-alike maid. As the film's title suggests, it offers double helpings of everything, especially of its nearly naked star, who, at this early stage of her career, was noted chiefly for the gorgeous amplitude of her breasts (plate 42). In *Serpent of the Nile*, also made in the early fifties, a dancer painted gold all over and attended by troupes of curvaceous assistants entertains Cleopatra's court in a lavishly dotty dinner-time entertainment (Plate 43). Voluptuous display for the purposeless, fleeting pleasure of it; banquets and jolly feasts enjoyed without thought of utility or economic consequences; the camp-Cleopatras bring with them some of the heady excitement of Rabelais's gleeful generosity. Spending money like there was no tomorrow, the makers of the Cleopatra films seem to emulate the Rabelaisian giants, who poured out bounty and ate their wheat in the blade, too impatient for pleasure to await the harvest. Pantagruel's father Gargantua wears a codpiece made from twenty-four and a quarter yards of wool, slashed with blue damask and 'well and gallantly fastened by two fine buckles with two enamelled clasps, in each of which was set a huge emerald the size of an orange, for . . . this fruit has an erective virtue, and is encouraging to the natural member'. This shameless and munificent giant wears a medallion on which is written. 'Charity seeketh not her own [profit]'.[51] There can be goodness in extravagance, even if common sense deplores it. It was for the prodigal, not the industrious, son that his father made merry.

In fact, of course, De Mille and the others sought their own and their producers' profit, just as any other commercial film maker does, but the legend of the camp-Cleopatra, queen of excess, takes no note of balance sheets, and the style of the cinema's Cleopatras continued to provide further material for the legend. When it opened in 1945 Gabriel Pascal's *Caesar and Cleopatra* was described by the *News Chronicle* as 'the most expensive film of all time'. Made over three wartime years in the British studios at Pinewood (where sets were menaced by flying bombs) and in Egypt, it was, in its day, almost as notorious as the Burton/Taylor version was to be twenty years later for delays, extravagance and its deleterious effect on the film industry in general. (The technicians' union passed a resolution deploring the amount of time and money and studio space monopolized by it.) Its total cost was said to be £1,300,000, perhaps even £1,500,000 (*Gone with the Wind*, as one reviewer pointed out, had cost only £800,000). 'And They Took a Sphinx to Egypt' ran a headline in the *Herald*. No authentic Egyptian sphinx looked as new as Pascal believed it would have done in the first century BC, so a model was constructed in Pinewood and transported to Egypt for the location scenes. Other such snippets (many of them doubtful, some obviously untrue) proliferate. A baby leopard was procured from a zoo (none is visible in the film). Cleopatra's coronation robe was made of real cloth of gold and embroidered with real gems (there is no coronation scene). Alexandria was rebuilt entire in Buckinghamshire and filled with peacocks. Oliver Messel's costumes were so beautiful and so exactly authentic that the chief of the Egyptian General Staff asked if he could buy them when filming was finished for use in military pageants.

According to one source huge quantities of sand were shipped to Egypt because Pascal did not like the colour of the authentic Egyptian article; according to another the Egyptian sand was found acceptable but then, for subsequent filming in Pinewood, four hundred further tons of the stuff, exactly matching it in colour and grain, had to be found – after a desperate search some meeting the specification was discovered in Cornwall.[52]

These stories speak not only of extravagance but also of a kind of exalted futility. Like the impossible tasks which the hero of a fairy story must perform before he wins the princess's hand, or like a spiritual exercise whose efficacy depends precisely on its unprofitability, they defy profane wisdom. They are heroic and absurd in equal measure. A camp-Cleopatra makes a mockery of reason and good behaviour, proposing instead a holy foolishness, an enchanted feast. 'Our desire to consume, to annihilate, to make a bonfire of our resources, and the joy we find in the burning, the fire and the ruin are what seem to us divine, sacred,'[53] wrote Georges Bataille. Such self-destructive self-indulgence is a proclamation of liberty from the limits of careful common sense.

Conspicuous expenditure was, by the 1960s, acknowledged to be Cleopatra's distinguishing characteristic. Even before shooting started on the Burton/Taylor *Cleopatra* the production was celebrated for its profligacy. Elizabeth Taylor's million-dollar fee (plus outsize expenses); the palm trees imported from California to Pinewood and trimmed with fresh palm fronds flown in daily from Egypt; the fifteen hundred spears which were simply mislaid, so vast was the mass of props; the 24-carat gold thread of Cleopatra's costumes; the fantastic sets constructed in Pinewood – eight and a half acres of Alexandria complete with temples and palaces – then scrapped when the production, with new director, new script and two new stars, shifted to Rome; the Roman Forum constructed in Cinecittà which was, according to the film's gleeful publicist, 'bigger than the original and about a hundred times as expensive';[54] these were the component parts of a story which the public read (and is still reading now, in the many biographies of Burton and/or Taylor) with mockery, outrage and unfailing avidity. 'The squandering of millions on an epic that nobody wanted to see', as Geoffrey O'Brien has rightly written, 'was itself the epic that people wanted to see.'[55] Like the ancient stories about Cleopatra's banquet – the nine roasted oxen, the gold plate given away on a whim, the drifts of rose petals, the dissolving pearl – all these stories about the making of the movie *Cleopatra* signify opulence, and a release from the wearisome fact that money has usually to be worked for before it can be spent. They also represent, though in an almost unrecognizably debased and tawdry form, something which has been associated since her own lifetime with Cleopatra's image – the sacred energy of Dionysiac excess.

Taylor-Cleopatra is a modern Maenad, a Bacchante who, possesed by an orgiastic spirit, turns her back on home and domestic duty in order to seek rapture. Elizabeth Taylor is said to have described Debbie Reynolds scornfully as Little Miss Homespun.[56] Homespun is the emblem of industrious domesticity, homespun is useful, homespun is ordinary, homespun is cheap. The image of Taylor, the modern Cleopatra, is everything that homespun is not. She is licentious ('What do you expect me to do . . . ?'). She has no respect for marriages, her own or other people's. She is extravagantly beautiful (or was in her teens and early twenties) and demands extravagant tokens of homage – yachts, furs, outsize gems. She is the Other Woman. 'I don't pretend to be an ordinary housewife,' she told an interviewer. 'I am not and couldn't be.'[57] Couldn't be – because a housewife's business is thrifty. She must save and store and plan ahead to ensure that her family gets enough. Taylor-Cleopatra, demanding luxury, disdaining sufficiency, taking no thought for the morrow, turns housekeeping on its head.

When Claudette Colbert first kissed her Antony in making De Mille's movie two hairdressers and a script girl are said to have fainted.[58] Even to her fellow workers in the production of an illusion a modern Cleopatra can seem to have superhuman sexual potency. During the shooting of Mankiewicz's film, the publicist Joseph Brodsky gained admittance to the set for a scene in which Cleopatra, stark naked, is massaged by her maids. Brodsky, a showbusiness professional and a married man who had doubtless seen female bodies more beautifully proportioned than Elizabeth Taylor's (she was going through a dumpy phase), was excited beyond measure. 'The kind of day that makes it all worth while,' he wrote to his partner. 'My Adam's apple seemed to be straining at my throat.'[59] The camp-Cleopatra may wink, but though her sexual glamour is a joke it is none the less irresistible.

This glamour lends a quality of wonder to the gossip column stories of Taylor's sexual appetite. She refused to collaborate with a ghost writer on her autobiography because she liked to spend all morning in bed with Eddie Fisher. She and Burton could not be persuaded to leave off kissing at the end of a screen embrace however often Mankiewicz shouted 'Cut!' They would regularly absent themselves from the *Cleopatra* set for 'matinees' in local hotels. 'I'm Cleo, the Nympho of the Nile,' sang Juliet Prowse in a review at the Winter Garden in the spring of 1962.

> She uses her pelvis just like Elvis . . .
> There was not a man she couldn't get
> That was Cleo's problem on and off the set.[60]

The prurient note of these jokes and stories is often ugly, but they are a part of a myth-making process by which Taylor-Cleopatra comes to embody 'Still More!' In the words of Roland Barthes, quoting William Blake, 'When amorous Expenditure is continuously affirmed, without limit, without repetition, there occurs that brilliant and rare thing which is called exuberance and which is equal to Beauty: "Exuberance is Beauty. The cistern contains, the fountain overflows." '[61]

The same recklessly festive spirit pervades the tales of the enormous amounts of money spent by, and spent on, Elizabeth Taylor. Even before her liaison with Burton began these were legion. Her first wedding, to Conrad Hilton, had been 'a fairy-tale wedding with Croesus writing the script'. When

357

she got engaged to Mike Todd he gave her a $30,000 pearl ring 'to keep her finger warm' until her 29½-carat diamond was ready. For the filming of *Cleopatra* a house was rented for her in London; she decided, without even setting foot in it, that she didn't like it and drove straight on in her Silver Cloud Rolls Royce to the Dorchester Hotel where she took two penthouse suites. In Rome she lived in a villa with fourteen rooms, or perhaps seventeen rooms, faced in pink marble. Every evening the cigarette holders, match books, candles, flowers and tablecloth were new, and matched her dress. She had full-length mirrors installed in her bathroom, where she bathed by candlelight. She brought three hundred dresses with her to Rome and threw each away after one wearing. In an attempt to keep her, Fisher bought her an emerald necklace worth a quarter of a million dollars, an antique mirror and a diamond ring. To win her away Burton bought her a necklace of Egyptian scarabs 'going back to the time of Cleopatra' and an emerald brooch. Even her nightdresses were made by Dior.[62]

Such futile expenditure is anarchic. It robs money, the stuff we work so hard to get and which we barter so carefully, of its meaning. Taylor-Cleopatra, squandering on fripperies the huge sums she acquired by the apparently effortless business of being herself (the public has never fully believed that acting, especially film acting, is work – hence the confusion between the stars and their screen personae), makes nonsense of economics. And once the connection between getting and spending is broken in the financial sphere, then all the laws governing social behaviour begin to feel flimsy. Self-denial will not necessarily earn respect. Fidelity will not be paid with love. Promiscuity need not devalue sex. The economic conventions of sexual behaviour are menaced, and with them the whole logical structure of action and consequence, transgression and regret. Taylor-Cleopatra vamps her man in 24-carat gold lamé, availing herself of an outdated typology of good girl-women and *femmes fatales*, and as she does it she winks, because this time the wicked temptress is not going to be vanquished at the end of the story. We are in the inconsequential realm of camp, where the rules no longer apply, where there are no rules, where nothing is serious enough to be sinful. Good and bad are indistinguishable: success is the only perceivable value and excess its token. This is Cleopatra's new banquet, the feast which is far, far better than enough. And it is in the nature of a feast that it has the power to suspend all laws and scramble all hierarchies. Taylor-Cleopatra is Mistress of Misrule.

Once Taylor-Cleopatra linked herself with Burton-Antony the orgy she seemed to personify was completed. She signified uninhibited sex and fabulous quantities of fairy gold. His contribution to the spectacle they jointly presented to the world was one appropriate to its Dionysiac nature – drunkenness. By Elizabeth Taylor's own account it was, perverse as it may seem, his boozing which made him attractive to her. When they first met on set his face was splotched with 'grog blossoms' and he had to ask her to hold his coffee cup to his mouth, so badly were his hands trembling. Later, when they went out to dinner, Eddie Fisher tried to persuade her to limit herself to one glass of wine. As she tells it, Burton helped her cheat by repeatedly swapping her empty glass for his full one. 'I thought, I absolutely adore this man.'[63]

The life they led together, during the making of *Cleopatra* and afterwards, was publicly understood to be a perpetual debauch. They ate, they drank, they fought, they made love, above all they shopped, and everything they did seemed somehow grander, looser, more extreme, than the same action or experience could have been to ordinary mortals. Reality, of course, was probably very different. Melvyn Bragg has suggested that Burton's big-spending, far from being blithely reckless, was the expression of a bitter fear of poverty,[64] while Elizabeth Taylor appears always to have been a shrewd manager who spent only what she could afford. Persistent drunkenness is, in reality, more likely to lead to rows and a diseased liver than to careless raptures, and a passion which ends twice in divorce must cause both parties as much wretchedness as joy. But such dreary facts concern the real Taylor and Burton. In the legend of 'Elizabeth Taylor' and

'Richard Burton' they have no place. In the fantasies of their public, Taylor-Cleopatra and Burton-Antony were exultant rebels. They turned the ancient rule for the care of the self on its head, reckless of self-improvement or any other restraint. Even Taylor's fatness and Burton's hangovers could be read as signs of plenty. The two of them were moderation's antithesis, anti-Apollonians audacious enough to demand everything in excess.

The manifestations of this profligacy were typical of their time, the big-spending era of the early sixties, the binge which eventually came to seem so gross that it made anti-materialists of a whole generation of young Westerners. The sacred excess of the Maenads found a modern equivalent in flashy displays which were outrages as much against good taste and upper-class refinement as they were against economic sense and morality. The jewels: the Krupp diamond, valued at $305,000, which Burton is said to have bought as a penalty for losing at table tennis and which he subsequently nicknamed 'the ice-rink'; the Cartier-Burton diamond which was even bigger; the La Peregrina pearl; the numerous necklaces, earrings, rings, brooches. All of these were probably in fact shrewd investments, registered as the holdings of tax-exempt companies, clever ways for Taylor and Burton to keep their savings, but the image of Taylor-Cleopatra has nothing to do with accountancy. As far as her legend goes, these huge sums spent on baubles represent the acme of frivolity, a gaudy exercise in potlatch. The yacht; the jet aeroplane ('I bought it so we could fly to Nice for lunch,' said Burton); the furs; the clothes ('This pink dress is to be thrown away – five or six hundred dollars' worth of ermine are on this cape,' said Taylor's couturier); the parties; the waste of it all. They bought paintings – Renoirs, Monets, Van Goghs – stashed them in a cellar and forgot about them. They chartered a luxury yacht for their dogs and moored it on the Thames to avoid the British quarantine regulations. The dogs were never house-trained: when the valuable carpets began to stink they were simply replaced. They travelled with a regal entourage; 'one hundred and fifty-six suitcases, four children, one governess, three male secretaries in mink battle jackets, one hairdresser, one nurse, four dogs, a turtle and two Siamese cats with diamond-studded collars'.

They were not just spending money, they were making a mockery of it, throwing it around so fast that in the speed of its going its value became invisible. They were careless of all proprieties, whether based on good taste or on morality, and both taste and morality proved vulnerable to the excitement they generated. 'That's the most vulgar thing I've ever seen,' Princess Margaret is reported to have said of the Krupp diamond. 'Want to try it on?' asked Taylor. 'Oh, yes, please,' said the Princess.[65]

During the filming of *Cleopatra* they were condemned for their adultery by upholders of propriety everywhere. Vatican Radio thundered against the 'insult to the nobility of the hearth'. Ed Sullivan hoped youngsters would not be 'persuaded that the sanctity of the marriage laws has been invalidated by the appalling example of Mrs Taylor/Fisher and married man Burton'. In the House of Representatives, Congressmen and -women demanded that the sinning couple be refused entry to the United States. In newspapers in Italy and around the world they were upbraided for their 'Mockeries of love and the sanctity of marriage'.[66] But all the protest served only to make their story the more titillating. The outraged Congressmen, the condemnatory Pope, the screaming headlines all became part of the legend of Taylor-Cleopatra, of her capacity to upset old verities and of her delicious carelessness. As the scandal grew, so did the market value of the scandalous lovers, and their glamour in the imagination of the public. 'I think the Taylor/Burton association is quite constructive,' noted *Cleopatra*'s producer Darryl Zanuck coolly.[67] The publicist, Nathan Weiss, was more emphatic: 'Everybody, but everybody, will go to see this picture to say that they can see on screen what's going on off it.'[68] Taylor-Cleopatra, the Other Woman, the female Ishmaelite, winks at her public, and the public winks back.

'Indiscriminate necking doesn't pay'[69] – that, according to one reviewer, was the moral of Cleopatra's story as told in

*Serpent of the Nile*, but the camp-Cleopatra presides over a realm where the prudent requirement that every mode of behaviour must 'pay' is in abeyance. It is an imaginary realm, apart from the real world. (The people who relished the stories of Taylor-Cleopatra's excesses did not, on the whole, intend to repeat them in their own lives: as actual sexual *mores* became more permissive, her popularity began to decline.) But unreal as it is, its image is exhilarating.

In De Mille's film Antony, leading two huge wolfhounds, goes to visit Cleopatra on her barge. As he crosses the gangplank an amazing spectacle greets him. He pauses, and commands the dogs to wait for him there (tokens of virility have no value where he is going). A double line of scantily clad women waft him onwards with enormous fans of ostrich plumes. He strides between them, and as he passes they raise and lower their fans so that he appears to be thrusting through a succession of soft impedimenta which caress him as they yield him passage into the body of the womanly ship. Beyond lies Claudette Colbert's Cleopatra, reclining before a vast elliptical (or vulvaic) mass of plumes. She is covered with pearls. Loops of pearls circle her neck, her head, her upper arms, her shoulders. (Born of the cunt-like oyster, pearls belong to the sea, to women and to sex. In Mary Butts's novel Cleopatra makes love to Antony in a perfectly spherical, shining-white bedroom, 'like the inside of a pearl'.)[70] 'I am dressed to lure you,' Colbert's Cleopatra tells Antony, and lure him she does, with dancing-girls and singing-girls, girls dressed as leopards, girls dressed as mermaids, girls riding bulls or leaping through burning hoops. She intoxicates him with women, with food and wine and rose petals and playfulness. His dogs take fright and run off home.

At last he succumbs, and as he lets his head fall on her breast she signals to her attendants. Silk curtains are unfurled to hide the lovers from view. Dancers sway, the music ripples and swoons, the plumed fans wave back and forth. Abruptly the rhythm of the score becomes stronger and more urgent. Rows of trumpets are raised for a triumphant fanfare. Banks of oars are seen thrusting and retracting, thrusting and retracting, until the sequence climaxes in a wonderful swirling tangle of lambent textiles, priapic trumpets and undulating female flesh. This gorgeous piece of cinematic euphemism conveys two meanings. Firstly, and most obviously, Cleopatra and Antony are fucking. Secondly, the oyster has closed on Antony. Lured by the pearly Cleopatra, he is now contained within her magical feminine space.

This is the space over which the camp-Cleopatra, queen of excess, presides. Within it everything the stern, thrifty world takes seriously is at risk of being laughed away. It is a woman's space, and women's traditional weapon (contrary to popular anti-feminist opinion) is humour. Colbert's Cleopatra teases her Antony and seduces him in the midst of a bout of hiccups by means of a game of hide-and-seek. The camp-Cleopatra makes fun (literally) of herself, and of everything else, giddily reducing all danger, all sin, all power, to play. In Rabelais's Abbey of Thélème a riddling poem is found. Its language is suggestive of solemn prophecies, but Gargantua's friend the Monk points out that its subject is actually nothing more portentous than a game of tennis, 'And here's good cheer!'[71] Cleopatra and Antony, wrote Hélène Cixous, 'abandoned the minuscule old world, the planet – the shell with its thrones and rattles, its intrigues, its wars, its rivalries, its tournaments of the phallus'.[72] Their new world is a kind of Thélème, where the ancient frenzy of Dionysus is combined with a modern impatience of crabby 'goodness' and thrift. In it nothing, including sexual identity, is quite stable. On Cleopatra's threshold De Mille's Antony leaves his dogs and lays aside his masculine, militaristic identity, and the power by which he previously presumed to judge Cleopatra and find her wicked. Before she takes him to bed she gives him back his virility, but first she camps it up (and camp is the humour of effeminacy). Tipsy and giggling, shimmering in satin and pearls, she picks up a peculiarly phallic club and hands it to her Antony, reminding him that if he so wished he could knock her head off with it. His manly potency is dependent on her favour, and in her custody masculinity is a joke – not a weapon but a toy. The winking

Cleopatra, consenting with one eye, denying with another, subverts all value, contradicts all certainty, and invites her admirers to squander their all for a laugh. She is not a good woman, but she is something resembling a great one, and the feast she offers is out of this world.

# Conclusion:
## THE TRIUMPH OF LOVE

THERE HAVE BEEN many Cleopatras. There will probably be many more. The forms the Queen of Egypt has so far assumed have far from exhausted her potential metamorphoses. In the mass of anecdotes and images which make up her legend it is possible to trace the outline of countless further Cleopatras – Cleopatras as yet unwritten, unpainted and unfilmed.

In her own era Cleopatra was likened to Helen, to Semiramis, to Omphale, to Dido, to Isis. Her image was first shaped by the impress of already existing moulds. It has since been refashioned to fit into numerous others, while gradually itself becoming a mould for further forms. 'Here comes my Cleopatra!' sang the British band the Flaming Mussolinis in 1985. A 'Cleopatra' is an identifiable object, however changeable. Elizabeth Taylor became a 'Cleopatra'. The advertisers hint that you or I can become one too, by the simple expedient of using Cleopatra soap. An image is a mask, and a mask can be lent and borrowed. A piece of empty artifice, it is easily detachable from the person whom it is supposed to represent. With equal ease it can be imposed on another body. The consumer of Cleopatra soap may not really be a 'Cleopatra', but then neither was Cleopatra herself.

'It is dangerous to unmask images,' wrote Jean Baudrillard. 'They dissimulate the fact that there is nothing behind them.'[1] I have not, in this book, attempted to strip away illusions and present Cleopatra plain. I cannot do it. I do not know her. I, like all the other writers whose works I have dissected, know only her depictions and descriptions, masks made by others in her image. Those representations, and their makers, have been my study. In conclusion I present not the real Cleopatra, but a sketch for one mask more, a Cleopatra for our times, a collage-Cleopatra made up from hints and traces scattered through the art and literature of two thousand years and assembled by a British woman writing in the last years of the twentieth century. In common with all the rest of those who have painted, narrated or filmed Cleopatra's story, I can speak only from my time and situation. Some of my prejudices and assumptions are too close for me to see them, but my topics I acknowledge as mine, and those of my culture. They are the infinite value and vulnerability of biological life, the questionable semiology of gender, the urgent need for international accord. As shamelessly as any of her other interpreters, I load these, my own preoccupations, on to Cleopatra.

In a painting by a sixteenth-century Venetian artist entitled *A Woman as Cleopatra*, a courtesan sits, richly dressed and bejewelled, in a chair like a throne. Behind her a bed, sumptuously hung, hints at her profession, but her gaze is solemn and her pose hieratic. She extends her arm at shoulder height, and in her hand she clutches a wriggling asp. The image is enigmatic, but its import is elucidated when it is juxtaposed with one which predates it by three thousand years. In the ruins of Knossos archaeologists found a faience figurine of a goddess. Her tight-fitting dress reveals her breasts, not through languid carelessness, but by emphatic design. Her arms, like those of the Cleopatran courtesan, are outstretched and, like her, she wields snakes. Flaunting her breasts, flourishing her phallic familiars, she is a potently hermaphroditic figure, goddess of generation and reconciliation, presider over a world where the gifts of woman and man could be combined. A deity revered in a culture which had links both with East and with West,[2] she defies difference, cultural as well as sexual. Proud equally of her breasts,

366

emblems of womanly kindness, and of her death-dealing snakes, she asserts that power and love need not be mutually exclusive. Such a goddess, such a Cleopatra, proclaims a unity, not blandly homogeneous, but dynamic and fertile. She challenges the simple oppositions which are so fundamental to all our thinking, and so fatally agonistic: oppositions like right/wrong, friend/foe/ east/west, man/woman, alive/dead.

Cleopatra has repeatedly been defined in terms of these mutually exclusive pairs. Over and over again she has been imagined to be her interpreters' antithesis. She has been weak when they were strong, lascivious when they were prudish, self-sacrificing when they were exorbitant in their demands. Her nationality and sex alike have stamped her different, and her story has traditionally been represented as that of the collision of opposites, of the contrast between Cleopatra/ 'them' and 'us'. A few voices have been raised on her behalf: there is a persistent, though never dominant, tradition within which Cleopatra's party is 'us', her opponents 'them'. Finally, all but submerged, there is within the Cleopatran literature and iconography a fragmentary third tradition, one in which neither party is exalted over the other but, instead, the alliance of opposites is celebrated.

In his play *Masra' Kliyupatra*, written in 1929, the Egyptian poet Ahmad Shawqui reversed the pro-Roman, anti-Oriental racism with which Cleopatra's story is usually imbued, describing the Romans, from an Egyptian perspective, as gross debauchees. Himself an ardent nationalist who was obliged to leave Egypt after falling foul of the British authorities during the First World War, Shawqui adapted Shakespeare's depiction of Cleopatra to make her a patriotic heroine, a defender of Egypt against the European imperialist. His Cleopatra's flight from Actium is a strategic move: it is her policy to allow the two Roman forces to annihilate each other, leaving Egypt mistress of the Mediterranean Sea.'[3] The Nigerian writer Wole Soyinka has recently argued that such a revision was unnecessary, urging that Shakespeare's Cleopatra is already possessed of 'steely patriotism'. Jokingly,

Soyinka suggests that Shakespeare must really have been an Arab, 'Shayk al-Subair', to have evoked so vividly 'tones, textures, smells and even tastes which were so alien to the wintry climes of Europe', and to have created a Queen whose musings on death seem to echo the Islamic *Book of the Dead*.[4] Such rereadings of the story serve as salutary counterbalances to the traditional, Eurocentric view, but it is still possible to imagine a more radically anti-racist image of Cleopatra, one in which the ancient dichotomy of West and East is not simply modified by being viewed from the less familiar, Eastern side, but is actually resolved.

The third-century Queen of Palmyra, Zenobia (or Bat Zabbi), claimed (untruthfully) to be descended from Cleopatra, and even took Cleopatra's name.[5] No doubt she was eager to claim kinship with a powerful female ruler, one whose kingdom she herself was intent on conquering, but it seems that she also understood and wished to associate herself with Cleopatra's internationalism. Like Cleopatra, Zenobia had a Roman partner, her husband Odenathus who was Rome's representative in Asia. When he died she ruled alone in the name of her sons, calling herself Queen of the East, reconquering Egypt and, in Gibbon's words, blending 'with the popular manners of Roman princes the stately pomp of the courts of Asia'.[6] It appears that Zenobia, at least, had grasped that it is possible to tell Cleopatra's story without contrasting East and West to the detriment of one or the other, to portray the Hellenistic Queen of Egypt, who aspired to rule an empire in which European and Asian could peacefully coexist, as the embodiment of a spirit of international fellowship, the person in whom East and West could finally meet. In *Goddess and God*, a play by John Balderston published in 1952, Cleopatra persuades Julius Caesar to turn his attention away from the narrow field of Roman politics and to lead an expedition into Parthia and India, an expedition which, although intent on conquest, might inaugurate a new age of multi-racial co-operation. She refers to Zeno, the philosopher who was Alexander the Great's contemporary, and quotes the ideals which, she believes, inspired Alexander. 'We are not to live nationally or parochially ... We are to consider all men fellow-countrymen, and our life and world are to be one – one flock living together in one fold.' Caesar is persuaded. 'All my thoughts are turning away from the West ... Our task is universal and not particular.[7] In the fertile duplicity of Cleopatra's person, in the image of a Queen whose capital stands at the junction of East and West and whose rule was extended over both, racial antagonism can be imagined to dissolve.

Cleopatra, along with her imitator Zenobia, has recently been identified as a fighter. Both the artist Judy Chicago and the historian Antonia Fraser have placed her in a category of 'warrior queens' headed by Boadicea. But there is an older tradition within which she is glorified as war's opponent, the pacifist queen of love. In Petrarch's 'Trionfi', written in the fourteenth century, Cleopatra appears in the crowd of those adorning the Triumph of Cupid. By her walks Julius Caesar:

> She triumphs over him: and right it is
> That he who conquered the world should be conquered in his
>   turn.[8]

The warrior's might is subdued by the gentler power of love. In the sixteenth-century poem by Guillaume Belliard, 'Les Delitieuses Amours de Marc Antoine et de Cléopâtre', Amour ask Mars, the god of war and Antony's patron, for permission to fire one of his arrows at the Roman hero. Mars, who, though terrible, is himself terrified of being smitten by love, consents and Antony is consumed by his ardour for Cleopatra as burning straw is consumed by the flame. The lover lays aside his cuirass and his lance and, furiously as Mars may tear his beard and roll his angry red eyes, his vassal is lost to him. Cleopatra, love personified, has him in thrall.[9] The story of the warrior Antony unarmed by the lovely Cleopatra is conventional, but in this version it has an emphasis far different from the censorious one that Octavius and countless subsequent interpreters have given it. Belliard's Antony loses his martial skill and his worldly glory for love's sake, but this time his bargain is understood to be a good one. Pluto assures him that in the Underworld he will live for ever in bliss with his Cleopatra, solaced by sweet zephyrs, the singing of Philomel and the fresh colours of flowers.[10]

The story of Cleopatra and Antony, of the warrior overcome by the lover, echoes the legend of Venus and Mars. Often the parallel has been explicitly drawn.[11] When Peter Hall directed Shakespeare's *Antony and Cleopatra* for the National Theatre in 1987, with Judi Dench and Anthony Hopkins in the title roles, the programme's cover illustration was a reproduction of Veronese's painting *Mars and Venus Bound by Cupid*. In the court entertainment devised for the king of France by Monsieur Fuzelier in 1746 Cleopatra appears as Venus in her barge. Antony is instantaneously struck with love for her, avowing that:

> One single instant is enough for Beauty
> To triumph over the conquerers of the world.

Cleopatra/Venus demurs: 'Rome forbids its heroes to dare to sigh', but Antony announces his changed allegiance – 'I read in your beautiful eyes more sovereign laws' – and his new-found mistress celebrates her victory with a song:

> Enjoy the pleasures of peace. In the breast of war suspend the
> terror of the Earth,
> Reign charming Love. Come give us lovely days![12]

Recently the mythological references have dropped away, but the dispute between the principles of war and love has survived as a major theme in Cleopatra's story. Plato, St Paul and all their followers may have distinguished between the gross cravings of the flesh and the pure passions of the soul, but there is a third kind of love, one neither celestial nor bestial but human, in which erotic desire and tenderness combine, and Cleopatra has occasionally been perceived as its advocate. In Sardou's play Antony is about to oversee the execution of a group of conquered officials, when, as though in mockery of the martial Roman trumpets, flutes and tambourines are heard.[13] Cleopatra, love's representative, is about to disrupt the killing business of war. In Delphine de

Girardin's play a more explicit pacifism is voiced. Cleopatra, recalling the Battle of Actium, explains that she withdrew in revulsion from the 'cowardly, stupid game' of warfare. A soldier on her own ship was killed, and when she saw him dead and bleeding she thought he resembled Antony and 'I forgot your great man's destiny, I saw only your spreading blood . . . What madness, when one could live beloved, to die for an empty name!'[14]

As it is possible to reverse Western racism and the code of manly virtue which declares Cleopatra wicked for having distracted Antony from his proper work of slaughtering enemies, so it is possible to subvert the puritanism which, having identified Cleopatra as the incarnation of terrestrial delights, proceeds to condemn her. Both Mary Butts and Lord Berners imagined exquisitely refined and charming Cleopatras expressing their contempt for the coarse Romans' incapacity for pleasure. A flourishing hypocrisy, as we have seen, has made the voluptuous Cleopatra as attractive as she is deplorable. Advertising copywriters, restauranteurs and travel agents all use her name to denote sensuous delight. The folklore of smut has it that she was able to work the muscles of her vagina so as to afford her lovers ineffably delicious sensations, a trick known as 'the Cleopatra grip' (the late Duchess of Windsor and the prostitutes of pre-war Singapore are among the many other sex heroines credited with the possession of this skill). The southern coast of Turkey is scattered with sites bearing her name – in memory, so local guides inform tourists, of the raptures of her honeymoon. There is 'Cleopatra's beach' near Bodrum, where the unusually fine and silky sand is said to have been imported from Egypt especially so that Cleopatra and Antony could lie all night on it, dallying beneath the stars. There is 'Cleopatra's spring', where fresh water rises into a cave flooded with seawater, forming a wonderful pearly green pool supposedly created on purpose for Cleopatra's bath. Face creams, shower cabinets and, most often, soaps have been named after her, as the manufacturers seek to borrow for their products some of the aura of erotic luxury lingering around her name. To

371

Claude Ferval, whose novel *The Private Life of Cleopatra*, written in 1930, is one of many more or less pornographic fantasies about her produced in this century, her 'radiant amber-coloured flesh' suggests 'luscious sunkissed fruit', and when she tumbles out of the carpet in Caesar's apartment, her dainty over-dress 'all rumpled', she is 'blooming, distracting, fascinating'. 'For the latest ethnic inspiration turn towards Egypt – and its devastating queen, Cleopatra,' counselled the caption on a fashion page in summer 1989. 'The look is sensual, exotic, bold.'[15]

This vision of Cleopatra as a material object of definable and therefore gratifiable desire has been frequently delineated. But the Cleopatra of pornographic or sybaritic fantasy has another, more luminous, but so far only vaguely apprehended alternative aspect. The real Cleopatra's enemies suggested that she was subhuman, surrounding her imagined figure with animal-headed idols. But to Shawqui her links with the non-human forces of nature give her a sublime grandeur. 'Water will flow in every chasm, thunder will sing and the lions will roar, giving strength to the throne.'[16] Cleopatra's nudity in Renaissance paintings suggests not only that she is an erotic object but also that she is divine, for deities are conventionally depicted naked or scantily draped. Her physicality, her affinity with the elements and with animals, do not necessarily reduce her. Constance Collier, who wore a headdress shaped like an ibis, a snake-scaled dress and a mantle of tiger and leopard skins when playing her in Frank Benson's 1898 production for Shakespeare's play, looks not only like a Romantic *femme fatale* but also like a Dionysiac priestess, a human commanding extra-human powers (Plate 49). Cleopatra can be seen to stand for the wilderness, for the body, for the beauty and energy of the physical world. In a song recorded by the Egyptian Mohamed Abdel Wahab in 1973 she personifies an ecstasy which is as much mystically pantheistic as sexual:

Cleopatra – dream of every man!
Our night reddens and the people sing,

God's smile grows and doubts fade.
My sweet love!
I have travelled about the seas while the oars sang.
You were my companion of joy.
The seven sails that shaded us knew that love was all before us.
O my love, everything sings.

Even to Ferval she is not only a luscious fruit but also 'that wonderful woman, who, with a lotus-flower in her hand, still stands with Antony, weaving the enchanting mists of romance and breathing the warm breath of passion over the crumbling ruins of the world . . .'[17] It is possible to imagine her as the embodiment of a pleasure in which the delights of the senses and those of the spirit unite. The Alexandrian poet C. P. Cavafy, in a haunting poem written in 1911, 'The God Abandons Antony', addresses Antony on the eve of his death and urges him to be worthy of the glorious life he has shared with Cleopatra, and to face his defeat honestly, without complaint but with a full appreciation of what has gone.

> Listen, your last enjoyment, to the sounds,
> The wonderful instruments of the mystic company,
> And say farewell, farewell to Alexandria you are losing.

That Alexandria Cavafy elsewhere describes as 'all the domain of pleasure'.[18] In Shawqui's play Cleopatra proclaims that 'unlike that of the Romans . . . our drinking will not be depraved but full of the treasures of love and compassion'.[19] It is possible to conceive of a Cleopatra who could typify an ideal of pleasure in which body and soul, libido and mind, shared equally. Thinkers of the Christian tradition, and their Graeco-Roman predecessors from whom, as Michel Foucault and Peter Brown have demonstrated, they drew their notion of the human being as a schizoid structure – soul and body opposed and only to be brought into a state of praiseworthy equilibrium by the exercise of constant self-culture and self-control – have fragmented happiness, dividing spiritual rapture from physical pleasure, intellectual excitement from erotic ecstasy. Cleopatra, who has been perceived both as a scholar and as a purveyor of extraordinary sexual delight, who has been harlot and queen, mother and warrior, goddess and sage, could be taken as a figure suggestive of human wholeness and the consequent possibility of guiltless human joy.

In his novel *Ararat*, published in 1983, D. M. Thomas repeats and modifies Pushkin's tale of the killer-Cleopatra. Pushkin left his story incomplete; Thomas provides it with an ending which significantly alters its nature. The third of the men who accept Cleopatra's offer of one night at the price of life, the flowerlike virgin boy who had spawned so many successors in nineteenth-century literature, turns out, in Thomas's version, to be Cleopatra's own son, offspring of her incestuous marriage to Ptolemy. The boy is ignorant of their relationship (she has had him fostered by a slave), but Cleopatra recognizes him by a birthmark. Undeterred, she takes her pleasure with him.

> Who knows if, struck by sudden terror
> Of slow decline, she wished to see
> Her youthful beauty in the mirror
> Of yet another Ptolemy? . . . [20]

Rapacious mother, leaching her own child of his vitality to keep herself young, heartlessly sacrificing his life for her own gratification, Thomas's Cleopatra is a dreadful figure, the devouring mother who gives life and destroys it, greedily sucking men back into the womb that gave them birth. She is akin to the Romantic killer-Cleopatras, but with one stark difference. Unlike them, she is not invincible. Thomas has her lover-son wake before dawn and offer Cleopatra wine spiked with mandragora. Then, stabbing the eunuch who guards the door, the boy escapes. His mother disposed of, a young man is free to enter adulthood. Once free of the fleshy, clinging female principle in which death and maternity combine, mankind is released to pursue a vigorous life, a life of the mind and the spirit.

Thomas's fable is a resonant one, but there are other, more positive, ways in which Cleopatra's image could be allied with that of the maternal archetype. The historical Cleopatra

374

identified herself in her own propaganda with Isis, mourning her Osiris/Caesar, and giving birth to his child and reincarnation Horus/Caesarion. Powerful goddesses linked with dying young men, as Venus is linked to Adonis, as Astarte is with Tammuz, are not necessarily malevolent. They are enacting a cycle of death and regeneration on which all life depends. When Cleopatra lures a youth into her fatal bed or, in the more nearly historical story, cradles the dying Antony in her arms, she is assimilated to a venerable iconographical tradition, emblematic of a general immortality ensured by an individual death. The seed must fall if the flower is to bloom. In the interior of an ancient Egyptian sarcophagus the goddess Nut is depicted holding out her arms as though to embrace the corpse. She is, as Erich Neumann pointed out, 'the same mother of death as the Christian pietà, the Madonna holding in her lap the dead Jesus, the child of death, who has returned to her'.[21] She is the earth-mother who – in true Dionysiac fashion, in true Christian fashion – demands death now so that the life to come may thrive.

Cleopatra, whose banquet is as gorgeous an icon of plenty and of nurture as any cornucopia, resembles the mother who loves, as well as the mother who kills. Emile Mâle describes Terra, a pagan goddess who was still appearing in paintings in twelfth-century France. She is benevolent, generous and 'the serpent, son of the earth, drinks at her breast'.[22] Cleopatra, exposing her breasts in painting after painting, calls attention to her maternal bounty as, like Terra, she puts a snake to her nipple. As Queen of Egypt, the land which provided the Roman world with its wheat, she makes a fit avatar for the benign deity who presides over all growth, all fertility. Calmly handling her asps she resembles both her own chosen patroness Isis, and Isis's Roman counterpart Ceres, goddess of the earth and of generation, who appears in a Hellenic relief holding ears of corn, signifying abundance, and snakes, signifying life-in-death.

The mother earth who absorbs the dying man into herself only to reproduce him contains both sexes. Cleopatra has always been associated with the confusion of genders, ever since, in her own lifetime, Octavius's friends identified her with Omphale and accused her of feminizing Antony. The creative energy of that confusion has seldom been given expression in versions of her story, but it can be recognized lying latent within it. Antony was likened, both by himself and his enemies, to Hercules. In legends which predate and may well underlie the story of his subjection by Omphale, Hercules deliberately disguises himself as a woman; and on the island of Cos, so Plutarch relates, the priest of Hercules used to wear a woman's robe and headdress when officiating at marriages while 'the newly-married husbands put on feminine clothes to receive their brides'.[23] Hercules, whom the Romans understood to have been emasculated when he assumed the appearance of a woman, can also be perceived to have gained in sexual potency by the disguise. Both man and woman, he is patron of marriage, the erotic sacrament which makes man and woman one flesh. Dionysus, Antony's other patron and the god to whom Cleopatra owed allegiance, was of indeterminate gender, and his androgyny conferred on him vast powers. Tiresias, who became a woman after he saw two snakes copulating, owed his wisdom and his clairvoyance to his bisexual nature. Male shamans, prophets and priests from ancient Germany to New Mexico have worn woman's dress to perform their sacred functions,[24] for the man-woman, the hermaphrodite, inspires not only disgust, but also holy dread.

When Cleopatra/Venus disarms Antony/Mars she becomes a potently ambivalent figure, Venus Victrix, or Venus Armata, who carried her conquered lover's sword. Shakespeare's Cleopatra dresses Antony in her tires and mantles and takes for herself his 'sword Philippan'. Thus armed and virile she is an abhorrent and terrifying figure, the castrating *femme fatale* who usurps the male role. But she can also be taken for an image of wholeness. She is not only the female embodiment of love who has defeated the male principle of war; she is a double being endowed with the virtues of both male and female, commanding and dispensing both love and force. In her person goodness and greatness finally combine.

Armed with Antony's sword, Cleopatra is a woman who has been spared the curse of womanly weakness. Holding the asp, the phallic beast which is one of her attributes and which does her will, she can lay claim to the wisdom of Tiresias, or of Athene who is accompanied always by a snake, or of Pythia, the oracular voice of Apollo, the priestess who knew all secrets, who was female person, male god and snake in one.

In the sixteenth-century painting by a follower of Leonardo Cleopatra stands majestically naked, holding the asp to her nipple. Her body is both powerful and voluptuous, her expression contemplative. This is a death scene but it communicates no violence, no sense of conflict or loss. The asp's undulations complete the curve of Cleopatra's arm. Her pose contains and controls of her own death, the biting which is also a suckling. her beautifully substantial body speaks of fecundity and strength. The woman and the serpent, between whom the god of Genesis put eternal emnity, meet and serve each other. And their union, the reconciliation of the irreconcilable, results not in an explosion, but in a tableau of transcendental peace.

Venus and Mars had a child, Harmony.[25] The fusion of opposites, the *discordia concors*, creates a blessed completeness. Venus Victrix wears arms, as Janet Adelman has pointed out, 'as the emblem of her conquest of Mars and of all the consequences, moral and cosmic, of that conquest'.[26] Among those consequences is not only the cessation of warfare, but also a jubilant abolition of the cramped compartments which divide humanity into pairs of antagonistic groups. Cleopatra, Queen of East and West, who contains both Venus and Mars, love and force, in her own person, who is both a mother and a phallic snake-woman, a woman and a man, is herself another Harmony, presiding genius of a Golden Age.

In that Golden Age even the ultimate division, that between life and death, can be healed. Visionary feminists from Virginia Woolf to Julia Kirsteva, as Toril Moi writes, have 'understood that the goal of a feminist struggle must precisely

377

be to deconstruct the death-dealing binary oppositions of masculinity and femininity'.[27] Early Christians abjured sex in the hope of escaping the frailty inherent in gender. When the 'either' of an equation merges with its 'or' all absolutes, even mortality, are called into question. In John Donne's words,

> As West and East
> In all flat maps (and I am one) are one,
> So death doth touch the Resurrection.[28]

If Mars could be permanently united to Venus, wrote the Renaissance neo-Platonist Pico della Mirandola, 'nothing would ever perish'.[29] By the same token androgyny confers immortality. Tiresias lived far beyond the normal span and the phoenix, the bird which can reproduce itself, being both male and female, lives for ever. If the sexes could become one, if love and power could be reconciled, if Orient and Occident could combine, death would be defeated. That concord and that hope appear epitomized in the person of my last Cleopatra.

I do not pretend that that Cleopatra is in any sense more real than the others I have described. Her claims to historicity are negligible. Like most of the other Cleopatras in this book, she is one part fact and nine parts a mixture of legend, symbol and wishfulness. Nor do I believe that the immortality offered by her is literally attainable. But her image, which I have cobbled together from fragments of ancient myth, Renaissance iconography and modern criticism, attracts and excites me much as – in their own times – Cleopatra the heroic suicide, Cleopatra the killer and Cleopatra the careless libertine must have moved those who imagined them. Cleopatra has frequently invited those who think of her to take the risk of abandoning themselves, to barter their workaday identities for the possibility of a richer life. So does this last Cleopatra, inviting us to dismantle the limiting dualistic structures within which we define ourselves and identify others as our enemies. The danger is grave. In following such a Cleopatra we risk losing most of what we have had and destroying most of what we have been (for how can I be both myself and my opposite?). But the possible gain is proportionately grand – harmony, and all it can create. Once again, as so often in the iconology of Cleopatra, self-destruction comes to seem desirable.

'All you have to do to see the Medusa is look her in the face,' wrote Hélène Cixous. 'She isn't deadly. She is beautiful and she laughs.' So too this imaginary Cleopatra turns out, when viewed steadily, to be benign. True, she is a woman endowed anomalously with masculine power. True, she is an exotic outsider who calls into question the cultural dominance of the West. True, she is a sensualist celebrating the mortal sins of the flesh. But her image, which flouts established order so comprehensively, can be read as a presage, not of chaos, but of greatly enlarged human possibility. Those who envisage her with minds cleared of sexual anxiety and racial arrogance, those who (unlike Baudelaire) can contemplate their own hearts and bodies without disgust, those who can lay aside a yearning for the ease and clarity of a moral sphere in which one side is always right and the other always wrong, may see her beauty, and hear her tolerant laughter.

# AFTERWORD

No story, however ancient, ever achieves its definitive form. Since this was first published Cleopatra has undergone at least two further metamorphoses beyond those I describe in it. Both of them have been imposed on her, not by any new information about the events of her lifetime, but by what has been happening in the world in the past two decades.

First, Cleopatra became an African. In writing about nineteenth-century orientalist images of Cleopatra I drew on the work of the American scholar Martin Bernal, the most prominent of a long line of Afro-centrist classical historians. Bernal argues that for centuries the culture of ancient Egypt has been under-estimated by racist historians unwilling to acknowledge that Greek, and therefore all European, civilisation had its origins in Africa. Gradually, while I was finishing my book, a version of that argument achieved common currency, and it became fashionable to assert that the ancient rulers of Egypt were black, but that their blackness had been shamefully denied. In the summer of 1991 there were two productions of Shakespeare's *Antony and Cleopatra* running in London. In each of them Cleopatra was played by a black actress: one of whom, Donna Croll of the Talawa Theatre Company, told a reporter 'the fable of the white Cleopatra is just another way of bleaching out history'. Soon, whenever I talked about Cleopatra in public, there was one question I was invariably asked: 'Was she black?'

It's a hard question to answer. Whether or not the Pharaohs should properly be described as black, Cleopatra was not one of them. Her father was a Ptolemy, the direct descendant of one of Alexander's generals, a Macedonian from an area of Northern Greece whose people can be quite fair. Theoretically he, and all his forebears for over two centuries, had been the offspring of incestuous brother-sister marriages, and therefore pure-bred (as well as in-bred) Greeks. In fact it occurred more than once that the heir to the throne of Ptolemaic Egypt was the child of a royal concubine of unrecorded origin. Cleopatra was one such case. We do not know who her mother was.

But the difficulty is not only one of lack of information. Certainly, as I have repeatedly demonstrated in this book, Romans of the first century BC saw Egypt as an alien place. But the fact that it was located on the African continent didn't make it any more alien than – say – the countries now known as France or Germany. It was more threatening, because infinitely more civilised and prosperous and therefore a far more formidable competitor, than either of those northern territories. But its people's skin-colour was not seen by their Italian-born contemporaries as being in any particular way significant, or indeed as noticeably different from their own. Cleopatra's contemporaries didn't divide the brownish-skinned people living around the Mediterranean into 'black' Africans and 'white' Europeans, as it has been conventional to do for the last five hundred years or so. Africa and Europe were not yet strange and mutually opposed universes: they were two shores of the same sea.

Besides, the words 'black' and 'white' were not fraught, as they are now, with the slave-trade's legacy of shame and grievance. Cleopatra's contemporaries had slaves, certainly, but slavery and slave-ownership were not colour-coded in ways now familiar. Lucan, in his extravagant description of the splendours of Cleopatra's court, describes her page-boys. Some of them are dark-skinned, curly-haired 'Nubians' from the Southern reaches of the Nile: others are blue-eyed, blond Germans. To Lucan (a Roman citizen of Spanish origin) they seem, as they would also have done to his contemporaries in Alexandria – equally curious, equally exotic, equally fit for servitude.

My guess is that Cleopatra was not noticeably darker than

the Romans with whom she came into contact. She had lived in Rome before Julius Caesar's death: there were plenty of people there who knew what she looked like. During the last stages of the conflict between her and Octavius, Roman poets and propagandists did their utmost to exaggerate her foreignness. They would surely have made use of anything in her appearance which marked her out as different from themselves, but I know of no ancient reference to the colour of her skin.

But blackness, of course, is a cultural condition and a state of mind as much as it is a matter of physical appearance. In the early 1990s the director of another version of Cleopatra's story asserted that identifying the Hellenistic Queen of Egypt as a black woman allowed her to do justice to Cleopatra's 'earthiness' and her kind of 'non-European regality which allows someone to sit on the floor'. Racial identity was the preoccupation of the moment. Just as Cleopatra had previously been co-opted into playing a part in discussions about the ethics of suicide, the status of a wife and the comparative merits of aristocratic or autocratic government, so in the last years of the twentieth century she found herself at the centre of a debate about race relations. Yet again, the terms of that debate were specific to the period that produced them. Yet again Cleopatra was being made over in conformity with anachronistic clichés and an interpreter's prejudices. Already, only a few years later, that director's language seems at best old-fashioned, at worst insulting: we do not now see 'earthiness' and a reluctance to use the furniture as characteristically black or African attributes. And they are certainly not attributes anyone could ever have safely assigned to Cleopatra, who was celebrated not for her instincts but for her scholarship and for the extreme formality of her court. We do not know her exact genetic inheritance, but we do know that the republican Romans were shocked by her propensity for sitting, not on the floor, but on a throne of solid gold.

More recently Cleopatra's African identity has come to seem less problematic, less urgently interesting, than her identity as a Middle Easterner. Any new account of her story would have to display an awareness that it describes a clash between what is now a predominantly Muslim state and a Western superpower. In the 1920s the Egyptian dramatist, Ahmad Shawqi, an active opponent of British colonial rule, made of Cleopatra a nationalist heroine defending her country from corrupting western influence. It is a theme ripe for further development.

Sixteen years ago I wrote that Westerners, ancient and modern, have repeatedly expressed the belief that Egyptians and other eastern Mediterranean peoples were effeminate, self-indulgent and sex-fixated while the Romans and their heirs – the peoples of the western democracies – seemed, according to the same code of prejudices, to 'embody the "masculine" virtues of patriotism, self-discipline, sexual abstemiousness and readiness for war'. Now those prejudices have been almost exactly reversed.

To a militant Islamicist, from Egypt or from anywhere else in the vast area – stretching from the coast of Lebanon to the eastern borders of the ancient Iranian empire – which Cleopatra and Antony dreamed of making their own, the West probably now seems as degenerate as Cleopatra's Egypt seemed to the Romans. Meanwhile to a Westerner unnerved by terrorists' threats the people of the Middle East now appear as stern, as morally censorious and as inhumanly brave as the Romans once fancied themselves to be.

This book will never be completely finished, neither is it likely ever to lose its contemporary relevance. Cleopatra keeps on changing, and will continue to do so until her name is forgotten, but the forces which shaped her life and which have shaped her legend – the forces of fear and fantasy and covert desire – are still at their lethal work in the world.

Lucy Hughes-Hallett
April 2006

# REFERENCES

(Full details of books referred to are to be found in the Bibliography)

## Introduction

1 Quoted in Halliwell, p. 301
2 Gautier, p. 8
3 Boccaccio, p. 192
4 Quoted in Ellmann, p. 292
5 Undated cutting from *News Chronicle* in British Film Institute Archive
6 Quoted in Steppat, p. 426
7 Quoted in Praz, p. 285

## Chapter 1: Fantasy and Fact

1 Plutarch (1965) 'Mark Antony', Ch. 85
2 Grant (1972), p. 225
3 Plutarch, op. cit., Ch. 27
4 Suetonius, 'Julius Caesar', Ch. 35
5 Grant (1982), pp. 202–3
6 Plutarch, op. cit., Ch. 27
7 Dio Cassius, Book LI, Ch. 21
8 Josephus, *De Bello Judaico*, Book I, Chs 360–2
9 Shakespeare, Act V, Scene II
10 Quoted in Washington
11 Appian, *The Civil Wars*, Book IV, Ch. 3
12 Quoted in Washington

## Chapter 2: The Story According to Octavius

1 Caesar, Book III, Ch. 107
2 Ibid
3 Suetonius, 'Julius Caesar', Ch. 51
4 Ibid, Ch. 52
5 Dio Cassius, Book LI, Ch. 21
6 Ibid, Book L, Ch. 28
7 Plutarch (1965), 'Mark Antony', Ch. 10
8 Ibid, Ch. 25
9 Ibid, Ch. 28
10 Appian, Book V. Ch. 1
11 Josephus, *Antiquities of the Jews*, Book XV, Ch. 93
12 Dio Cassius, Book XLVIII, Ch. 24
13 Plutarch, op. cit., Ch. 36
14 Ibid, Ch. 37
15 Ibid, Ch. 51
16 Dio Cassius, Book XLIX, Ch. 34
17 Plutarch, op. cit., Ch. 62
18 Ibid, Ch. 66
19 Dio Cassius, Book XLV, Ch. 2
20 Plutarch, 90. cit., Ch. 55
21 Ibid, Ch. 58
22 Ibid
23 Grant (1972), p. 193
24 Plutarch, op. cit., Ch. 58
25 Suetonius, 'Augustus', Ch. 31
26 'Res Gestae Divi Augusti', in Lewis and Reinhold, p. 9
27 Dio Cassius, Book L, Ch. 11
28 Ibid, Ch. 24

29  Tarn (1934), p. 35
30  Virgil (1956), Book VIII, p. 222
31  Schwab, p. 1
32  Caesar, 'The Alexandrian War', Ch. 24
33  Ibid
34  ibid, Ch. 7
35  Lucan, Book IX
36  Dio Cassius, Book XXXIX, Ch. 57
37  Lucan, Book X
38  Plutarch, op. cit., Ch. 53
39  Dio Cassius, Book LI, Ch. 12
40  Propertius (1985), Book III, Ch. 11
41  Dio Cassius, Book XXXIX, Ch. 57
42  Quoted in Rawson
43  Dio Cassius, Book L, Ch. 24
44  Propertius, op. cit.; Virgil, op. cit.
45  Dio Cassius, Book LI, Ch. 16
46  Propertius, op. cit.; Virgil, op. cit.
47  Plutarch, op. cit., Ch. 54; Dio Cassius,
    Book XLIX, Chs 40–1
48  Lucius Florus, Book II, Ch. 21
49  Virgil (1984), Book VI, pp. 187, 190
50  Velleius Paterculus, Book II, Ch. 85
51  Dio Cassius, Book L, Ch. 24
52  Ibid, Ch. 33
53  Appian, Book V, Ch. 1
54  Dio Cassius, Book XLVIII, Ch. 27
55  Plutarch, op. cit., Chs 28, 29
56  Ibid, Ch. 56
57  Ibid, Ch. 71
58  Pomeroy, p. 126
59  Hopkins (1983), pp. 90–1
60  Horace, Epode 9, p. 57
61  Propertius, Book III, 11
62  Hopkins (1978), p. 119
63  Suetonius, 'Augustus', Ch. 67; Hopkins,
    op. cit., p. 119
64  Lucan, Book X, p. 212
65  Josephus, *Antiquities of the Jews*, Book
    XV, Ch. 97
66  Lucan, Book X
67  Propertius, op. cit.
68  Fraser (1988), pp. 11, 29
69  Velleius Paterculus, Book II, Ch. 74
70  Cicero, *Pro Caelio*
71  Martial, Book XI, 20
72  Volkmann, p. 105
73  Propertius, op. cit.
74  Apollodorus in Kerenyi (1959), p. 192
75  Ovid, Heroides IX, 54 ff
76  Volkmann, p. 139
77  Plutarch (1960), 'Pericles', Ch. 2
78  Plutarch (1927), 'Comparison of
    Demetrius and Antony', Ch. 2
79  Volkmann, Plate VII
80  Dio Cassius, Book L, Ch. 27
81  Suetonius, 'Augustus', Ch. 69. Trans-
    lation in Grant (1972), p. 185

82  Plutarch (1965), 'Mark Antony' Ch. 4
83  Ibid, Ch. 36
84  Plato (1973), Ch. 253
85  Foucault, Vol. III, pp. 89–90
86  Suetonius, 'Julius Caesar', Chs 45, 49
87  Dio Cassius, Book XLVI, Ch. 18
88  Suetonius, 'Augustus', Ch. 68
89  Dio Cassius, Book L, Ch. 27
90  Plutarch, op. cit., Ch. 60
91  Homer, Book X, p. 191
92  Lucan, Book X
93  Plutarch, op. cit., Ch. 33; Dio Cassius,
    Book L, Ch. 5
94  Ibid, Ch. 27
95  Ibid, Ch. 5
96  Lucius Florus, Book II, Ch. 21
97  Dio Cassius, Book L, Ch. 27
98  Propertius, Book II, 1
99  Virgil (1940), Book III, p. 29
100 Propertius, Book II, 34b
101 Virgil (1984), Book IV, pp. 95–120
102 Dio Cassius, Book LI, Ch. 12
103 Quoted in Rose (1986), p. 219
104 Lucan, Book X; Plutarch, op. cit., Ch.
    26; Pliny, Book IX, Ch. 57; Athenaeus,
    Book IV, pp. 147–8
105 Plutarch, op. cit., Ch. 28
106 Lucan (1961), p. xi
107 Lucan, Book X
108 Plutarch, op. cit., Ch. 28
109 Josephus, *Antiquities of the Jews*, Book
    XV, Ch. 90
110 Plutarch, op. cit., Ch. 26
111 Athenaeus, op. cit.
112 Plutarch, op. cit., Ch. 28
113 Athenaeus, op. cit.
114 Suetonius, 'Augustus', Ch. 71
115 *Historiae Augustae*, 'Tyranni Triginta',
    Ch. 30
116 Suetonius, 'Julius Caesar', Ch. 47
117 Pliny, Book IX, Chs 54, 57 and Book
    XXXVII, Ch. 6
118 Pliny, Book XXXVII, Ch. 6
119 Rabelais, Book II, Ch. 30, p. 268
120 Pliny, Book IX, Ch. 57
121 Suetonius, 'Gaius', Ch. 37
122 Quoted in Ullmann, p. 193
123 De Jongh, p. 76
124 Revelation, Ch. 17, v. 4
125 Heckscher, p. 9
126 Bullough, p. 220
127 Lucan, Book X
128 Dio Cassius, Book XLII, Ch. 34
129 Petronius, p. 148
130 Bullough, p. 343
131 Beer, pp. 158–60
132 Lucius Florus, Book II, Ch. 21

# Chapter 3: Cleopatra's Version

1 Boccaccio, p. 192
2 Becher, p. 179
3 John of Nikiu, Ch. 67, p. 50
4 Al-Masūdi, Ch. 27, p. 287
5 Shakespeare, Act I, Scene II
6 Pseudo-Acro, quoted in Tarn (1934), p. 36
7 Plutarch (1965), 'Mark Antony', Ch. 86
8 Josephus, *Against Apion*
9 Plutarch, op. cit., Ch. 27
10 Ibid, Ch. 29
11 John of Nikiu, Ch. 67, p. 50
12 Al-Masūdi, Ch. 67, p. 50
13 Cicero, XV, 15
14 Appian, Book V, Ch. 1
15 Plutarch, op. cit., Ch. 27
16 Tarn (1934), p. 38
17 Ibid, p. 37; Lemprière, entry on Cleopatra; F. S. Taylor, p. 116
18 Tarn (1934), p. 36
19 F. S Taylor, p. 116
20 Grant (1972), p. 181
21 Al-Masūdi, Ch. 27, pp. 285–7
22 Ammianus Marcellinus, Book XXII, Ch. 16; Malalas, Book X
23 Tarn (1934), p. 38
24 John of Nikiu, Ch. 67, p. 50
25 Lucius Florus, Book II, Ch. 13
26 'Res Gestae' in Lewis and Reinhold, p. 16
27 Plutarch (1958), 'Life of Julius Caesar', Ch. 49
28 Dio Cassius, Book XLII, Ch. 35
29 Suetonius, 'Julius Caesar', Ch. 52
30 Grant (1982), p. 202
31 Plutarch (1965), 'Mark Antony', Ch. 26
32 Ibid
33 Grant (1972), p. 22
34 Dio Cassius, Book LI, Ch. 5
35 Grant (1972), p. 47
36 Valerius Maximus, Book I, Ch.3
37 Propertius, Book II, 33a
38 Juvenal, Satire VI, p. 126
39 Godwin, p. 120
40 Appuleius, pp. 226–8
41 Grant (1972), p. 87
42 Plutarch, op. cit., Ch. 54
43 Apuleius, pp. 226–7
44 Plutarch (1936), *Of Isis and Osiris*, Vol. V, 382
45 Quoted in Grant (1972), pp. 119-20
46 Diodorus Siculus, Book I, Ch. 25
47 Witt, p. 16
48 Diodorus Siculus, Book I, Ch. 14
49 Plutarch, op. cit., pp. 356–8
50 Ibid, p. 363
51 Quoted in Grant (1972), p. 119
52 Witt, p. 19
53 Ibid, p. 15
54 Ibid, p. 30
55 Godwin, p. 26
56 Witt, pp. 64, 121
57 Grant (1972), p. 85
58 Witt, p. 37
59 Dio Cassius, Book L, Ch. 5
60 Diodorus Siculus, Book I, Chs 17–19
61 Apuleius, p. 236
62 Witt, pp. 19, 43, 178, 259, 264
63 Ibid, pp. 243, 256–7
64 Ibid, p. 39
65 Ibid, p. 126
66 Hymn to Anubis, quoted in Witt, p. 126
67 Witt, pp. 85, 86, 138
68 Plutarch (1965), 'Mark Antony', Ch. 26
69 Hekscher
70 Apuleius, p. 99
71 Hekscher, p. 16
72 Plutarch, op. cit., Ch. 26
73 Ibid, Ch. 44
74 J. M. Carter, p. 21
75 Lane-Fox, p. 26
76 Plutarch, op. cit., Ch. 22
77 Ibid, Ch. 4
78 Kerenyi (1959), p. 205
79 Plutarch, op. cit., Ch. 4
80 Kerenyi (1959), pp. 167–9
81 Plutarch, op. cit., Ch. 24
82 Ibid, Ch. 9
83 Lucian, 'Dionysus'
84 Grant (1972), p. 24
85 Witt, p. 55
86 Kerenyi (1976), passim
87 Diodorus Siculus, Book I, Ch. 13
88 Plutarch (1936), *Of Isis and Osiris*, 365
89 Apuleius, p. 244
90 Livy, Book XXXIX, Chs 8–18
91 Grant (1972), p. 172
92 Sibylline Oracles, Book III, 1.410 ff
93 Quoted in Tarn (1932), p. 144
94 Sibylline Oracles, Book IX, 1.316 ff
95 Quoted in Grant (1972), p. 173
96 Ibid
97 Suetonius, 'Augustus', Ch. 94
98 Ibid, Ch. 57
99 Ibid, Ch. 70
100 Dio Cassius, Book LI, Ch. 1
101 Propertius, Book III, 11
102 Virgil (1974), Book VIII, p. 255
103 Virgil (1956), Book VIII, p. 223
104 Huizinga, p. 104
105 Shakespeare, Act IV, Scene III
106 Nietzsche (1967), passim
107 Athenaeus, Book IV, 148
108 Plutarch (1965), 'Mark Antony', Ch. 50

109 Velleius Paterculus, Book II, Ch. 82
110 Plutarch, op. cit., Ch. 75
111 Virgil (1956), Book II, p. 61; Grant (1972), p. 222; Suetonius, 'Domitian', Ch. 15
112 Horace, Odes, Book I, 37
113 Pliny, Book XIV, Ch. 22
114 Plutarch, op. cit., Ch. 75; Plutarch (1988), p. 195; Anthologia Palatina, quoted in Tarn (1934), p. 38
115 Briffault, Vol. III, p. 130
116 Graves (1955), p. 104
117 Nietzsche (1967), p. 59
118 Appian, Book V, Ch. 1
119 Plutarch, op. cit., Ch. 28
120 Ibid, Ch. 54
121 Grant (1972), p. 142
122 Tarn (1934), p. 68
123 Quoted in Grant (1972), p. 174
124 Diodorus Siculus, Book II, Ch. 59
125 Tarn (1932), pp. 144–9
126 Buchheim, passim
127 Quoted in Tarn (1932), p. 140
128 Plutarch, op. cit., Ch. 56
129 Ibid, Ch. 71
130 Ibid

131 Ibid, Ch. 73
132 Dio Cassius, Book LI, Ch. 5
133 Plutarch, op. cit., Chs 76–8
134 Ibid, Chs 82–4
135 Iid, Ch. 86
136 Ibid, Ch. 85
137 Ibid
138 Ibid, Ch. 86
139 Findlay E. Russell, p. 444
140 Fitzsimmons, p. 14
141 Ibid, p. 13
142 Browne, pp. 251–2
143 Propertius, Book III, 11; Horace, Odes, Book I, 37; Virgil, Book VIII
144 Lurker, entry for 'uraeus'
145 Witt, Plates 27 and 30
146 Grant (1972), p. 227
147 Propertius, op. cit.; Horace, op. cit; Virgil, op. cit.
148 Galen, De Theriacis, Ch. 7
149 Findlay E. Russell, pp. 444–6
150 The Book of the Dead, Ch. 37
151 F. S. Taylor, p. 117
152 Findlay E. Russell, p. 446
153 Plutarch (1936), Of Isis and Osiris, 63
154 Horace, op. cit.

## Chapter 4: The Suicide

1 Augustine, Book I, Ch. 20
2 Chaucer (1966), 'The Legend of Good Women', p. 496
3 Ibid, p. 482
4 Gower, Confessio Amantis, Book VIII, 11.2571 ff
5 G. B. Giraldi Cinthio, 'Cleopatra', in Bullough, p. 349
6 Chaucer (1966), pp. 496–7
7 Ibid, p. 481
8 Tertullian, Ad Martyras, Vol. I, p. 5
9 Ibid, On Exhortation to Chastity, Vol. III, p. 14
10 Rist, pp. 234–44
11 Lecky, Vol. I, p. 213
12 Virgil (1984), Book VI, p. 175
13 Quoted in Rist, p. 237
14 Ibid, p. 249
15 Spenser, The Faerie Queene, Book I, 5
16 Shakespeare, Act IV, Scene XV
17 Augustine, Book I, Chs 17–26
18 Burton, pp. 436–8
19 Sym, p. 178
20 Augustine, Book I, Ch. 22
21 Jeremy Taylor, pp. 73–4
22 Jodelle, Act I, p. 38
23 Ibid, Act V, p. 101
24 Garnier, in Bullough, p. 388
25 Tacitus, Book XV, Ch. 62
26 Carcopino, p. 87

27 Tertullian, op. cit., Vol. III, p. 13
28 Jerome, Against Jovianus, Book I, p. 381
29 Lecky, Vol. II, p. 46
30 Augustine, Book I, Ch. 17
31 Ibid
32 Lloyd, p. 42
33 Shakespeare, p. xxxiii
34 Propertius, Book III, 13
35 Jerome, op. cit., p. 381
36 Garnier, in Bullough, pp. 405–6
37 Quoted in P. Thomas, p. 235
38 Ibid, p. 295
39 Jodelle, Act I, p. 31
40 Chaucer, op. cit., pp. 496–7
41 Giraldi Cinthio, in Bullough, p. 354
42 Daniel, in Bullough, p. 435
43 Garnier, in Bullough, p. 372
44 Daly, p. 131
45 Garnier, in Bullough, p. 374
46 Daniel, in Bullough, p. 411
47 Chaucer (1966), 'The Parson's Tale', p. 257
48 Delfino, pp. 9, 156
49 Chaucer (1968), appendix p. vi
50 Davies, p. 191
51 Chalmers, Vol. II, p. 611
52 Lilly, p. 113
53 Mayo, p. 81; Thompson, p. 48
54 Jodelle, Act I, p. 33

55 Giraldi Cinthio, in Bullough, p. 356
56 Garnier, in Bullough, pp. 401–2
57 Daniel, in Bullough, p. 408
58 Dante, *Inferno*, Canto V, 1.63
59 Lydgate, Book VI, 1.3632 ff
60 Spenser, op. cit., Book I, v
61 Boccaccio, pp. 192–7
62 Chaucer (1966), 'The Parson's Tale', p. 252
63 Quoted in Waddell
64 Abelard, p. 148
65 Quoted in Economou, p. 18

66 Ferrante, p. 19
67 Abelard, p. 131
68 Garnier, in Bullough, p. 370
69 Kramer and Sprenger, Part I, p. 46
70 Cixous and Clément, 'The Guilty One', passim
71 Garnier, in Bullough, p. 369
72 Spenser, op. cit., Book V, viii
73 Chaucer (1966), 'The Legend of Good Women', p. 496; Jodelle, Act II, p. 61; Garnier, in Bullough, p. 376

## Chapter 5: The Lover

1 Shakespeare, Act III, Scene XI
2 Quoted in Steppat, p. 416
3 Tarn (1934), p. 66
4 Petrarch, 'Triumphus Fame', p. 541
5 Dickey, pp. 26, 6
6 Ibid, p. 37
7 Virgil (1984), Book IV, p. 29
8 Jodelle, Act I, pp. 27–9
9 Giraldi Cinthio, in Bullough, p. 346
10 Dickey, p. 35
11 Shakespeare, Act I, Scene I
12 Quoted in Dusinberre, p. 79
13 Brandon, 'Letter from Octavius to Antonius', 11.226 ff
14 Fraser (1984), pp. 32–4
15 Brandon, Act II, Scene II, 865 and chorus, 961 ff
16 De Rougemont, p. 42
17 Economou, p. 22
18 I Corinthians, Ch. 13
19 Freud, Vol. 12, 'Civilisation and its Discontents', p. 313
20 Abrams, p. 294
21 Shakespeare, Sonnet 129
22 Pascal, p. 50
23 Marston, 'Inamorato Curio', quoted in programme for *The Changeling*, by Thomas Middleton and William Rowley, National Theatre, London 1988
24 Quoted in Dickey, p. 23
25 Hamlet, Act III, scene II
26 Giraldi Cinthio, in Bullough, p. 344
27 Shakespeare, *A Midsummer Night's Dream*, Act III, Scene I
28 Jondorf, p. 34
29 Garnier, in Bullough, p. 387
30 Brandon, 'Letter of Octavia to Antonius', 1.115
31 Bullough, p. 216
32 Garnier, in Bullough, p. 387
33 Dickey, p. 58
34 Shakespeare, Act I, Scene I

35 Bertrand Russell, p. 442
36 Quaife, p. 244
37 Angela Carter, p. 16
38 Giraldi Cinthio, in Bullough, p. 344
39 Bataille, p. 62
40 Ibid, p. 171
41 Brandon, *The Virtuous Octavia*, Act IV, Scene I, 1.2029 ff
42 Daniel, in Bullough, p. 438
43 Act I, Scene IV
44 Act II, Scene VI
45 Act II, Scene II
46 Act I, Scene I
47 Cixous and Clément, 'The Guilty One', p. 9
48 Thewelheit, p. 59
49 Act III, Scene XI
50 Quoted in Ian Scott-Kilvert's Introduction to Plutarch (1966), p. 8
51 Act III, Scene XIII; Act IV, Scene XIV
52 Ibid
53 Garnier, in Bullough, p. 362
54 Act I, Scene II
55 Dickey, p. 39
56 Act II, Scene V
57 Garnier, in Bullough, p. 386
58 Quoted in Dickey, p. 174
59 Act I, Scene I; Act I, Scene IV; Act II, Scene V
60 Douglas, p. 53
61 Ibid, pp. 47–57
62 Deuteronomy, Ch. 22, v. 5
63 Dusinberre, pp. 233–4
64 Ibid, p. 232
65 Warner, p. 157
66 Lucan, Book X
67 Act II, Scene II; Act I, Scene III
68 Abrams, p. 415
69 Plutarch (1966), 'Mark Antony', Ch. 71
70 Quoted in Bataille, p. 11
71 Act IV, Scene XV
72 Act V, Scene II

73 Act IV, Scene XV
74 Cixous and Clémet, 'Sorties', p. 98
75 Act I, Scene II
76 Williamson, p. 93
77 Brandes, p. 143
78 Daniel, in Bullough, p. 444
79 Quoted in Williamson, p. 59
80 Unpublished essay in Warburg Institute Library (author unidentified)
81 Eagleton, p. 87
82 Act IV, Scene XIV
83 Act V, Scene II
84 Plutarch (1936), Of Isis and Osiris
85 Act V, Scene II
86 Dante, Canto V
87 Ortega y Gasset, p. 56
88 Shaw, p. xxx

89 Adelman, p. 52
90 Act V, Scene II
91 Cook, p. 135
92 Steppat, p. 408
93 Act II, Scene II
94 Act I, Scene II
95 Lacan, p. 143
96 Quoted in Lacan, p. 6
97 Lacan, p. 81
98 Steppat, p. 108
99 Dickey, pp. 41, 116
100 The Doors, 'Light My Fire'
101 Bruce Springsteen, 'Born to Run'
102 Peckham, pp. 249–96
103 Brandes, p. 144
104 Foucault, Vol. III, pp. 53–6

## Chapter 6: The Woman

1 Dryden, p. 73
2 Quoted in Fraser (1984), p. 205
3 Ibid, pp. 164–8, 171–4, 197
4 Effinger, p. 374
5 Goncourt, p. 245
6 Fraser (1984), p. 365
7 Dryden, p. 37
8 Christie's catalogue for sale of 21 May 1976, Lot 53
9 Haym, Act III, Scene II
10 Sedley, p. 247
11 Haym, Act I, Scene III
12 Ibid, Act II, Scenes I and III
13 Fielding, p. 14
14 Sedley, p. 216
15 Dryden, p. 66
16 Brooke, p. 334
17 Sedley, p. 215
18 Cibber, p. 62
19 Dryden, p. 10
20 Quoted in Fraser (1984), p. 43
21 Brandon, Act II, Scene I
22 Sedley, p. 213
23 Brandon, Act I, Scene I
24 Mairet, pp. 22–9
25 Sedley, p. 230
26 Brooke, pp. 344–5
27 Mairet, pp. 13, 40, 45, 50
28 Sedley, p. 258
29 Dryden, p. 38
30 La Calprenède, pp. 34–7
31 Dryden, p. 9
32 Stone, pp. 30–5
33 Garnier, in Bullough, p. 405
34 Brandon, Act V, Scene III
35 Stone, p. 135
36 Tertullian, Vol. III, 'On Exhortation to Chastity', p. 14
37 Brandon, Act I, Scene III and Act III,

chorus
38 Dryden, p. 67
39 Ibid, p. 39
40 Brandon, 'Letter of Octavia to Antonius'
41 De Girardin, pp. 173, 183, 206
42 Lennox, pp. 105–6
43 Brooke, pp. 353, 359–60
44 Ibid, p. 346
45 Dryden, p. 67
46 Ibid, p. 80
47 Ibid, p. 57
48 Quoted in Fraser (1984), p. 393
49 May, sig. B
50 Daniel in Bullough, p. 411
51 Fraser (1984), p. 419
52 Ibid, p. 425
53 Quoted in J. H. Wilson
54 May, sigs B2, B5, D4
55 Fletcher, pp. 315, 327, 329
56 Unpublished translation
57 Cibber, p. 29
58 Volkmann, p. 109
59 Quoted in Lawner, p. 32
60 Quoted in Dusinberre, p. 115
61 Fielding, pp. 2, 28, 33, 167
62 Brandon, Act II, Scene II
63 Fletcher, pp. 340-2
64 Cibber, pp. 54–5
65 Quoted in Fraser (1984), p. 393
66 Sedley, p. 259
67 Cibber, p. 80
68 Gillray, Plate 71
69 Coleridge, p. 400
70 Lamb, p. 53
71 Steppat, p. 416
72 Abbot, pp. 104, 122
73 Brontë, pp. 275–8; Ewbank, pp. 64–8

# Chapter 7: The Queen

1 May, sig. B2
2 Hobbes, pp. 369–70
3 Bodin, p. 193
4 Filmer, p. 90
5 La Calprenède, p. 42
6 Yavetz, p. 21
7 Bernal, p. 177: Voltaire, p. 270; Mitford, pp. 9, 52
8 De Benserade, p. 52
9 Lucan, p. vi
10 Lucan, Book VIII
11 Bodin, p. 64
12 Machiavelli, p. 85
13 Fletcher, p. 310
14 Dio Cassius, Book LII, Ch. 14
15 Sedley, pp. 216, 217, 231
16 Marmontel, pp. 224, 231
17 Eagleton, p. 85
18 Capponi, pp. 11, 70
19 Sedley, p. 218
20 Capponi, p. 27
21 Soumet, p. 23
22 Dio Cassius, Book LII, Ch. 19
23 Filmer, p. 80
24 Bossuet, p. 13
25 Garnier, in Bullough, p. 394
26 Bodin, p. 40
27 Jondorf, p. 53
28 Capponi, p. 52
29 Filmer, pp. 84, 62
30 Bodin, p. 199
31 Sedley, p. 216
32 Ibid, pp. 199, 227
33 Dryden, p. 23
34 May, sig. C2
35 Plutarch (1965), 'Mark Antony', Ch. 84
36 *Shorter Oxford English Dictionary*
37 Dusinberre, p. 35
38 Corneille, Act III, Scene II
39 Cibber, p. 31
40 Daniel, in Bullough, p. 417
41 Fletcher, pp. 366, 369
42 Corneille, Act III, Scene I
43 Capponi, p. 68
44 Sedley, p. 221
45 Delfino, p. 94
46 Corneille, Act II, Scene I and Act I, Scene III
47 Fletcher, p. 366
48 Capponi, p. 18
49 Sedley, p. 223
50 Aristotle, Book I, ii
51 Bodin, pp. 191–3
52 Sedley, p. 222
53 Reproduction in Warburg Institute Library
54 Dio Cassius, Book LII, Ch. 30
55 Christie's catalogue for sale of 4 July 1981, lot 36
56 Levy (1986), p. 148
57 Besterman, p. 4
58 Lamb, p. 44
59 Vansittart (1989), p. 333
60 Cibber, p. 7

# Chapter 8: The Foreigner

1 Michelet, pp. 369, 392
2 Lamb, p. 31
3 Greene, pp. 26–7
4 Brandon, Act III, Scene I
5 Cibber, p. 49
6 Beer, p. 160
7 Belliard, p. 3, 22
8 Garnier in Bullough, p. 376; De Benserade, p. 52
9 Baudelaire, p. 140
10 Michelet, pp. 369, 392, 400
11 Bernal, p. 218 and passim
12 Houssaye, p. 119
13 Blaze de Bury, p. 128
14 Kabbani, p. 74
15 Ibid, p. 72
16 Said, p. 100
17 Praz, p. 214
18 Curl, jacket illustration
19 Kabbani, p. 67
20 Bernal, p. 269
21 O'Shaughnessy, p. 93
22 Sografi (1801), p. 25
23 Quoted in Norman Lewis, p. 13
24 Sardou, p. 226
25 Swinburne (1866), p. 333
26 Steppat, p. 409
27 Said, p. 100
28 Newby, p. 38
29 Kabbani, pp. 52, 45
30 Ibid, p. 27
31 Ibid, p. 30
32 Byron, *Don Juan*, Canto I, 63
33 Sardou, p. 219
34 De Girardin, pp. 177, 178
35 Cantel, pp. 27, 41, 194, 152
36 Gautier (1886), p. 19
37 Sardou, p. 264
38 Samain, pp. 107–8
39 Lamb, p. 117
40 O'Shaughnessy, p. 93
41 Houssaye, pp. 85, 116–19; De Girardin, p. 149; Sardou, p. 265; Cantel, pp. 251, 109 and passim
42 Houssaye, p. iii
43 Gautier (1886), p. 63
44 Sardou, p. 199
45 Ibid, pp. 244–5

46 Daniel, p. 51
47 Said, p. 187
48 Sardou, p. 236
49 Flaubert, p. 10
50 O'Shaughnessy, p. 93
51 Brodie, p. 93
52 Bernal, pp. 154, 166
53 Said, p. 84
54 Sografi, Delfino and de Girardin, passim
55 O'Shaughnessy, p. 93
56 Ebers, Vol. I, pp. 25, 237, Vol. II, p. 122
57 Symons, p. 144
58 De Banville, 'Cléopâtre', p. 28
59 Heine, p. 310
60 Gautier, pp. 2, 6, 12
61 De Girardin, p. 152
62 Mommsen, p. 530
63 Bernal, p. 199
64 De Quincey, pp. 267–8
65 Said, p. 208
66 De Girardin, p. 140
67 Bernal, p. 249
68 De Girardin, Introduction by Gautier, p. xiii
69 Gautier, p. 56
70 Lloyd, p. 42
71 Von Wertheimer, pp. 39, 109
72 Kabbani, p. 59
73 Michelet, Introduction
74 Blaze de Bury, p. xxvi
75 Michelet, pp. 400–1
76 Ebers, Vol. II, pp. 154, 272
77 Plutarch (1965), Introduction, p. 10
78 Paraphrased in Praz, p. 210

## Chapter 9: The Killer

1 Cantel, pp. 35–41
2 Ironmonger, pp. 38, 56
3 Steiner, p. 213; Alfieri, pp. 10, 55
4 Soumet, pp. 1, 69–71
5 Kotzebue, unpublished translation
6 Haggard, p. 26
7 O'Shaughnessy, 'Creation', p. 103
8 Heine, p. 306
9 Ibid, p. 308
10 Biographie Universelle, Vol. VIII, p. 426
11 Haggard, pp. 91, 206
12 Cantel, pp. 171–5
13 Praz, p. 214
14 Ebers, Vol. I, p. 98
15 Cantel, p. viii
16 Ibid, p. 244
17 Praz, p. 159
18 Payen, pp. 68, 40
19 Freud, Vol. XI, pp. 416, 424
20 Praz, p. 286
21 De Girardin, Introduction, pp. xiii–xv
22 De Girardin, p. 147
23 Sardou, p. 225
24 Saadeh, p. 69
25 Gautier, pp. 31, 36
26 Hugo, pp. 568–70
27 Von Wertheimer, p. 77
28 Saadeh, pp. 369, 119
29 Sardou, pp. 352, 334
30 Gautier, pp. 26, 54
31 Bataille, pp. 164, 167
32 Michelet, p. 391
33 De Girardin, pp. 138, 146
34 Swinburne (1866), pp. 331–3
35 De Banville, p. 28
36 Bryusov, unpublished translation
37 Haggard, p. 162
38 Aurelius Victor, 'Cleopatra Regina'
(unnumbered pages)
39 Dostoevsky, p. 583
40 Fraser (1988), pp. 29, 168
41 Pushkin, p. 521
42 Ibid, pp. 258–60
43 Gautier, p. 60
44 Peckham, pp. 242–9
45 Freud, Vol. XI, p. 413
46 Sardou, p. 238
47 Dijkstra, pp. 352–4
48 Freud, Vol. XI, p. 328
49 Lamb, p. 75
50 Landor, pp. 12–13
51 Cantel, p. 293
52 Payen, p. 45
53 Story, p. 147
54 De Banville, p. 28
55 Swinburne (1973), p. 127
56 Michelet, pp. 400–1
57 Sardou, pp. 353–63
58 Blaze de Bury, p. 7
59 Von Wertheimer, p. 109
60 Symons, p. 141
61 Blaze de Bury, p. 29
62 Story, pp. 147–54
63 Praz, p. 222
64 Haggard, p. 90
65 Heine, p. 305
66 Swinburne, 'Memorial Verses on the Death of Théophile Gautier'
67 Praz, pp. 250–1
68 Haggard, pp. 45, 50, 91
69 Saadeh, p. 134
70 Cantel, p. 74
71 Ebers, Vol. 1, p. 277
72 Cantel, p. v
73 Goethe, Part 2, p. 252
74 Freud, Vol. 2, p. 112

75 Haggard, p. 115
76 De Hérédia, p. 77
77 Vansittart (1988), p. 50
78 Haggard, pp. 116, 90
79 Hugo, p. 570; Swinburne (1866), p. 331; Cantel, p. 110
80 Praz, p. 286
81 Gautier, p. 62
82 Cantel, p. 128
83 De Girardin, p. 152
84 Cantel, pp. 44, 251
85 Knott, pp. 89–92
86 Blaze de Bury, p. 41
87 Swinburne (1866), p. 133
88 O'Shaughnessy, p. 103
89 Swinburne (1866), p. 331
90 Saadeh, p. 279
91 Cantel, pp. 376–82
92 Bernal, p. 175
93 Wintle, p. 286
94 Buckle, p. 347
95 Haggard, pp. 178–92
96 Freud, Vol. 11, pp. 424–5
97 Heine, p. 309
98 Gautier, pp. 24–5
99 De Girardin, p. 145
100 Cantel, pp. 83, 100, 109
101 Pushkin, p. 247
102 Praz, p. 275
103 Nietzsche (1910), p. 20
104 Baldick, p. 104
105 Baudelaire, p. 123
106 Eliot (1953), p. 194
107 Baudrillard, p. 27
108 Alfieri, p. 55
109 Pushkin, p. 248
110 Payen, p. 53
111 Buckle, pp. 150–1
112 Symons, p. 144
113 Freud, Vol. 12, p. 79

## Chapter 10: The Child

1 Shaw, pp. xxi–xxii, xxxi
2 Ibid, pp. 149–50
3 Ibid, p. 154
4 Deans, Preface
5 *Sunday Times*, 30 August 1951
6 Weigall, p. 18
7 De Bernath, pp. 136, 197
8 Ibid, pp. 175–6, 152
9 Saadeh, p. 118
10 Weigall, p. 21
11 Ebers, Vol. 1, pp. 229–30
12 Knott, p. 85
13 Weigall, p. 112
14 Ibid, p. 304
15 De Bernath, p. 196
16 Blaze de Bury, p. 126
17 De Bernath, p. 315
18 Weigall, p. 187
19 Blaze de Bury, p. 72; Houssaye, p. 178; Sergeant, p. 318; de Bernath, p. 268; MacKereth, p. 37
20 Wells, p. 319
21 Saadeh, p. 189
22 Weigall, p. 186
23 Ebers, Vol. 1, pp. 239, 243, Vol. 2, pp. 158, 266
24 Houssaye, p. 200; Knott, p. 93; Ebers, Vol. 2, p. 292
25 Ebers, Vol. 1, p. 185
26 Von Wertheimer, Preface
27 Shaw, p. 249
28 Ibid, p. xxx
29 Houssaye, p. 196
30 Knott, p. 20
31 MacKereth, pp. 34, 44
32 Ironmonger, pp. 2, 19
33 Weigall, p. 18
34 Ibid, pp. 85–90
35 De Bernath, p. 174
36 Shaw, p. xxxi
37 Dickens, p. 362
38 Shaw, p. 202
39 Higham, p. 66
40 Wilson (1958), 'The Greatest Show On Earth'
41 Wilson (1952), 'The National Winter Garden'
42 Wilson (1952), p. 280

## Chapter 11: Cleopatra Winks

1 Saadeh, p. 372
2 Bodeen, pp. 13–15; Kyrou, p. 434; *Photoplay* (undated); Publicity material in Kobal Collection
3 Kyrou, pp. 434–5; Pratt, Vol. II, pp. 204–7
4 Eliot (1961), pp. 54, 66
5 Core, p. 7
6 Sontag, p. 110
7 *Monthly Film Bulletin,* January 1954; Unidentified cutting in British Film Institute Archive
8 *Sunday Times,* 4 August 1963
9 Halliwell, p. 301
10 De Bernath, p. 187
11 Weigall, p. 208

12 Stone, pp. 37, 12, 60, 79
13 Butts, p. 22
14 Berners, pp. 60, 106; Baring, pp. 225–30
15 Wilder, p. 73
16 Blaze de Bury, pp. 20–2
17 Butts, p. 141
18 Cantel, p. iii
19 Wilder, pp. 72, 96, 111, 114
20 Stone, p. 26
21 Butts, p. 224
22 Stone, p. 36
23 Mundy, p. 50
24 Butts, p. 71
25 Berners, pp. 29, 200
26 Bodeen, pp. 13–15; Kyrou, p. 434; Publicity material and undated cutting from *Photoplay* in Kobal Collection
27 Walker, p. 127
28 Ibid, p. 149
29 Kelley, p. 116
30 Waterbury, p. 158
31 Zec, cover
32 Massie, p. 147
33 Sontag, p. 116
34 *Aspel and Company,* London Weekend Television, 8 February 1988
35 Brewer, p. 240
36 Levey (1986), p. 148
37 Richardson (1959), pp. 121–2
38 Ellmann, pp. 112, 107
39 Murphy, pp. 83, 117–18
40 Wharton, p. 154
41 Cooper, p. 247
42 Walker, pp. 79, 153, 204, 206
43 Brodsky, p. 28
44 Kelley, p. 107
45 Cixous, pp. 123–4
46 *Bioscope,* 23 May 1918; Publicity material in British Film Institute Archive
47 British Film Institute Archive, unidentified source
48 *Kinematograph Weekly,* 16 August 1934 and 23 August 1934; Press cuttings and handouts in British Film Institute Archive; Higham (New York 1973), p. 234
49 Rabelais, p. 292
50 Ibid, p. 155
51 Ibid, pp. 55–6
52 *The Herald,* 12 December 1945; Reviews and cuttings in British Film Institute Archive
53 Bataille, pp. 68, 168–9
54 Kelley, pp. 134, 135; Elizabeth Taylor, pp. 106, 110; Brodsky, p. 4
55 O'Brien, p. 25
56 Kelley, p. 120
57 Brodsky, epigraph
58 Higham (New York 1973), p. 234
59 Brodsky, p. 23
60 Kelley, pp. 145, 164; Brodsky, pp. 35, 59
61 Barthes, p. 85
62 Zec, pp. 6, 14; Kelley, pp. 133, 203; Elizabeth Taylor, p. 114; Waterbury, pp. 199, 201, 203
63 Elizabeth Taylor, pp. 103–4
64 Bragg, pp. 123–4, 194
65 Kelley, pp. 200–4; Junor, p. 147
66 Kelley, pp. 160–4
67 Ferris, p. 109
68 Brodsky, p. 55
69 *Monthly Film Bulletin,* January 1954
70 Butts, p. 229
71 Rabelais, p. 163
72 Cixous and Clément, p. 128

## Chapter 12: The Triumph of Love

1 Baudrillard, p. 9
2 Bernal, p. 34 and passim
3 Shawqui, Act I
4 Soyinka, pp. 207–11
5 *Historiae Augustae,* Vol. 2, 'Tyranni Triginta', Chs xxvii–xxx
6 Gibbon, p. 114
7 Balderston, pp. 12, 17
8 Petrarca, p. 484
9 Belliard, pp. 1–3, 9, 12
10 Ibid, p. 18
11 May, sig. B5
12 Fuzelier, pp. 11–19
13 Sardou, p. 206
14 De Girardin, p. 194
15 Ferval, pp. 5–6; *Telegraph Weekend Magazine,* 17 June 1989
16 Shawqui, Act I
17 Ferval, p. vi
18 Cavafy, pp. 41, 46
19 Shawqui, Act I
20 D. M. Thomas, pp. 85–7
21 Neumann, p. 222
22 Adelman, p. 205
23 Kerenyi (1959), p. 163; Delcourt, pp. 20–1
24 Briffault, p. 531
25. Wind, p. 86
26 Adelman, p. 92
27 Moi, p. 13
28 Donne, 'Hymn to God my God, in my Sickness', p. 177
29 Wind, p. 89

# BIBLIOGRAPHY

Classical texts are in the Loeb Classical Library edition unless otherwise specified. Translations not otherwise credited are my own.

Abbott, Jacob, *The History of Cleopatra* (London 1852)

Abelard and Heloise, *The Letters*, trans. Betty Radice (Harmondsworth 1974)

Abrams, M. H., *Natural Supernaturalism: Tradition and Revolution in Romantic Literature* (Oxford 1971)

Adelman, Janet, *The Common Liar: An Essay on Antony and Cleopatra* (New Haven 1973)

Alfieri, Vittorio, *Tragedie Postume* (Bari 1947)

Al-Masūdī, *Les Prairies D'Or*, trans. C. Barbier de Meynard and C. Pavet de Courteille (Paris 1861)

Appian, *Roman History: The Civil Wars*, trans. Horace White (London and New York 1913)

Apuleius, Lucius, *The Golden Ass*, trans. Robert Graves (Harmondsworth 1950)

Arber, Edward (ed.), *The Dunbar Anthology* (London 1901)

Aristotle, *The Politics*, trans. T. A. Sinclair (Harmondsworth 1981)

Athenaeus, *Deipnosophistae*, Book IV (London and New York 1927)

Augustine, St, *The City of God Against the Pagans* (London 1957)

Aurelius Victor, *De Viris Illustribus* (London 1759)

Balderston, John L., *Goddess and God* London 1952)

Baldick, Robert, *Dinner at Magny's* (Harmondsworth 1973)

Banville, Théodore de, *Les Exiles et les Princesses* (Paris 1890)

Baring, Maurice, 'Three Minutes', in *The London Magazine*, Vol. XXX (London, 1934)

Barthes, Roland, *A Lover's Discourse*, trans. Richard Howard (New York 1978)

Bataille, Georges, *Eroticism*, trans. Mary Dalwood (London 1987)

Baudelaire, Charles, *Les Fleurs du Mal* (Oxford 1970)

Baudrillard, Jean, *Simulations* (New York 1983)

Becher, Ilse, *Das Bild der Kleopatra in der Griechischen und Lateinischen Literatur* (Berlin 1966)

Beer, Jeanette, *A Mediaeval Caesar* (Geneva 1976)

Belliard, Guillaume, 'Les Delitieuses Amours de Marc Antoine et de Cléopâtre' in *Le Premier Livre des Poèmes de Guillaume Belliard* (Paris 1578)

Benserade, Isaac de, *Cléopâtre: Tragédie* (Paris 1636)

Bernal, Martin, *Black Athena: The Afroasiatic Roots of Classical Civilisation*, Vol. I (London 1987)

Bernath, Désiré de, *Cleopatra* (London 1907)

Berners, Lord, *The Romance of a Nose* (London 1941)

Besterman, Theodore, *A Bibliography of Cleopatra* (London 1926)

Bethell, A. J., *From Cleopatra to Christ* (unpublished)

*Biographie Universelle Ancienne et Moderne*, ed. A. Thoisnier Desplaces (Paris 1844)

Blaze de Bury, Henri, *Les Femmes et la Société au Temps d'Auguste* (Paris 1875)

Boccaccio, *De Claris Mulieribus*, trans. Guido A. Guarino (London 1964)

Bodeen, De Witt, *From Hollywood* (London 1976)

Bodin, Jean, *Six Books of the Commonwealth*, trans. M. J. Tooley (Oxford 1955)

Bossuet, J. B., *The Political Science Drawn from Holy Scriptures* (London 1842)

Bragg, Melvyn, *Rich: The Life of Richard Burton* (London 1988)

Brandes, George, *William Shakespeare* (London 1898)

Brandon, Samuel, *The Tragicomoedia of the Vertuous Octavia* (Oxford 1909)

Brewer's Dictionary of Phrase and Fable (London 1987)

Briffault, Robert, *The Mothers* (London 1927)

Brodie, Fawn M., *The Devil Drives: A Life of Sir Richard Burton* (London 1986)

Brodsky, Jack and Weiss, Nathan, *The Cleopatra Papers* (New York 1963)

Brontë, Charlotte, *Villette* (Harmondsworth 1985)

Brooke, Henry, *Poems and Plays*, Vol. II (London 1789)

Browne, Sir Thomas, *Pseudodoxia Epidemica*, Book V (London 1646)

Bryusov, Valery Yakovlevich, *Cleopatra*, trans. Timothy Binyon (unpublished)

Buchheim, H., *Die Orientpolitik des Triumvirs Marcus Antonius* (Heidelberg 1960)

Buckle, Richard, *Diaghilev* (London 1979)

Bullough, Geoffrey (ed.), *Narrative and Dramatic Sources of Shakespeare*, Vol. V, *The Roman Plays* (London 1964)

Burton, Robert, *The Anatomy of Melancholy* (London 1932)

Butts, Mary, *Scenes from the Life of Cleopatra* (London 1935)

Caesar, *The Civil War*, trans. Jane F. Mitchell (Harmondsworth 1967)

*Cambridge Ancient History*, Vol X, 1934 (see Tarn)

Cantel, J., *La Reine Cléopâtre* (Paris 1914)

Capponi, Giovanni, *Cleopatra: Tragedia* (Bologna 1628)

Carcopino, J., *Daily Life in Ancient Rome* (London 1941)

Carter, Angela, *The Sadeian Woman* (London 1979)

Carter, J. M., *The Battle of Actium* (London 1970)

Cassius Dio, *see* Dio Cassius

Cavafy, C. P., *Poems* trans. John Mavrogordato (London 1951)

Chalmers, A. (ed.), *The Works of the English Poet*, Vol. II (London 1810)

Chaucer, Geoffrey, *Odd Texts of Chaucer's Minor Poems*, ed. F. J. Furnivall (London 1868)

——*The Works*, ed. F. N. Robinson (London 1966)

Chicago, Judy, *The Dinner Party*, exhibition catalogue (London 1985)

Cibber, Colley, *Caesar in Aegypt*, in *The Dramatick Works*, (London 1736)

Cicero, *Letters to Atticus*, trans. E. O. Winstedt (London and New York 1918)

Cixous, Hélène, and Clément, Catherine, *The Newly Born Woman*, trans. Betsy Wing (Minneapolis, 1986)

Coleridge, S. T., *Select Poetry and Prose* (London 1933)

Cook, Judith, *Women in Shakespeare* (London 1980)

Cooper, Diana, *Trumpets from the Steep* (London 1960)

Core, Philip, *Camp: The Lie That Tells the Truth* (London 1984)

Corneille, Pierre, *Pompée*, in *Oeuvres de Pierre Corneille* (Paris 1862)

*Cornhill Magazine* (London 1866)

Curl, J. S., *The Egyptian Revival* (London 1982)

Daly, Mary, *Gyn/Ecology: The Metaethics of Radical Feminism* (London 1979)

Daniel, Norman, *Islam, Europe and Empire* (Edinburgh 1966)

Dante Alighieri, *Inferno* (New York 1961)

Davies, R. T. (ed.), *Mediaeval English Lyrics* (London 1963)

Deans, Marjorie, *Meeting at the Sphinx* (London 1946)

Delcourt, Marie, *Hermaphrodite*, trans. Jennifer Nicholson (London 1961)

Delfino, Giovanni, 'La Cleopatra' in *Parnaso de Eminentissimo Cardinal Delfino* (Utrecht 1730)

De Quincey, Thomas, *Confessions of an English Opium Eater* (Edinburgh 1862)

De Rougement, Denis, *Passion and Society*, trans. Montgomery Belgion (London 1940)

Dickens, Charles, *Dombey and Son* (Harmondsworth 1970)

Dickey, F. M., *Not Wisely But Too Well* (California 1966)

Dijkstra, Bram, *Idols of Perversity: Fantasies of Feminine Evil in Fin-de-Siècle Culture* (Oxford 1987)

Dio Cassius, *Dio's Roman History*, with translation by Ernest Cary (London and New York, 1917)

——*The Roman History: the Reign of Augustus*, trans. Ian Scott-Kilvert (Harmondsworth 1987)

Diodorus Siculus, *The Library History*, trans. C. H. Oldfather (London and New York 1933)

Donaldson, Ian, *The Rapes of Lucretia* (Oxford 1982)

*John Donne: A Selection of his Poetry* (Harmondsworth 1950)

Dostoevsky, Fyodor, *The Idiot*, trans. Constance Garnett (London 1975)

Douglas, Mary, *Purity and Danger* (London 1984)

Dryden, John, *Complete Works*, ed. George Saintsbury, Vol. 2 (London 1950)

Dusinberre, Juliet, *Shakespeare and the Nature of Women* (London 1975)

Eagleton, Terry, *William Shakespeare* (Oxford 1986)

Ebers, Georg, *Cleopatra*, trans. Mary J. Safford (London 1894)

Economou, George D., 'The Two Venuses and Courtly Love', in *In Pursuit of Perfection*, ed. George D. Economou and Joan Ferrante (Port Washington, NY 1975)

Effinger, John, R., *Women of the Romance Countries* (Philadelphia 1907)

Eliot, T. S. *Selected Prose* (London 1953)

——*Selected Poems* (London 1961)

Ellmann, Richard, *Oscar Wilde* (London 1987)

Ewbank, Inga-Stina, 'Transmigrations of Cleopatra', in *The University of Leeds Review*, Vol. 29 (Leeds 1986–7)

Ferrante, Joan M., *Woman as Image in Mediaeval Literature* (New York 1975)

Ferris, Paul, *Richard Burton* (London 1981)

Ferval, Claude, *The Private Life of Cleopatra*, trans. M. Poindexter (London 1930)

Fielding, Sarah, *The Lives of Cleopatra and Octavia* (London 1928)

Filmer, Sir Robert, *Patriarcha* (Oxford 1949)

Fitzsimons, F. W., *Snakes and the Treatment of Snake Bite* (Cape Town 1929)

Flaubert, Gustave, *Salammbô*, trans. A. J. Krailsheimer (Harmondsworth 1977)

Fletcher, John, 'The False One', in *The Works of Francis Beaumont and John Fletcher*, Vol. III (Cambridge 1906)

Florus, Lucius Annaeus, *Epitome of Roman History*, trans. Edward S. Foster (London 1929)

Foucault, Michel, *The History of Sexuality*, trans. Robert Hurley (Vol. 1 Harmondsworth 1981, Vol. 2 Harmondsworth 1987, Vol. 3 London 1988)

Fraser, Antonia, *The Weaker Vessel* (London 1984)

——*Boadicea's Chariot* (London 1988)

Freud, Sigmund, *The Pelican Freud Library*, Vols 11, 12

Fuzelier, 'Cléopâtre: Ballet Heroïque', in *Recueil des Comédies et Ballets Représentés sur le Théâtre des Petits Appartements* (Versailles 1748)

Gautier, Théophile, *Une Nuit de Cléopâtre* (Paris 1894)

——*One of Cleopatra's Nights*, trans. Lacfadio Hearn (New York 1886)

Gibbon, Edward, *The Decline and Fall of the Roman Empire* (Harmondsworth 1963)

Gillray, James, *The Satiric Etchings* ed. Draper Hill (New York 1976)

Girardin, Delphine de, *Oeuvres Complètes* (Paris 1861)

Godwin, Joscelyn, *Mystery Religions in the Ancient World* (London 1981)

Goethe, Johann Wolfgang von, *Faust*, trans. Philip Wayne (Harmondsworth 1959)

Goncourt, E. and J., *The Women of the Eighteenth Century* (London 1928)

Gower, John, *Complete Works* (Oxford 1901)

Grant, Michael, *Cleopatra* (London 1972)

——*From Alexander to Cleopatra: The Hellenistic World* (London 1982)

Graves, Robert, *The Greek Myths* (Harmondsworth 1955)

Greene, Robert, *Ciceronis Amor, or Tullie's Love* (Gainesville 1954)

Grosrichard, Alain, *Structure du Sérail* (Paris 1979)

Haggard, Henry Rider, *Cleopatra* (London 1889)

Halliwell, Leslie, *Halliwell's Filmgoer's Companion*, 8th edition (London 1985)

Haym, Nicola, and Handel, George Frederic, *Julius Caesar*, libretto trans. Brian Trowell (London 1985)

Hazlitt, William, *The Characters of Shakespeare's Plays* (Oxford 1917)

Heckscher, W. S., 'The Anadyomene in the Mediaeval Tradition', in *Nederlands Kunsthistorisch Jaarboek* VII, 1956.

Hérédia, José-Maria de, *Les Trophées* (Paris 1893)

Heine, Heinrich, 'Shakespeare's Maidens and Women', in *The Works*, Vol. I (London 1891)

Higham, Charles, *Cecil B. De Mille* (New York 1973)

—*Ziegfeld* (London 1973)

*Historiae Augustae* (London 1922)

Hobbes, Thomas, *Leviathan* (Harmondsworth 1968)

Homer, *The Odyssey*, trans. Robert Fitzgerald (London 1961)

Hopkins, Keith, *Sociological Studies in Roman History: Volume I, Conquerors and Slaves* (Cambridge 1978)

—*Volume II, Death and Renewal*, (Cambridge 1983)

Horace, *The Complete Odes and Epodes*, trans. W. G. Shepherd (Harmondsworth 1983)

Houssaye, Henry, *Aspasie: Cléopâtra: Theodora* (Paris 1896)

Hugo, Victor, *Oeuvres Poétiques Complètes* (Paris 1961)

Huizinga, Johan, *The Waning of the Middle Ages*, trans. F. Hopman (Harmondsworth 1955)

Ironmonger, C. Edith, *Cleopatra* (Birmingham 1924)

Jerome, St, *The Principal Works of St Jerome*, trans. W. Fremantle (Oxford 1893)

Jodelle, Estienne, *Cléopâtre Captive* (Paris 1925)

John, Bishop of Nikiu, *The Chronicle*, trans. R. H. Charles (London 1916)

Jondorf, Gillian, *Robert Garnier and the Themes of Political Tragedy in the Sixteenth Century* (Cambridge 1969)

Jongh, E. de, 'Pearls of Virtue and Pearls of Vice' in Netherlands Quarterly for the History of Art, Vol. 8, no 2 (Utrecht 1975)

Josephus, *The Works*, with translation by Louis H. Feldman (London 1926)

Junor, Penny, *Burton* (London 1985)

Juvenal, *The Satires*, trans. G. G. Ramsay (London 1918)

Kabbani, Rana, *Europe's Myths of Orient* (London 1986)

Kelley, Kitty, *Elizabeth Taylor* (London 1981)

Kerenyi, C., *The Heroes of the Greeks*, trans. H. J. Rose, (London 1959)

——*Dionysos: Archetypal Image of Indestructible Life*, trans. Ralph Manheim (London 1976)

Knott, Vernon, *Cleopatra with Antony* (London 1904)

Kotzebue, August von, *Octavia*, unpublished translation by Charity Scott-Stokes

Kramer, Fr Henry and Sprenger, Fr James, *Malleus Maleficarum*, trans. M. Summers (London 1928)

Kyrou, Aldo, *Amour-Erotisme et Cinéma* (Paris 1957)

La Calprenède, G. de C., *Cléopâtre*, trans. Robert Loveday as *Hymen's Praeludia or Love's Masterpiece* (London 1698)

Lacan, Jacques, *Feminine Sexuality*, ed. Juliet Mitchell and Jacqueline Rose (London 1982)

Lamb, Margaret, *Antony and Cleopatra on the English Stage* (London and Toronto 1986)

Landor, Walter Savage, *Antony and Octavius: Scenes for the Study* (London 1856)

Lane Fox, Robin, *Alexander the Great* (Harmondsworth 1986)

Lawner, Lynne, *Lives of the Courtesans: Portraits of the Renaissance* (New York 1986)

Lecky, W. E. H., *History of European Morals from Augustus to Charlemagne* (London 1911)

*Lemprière's Classical Dictionary Writ Large* (London 1788)

Lennox, Charlotte, *The Female Quixote, or, The Adventures of Arabella* (Oxford 1970)

Levey, Michael, *Giambattista Tiepolo: His Life and Art* (New Haven and London 1986)

Lewis, Naphtali and Reinhold, Meyer, *Roman Civilization – Sourcebook II: The Empire* (New York 1966)

Lewis, Norman, *The Changing Sky* (London 1959)

Lilly, Joseph (ed.), *A Collection of Seventy-nine Black-Letter Ballads and Broadsheets* (London 1559–97, reprinted 1867)

Lindsay, Jack, *Cleopatra* (London 1971)

Livy, *Works*, trans. E. T. Sage and A. C. Schlesinger (London 1919–59)

Lloyd, John, *Great Women* (New York 1885)

Lucan, Marcus Annaeus, *Pharsalia*, trans. Robert Graves (London 1961)

Lucian, *Works*, trans. A. M. Harmon (London 1921)

Lurker, Manfred, *Gods and Symbols of Ancient Egypt* (London 1980)

Lydgate, John, *The Fall of Princes*, ed. H. Bergen (London 1924)

Machiavelli, Niccolò, *The Prince* (New York 1965)

MacKereth, James, *The Death of Cleopatra* (London 1920)

Mairet, Jean, *Le Marc-Antoine ou La Cléopâtre* (Paris 1637)

Malalas, John, *The Chronicle*, trans. Matthew Spinka (Chicago 1940)

Marcellinus, Ammianus, *Works* trans. John C. Rolfe (London 1935)

Marmontel, *Théâtre de M. Marmontel*, (Paris 1787)

Massie, Allan, *Augustus* (London 1987)

May, Thomas, *The Tragedie of Cleopatra Queen of Egypt* (London 1654)

Mayo, Katherine, *Mother India* (New York 1927)

Michelet, J., *The History of the Roman Republic*, trans. William Hazlitt (London 1848)

Millar, F. and Segal, E., *Caesar Augustus* (Oxford 1984)

Mitford, Nancy, *The Sun King* (London 1969).

Moi, Toril, *Sexual/Textual Politics* (London 1985)

Mommsen, Theodor, *History of Rome*, trans. W. Dickson (London 1868)

Mundy, Talbot, *Queen Cleopatra* (London 1929)

Murphy, Sophia, *The Duchess of Devonshire's Ball* (London 1984)

Neumann, Erich, *The Great Mother*, trans. Ralph Manheim (London 1955)

Newby, Eric (ed.), *A Book of Travellers' Tales* (London 1985)

Nietzsche, Friedrich, *The Birth of Tragedy*, trans. Walter Kaufmann (New York 1967)

——*The Genealogy of Morals*, trans. Horace Samuel (London 1910)

O'Brien, Geoffrey, *Dream Time* (London 1988)

Ortega y Gasset, José, *On Love*, trans. Tony Talbot (London 1959)

O'Shaughnessy, Arthur W. E., *An Epic of Women and Other Poems* (London 1870)

Pascal, Blaise, *Pensées* (London 1950)

Payen, Louis, *Cleopatra* (New York 1915)

Peckham, Morse, 'Eroticism = Politics; Politics = Eroticism', in *Victorian Revolutionaries* (New York 1970)

Petrarca, Francesco, *Rime, Trionfi e Poesie Latine* (Milan 1951)

Petronius, *Fragmentum* (Amsterdam 1671)

Plato, *Phaedrus*, trans. Walter Hamilton (Harmondsworth 1973)

——*The Symposium*, trans. Walter Hamilton (Harmondsworth 1951)

Pliny the Elder, *Naturalis Historiae*, trans, H. Rackham (London 1938)

Plutarch, *The Lives of the Noble Grecians and Romanes*, trans. Sir Thomas North (Oxford 1927)

—— *Moralia*, trans. Frank Cole Babbit (London 1936)

—— *The Rise and Fall of Athens*, trans. Ian Scott-Kilvert (Harmondsworth 1960)

—— *Makers of Rome*, trans. Ian Scott-Kilvert (Harmondsworth 1965)

—— *Fall of the Roman Republic*, trans. Rex Warner (Harmondsworth 1972)

—— *Life of Antony*, ed. C. B. Pelling (Cambridge 1988)

Pomeroy, Sarah B., *Goddesses, Whores, Wives and Slaves* (New York 1975)

Pratt, George C., *Spell-bound in Darkness: Readings in the History and Criticism of the Silent Film* (Rochester, New York 1966)

Praz, Mario, *The Romantic Agony* (Oxford 1970)

Propertius, *The Poems*, trans. W. G. Shepherd (Harmondsworth 1985)

Pushkin, Alexander, *Complete Prose Fiction*, trans. P. Debreezyn and W. Arndt (Stanford 1983)

Quaife, Geoffrey, *Wanton Wenches and Wayward Wives* (London 1979)

Rabelais, François, *Gargantua and Pantagruel*, trans. J. M. Cohen (Harmondsworth 1955)

Rawson, Elizabeth, *Intellectual Life in the Late Roman Republic* (London 1985)

Richardson, Joanna, *Sarah Bernhardt* (London 1959)

Rist, J. M., *Stoic Philosophy* (Cambridge 1969)

Rose, Jacqueline, *Sexuality in the Field of Vision* (London 1986)

Rostovtzeff, M., *Social and Economic History of the Hellenistic World* (Oxford 1941)

Russell, Bertrand, *A History of Western Philosophy* (London 1984)

Russell, Findlay E., *Snake Venom Poisoning* (Philadelphia 1980)

Saadeh, Khalil, *Caesar and Cleopatra* (London 1898)

Said, Edward W., *Orientalism* (London 1985)

Samain, Albert, *Au Jardin de L'Infante* (Paris 1922)

Sardou, Victorien, *Théâtre Complet*, Vol. 4 (Paris 1935)

Schwab, Raymond, *The Oriental Renaissance*, trans. G. Patterson-Black and V. Reinking (New York 1984)

Sedley, Charles, *Antony and Cleopara: A Tragedy*, in *Poetic and Dramatic Works* (London 1928)

Sergeant, Philip Walsingham, *Cleopatra of Egypt: Antiquity's Queen of Romance* (London 1909)

Shakespeare, William, *The Arden Shakespeare: Antony and Cleopatra*, ed. M. R. Ridley (London 1954)

Shaw, George Bernard, *Three Plays for Puritans* (Harmondsworth 1946)

Shawqui, Ahmad, *Masra' Kliyuptra*, trans. Kate Figes (unpublished)

*Sibylline Oracles*, trans. Milton S. Terry (New York 1890)

Sografi, *La Morte di Cleopatra* (London 1806)

Sontag, Susan, *A Susan Sontag Reader* (London 1983)

Soyinka, Wole, *Art, Dialogue and Outrage* (Ibadan 1988)

Soumet, Alexandre, *Cléopâtre: Tragédie* (Paris 1825)

Spenser, Edmund, *The Faerie Queene* (London 1955)

Stahr, Adolf, *Cleopatra* (Berlin 1879)

Steiner, George, *The Death of Tragedy* (London 1961)

Steppat, Michael, *The Critical Reception of Shakespeare's Antony and Cleopatra from 1607 to 1905* (Amsterdam 1980)

Stone, John, *Great Kleopatra* (London 1911)

Stone, Lawrence, *The Family, Sex and Marriage 1500–1800* (London 1977)

Story, William Wetmore, *Graffiti D'Italia* (Edinburgh 1868)

Suetonius, *The Twelve Caesars*, trans. Robert Graves (Harmondsworth 1957, revised edition 1979)

Swinburne, Algernon, *A Choice of Swinburne's Verse* (London 1973)

——'Cleopatra', in *The Cornhill Magazine* (London 1866)

Sym, John, *Life's Preservative Against Self-Killing* (London 1637)

Syme, R., *The Roman Revolution* (Oxford 1960)

Symons, Arthur, *Tragedies* (London 1916)

Tacitus, *The Annals of Imperial Rome*, trans. Michael Grant (Harmondsworth 1977)

Tarn, W. W., 'Alexander Helios and the Golden Age', in *Journal of Roman Studies*, xxii (London 1932)

——*Cambridge Ancient History*, Vol. x, Chs 2–4 (Cambridge 1934)

Tasso, Torquato, *Gerusalemme Liberata* (Florence 1895)

Taylor, Elizabeth, *Elizabeth Taylor* (New York 1964)

Taylor, F. S. 'Alchemy in Egypt', in *Journal of Hellenic Studies*, L(London 1936)

Taylor, Jeremy, *Ductor Dubitantium or The Rule of Conscience* (London 1660)

Tertullian, *The Writings*, ed. A. Roberts and J. Donaldson (Edinburgh 1869)

Thewelheit, Klaus, *Male Fantasies*, trans. Stephen Conway (Cambridge 1987)

Thomas, D. M., *Ararat* (London 1983)

Thomas, P., *Indian Women through the Ages* (London 1964)

Thompson, Edward, *Suttee* (London 1928)

Ullman, 'Cleopatra's Pearls', in *The Classical Journal*, Vol. 52, no. 5 (1957)

Vansittart, Peter (ed.), *Happy and Glorious* (London 1988)

——(ed.), *Voices of the Revolution* (London 1989)

Velleius Paterculus, Caius, *Compendium of Roman History*, trans. Frederick W. Shipley (London 1924)

Virgil, *Aeneid*, trans. Robert Fitzgerald (London 1984) and tran. Jackson Knight (Harmondsworth 1956)

——*Georgics*, trans. C. Day Lewis (London 1940)

Volkmann, Hans. *Cleopatra: Politics and Propaganda*, trans. T. J. Cadoux (London 1958)

Voltaire, *The Age of Louis XIV*, trans. Martyn Pollack (London 1958)

Wadell, Helen, *The Wandering Scholars* (Harmondsworth 1954)

Walker, Alexander, *Vivien: The Life of Vivien Leigh* (London 1987)

Warner, Marina, *Joan of Arc* (London 1981)

Washington, Peter, *Versions of Paradise* (unpublished)

Waterbury, Ruth, *Elizabeth Taylor* (New York 1982)

Weigall, Arthur, *The Life and Times of Cleopatra* (London 1914)

Wells, H. G., *The Outline of History* (London 1919)

Wertheimer, Oskar von, *Cleopatra – A Royal Voluptuary*, trans. Huntley Paterson (London 1931)

Wharton, Edith, *The House of Mirth* (Harmondsworth 1979)

Wilder, Thornton, *The Ides of March* (London 1948)

Williamson, Marilyn L., *Infinite Variety: Antony and Cleopatra in Renaissance Drama and Earlier Tradition* (Mystic, Connecticut 1974)

Wilson, Edmund, *The Shores of Light* (London 1952)

——*The American Earthquake* (London 1958)

Wilson, John Harold, *All The King's Ladies* (Chicago 1958)

Wind, Edgar, *Pagan Mysteries in the Renaissance* (London 1967)

Wintle, Justin (ed.), *Makers of Nineteenth Century Culture* (London 1985)

Witt, R. E., *Isis in the Graeco-Roman World* (London 1971)

Yavetz, Zvi, 'The Res Gestae and Augustus's Public Image', in *Caesar Augustus*, ed. F. Millar and E. Segal (Oxford 1984)

Zec, Donald, *Liz: The Men, The Myths and The Miracle* (London 1982)

# INDEX

410

414